Eighth Edi

AMERICAN REALITIES

HISTORICAL EPISODES FROM FIRST SETTLEMENTS TO THE CIVIL WAR

VOLUME 1

J. William T. Youngs

Eastern Washington University

Text illustrations by Cecily Moon

Longman

Boston   Columbus   Indianapolis   New York   San Francisco   Upper Saddle River
Amsterdam   Cape Town   Dubai   London   Madrid   Milan   Munich   Paris   Montreal   Toronto
Delhi   Mexico City   São Paulo   Sydney   Hong Kong   Seoul   Singapore   Taipei   Tokyo

Editorial Director: Craig Campanella
Executive Editor: Ed Parsons
Editorial Project Manager: Tracy Clough
Director of Marketing: Brandy Dawson
Senior Marketing Manager: Maureen E. Prado
  Roberts
Marketing Assistant: Marissa O'Brien
Production Manager: Fran Russello
Art Director: Jayne Conte

Cover Designer: Axell Designs
Manager, Cover Visual Research & Permissions:
  Karen Sanatar
Cover Art: Hulton Archive Photos/Getty Images
Full-Service Project Management: Suganya
  Karuppasamy/GGS Higher Education
  Resources, PMG
Printer/Binder: RR Donnelley & Sons, Inc.
Text Font: Minion

Credits and acknowledgments borrowed from other sources and reproduced, with permission, in this textbook appear on page 263.

Many of the designations by manufacturers and seller to distinguish their products are claimed as trademarks. Where those designations appear in this book, and the publisher was aware of a trademark claim, the designations have been printed in initial caps or all caps.

Library of Congress Cataloging-in-Publication Data
Youngs, J. William T. (John William Theodore)
  American realities : historical episodes / J. William T. Youngs. — 8th ed.
    p. cm.
  Includes bibliographical references and index.
  ISBN-13: 978-0-205-76412-9
  ISBN-10: 0-205-76412-6
  ISBN-13: 978-0-205-76413-6
  ISBN-10: 0-205-76413-4
  1. United States—History.   I. Title.
  E178.6.Y68 2011
  973—dc22

                                        2009054329

10 9 8 7 6 5 4 3 2

Longman
is an imprint of

www.pearsonhighered.com

ISBN 10:   0-205-76412-6
ISBN 13: 978-0-205-76412-9

To the memory of my mother and my father

CONTENTS

PREFACE

American history is an epic composed of many events: colonists made their homes in a new world; soldiers fought for independence; capitalists built giant industries; and civil rights activists struggled for equality. In such episodes we encounter the emotions, thoughts, and experiences that made up the distinct worlds of the past. In the two volumes of *American Realities,* my goal has been to recreate some of those worlds and to capture the immediacy—the reality—of life as lived in other eras. I have not tried to reduce all these events to a single pattern, but in the aggregate, the chapters trace the course of American history from the distant past to the present.

Each chapter is designed to lead the reader to a better understanding of major themes in United States history. Each volume can be read by itself or in tandem with a conventional American history textbook. The standard surveys present the general patterns of the past; this book reveals in greater depth the life beneath those patterns.

These stories describe the broad contours of American history as well as the illustrative particulars. The death of Thomasine Winthrop leads us to know Puritanism better, and the flight of the *Enola Gay* to Hiroshima exhibits the harsh outlines of total war. The Lewis and Clark Expedition reveals the marvelous land on which the nation developed, and Joseph McCarthy's career illuminates the turmoil of cold war politics.

While writing *American Realities*, I have often wished I had the novelist's poetic license to fill gaps not covered by the sources. But fortunately, facts can be as engaging as fiction. Documents are often colorful and evocative, allowing us to listen to the deathbed conversation of John and Thomasine Winthrop, to see the light of the South Pacific from a B-29, and to enter imaginatively into the realities of other men and women.

Like ourselves, the people of the past were immersed in their times. But even while living fully in their own worlds, they bequeathed us ours. We can find historical kinship in the ordinary circumstances of daily life. George Washington is comprehensible because he was stunned when his army in Manhattan collapsed. John Muir is like most of us because he was troubled once about choosing a career. My touchstone in choosing topics for *American Realities* was that each should suggest our common humanity, even while revealing worlds distinct from our own. More simply, I had to care about the subjects and believe others could care about them as well. Through such sympathy, we come actually to live in history and feel our involvement with the past: his story and her story become our story.

The eighth edition of *American Realities* includes two new chapters, changes in others, and revised bibliographies and study guides. These guides are intended to help readers understand the chapters better with identification topics and study questions. In Volume I, I have broadened my treatment of the Texas Revolution to include the story of Sam Houston as well as Lorenzo de Zavala, showing how the careers of these fascinating individuals came together in frontier Texas. In Volume II, I have described one of the outstanding Indian leaders of the nineteenth century, Chief Joseph, and explored his role in the Nez Perce War. I have also revised the chapters on Steve Jobs and Colin Powell, bringing their stories to the present.

The effort in *American Realities* to recreate history in words is supplemented by the imaginative drawings of Cecily Moon. Ms. Moon based her illustrations on careful reading of each chapter and on personal research in historical paintings and photographs. Each drawing highlights a major theme in the chapters.

SUPPLEMENTS

An Instructor's Manual is available to accompany *American Realities*. Written by Jeffrey D. Carlisle of Oklahoma City Community College in consultation with the author, this tool is designed to aid both the novice and experienced instructor in teaching American history. Each chapter includes a concise chapter overview, multiple choice questions, identification questions, and a list of topics for online research.

ACKNOWLEDGMENTS

American Realities arrived at its present form with the help of many other scholars, writers, and editors. I am particularly grateful to Marian Ferguson, Dave Lynch, and Katie Carlone for their help on the first edition. A writer could not ask for more congenial and intelligent assistance in nurturing his ideas than these editors provided. This book also owes a great deal to the assistance of Clair Seng-Niemoeller, Frank Kirk, Lois Banner, Ron Benson, Peter Carroll, Joseph H. Cartwright, David Coon, Doris Daniels, Emmett M. Essin, Don Glenn, James Hunt, Donald M. Jacobs, Maury Klein, Ralph Shaffer, Julius Weinberg, Charles Baumann, Joseph Corn, James Gale, Richard Johnson, William Kidd, Nancy Millard, Sue Murphy, Robert Toll, Albert Tully, and my students in American History. For their help on previous revisions I am particularly grateful to Linda Stowe, Jay Hart, Russ Tremayne, Madeleine Freidel, August W. Giebelhaus, Emmett M. Essin, Paul W. Wehr, James L. Gormly, Guy R. Breshears, Larry Cebula, Matthew A. Redinger, Jason Steele, Brenda Cooper, David Danbom, Paul Mertz, Carole Shelton, Bruce Borland, Michele DiBenedetto, Carol Einhorn, David Nickol, Matthew Kachur, Lily Eng, Jessica Bayne, Peter S. Field, Jim Hunt, Timothy Koerner, Jeffrey Roberts, Tom Russell, Laura White, Laura Loran, Jim Keenan, Jay O'Callaghan, Jennifer Ahrend, Victoria Fullard, Terri O'Prey, Eileen O'Sullivan, Kerrie Ann Pearson, Seán Reagan, Erin C. Stetler, V. Keven Shipman, Anna S. Meigs, Robert Dean, Ashley Dodge, Jacob Drill, Everett W. Kindig, Bruce Cohen, Catherine Tobin, James Hedtke, Scott Barton, Jolane Culhane, Wilson J. Warren, Dixie Haggard, and David Price.

For the Eighth Edition, I would especially like to thank Tony Baracco, Oakland Community College; Jeffrey Carlisle, Oklahoma City Community College; Tona Hange, Worcester State College; Peter Holloran, Worcester State College; Andrew Huebner, University of Alabama; Rowena McClinton, Southern Illinois University at Edwardsville; Gary Tucker, West Virginia University at Parkersburgh; Tracy Clough, assistant editor for U.S. history; and Amanda Dykstra, editorial assistant for U.S. history. I would like to extend my thanks to Fran Russello, project manager at Pearson; Suganya Karuppasamy, production editor; and Shanthi Lakshmipathy, copyeditor at GGS Higher Education Resources.

Linda Youngs gave me many valuable suggestions when I began writing the book while she was busy pursuing her own schedule as a mother and an attorney. Finally, in dedicating *American Realities* to the memory of my mother, Marguerite Youngs, and my father, J. W. T. Youngs, I wish to recognize their part in helping me find my own place in history.

J. William T. Youngs
Eastern Washington University
jyoungs@ewu.edu

NORTH
AMERICA

ATLANTIC
OCEAN

Timuquan

Tenochtitlán

Tulum

CUBA

Columbus's Route in 1492

HISPANIOLA

WEST
INDIES

Tulum

GULF OF
MEXICO

MAYA

CHAPTER 1

The Native Americans
October 11, 1492

American history did not begin with Christopher Columbus in 1492 or with John Smith in 1607. Long before Europeans reached what they called the New World, Native Americans settled the whole of the Western Hemisphere and created hundreds of civilizations, some as large and complex as fifteenth-century European states. They made pottery, built cities, founded empires, wrote poetry, and plotted the course of the sun and the stars. Eventually their lives would be changed by massive invasions of European soldiers and immigrants, but they did not exist simply to interact with Europeans. They began the human story in America long before 1492, and the story of their lives constitutes the first chapter of American history.

On October 11, 1492, the people of Tulum on the eastern coast of Mexico's Yucatán Peninsula lived in an important coastal community, atop a high bluff overlooking the sea. On three sides stone walls marked the boundary between the town and the thick green bush beyond. On the fourth side limestone cliffs dropped away sharply to the white sands of a narrow beach and the warm turquoise waters of the Caribbean.

Compared with other Mayan cities, Tulum was built on a modest scale. Its *castillo*, or main temple, stood only forty feet high, less than one-fifth the height of the great castillo at Chichén Itzá in the interior. The city housed no more than five or six hundred people, whereas tens of thousands had lived in the great Mayan cities of the past. These coastal Mayas were nonetheless the heirs of a proud tradition. Their ancestors had charted the sun's and stars' courses from great stone observatories and developed the world's most accurate calendar. They employed a sophisticated numerical system, chronicled their history in hieroglyphs, and honored their gods with elaborate carvings and massive temples.

Most of the ancient centers had been abandoned several centuries before when the Mayan people had come under the sway of invading Toltecs, and in 1492 the Mayas were living in more than a dozen small states, their former glory long lost. But in a few places like Tulum, whose neatly plastered and painted stone walls and buildings stood out brightly from the sea, something of that ancient splendor endured. Statues carved on building façades as well as frescoes testified to Mayan piety. The most striking figure was the "diving god," a divine figure apparently plunging earthward from the sky.

Tulum was a convenient embarkation point for trips in long wood canoes to the offshore island of Cozumel, where pilgrims made offerings to Izchel, the goddess of medicine, sought out particularly by expectant mothers. They came before a large pottery figure representing the deity and were addressed by priests hidden behind the shrine.

The people of Tulum prospered on generous crops from land and sea by raising maize, beans, squash, and chilies; by hunting deer and turkey; and by taking fish, lobster, clams, and conchs from the clear waters of the Caribbean. They traded in canoes along the populous coast, exchanging native honey and shells for cacao (beans used to make cocoa), feathers, and other exotic products.

In 1492 trade and piety connected the people of Tulum with a wide area of Caribbean coastline and Yucatán interior. But their world was limited to the tropical skies of Meso-America. They were only one of hundreds of peoples who occupied the American continents. A thousand miles from the Mayan lands lay another world, impressive beyond what they could have imagined. Here, in the Valley of Mexico, the Aztec Empire was at its height; in contrast to its grand capital, a place such as Tulum was a mere village.

Travelers who approached the great Aztec city of Tenochtitlán for the first time must have been struck with wonder. Before them across a long causeway in the middle of Lake Texcoco lay a city of incredible size, home of some three hundred thousand people. On its fringes lay hundreds of small, man-made islands called *chinampas*, whose rich soil provided much of the city's maize.

Thousands of neat houses, made of adobe or stone and stucco, lined the streets, their whitewashed walls reflecting the bright sun and their flower-dense interior gardens filling the air with fragrance. Beyond these modest houses were larger buildings where the great lords and high priests lived. The greatest of these dignitaries was the emperor, a man elected from among the members of the royal family by the council of noblemen. He was venerated, almost isolated, by worshipful ceremony—riding from place to place in a litter carried by noblemen or walking on cloths cast before him to keep his feet from touching the ground. He ate his meals behind a gilded screen, shielded from the prying eyes of lesser mortals.

Near the palaces were temples dedicated to some forty major deities worshiped in Tenochtitlán. Some were traditional Aztec gods; others came from peoples conquered in the empire's endless wars. The greatest temple belonged to Huitzilopochtli, Left-Handed Hummingbird, whose pacific name seems ill-suited to his stern character.

The history of Huitzilopochtli was inextricable from the history of the Aztecs. Long before being honored by a stone monument more than a hundred feet tall, he had been represented by a wooden image carried by four priests in the company of a wandering band of nomads. These were the original Aztecs who, with their foremost god, had come to the Valley of Mexico several centuries before. Poor and despised, they were forced into a small section of desert by their more prosperous neighbors, then driven even from this land into the marshes of Lake Texcoco. Here the god Huitzilopochtli told the priests to find an eagle perched on a cactus with a rattlesnake in its mouth and to build a city at that place. The foretold apparition was discovered on an island in Lake Texcoco, and in 1325 the Aztecs began to construct their great city, Tenochtitlán.

It proved an admirable seat for the new empire. The lake was shallow, allowing the Aztecs to build up arable land from the silt and rocks of the lake bottom. The surrounding waters discouraged attack by enemy tribes while enabling their own armies to set out and make war. As their power grew, warriors from other tribes joined the Aztecs, swelling their numbers and augmenting their power. By 1492 Aztec armies had marched hundreds of miles to the seas on the east and the west and into the interior both north and south, demanding and receiving tribute from dozens of neighboring states.

Throughout this period of remarkable growth, Huitzilopochtli, once the frail image of a wandering people, grew into a mighty god with an insatiable need for human sacrifice. The Aztecs believed their god would make them victorious in battle if they offered him the hearts of captives. Hardly a week passed in Tenochtitlán without such a sacrifice. At the crest of the temple pyramid each victim was held over a sacrificial stone by four priests while a fifth cut the heart from the body with an obsidian knife.

Often the Aztecs made multiple sacrifices, and only a few years before 1492, at the dedication of the great temple, long lines of captives had gone one by one to the sacrificial stone in rites lasting four days and consuming between twenty and eighty thousand lives.

Mayan boatmen in the Caribbean near Tulum. Along hundreds of miles of Yucatán coastline, they traded and visited religious sanctuaries.

Often the victims accepted their fate with religious resolve, believing that their blood would feed the sun and unite them with the gods. Some even preferred death and refused the chance to live an honorable life among their captors. But many must have trembled as they began the long ascent up the stone steps of the pyramid on the way to the sacrificial stone.

Under the shadow of the temples one might think that life in Tenochtitlán had a ghostly pallor, that the proximity of so much death would distort the whole of life. But the city's daily routine does not appear to have had a morbid flavor. The people moved along the narrow sidewalks or through the smooth canals in brightly colored garments and gathered in huge marketplaces to exchange their wares. At the nearby island of Tlaltelolco, as many as sixty thousand merchants and customers assembled on a single day. Here one could obtain maize, beans, venison, robes and other clothes, jewelry, swords, and spears. Because cacao beans, cloths, and gold dust were the only forms of currency, much of the trade was done by barter, and almost everyone was a merchant as well as a customer.

Aztecs engaged in dozens of professions—working as administrators, merchants, priests, goldsmiths, feather workers, painters, messengers, and teachers. Although most of the citizens worked in such material occupations as raising crops or making jewelry, there was also an intellectual class in Tenochtitlán. The Aztecs possessed a considerable body of philosophy and theology, passed down from generation to generation in an oral tradition of poetry, song, and story. The priests taught the people rules to guide their lives and furnished the ideological framework for an orderly world.

The Aztecs kept their streets clean and conducted their transactions in the markets with decorum. They punished thievery, drunkenness, and adultery with death and raised their progeny in a strong home environment. When children were three years old, they received toys such as looms and grindstones to familiarize them with the tools of adult life. Their parents encouraged them to choose their vocations carefully and taught them a code of social conduct. One Aztec rule stressed the need to value goodness more than pride:

> Not with envy,
> not with a twisted heart,
> shall you feel superior,
> shall you go about boasting.
> Rather in goodness shall you make true
> your song and your word.
> And thus you shall be highly regarded,
> and you shall be able to live with others.

One of the most important social arrangements was marriage. Parents usually chose their children's spouses and taught young people to wait patiently for the proper moment for marriage. The priests declared:

> This is how you must act:
> before you know woman
> you must grow to be a complete man.
> And then you will be ready for marriage;
> you will beget children of good stature,
> healthy, agile, and comely.

Postponement was not a tremendous hardship, however, because most marriages took place when men were about twenty and women about sixteen.

On the evening of October 11, 1492, many wedding ceremonies must have been in progress during the twilight hours in Tenochtitlán. Each bride was carried to her groom's house; there she stood with him before the hearth, and friends tied his shirt to her dress as a sign of their union. After the ceremony the bride and groom burned incense to the gods for four days before being allowed to consummate their marriage.

We may imagine such a couple on this night, alone together, contemplating their lives and their gods, glad of each other's company in the crisp night air, anticipating with pleasure the time when they would "beget children of good stature, healthy, agile, and comely."

Several thousand miles away in Florida, a region unknown even to the far-traveling Aztecs, the Timuquan Indians lived along what was later named the Saint Johns River. They inhabited small circular villages surrounded by simple log fortifications. Their houses were made of wood and thatch, and they wore loincloths. The Timuquans may seem at first to have been a simpler people than the Mayas or the Aztecs. They did not build great stone cities, paint hieroglyphs, or accurately calculate the length of the year. Their culture had a richness of its own, however, reflected in their economy, recreation, and ceremonies.

The Timuquans tilled the soil with hoes made of heavy fishbones attached to wood handles; the men hoed and the women planted beans and maize. They gathered fruit from the islands at the mouth of the Saint Johns and hunted the abundant wildlife of the region, including snakes, deer, and alligators. Pursuit of the alligator required the coordinated efforts of many men. First some of the hunters skewered the alligator through the mouth with a long, pointed log; then they flipped it over and other men shot arrows into its soft belly. These beasts, along with fish and other game, were carefully smoked over fire to preserve them through the winter. The smoked flesh was stored along with fruit and grain in large round buildings owned by the tribe or cooked in large earthenware vessels that could be set directly on a fire.

A council of state assembled periodically on a long, curved wood bench with the chief at the center. The councilors approached ceremoniously in order of age, and the chief listened to their advice. The council probably decided when crops should be planted, whether alliances should be formed, where the tribe should make its winter quarters, and other important matters.

Most of the tribe's business followed a pattern determined by natural elements and native customs. Even warfare had a stylized, ritual quality. If the Timuquans wished to declare war, men were sent to post arrows in the paths near the enemy. The leader then assembled his warriors and voiced incantations asking for victory. They marched out in an orderly procession, well armed with heavy bows and arrows or large wood clubs. At nightfall they made camp in regular lines divided into squads of ten. Often their only nourishment came from a drink called *casina*, carried by porters.

On the battlefield these tribes usually fought in large squares, with the leader protected in the middle and directing the action. If victorious, they dismembered their fallen enemies' bodies and carried home the limbs and heads as trophies. Even the

Timuquan activities. This composite of Indian practices is based on a drawing by a sixteenth-century French colonist, Jacques Le Moyne, and depicts a war council, meat being smoked, hunters disguised as deer, and a native boat.

wives of slain warriors had a ceremonial function to perform. They came before the chief to ask his protection and then went to their husbands' graves to mourn. They decorated the graves with drinking cups and weapons, as well as with most of their hair, cut short in a sign of sorrow. They were allowed to remarry only after their hair had once more grown to shoulder length.

In peaceful times the Timuquans enjoyed wading to the pleasant offshore is-lands, carrying children and baskets of food in their arms. For sport they ran footraces and practiced with the bow and arrow. Their taste for beauty was reflected in the bright feathers worn in men's hair, the colorful ornaments in women's ears, and the animal skins that adorned the chiefs. The principal men and women of the tribe were decorated with elaborate tattoos; on important occasions the chief wore a brightly painted deerskin, and the women wore belts of silken moss.

The Timuquan existence was continually enlivened with rituals. In the spring a large stagskin filled with roots was placed atop a pole as an offering to the sun. The chief then prayed while the people responded. After a victory in war the tribe assembled around the trophies and listened while a priest recited a victory chant, accompanied by the beating of gourds and a drum. During the greatest celebration of all, the marriage of the chief, the bride was brought forth on a litter behind heralds who blew through trumpets of bark to announce her coming. Then young girls, gold and silver ornaments tinkling around their hips, danced before the couple, praising the chief in unison.

On October 11, 1492, the Timuquans were probably occupied with more practical matters, for they would soon move from their summer dwellings into the forest to spend the cold months. Thus, they would be busy gathering and storing as much food as land and sea would yield.

Halfway across America lived the Natchez, one of many cultures concentrated near the banks of the Mississippi River from the Gulf of Mexico to Minnesota and along several tributaries including the Missouri, Ohio, and Tennessee Rivers. Known as Mississippians, the tribes in this region were mound builders. In 1492 Mississippians numbered in the millions. Their largest city, Cahokia, near the present-day St. Louis, had at its peak a population of at least twenty thousand. Its main mound, shaped like an Aztec pyramid—with a flat top for a temple—was one hundred feet tall and one thousand feet long. The kings of the various tribes were known as Great Suns, and their ornate robes were made from furs and intricately woven feathers. They could assemble war parties of two hundred canoes.

The Natchez people lived on the Mississippi a few dozen miles upstream from the Gulf of Mexico. They preserved in legend a time when their ancestors had lived on the plains of Mexico. According to the story, threatened by their enemies, the ancestors had sent out explorers, who came back with news of a pleasant country along the eastern shore of a great river, the Mississippi. And so, as a Natchez priest recalled, the ancestors decided to remove into this land, here "to build a temple and to preserve the eternal fire." They may have brought corn with them. The Natchez planted eastern flint corn, which thrived in moist soil and was likely domesticated in highland Guatemala.

The Natchez leader, the Great Sun, was thought to have tremendous powers, including control over the weather and the sun itself. When a Great Sun died he was buried with earthly valuables and a group of relatives and associates (which might include wives, a sister, and servants), sometimes a half dozen or more, were killed and buried with him. The act of dying with the ruler was so honorific that other men and women would sometimes request to be killed.

The principal ceremonial site among the Natchez was the Emerald Mound, located near present-day Natchez, Mississippi. The mound was about four hundred by seven hundred feet and was built some thirty-five feet above the surrounding countryside. It was topped by two truncated pyramids each about thirty-five feet high, putting their flat tops seventy feet above the base of the mound. Each morning the human Great Sun welcomed his brother, the celestial sun, with song and prayer. Once a month the people gathered at the temple to pay tribute to the Great Sun. He was brought before them in a litter carried by eight bearers; he wore a crown of swan's feathers.

Despite the exalted status of the Great Sun, he was limited in one remarkable way. He was required to marry far below his station in life. The Natchez had three orders of nobility: the Suns (among whom the Great Sun was the foremost), the Nobles, and the Honored People. The rest of the people, the common folk, were known as Stinkards. The Great Sun and other Suns were required to marry Stinkards, and in the case of the Sun men their progeny dropped one rank and became Nobles. Male Nobles and Honored People also married Stinkards, and their children became Stinkards. The status of the child followed that of the mother; so although the children of elite women were also required to marry Stinkards, their children inherited elite status. The son of the Great Sun's sister and the Stinkard whom she married inherited the position of Great Sun. Although a Stinkard could marry into the elite, his or her status remained humble. A Stinkard could not eat in the presence of the elite spouse and had to stand in his or her company. A female Sun could divorce her Stinkard spouse at will, and she could have him executed for adultery. She, on the other hand, was allowed to have affairs. This complex system, a form of exogamy, would puzzle scholars for centuries into the future, but in 1492 it was simply the accepted custom among the Natchez, another example of the diversity of Native American life.

The Mayas, Aztecs, Timuquans, and Natchez were only four of the hundreds of cultures that flourished in the Americas in 1492. Some, such as the Incas of South America, were great empires, as powerful as the Aztecs. Others, like the Delawares, Abenakis, Hurons, Kickapoos, Sioux, Nez Percés, Navajos, and Hopis, were smaller tribes but had nevertheless created distinctive cultures.

Most of the tribes were familiar with only a small territory near their own homes, but almost all of them traded with other tribes over long distances. Thus, copper from the south shore of Lake Superior was exchanged—through middlemen—for tobacco and shells from Virginia. Red pipestone from Minnesota found its way to upper New York; unfinished blanks of flint were carried from Ontario to the Rockies; and obsidian from the Rockies found its way to the Hopewell mounds in Ohio. On a more local scale, fairs throughout the Americas periodically attracted Indians from fifty to sixty miles away.

In 1492 there were approximately one hundred million inhabitants in North and South America; perhaps ten million lived in the region that would become the United States. Each tribe had developed hunting skills, and most planted crops. Each built dwellings suitable to its own needs, developed its own political system, and had its own religion. On the night of October 11 that life was reflected in the thoughts of one hundred million human beings: a Mayan boy lay thinking about his plans to go diving for conchs the next day with his father; an Aztec scholar contemplated a sacred poem; a Timuquan woman silently mourned her husband killed in a recent battle; a Great Sun welcomed the dawn breaking over the Natchez lands. Surely people had always had such thoughts, and they always would.

A few score miles away men of another civilization, economy, and faith were preparing for their own night's rest in three crowded ships. Only the captains had the privacy of sleeping berths; the crewmen slept in their clothes wherever they could find space. The captain general, Christopher Columbus, had sailed many miles and would soon be a famous man. But few men in history have ever been as lost as Christopher Columbus was at that moment; he had miscalculated the circumference of the world and believed himself to be on the edge of China, eight thousand miles to the west.

His men had caught a last glimpse of the mountain of Tenerife in the Canary Islands on September 9 and had not seen land since. To the knowledge of the ships' companies, no other vessels had ever been so long at sea. The men had eaten nothing for days but peas, dried bread, and salt meat, cooked on deck over wood fires set in beds of sand. And they were rebellious.

Like the Native Americans, they lived a life that was rich in sacred observances, and on these anxious days their accustomed sailors' pleas for divine assistance must have seemed more than routine. Each morning a boy awakened the crew with the verse:

> Blessed be the light of day
> And the Holy Cross we say.

He then recited the Ave Maria and the Lord's Prayer. In the evening the whole crew joined in reciting the Creed, the Lord's Prayer, and the Ave Maria and sang the Latin hymn, *Salve Regina*.

Many crewmen wanted to turn back before their supplies ran out rather than sail on day after day looking for land that might not exist. Even Columbus had been discouraged until signs appeared that land was nearby—branches in the water and flocks of migrating birds in the sky. On October 11 additional indications gave them even more hope: sandpipers flying overhead and, in the water, a branch covered with berries and wood that had apparently been worked with iron.

On the evening of October 11 Columbus reminded his men of a reward that had been promised to the first sailor who sighted land. Sailing that night over warm seas, with a strong following wind, Columbus thought he saw two lights flickering like wax candles in the distance. But they disappeared, and as the moon rose the ships were still in the middle of an empty sea.

Then at 2:00 A.M. on October 12 the lookout aboard the lead ship, the *Pinta*, cried "Land! Land!" Columbus came alongside in the *Santa Maria* and confirmed the sighting. The three ships hauled in sail and drifted south along the coast, waiting until dawn to seek a safe place to land. On the shore the Arawak natives, who called their island Guanahani, slept as the three boats approached on the moonlit sea.

The next morning Columbus found a safe passageway between the reefs on the western shore of the island and anchored his ships near a white coral beach. Ashore the men knelt and gave thanks to God for their safe voyage and named the island San Salvador (Holy Savior).

The natives, who had seen the three ships and run off in fear, were now subjects of the king and queen of Spain, according to the European explorers, who simply assumed lands not possessed by other European states belonged to the first "civilized" nation to visit them.

Fortunately, the Arawaks were unaware of the annexation, and the Spanish had no interest in backing up their claim with a garrison, so Columbus's first meeting with these Indians of the New World took place in a peaceful atmosphere. After watching the strangers from the ships, some of the young Arawak men approached them cautiously. Each side wanted to trade, and soon a spirited exchange took place, the Arawaks offering parrots, darts, and cotton thread for red caps, glass beads, and hawk bells.

Columbus believed the natives were simple and innocent. They painted their bodies, wore almost no clothing, and were exceptionally friendly. He concluded that they had no religion of their own and could easily be converted to Christianity. The natives, of course, having seen the Spaniards only as traders, might as easily have concluded that these visitors had no religion and might benefit from being introduced to the Arawak faith.

From San Salvador, Columbus sailed west, always looking for indications that he was somewhere in the Far East. Guided by several natives from San Salvador, he sailed through more small islands, then reached the larger islands of Cuba and Hispaniola. He sought gold primarily, but was also interested in other products of the islands, including maize and potatoes—foods that in the long run would prove more important to Europe than all of America's precious metals. Columbus also became the first white man to observe the use of tobacco.

On Christmas Day, Columbus's flagship, the *Santa Maria*, rammed into a reef on the north coast of Hispaniola and sank. Columbus and his men were rescued by the *Niña*, and he regarded the event as a sign from God that he should found a colony on the shore nearby. After seeing that thirty-nine of his men were comfortably settled in the new colony, which he named La Navidad, he boarded the *Niña* and set out on the long voyage home.

During his three months in the West Indies, Columbus had been warmly received by the natives on the islands he visited. He manifested no aggressive intentions and insisted that his men trade fairly, giving the natives something in exchange for goods they received. Toward the end of the voyage his patience was rewarded when chiefs on the larger islands gave him gold ornaments—treasures with which he could impress his patrons, the king and queen of Spain.

When Columbus returned to Spain, news of his achievement spread rapidly. Whereas the Viking "discovery" and colonization of America five centuries earlier went virtually unnoticed in Europe, the news of Columbus's voyage reached nations that were capable of sending hundreds of expeditions to explore, colonize, and ravage the new land. Columbus himself led three more voyages, in 1493–1494, 1498–1500, and 1502–1503.

The joining of the Old and New Worlds in the years ahead would radically alter the history of both—a process sometimes called the "Columbian exchange." American silver, gold, maize, potatoes, and tobacco changed the economic and agricultural history of Europe. Old World diseases, especially smallpox, but also chicken pox and measles, decimated the Native American populations. European conquerors became the masters of lands once held by the Mayas, Aztecs, Timuquans, Arawaks, and other peoples.

Columbus died unaware that he had discovered a new world rather than a new route to Asia. An Italian navigator named Amerigo Vespucci, who made several transatlantic voyages after Columbus, was the first to realize that the lands he visited were indeed a "new world" and not the fringes of Asia. Following this lead, a German cartographer, Martin Waldseemüller, drew a map in 1507 showing these lands as a separate continent; in Vespucci's honor, he named the place "America." It was Columbus's daring voyage, however, that made possible Vespucci's expedition and led to the merging of the two hemispheres.

If the Native Americans Columbus met on his first voyage through the Caribbean had been united into one nation, and if they had known that disease and conquest would follow in Columbus's wake, they might easily have prevented his return to Spain. His men might have been absorbed into the native cultures, their tales of the land beyond the sea drifting eventually into the world of Indian mythology. European monarchs, hearing of Columbus's failure, would not have sent another fleet into the unknown waters of the western seas, preferring instead to reach China by a new route around the coasts of Africa. Two or three generations might have passed before another explorer had the audacity—and the financial backing—to sail due west from the known world.

Even as it was, many Native Americans did not see a white man until long after the Columbus expedition. The Aztec Empire survived for thirty years before Hernando Cortés led a conquering army through the streets of Tenochtitlán. In the remote mountains and jungles of both American continents Indian tribes remained independent of Euro-American domination until the twentieth century. If the one hundred million Indians alive in the Americas in 1492 had been told that they were about to be "discovered," they would have smiled in disbelief. Surely it was their own ancestors who first settled the land. Had they not reared families, formed governments, waged wars, manufactured pottery, constructed temples, conducted religious ceremonies, and speculated about the meaning of life—making the land their own?

The Native American influence would remain long after the arrival of Europeans, and later, Africans and Asians. More than half the food consumed on a typical day in the present-day United States is of Indian origin, including corn, beans, squash, potatoes, tomatoes, and peanuts. The Indians also developed enduring ways of preparing food: stewed tomatoes, tamales, succotash, pumpkin pudding, and salted peanuts, for example. Indian language, medicine, entertainment, and clothing continue to influence modern America. American English absorbed Indian words, including buccaneer, barbecue, caucus, chipmunk, chocolate, hurricane, klondike, powwow, raccoon, tapioca, and wampum. More than two hundred drugs, including quinine, today recognized for their pharmaceutical value, were developed by Native Americans. They taught Old World immigrants the value of the canoe, the snowshoe, and the toboggan and the pleasures of lacrosse and the hammock; and they invented the moccasin and the panama hat.

The impact of Indians on their world was so great that modern scholars have come to reject what has been called the "pristine myth" of native life—the idea that America was an Eden, undisturbed by the touch of human control until Europeans arrived. Native Americans, to the contrary, were so successful in shaping the landscape that one scholar credits them with having created across the Americas "the world's largest garden."

The story of the Natchez provides evidence of the controlled landscape of the Americas. When Hernando De Soto, a Spanish explorer, passed through their country in 1541, he saw thousands of human beings, but no buffalo. And yet when the French visited the region more than a century later, they saw relatively few people, but lots of buffalo. What had changed? Disease had ravaged the indigenous population, which had previously killed off most of the local buffalo. With the decline of the human population, the buffalo population along with elk and other creatures thrived.

From the European point of view, Columbus did discover America, but in a more meaningful way he began the long exchange between two worlds. Contact brought change, but the Indians were already familiar with change, with the ebb and flow of their own civilizations. Nor would the new conquerors and colonizers be immune from change. The English and Spanish nations would establish American empires, but these would crumble. The new American nations born in the revolts of the late eighteenth and early nineteenth centuries would in turn suffer shocks from economic growth.

At the height of the Aztec civilization a philosopher-king, Nezahualcóyotl, wrote a poem expressing his sense of the transitoriness of life:

> Is it true that on earth one lives?
> Not forever on earth, only a little while.
> Though jade it may be, it breaks;
> though gold it may be, it is crushed;
> though it be quetzal plumes, it shall not last.
> Not forever on earth, only a little while.

In such thoughts, as well as in the portraits we may construct of early life in the Yucatán, Mexico, Florida, and Mississippi, we are reminded that the humanity of American history had its beginnings long before ninety sea-weary sailors from another world fell to their knees on the island they called San Salvador.

Bibliography

Calloway, Colin G. *New Worlds for All: Indians, Europeans, and the Remaking of Early America* (1997). Excellent synthesis of recent work on early history of contacts between Europeans and Native Americans.

Collis, Maurice. *Cortés and Montezuma* (1954). Stirring account of Cortés's conquest of Mexico.

Crosby, Alfred W. *The Columbian Exchange: Biological and Cultural Consequences of 1492* (1972). Describes changes in European and Native American life resulting from contact between the two cultures.

Hudson, Charles. *The Southeastern Tribes* (1976). Scholarly account of the tribes of the region including the Natchez.

Krech, Shepard, III. *The Ecological Indian: Myth and History* (1999). Describes the many ways that Native Americans transformed the landscape long before Columbus.

León-Portilla, Miguel. *Aztec Thought and Culture* (1963). Sensitive analysis of Aztec intellectual life.

Mann, Charles C. *1491: New Revelations of the Americas Before Columbus* (2005). A thoughtful and entertaining overview of recent findings about the ancient peoples of the Americas.

Morison, Samuel Eliot. *Christopher Columbus, Mariner* (1955). Classic account of Columbus's voyages.

Sale, Kirkpatrick. *The Conquest of Paradise: Christopher Columbus and the Columbian Legacy* (1990). Presents Columbus and his successors as despoilers of an agrarian paradise.

Viola, Herman J., and Carolyn Margolis, Editors. *The Seeds of Change* (1991). Beautifully illustrated anthology of articles on the environmental impact of Columbus's "discovery" of America.

Identification Topics

Mayas, Tulum, Aztecs, Tenochtitlán, Huitzilopochtli, Lake Texcoco, Timuquans, Natchez, Cahokia, the Great Sun, Emerald Mound, Christopher Columbus, Arawaks, San Salvador, Hernando Cortés, Nezahualcóyotl

Study Questions

1. Why do we say that Columbus discovered America when there were already one hundred million people here?
2. Describe the religious customs of the Mayas, Aztecs, Timuquans, Natchez, and Spaniards as noted in the essay. In what ways were the various customs similar? In what ways were they different?
3. Describe the principal political, economic, and social characteristics of the four Native American groups described in this chapter.
4. What do the Aztec poems indicate about Aztec values?
5. In what ways were the civilizations of America equal to those of Europe in 1492? In what areas were they more advanced? Less advanced?
6. Describe the important elements of the Columbian exchange. In what ways did Native Americans shape the environment—for better and for worse—before the arrival of Columbus?

CHAPTER 2

The English Background
A Puritan Death: John and Thomasine Winthrop

The first European immigrants to the United States carried with them Old World ideas and experiences that influenced the way they farmed their land, organized their governments, and worshiped their deity. One of these imported customs was the Puritan faith, a product of the Protestant Reformation. Nourished in thousands of European homes in the early seventeenth century, Puritanism grew to maturity in its native environment before it was brought to America. It taught men and women how to honor God and deal justly with one another and how to live fully on earth and prepare bravely for heaven. A living faith, it entered the lives of John Winthrop, a founder of Massachusetts, and his wife, Thomasine, molding their daily thoughts and preparing them for their separation in death.

The county of Suffolk, England, was a region of great beauty and industry. During the fall of 1616, travelers walking or riding horses along one of the narrow lanes that led from town to town would be impressed by the meadows dotted with sheep, the fields of dark soil newly plowed for winter crops, and the fine villages. They would see men and women busy at their tasks: farmers plowing fields behind sturdy horses; dairymaids cleaning stalls and preparing milk, butter, and cheese; housewives making soap or gathering herbs from house gardens; woodsmen cutting timber; and townspeople weaving cloth. In a tavern the visitor might hear men discussing their fields, orchards, and livestock; the land dispute between Smith and Sibley; the marriage of the daughter of a local nobleman; or the religious situation in Germany.

If they had an eye for such things, visitors could also see God in Suffolk County. The Lord was not as discernible as apples or woolens. But He moved over the land, preserving a good person from a bad fall, prospering the fruit crops, punishing a recalcitrant sinner, and engendering a sense of peace and joy in a believer's heart. It was possible, of course, to live one's life without being aware of God. Many men and women conducted themselves—their planting and harvesting, cooking and cleaning, begetting and child rearing—as if there were no God. But many others were aware of the presence of the Lord and worshiped Him in their homes and churches. Occasionally one of the people of Suffolk left his or her trim cottage and pleasant fields to dwell in heaven with the Lord.

Such a person was Thomasine Winthrop, wife of John Winthrop of Groton Manor. In fall 1616 she would die in childbirth, a common event in seventeenth-century England. In those times one could not enter pregnancy without realizing that death, as well as new life, might be the issue. There is nothing unusual in the fact of Thomasine Winthrop's passing, but if her death in childbirth was commonplace, the record of it is not. Her husband, John, reported the incident in minute detail; his account allows us to stand beside Thomasine in her final days, see people enter and leave her chamber, and listen to the words and gestures exchanged between husband and wife. It also tells us something about the world Thomasine left behind and enables us to study a presence as real as any of these physical events, the relationship between John and Thomasine and their Puritan God.

John and Thomasine were both children of East Anglian gentry. In the mid-sixteenth century John's grandfather, Adam, had purchased a church property known as Groton Manor when Henry VIII sought to further the Reformation and enrich himself by dissolving the monasteries. A second Adam Winthrop, John's father, inherited the manor.

John Winthrop was born in 1588, the year the English defeated the Spanish Armada. The England he grew up in was changing rapidly. In the half century after 1575 there was a fivefold to tenfold increase in the production of coal, salt, iron, steel, lead, ships, and glass. In addition, new industries were established producing copper, brass, paper, soap, sugar, and tobacco. The English began to form great trading companies to tap the wealth of Asia, Africa, and America. Economic historians generally characterize this era of growth as England's first industrial revolution. The energy and resourcefulness that sent miners into the bowels of the earth and drove merchant traders halfway around the world were also reflected in England's nationalism. The defeat of the Spanish Armada had established England as one of the preeminent powers in Europe. When Shakespeare's John of Gaunt called England "This dear, dear land," he was articulating the feelings of most of his countrymen.

These developments in the outside world were not all found, however, at Groton Manor. The Winthrops' involvement in the market economy was on a small scale. When John's mother, Anne, sent to his father in London a woolen shirt and five pairs of socks to sell, she added, "If you would have any for your own wearing, I have more a knitting." Such economic changes as the increase in paper and iron manufacturing might have made it easier to acquire a new Bible or plow, but most of the products at Groton Manor were made locally in ways that had changed little over the centuries.

The land where the Winthrops lived was in the southern part of Suffolk County, near the border of Essex. The rolling countryside was covered with rich farmland, green marshes, ponds, and forests of oak, beech, and willow trees. The county was the first in England to enclose its fields, and the land was intersected with innumerable hedgerows that served as fences. It was noted for its mutton, beef, butter, and cheese. It was a pastoral land, but the white gulls that fed at the Groton ponds often reminded the people that the sea was only a few miles away.

The Winthrops produced most of what they consumed. John's father, Adam, kept careful accounts of everything he bought and sold on the manor, most of his payments going to men who worked the land—a few shillings for mowing, digging a ditch, harvesting grain, or thatching a roof. They purchased only a few products: shoes, a plow, nails, and paper. Income came from the lands they rented to tenants and from the sale of surplus produce such as grain, wood, and livestock.

John was raised on the manor until age fifteen, when he went to Cambridge to attend Trinity College. He stayed at Cambridge for only two years, returning at age seventeen to help his father manage Groton Manor. He so impressed his parents with his maturity that they consented to his marriage to Mary Forth, the twenty-year-old daughter of a neighboring gentryman. John and Mary lived together for ten years until her death in 1615, when she left him with four children.

Although John lamented Mary's passing, in those days a bereaved spouse seldom remained single for long. Marriage was a practical as well as a personal and romantic relationship, for a wife's help was essential in raising children and overseeing a household. Thus, shortly after Mary's death John began courting Thomasine Clopton, whom he undoubtedly knew already. She was the daughter of William Clopton, squire of a nearby estate. The couple was married in fall 1615. Thomasine was a good wife, "industrious," "plainhearted," and "patient of injuries." She showed her love of God in public and private worship and cared for John's children as if they were her own. John was so attracted to her that he would recall after her death their affection "had this only inconvenience, that it made me delight too much in her to enjoy her long."

During their year together John and Thomasine spent most of their time in the day-to-day tasks of managing their country estate. The Winthrop papers and descriptions of other households allow us to draw a picture of their life. On a typical spring day they would awake with the crowing of the cock. They would dress quickly in their chilly room and hurry downstairs to a warm fire prepared by the servants. John's four children would soon arrive and huddle near the flames to warm themselves as servants came in from the kitchen. Each morning Winthrop read to the family from the Bible and offered a prayer asking for God's favor in the day ahead.

After this simple service, parents, children, and servants sat down at a large table near the fire and began to eat. The presence of servants at the family table was customary in households like the Winthrops'. It was only in a later period that the lives of the servants and masters were sharply divided. Servants at Groton Manor were subject to the same discipline and much of the same training as John's own children. In many households servants were included in such family activities as card games. Advertisements for help sometimes even stipulated that the prospective employee should be adept at cards. In 1616 John had decided that cards were not a proper pastime in a Christian household, but he did share other activities with his servants.

At breakfast John and Thomasine might discuss the day's activities with the children and servants. After they finished the meal, John would be likely to tour the manor to see that all was in order, inspecting cattle and pigs and supervising his servants in the fields or woodlot. On many spring mornings the air was damp and cold, but there were pleasant days when the sun broke through the clouds to the east and the wind bore the scent of salt water from the North Sea. Since most physical labor at Groton was done by servants, Winthrop could devote time to studying the Bible and performing religious works. We may imagine him retiring to his study after touring the manor.

Thomasine would probably supervise the domestic chores, seeing that the rooms were dusted, the floors swept, the butter churned, and the meals prepared. She might attend personally to a garden of flowers, vegetables, and herbs. Whereas the men supervised grain cultivation, English women usually planted radishes, beets, carrots, cabbage, cucumbers, onions, melons, parsley, and other garden crops.

At noon the cook would ring a bell summoning the household for the main meal of the day. Afterward, glad to have the excuse to ride through the country lanes, leading a small packhorse as he went, John might visit a neighboring tenant to collect rent in the form of grain. If the tenant were also a friend, they might discuss last Sunday's sermon, both men recognizing their Christian duty to extend the religious training of the Sabbath through the week.

At the manor Thomasine and the servants might spend the afternoon washing clothes, an arduous task performed only once monthly. They must first carry water by hand and then heat it over the fire and pour it into a large tub, where dirty clothes were soaped and scrubbed. Once Thomasine and the servants had thoroughly cleaned the clothes, they would put them in a second tub to rinse and hang them on a line. All the women, including Thomasine, would take turns at the work. At supper the family might discuss the day's events. John would again read from the Bible, and they would sing a psalm.

In spring 1616 Thomasine learned that she was pregnant. She and her husband must have often discussed the new baby, John wondering whether she felt well, and Thomasine worried about the older children's reaction to a new brother or sister. John might have told her, as he later wrote in his diary, that his children already loved her like a mother.

On the surface, life at Groton Manor seems a kind of agrarian paradise. The family is close; everyone is well fed, clothed, and housed; the men and women spend their days in honest toil. There is, however, another side to life at Groton. Like human beings of other times and places, John and Thomasine were troubled by domestic and political problems.

Most of the Winthrops' servants were reliable, but some were not. Thomasine characterized one as a "stubborne wenche" and believed another had been spoiled by a background of "badd servinge" in an alehouse. The world around them presented other problems. Families once wealthy were ruined by new economic forces. Changes in land use threw men out of work and filled the roads with "sturdy beggars," men physically able to work but unable to find employment. Some turned to petty crime—John's father, Adam Winthrop, was robbed at least once by "false knaves." His diary includes frequent references to violence in the neighborhood—assaults, murders, suicides. Disease also scourged the country, sometimes killing large numbers in epidemics.

In a world full of confusion and change the Winthrops' God provided them with a sense of peace and stability. John and Thomasine believed that they should think constantly about their relationship to God rather than become overly absorbed in the joys and sorrows of everyday life. John and Thomasine believed in salvation by faith, the main doctrine of the Protestant Reformation on the Continent and in England. The Reformation had begun with Martin Luther's conviction that people must be saved by God's grace rather than by their own good works. The emphasis on grace was absorbed by John Calvin, who in turn influenced the early English Reformers. Under Queen Elizabeth, who ruled England in the latter part of the sixteenth century, and King James, who reigned in the first quarter of the seventeenth, the doctrine of salvation by faith held a high position in English worship. Some Englishmen did want further reformation of the church, but most were willing to accept the status quo. John Winthrop and others like him would eventually disagree with the church policies of the 1620s and identify themselves as "Puritan" opponents of the established religion, but in his early years his piety was nourished by Church of England ministers.

We can better understand Puritanism, and the elusive doctrine of faith, if we survey its influence on John Winthrop as recorded in his papers. At age ten he had come to have "some notions of God," but he characterized himself as being "lewdly disposed," "wild and dissolute," and dominated by a "voluptuous heart." This description does not mean that he spent his time drinking, whoring, and stealing. In fact, the only youthful sin he specifically mentions in his later writings is the theft of two books as a small boy. When Winthrop refers to himself as possessing a "voluptuous heart," he is probably describing his imagination rather than his actual behavior. Although mere thoughts may not seem to qualify as "dissolute behavior" today, this failure to master his desires grieved Winthrop. He believed that a good Christian would discipline his heart and think about God in all his free moments. There was sin, he believed, in "all such works as are done to fulfill the will of the flesh rather than of the spirit."

By age eighteen John Winthrop was deeply perturbed about his spiritual condition. Now for the first time the word came into his "heart with power." He would walk for miles to hear a good sermon, and he developed a reputation for giving spiritual advice to others. But he also became too proud, and because he realized that without Christ's grace all his good works could not save him, he began to despair, feeling that perhaps he was only a hypocrite.

Throughout his twenties Winthrop's religious life consisted of alternating periods of assurance and doubt. He abandoned hunting and cards because he felt that they interfered with his religious life. He attempted to devote more time to prayer, meditation, and religious reading but frequently failed to meet his own high standards of conduct. He accused himself of having become too frivolous in his relationships with friends and of having eaten and drunk more than was appropriate. Once he condemned himself because during a church service his mind wandered to a journey he was about to take into Essex, and soon he was "possessed with the world." He sought to "tame his heart" by regulating his diet, singing psalms while traveling, and reading religious tracts. But he found that complete abstinence from the pleasures of the world left him "melancholy" and "dumpish." He discovered that complete asceticism was as destructive to his spiritual equilibrium as excessive worldliness. The problem was to find a moderate course between these two extremes. The Puritans had a phrase that aptly described their relationship to material pleasures: "Wine is from God, but drunkenness is from the devil."

The goal of Winthrop's constant self-regulation was a relationship with Christ that he could feel. Puritans believed that grace came when one preferred heavenly to earthly treasures. Moments of spiritual illumination were rare but compelling. In 1612, for example, after comforting an old man with spiritual advice, Winthrop went to bed and dreamed that he was with Christ. "I was so ravished with his love towards me," he writes, "that being awakened it had made so deep impression in my heart, as I was forced to unmeasurable weepings for a great while."

Despite the experience of such periods of ecstatic acceptance, John often felt that he was too concerned with the world. His religious life was a constant struggle to "tame" his heart to complete service to God. On the manor he was responsible for overseeing a complex economy, planting crops, buying and selling livestock, gathering rents, and a dozen other duties. But important as these activities were, when he wrote about his own life or went to bed at the end of the day, his greatest worry was frequently whether his rebellious heart had indulged itself too much in the world.

We know less about Thomasine's religious life than we do about John's, but it is apparent that she too was a serious Christian and believed that salvation came through God's grace. John later praised her for her reverent attention to religious services at home and in church and remarked that she avoided "all evil" herself and reproved sin in others. Undoubtedly on many evenings after they had discussed crops, children, or servants, they would end the day by praying or reading Scripture. Together they would pursue the path of moderation.

John and Thomasine thus spent their days attending to matters temporal and spiritual. The year 1616 progressed from season to season. In the summer there were bright days interrupted by occasional sharp storms of thunder and lightning. Then came time to harvest and thresh the wheat. In October gray clouds hung over the countryside, and the crisp night air and the geese flying overhead announced the approach of winter. The hearth with its crackling fire drew the family to it in the morning. John and Adam dragged their main pond, catching carp for dinner. In preparation for winter the family salted fish and pressed apples into cider to store in the cold cellar.

Now that Thomasine was pregnant, she was less active. She occupied her days by preparing for the new baby, making blankets and a bunting. She also spent more time with the children, playing games and helping them read. In November she had difficulty moving and sleeping comfortably. Then on Saturday, November 30, she felt that her time had arrived. John summoned a midwife, who came to the house with several neighbor women. They heated kettles of water and encouraged Thomasine, who bore her pains patiently and asked constantly about the child. People would later remark "how careful she was" for the life of the baby in her travail. At last the infant was born, a tiny girl. She was washed by the women and then placed alongside her mother. John now entered the chamber and sat beside Thomasine and their new daughter. He offered prayers of thanks for the safe delivery.

That night John slept in a separate room, leaving Thomasine under the watchful eye of a "keeper," a woman who made sure that mother and child were well. On the following morning, a Sunday, John arose early and came to the room. When Thomasine awoke, he sat with her and prayed for the continuing health of his wife and daughter. After breakfast John, his parents, and the other children went to church.

Later that Sunday the child began to weaken, and on Monday morning the Winthrops' new daughter was dead. John later reported that Thomasine took the child's death with "patience," by which he meant that she accepted the loss as God's will. Thinking of Thomasine's earlier worry about the baby girl, people now "marvelled" at her ability to accept her death.

But John had little time to think about the loss of his infant daughter. Thomasine now became ill, suffering from a violent fever and a cough. The next morning these symptoms were allayed, but she was hoarse, her mouth was sore, and her throat bled. John began to fear for her life and on Wednesday sent for his cousin, a doctor.

When she heard that a physician was coming, Thomasine told John that she expected to die. His account of their conversation at this moment is so detailed that we can virtually hear their words. Frequently, ill persons were not told the truth about their ailments for fear of upsetting them, but Thomasine did not wish to be deceived. "John," she said, "when cousin Duke comes, I hope that he will deal plainly with me and not fill me with vain hopes."

Forced by his wife to acknowledge the seriousness of her condition, John began to cry. Thomasine was moved by his concern and begged him "to be contented"—to accept her condition with patience—"for you break my heart," she said, "with your grievings."

John replied, "I can do no less when I fear to be stripped of such a blessing."

Bedridden, seriously ill, Thomasine sought to comfort her husband. John later recalled that "always when she perceived me to mourn for her, she would entreat and persuade me to be contented, telling me that she did love me well, and if God would let her live with me, she would endeavour to show it more." She urged him to pray for her and stay as near as possible.

At noon Thursday the doctor arrived, and after examining Thomasine he declared that her condition was dangerous. When John told her this, she was "no whit moved at it, but was as comfortably resolved whether to live or to die." In this condition of resignation, of willingness to accept life or death from God, she fell asleep. She awoke at midnight, and feeling that death was near called to John to help her prepare. She wanted also to see her two ministers and other friends and so desired "that the bell might ring for her." In the early morning hours neighbors came one by one to talk by candlelight "quietly and comfortably" with Thomasine. Then the bell began to ring. John tells us, "Some said it was the 4 o'clock bell, but she conceiving that they sought to conceal it from her, that it did ring for her, she said they needed not, for it did not trouble her."

The ringing of the bell was a traditional way of telling a community that someone was critically ill. It allowed men and women in and around Groton who knew of Thomasine's illness to visit her or say prayers or simply think of her. The bell did not always announce a person's death—some for whom it rang recovered—but it always meant that the community might be losing one of its members. It was with this tradition in mind that the seventeenth-century English poet John Donne concluded a meditation on the interdependence of humanity with the line, "never send to know for whom the bell tolls; it tolls for thee."

In a small community like Groton, everyone knew for whom the bell tolled, and eventually the two ministers and more friends arrived. When the Reverend Mr. Sands appeared, Thomasine "reached him her hand, being glad of his coming." He questioned her about various religious matters and was surprised at the maturity of her answers. He said that he had "taken her always for a harmless young woman" but did not expect to find her so well "grounded" in religion. The second minister was impressed with her patience in the face of death and her "great comfort in God" and concluded "that her life had been so innocent and harmless as the devil could find nothing to lay to her charge."

At six o'clock the next morning the doctor came again. First he concluded that she had "received her death's wound" in the night but might languish for another day or two. Then, after feeling her pulse, he said that there was "some hope left." During the day Thomasine improved, and her next night was good; she "began to entertain some thought of life, and so," says John, "did most of us who were about her."

On Saturday, however, her condition worsened. She felt cold and told John to set his heart at rest; now, she said, "I am but a dead woman." She believed that her left hand was already dead and could not be persuaded that it was merely numb because she had slept on it. When John asked Thomasine to replace her gloves—in keeping with tradition, she was completely dressed—she at first refused, saying that it was vanity to cover a dead hand, but then she consented to please her husband.

In the next few hours she became increasingly disturbed. She complained of pain in her breast and appeared distracted. She believed that she was fighting with Satan; in her struggle she spat, clenched her teeth, fixed her eyes, and shook her head. Then she became calm, lifted herself in bed, and prayed "earnestly that she might glorify God, although it were in hell." She exhorted those around her to serve God and asked that the window curtains be opened. Formerly she had wanted them closed, but now she desired light.

Now certain that she would die, she asked to see each member of her family one at a time to give them her final advice. Her parting words to her sister included admonitions to serve God, marry for religious rather than worldly considerations, avoid lying, and raise her children well. Then she spoke to her mother, remarking that she, Thomasine, was the first child her mother would bury, and praying that she would not be "discomforted." Her mother, a pious woman, replied, "I have no cause to be discomforted. You will go to a better place, and you will be with your father again." The thought must have comforted the mother, but Thomasine, perhaps overly self-righteous now, said that since she would go to God she would be with "a better father than her earthly father."

She next spoke to members of John's family, thanking his parents for their kindness and blessing the children. She spoke to the servants, praising some and scolding others, and encouraging them to behave well and to observe the Sabbath. Finally, she told the woman who had served as her keeper not to blame herself if she died.

Thomasine was still in great pain. Her breasts were so swollen that her friends cut her waistcoat to give her some relief. She uttered many prayers and urged those around her to prepare to die, telling them they did not know "how sharp and bitter the pangs of death were." Reflecting on the church, she asked God to "bless good ministers, and convert such ill ones as did belong to him, and weed out the rest."

It was apparent that "God had given her victory" in her spiritual struggle. In the afternoon her pains lessened, and she told John she expected to live for another twenty-four hours. Through the afternoon and evening he read the Scriptures to her. Thomasine was attentive, asking John "earnestly" to read on whenever he paused and remarking on his texts. "This is comfortable," or "This is a sweet psalm," she would say.

In the evening the Reverend Mr. Sands came and prayed. Thomasine took him by the hand to say farewell. John retired, leaving his wife in the care of a woman who continued to read to her into the night. Thomasine frequently asked about John, and at two o'clock on Sunday morning he got up and came to her again.

At times Thomasine again had doubts about her conversion, saying that the devil wanted her to cast off her "subjection" to her husband. At noon, when others were at dinner, John and Thomasine continued to talk. John assured her of Christ's love for her and told her "how she should sup with Christ in paradise that night." From Groton Manor in Suffolk, England, she would actually go into the presence of Abraham, Isaac, Jacob, and the other patriarchs, apostles, and saints. This thought so encouraged Thomasine that she said, "if life were set before her she would not take it."

Thomasine and John conversed throughout the afternoon. He told her that the previous day had been the first anniversary of their marriage and that now she was going to Christ, who would "embrace her with another manner of love." She misunderstood him and replied, "O husband, I must not love thee as Christ."

After a while she could no longer speak but lay back, her eyes "steadfastly" on John as he spoke to her about the promises of the gospel and the "happy estate" she was "entering into." If he paused, she would signal him feebly with her hands, urging him to continue. A minister came to pray with her at five o'clock on Sunday afternoon. At the end of the prayer she sighed and fell "asleep in the Lord." Three days later she was buried beside John's first wife in Groton chancel. Her child was taken from its tiny grave and laid by her.

Thomasine's death led John to a period of intense self-scrutiny. He regarded his loss as punishment from God. This was a typical Puritan response to the death of a loved one. One had to recognize his or her dependence on Christ in order to be saved. One sought, but frequently could not find, this sense of dependence. But the death of a loved one proved the frailty of human life and led one to seek the God who transcended human life. During Thomasine's illness John had felt his heart "humbled and God's free mercy in Christ more open to me than at any time before to my remembrance."

Although he does not tell us exactly what happened in the moments immediately after Thomasine died, we can readily imagine his behavior. He must comfort his children, who had come to regard Thomasine as their own mother. He would encourage and exhort everyone: Thomasine had died bravely; she was now in heaven; God had his reason for taking her and must be loved. As he spoke his mind must have been feverish with thought: *She is dead, God has punished me, I have relied too much on worldly comforts, I will not set my mind on the world again. This life is transitory. Our home is in heaven.*

We know that in the days that followed Winthrop thought often about the course of his life. A small sin committed many years before troubled him. As a boy visiting a house he had spied two small books. Reasoning that the owner had thrown them away, he took them with him. The memory of that act grieved him, especially in times of affliction. Now, troubled once more, he made "satisfaction" for the books, probably by paying something to the former owner.

In January 1617 Winthrop attended a court session, usually an occasion for entertainment and frivolity as well as judicial business. This time he felt detached and was bemused by the respect paid by other men to wealth and pleasure. Later, on a trip to London, he mentioned that he used to "lose all my time in my journeys, my eyes running upon every object, and my thoughts varying with every occasion." But now he passed the time in prayer, psalm singing, and meditation.

Groton Church. In small English parish churches such as this, men and women like John and Thomasine Winthrop first encountered the Puritan God. Many, like John Winthrop, took their faith to the New World.

In later years Winthrop would identify this period as his time of greatest piety, and he felt powerfully that Christ accepted and loved him. This was not merely an intellectual conclusion but rather a pressing conviction of Christ's presence. He wrote, "I was now grown familiar with the Lord Jesus Christ. He would oft tell me he loved me. I did not doubt to believe him. If I went abroad he went with me, when I returned he came home with me. I talked with him upon the way, he lay down with me and usually I did awake with him. Now I could go into any company and not lose him."

Thus, after Thomasine's death John Winthrop spent many hours meditating about a being whom he could love without fear of loss. He took comfort in the belief that there is in this world a reality that transcends human life. Some men and women who have been possessed by this realization have concluded that they should withdraw from the world and worship God in a monastery or convent. Some, like Thomasine, have anticipated a moment when their spirit would leave the world and actually dwell with God. But John Winthrop did not withdraw from the world. Another aspect of Puritanism helped him find his way.

Puritanism taught that life was precious as well as transitory and that men have a duty to make their lives and their societies conform to the will of God. In 1618 John Winthrop married Margaret Tyndal, daughter of Sir John Tyndal, a local magnate. Their letters reveal a strong human attachment and a mutual effort to transform earthly love into divine love. With Margaret, John had more children. They might well have lived out their lives in England, but in 1629 a group of Puritans received a charter incorporating the Massachusetts Bay Company and began planning a holy community in America. Winthrop was interested in their work, and because of his legal experience as well as his Puritan piety, he was persuaded to serve as governor of the enterprise. In 1630 he led a fleet of eleven ships to the shores of New England and chose a site on a hilly peninsula in Massachusetts Bay, which the Puritans named Boston, to be his home in the new land. He must have missed his English home, but he could console himself for the loss of his native land by recalling that human fulfillment comes only through the life of the spirit. In that way the piety that had prepared him for Thomasine's death also prepared John for life in the wilderness of America.

During the first winter in New England, many settlers lived in tents; two hundred died of hunger and exposure. Nonetheless, Winthrop wrote home to his wife that he was in a "paradise." For him as for many other Puritans, nothing could be more rewarding than the opportunity America offered to create communities attuned to the will of God. During John Winthrop's twenty-year association with Massachusetts Bay, he was elected governor sixteen times. Occasionally he took an unpopular stand, or the freemen worried about creating a hereditary ruler and Winthrop lost the governorship. But always the job returned to him. In him were mingled the qualities of piety, good humor, intelligence, and vision. The people had the wisdom to reward him and themselves by accepting his leadership.

John Winthrop is remembered particularly for some of the words he used in expressing Puritan ideas. The most famous of all John Winthrop's pronouncements was his description of the ideal community, set forth in a sermon aboard the *Arbella* bound for America. He began by saying, "God Almighty in His most holy and wise providence hath so disposed of the condition of mankind as in all times some must be rich, some poor; some high and eminent in power and dignity, others mean and in subjection." That aristocratic conception of government would meet opposition even in his own lifetime. Other phrases, however, were repeated again and again in Puritan New England and echo still in our own times. "There are two rules whereby we are to walk, one towards another, justice and mercy," Winthrop said. "We must be knit together in this work as one man.... We must delight in each other, make others' conditions our own, rejoice together, mourn together, labor and suffer together." New Englanders must be so virtuous that other peoples would look on their community as a model of Christian charity. "We must consider that we shall be as a city upon a hill," Winthrop said. "The eyes of all people are upon us."

The grandeur of the Puritan scheme is apparent in phrases such as these. It is also apparent in more prosaic experiences, such as John Winthrop's night spent in a forest. One fall evening in 1631 he went for a walk near his farmhouse, taking along a gun in case he should come across a wolf. When he was about a half mile from his house, night fell, and Winthrop could not find his way home. Fortunately he came on a native house, then empty. He built a fire outside and lay down on Indian mats. But he was unable to sleep; he spent the night gathering wood, walking by the fire, and singing psalms. The religious spirit that had sustained him many years before as he watched beside Thomasine's bed encouraged him now when his own life was in danger.

The next day Winthrop located his house, to the great relief of the servants, who had shouted and shot off their guns the night before, hoping to attract his attention. It was a small adventure, happily ended. But nothing in John Winthrop's life better typifies his piety, or the pervasive religiosity of the early Puritans, than the image of the governor of Massachusetts alone by a fire in the middle of the night—singing psalms.

Bibliography

Bremmer, Francis. *The Puritan Experiment* (1976). Historical survey of Puritanism.

————. *John Winthrop: America's Forgotten Founding Father* (2003). Definitive and well-written Winthrop biography based on exhaustive use of the sources.

Geddes, Gordon E. *Welcome Joy: Death in Puritan New England* (1981). Argues that Puritans often associated death with the journey to Heaven.

Hambrick-Stowe, Charles E. *The Practice of Piety* (1982). Excellent account of Puritan devotional practices.

Middlekauff, Robert. *The Mathers: Three Generations of Puritan Intellectuals 1596–1728* (1971). Vivid intellectual biography of three Puritan ministers.

Miller, Perry. *The New England Mind* (2 vols., 1939, 1953). Standard intellectual history of the Puritans.

Morgan, Edmund S. *The Puritan Dilemma* (1958). Excellent short biography of John Winthrop.

————. *The Puritan Family* (1966). Survey of domestic life.

Morison, Samuel Eliot, et al., Editors. *Winthrop Papers* (2 vols., 1929, 1968). Includes John Winthrop's spiritual musings and his account of Thomasine's death.

Youngs, J. William T. *The Congregationalists* (1990). Survey of Puritan history in America with biographical sketches of principal leaders.

Identification Topics

John Winthrop, Thomasine Winthrop, Groton Manor, salvation through God's grace, Puritan moderation, the ringing of the bell, "Holy community"

Study Questions

1. The Puritans believed in salvation through Christ's grace. How did they attempt to bring themselves closer to Christ?
2. What kinds of thought and behavior did Puritans discourage? Give specific examples and explain the reasoning behind each.

3. What did Puritans mean when they said "wine is from God but drunkenness is from the devil"?
4. What are the chief characteristics of Puritan family life as exemplified by the Winthrops?
5. How did Thomasine's behavior in childbirth and death reflect her Puritan piety?
6. In view of their emphasis on the life of the spirit, why did Puritans allow themselves to enjoy good meals and alcoholic beverages?
7. The Winthrop household was typical of preindustrial households in England and America. Describe the "economy" of the household (how products were produced, exchanged, and consumed), and describe the roles of husband and wife in the household.

CHAPTER 3

The British American
William Byrd in Two Worlds

Europeans lived in the New World for several generations before they began to think of themselves as Americans. Britain dominated their government and culture: the colonists honored a British ruler and admired British literature, music, and architecture. By 1700 Americans possessed most of the coastal regions, but looked eastward across the Atlantic rather than westward over the Appalachians to discover who they were. William Byrd's career demonstrates the colonists' tendency to regard England as home. He spent much of his life in England pursuing his fortune. However, it was in America that he and other settlers found the greatest use for their talents.

The sun went down behind the steep, forested ridge of the Alleghenies. Resplendent stars shone brightly in the clear autumn sky while bear, deer, and opossum foraged among the darkened trees. In the midst of a vast and potent wilderness there glowed a solitary campfire, a flickering circle of light illuminating tents, horses, and a cluster of men.

The men standing by the campfire were working their way through swamps and brush surveying a dividing line between the colonies of Virginia and North Carolina. Their supplies had long since run low, and most of their horses were lame. Nonetheless, their camp was festive: this was October 30, 1728, the king's birthday, and patriotism led them to consume spirits and discharge fireworks in celebration. The men were doing their best, toasting King George II with the last of their liquor, a bottle of cherry brandy carefully preserved by their leader, William Byrd, and drinking to the queen and all her royal progeny with drafts of pure water from an Allegheny tributary. To complete the celebration, they set off explosives, fashioned of green cane from a nearby field and laid in the fire. The air within the cane joints expanded and punctured the night air with loud and satisfying bangs.

When William Byrd recorded this episode, he considered it natural to honor the English king. Although he was a second-generation Virginian, he regarded himself as an Englishman and was accustomed to celebrating his transatlantic heritage. In the middle period of colonial history, Byrd lived in two worlds—provincial Virginia and Georgian England. It was as natural for him to observe the king's birthday in the American wilderness as for any British subject in London.

Byrd's history, remarkable for his dramatic and wide-ranging achievements, highlights important features of British-American life. Byrd was many things—planter, gentleman, politician, writer, and lover. A contemplative as well as an active man, he sought to live a full and dignified life alternately as a London gentleman and as a southern planter. In certain respects he succeeded in standing astride the Atlantic, half British and half American; yet his life also exhibits a tension between the two worlds. As an American he was unable to achieve the stature he sought in London; as an Englishman he had difficulty feeling at ease in Virginia.

William Byrd can be seen as a man trying to locate himself, to find a "home." His quest for personal satisfaction in two worlds was full of contradictions. He was a moralistic libertine, a contemplative gadabout, a provincial cosmopolitan. In some ways he was an unattractive figure; he was arrogant, undisciplined, and insensitive. But at the same time he was peculiarly open, forthright, and perceptive. Because he lived fully and left accounts that reveal his multifaceted personality, he appears to us as a peculiarly vital and accessible human being, a representative figure in an America that did not yet know itself as America.

The William Byrd of our story was the second Virginian of that name. His father and namesake, William Byrd I, was the son of a prosperous London goldsmith named John Byrd. The elder William, born in 1652, might well have stayed in England and followed his father's trade, but he was drawn to Virginia in 1670 by an invitation from his uncle, Capt. Thomas Stegg. It was through the Stegg family that the Byrd dynasty in Virginia made its start. Capt. Thomas Stegg was the son of an earlier sea captain of the same name, an Atlantic trader who was appointed by Parliament during the English Civil War to sail to Virginia and demand that the colony acknowledge the rule of Oliver Cromwell. Stegg completed his mission but was lost at sea on his return passage in 1651. He left his property to the younger Captain Stegg, whose sister married John Byrd and bore the nephew whom Thomas recalled in his later years. Because he lacked an heir, he invited this nephew, William Byrd I, to come to Virginia and, by implication, to take over his land.

Thus, as a youth of eighteen, William Byrd I went to Virginia to seek his fortune. Unlike the pioneers who died by the hundreds from starvation, disease, exposure, and Indian attacks in the first bleak years at Jamestown, and unlike the Pilgrims of Plymouth Rock who found no "inns to refresh their weather-beaten bodies," William Byrd I arrived in a wilderness that was already somewhat civilized. He sailed up the James River in 1670 and landed near his uncle's substantial two-story stone plantation house.

William Byrd I hardly had time to settle into his new surroundings before his uncle died, leaving the young man a Virginia estate. Byrd took good care of his inheritance, thanks in part to the help of a young woman named Mary Horsemanden Filmer, whom he married in 1673. She was the daughter of Sir Warham Horsemanden, a staunch supporter of King Charles II. Her family would supply the Byrds with valuable connections in England.

In 1674 the couple's first child was born. Named William Byrd II, he spent his early years on his father's Virginia plantation, the hub of extensive agricultural and trading activity. The elder Byrd raised tobacco, which he exchanged for African slaves and English manufactured goods. His plantation was an entrepôt for trade with smaller planters and with remote Indian tribes. As a boy, William could watch large packtrains with several score horses forming near his house in preparation for their journey along the Trading Path four hundred miles into the interior to the lands of the Catawbas and the Cherokees. In those distant regions they exchanged cloth, blankets, beads, pots, pans, hatchets, guns, lead, and rum for the hides of bear, deer, beaver, otter, mink, and buffalo.

By engaging in such activities the elder Byrd increased his fortune, and in colonial America wealth generally led to political influence. The colonists had already broken with some of the aristocratic traditions of England. The colonial electorate was proportionately larger than the English. In both places only free adult males with fifty acres of land or fifty pounds in property could vote, but in America the widespread availability of land made it much easier to acquire the fifty acres. Although Virginians could not vote for the governor or for members of the upper house of their legislature—in most colonies they were appointed by the crown—they could elect the lower house, called the House of Burgesses.

Widespread political participation did not, however, undermine the relationship of wealth, social position, and political influence. The colonial ruling elite as well as the English aristocracy assumed that these forms of power belonged together. The upper house of the legislature consisted of the wealthiest colonists, and even the House of Burgesses was mainly composed of well-to-do planters. They alone could afford to leave their plantations in the care of overseers and serve without pay in the legislature. It was generally assumed that the wealthy were the fittest to rule. Their plantation experience educated them in government, and their superior social position reminded colonists of their accustomed rulers in Europe. It seemed natural to think of such men as leaders.

With his success as trader and planter, it was inevitable that the elder Byrd should join the provincial elite. But his career was almost ruined by an event that occurred while he was still in his twenties, a curious episode in Virginia history known as Bacon's Rebellion. In 1676 an unauthorized frontier war against Indians culminated in a revolt against the colonial governor, Sir William Berkeley. The revolt was once interpreted as a democratic upheaval, but is now generally understood as having been a conflict for privilege among factions of Virginia gentry. The minor reforms that followed the fall of the rebels somewhat broadened the circle of privilege in Virginia, but it did not end the assumption that wealth and power should be closely intertwined.

William Byrd I nearly became one of the victims of the rebellion. A frontier planter, he was so worried by the Indian attacks that in 1676 he sent his wife and child to England to escape the conflict. In their absence he joined rebel Nathaniel Bacon's attacks on the Indians. But when Bacon waged war on the governor, Byrd wisely sided with Berkeley.

His wife and son returned from their short exile in 1677 to find that Byrd had chosen the winning side and had thus launched a political career that would take him to the House of Burgesses, the Provincial Council, and in 1687 to the position of auditor of public accounts and receiver general of Virginia. When his son reached age seven, Byrd sent him to England to attend school, as was customary among the Virginia gentry. Lacking a local college, the Virginia aristocrats assumed that a child must go abroad to receive a good classical education and become familiar with the larger world. Thus, in 1681 William Byrd II left home on his first long pilgrimage to England.

In London he was placed under the care of his maternal uncle, Daniel Horsemanden, who sent him to Felsted School, thirty-five miles northeast of London. Felsted was a tiny island in the rolling fields of Essex but was well respected because its headmaster, Christopher Glasscock, was reputed to be one of the best schoolmasters in England. William Byrd passed his early youth at Felsted. In the chill fogs of rural Essex, far from the hot sultry air of plantation Virginia, he learned, played, ate, and lived in a world of boys; his earlier world, the place of father, mother, servants, slaves, and traders, must have seemed as remote and unreal as a dream.

William Byrd's classical education influenced his thought and behavior for the rest of his life. Felsted taught him Latin, Greek, and probably Hebrew. It introduced him to the history of ancient civilizations and grounded him in biblical and classical philosophy. In later years he read the ancient texts almost daily, perhaps because he had first encountered them after he had lost his family and his native land. They may have given him a sense of continuity and stability in the changing environments, cultural as well as personal, of his existence.

In 1689, at age fifteen, Byrd was ready to leave Felsted to embark on the second phase of his education. His father was eager that his son, who would inherit the Virginia estate, should not be an untutored provincial in the world of commerce. Thus he sent him to the Netherlands to learn the "fine business sense" of the Dutch merchants. In the following year, he transferred the boy to the London firm of Perry and Lane, merchants who handled the family dealings in tobacco and furs.

Byrd's education took another turn in 1692 when he entered the Middle Temple in London to study law. The Temple, one of the most ancient and respected educational institutions in England, was a school for dramatists, scientists, and merchants as well as lawyers. Its emphasis on culture and gentlemanly behavior attracted the sons of many leading English families. At the Temple, Byrd studied law and qualified for the bar in 1695; during this time he also developed a taste for drama, science, conversation, and women.

His interest in drama was encouraged by three of the leading English dramatists of his generation, William Wycherley, William Congreve, and Nicholas Rowe, all of whom studied with Byrd at the Temple. Many great plays, including Shakespeare's *Twelfth Night*, had premiered at the Temple Theatre. Byrd's devotion to drama continued through many evenings at Drury Lane and the Queen's Theatre in London; in later years his extensive library in Virginia would include several hundred plays, probably the largest collection in America.

Byrd also maintained an active amateur interest in science. Through a family friend and personal confidant, Sir Robert Southwell, he was admitted to the Royal Society in 1696. This organization brought together the greatest scientific minds in England; Byrd's colleagues included such eminent men as Sir Isaac Newton. Byrd's contributions were limited, but he maintained an avid interest in the society throughout his life and corresponded for many years with some of its members, including Charles Boyle, Earl of Orrery.

Science and drama contributed to his third area of activity in London—Byrd's interest in polite conversation. If one activity stands out above all others in Byrd's life, it is human discourse. Many of his days seem to have been spent in talking with friends about literature, drama, science, and society. They met in each others' rooms, in coffee-houses, and at fashionable spas, such as Tunbridge Wells.

Finally, Byrd was interested—to the point of obsession—in the opposite sex. Many years after he left the Middle Temple he recalled his youthful "intrigues" with "naughty jades" in a letter to his former partner in lust, Benjamin Lynde, by then a staid and proper chief justice of Massachusetts. William Wycherley, another Temple friend, is supposed to have introduced Byrd to the taverns, gambling, and women that made up much of London's nightlife. We have no diary of these early activities, but Byrd hints at them in a letter to a godson, whom he counsels: if you must be punished at school, don't let it be for failure to study, "but for some sprightly action or gaiety of heart." Byrd's own sprightliness is indicated in a brief autobiographical piece entitled "The Enamored Bird." Writing of himself in the third person, he says, "Love broke out upon him before his beard, and he could distinguish sexes long before he could tell the difference betwixt good and evil." He continues that it was fortunate that he did not have a twin sister, for he might have had an affair with her in their mother's womb.

There were numerous opportunities for a young man to find sexual companion-ship among London's prostitutes and with women looking for temporary alliances, and Byrd appears to have known many of them during his twenties. But as he neared his thirtieth birthday he began to think of marriage. Lady Elizabeth Cromwell, a bright, clever, attractive young woman, seemed a likely candidate. She promised to be a stimu-lating companion to a successful suitor, and she would bring her husband an annual income of £2,000 a year, enough to enable Byrd to live easily in England for the remain-der of his life. But Lady Elizabeth had other plans. In summer 1703 she went to Ireland, leaving Byrd, as he complained to her, with his soul "perfectly out of tune." He wrote that she was wasting herself on Ireland, a country "so disagreeable that even toads and spiders disdain to live in it." But this effort was all to no avail: she married another man.

In disparaging Ireland, Byrd revealed sentiments he may have harbored toward his remote homeland in America. He had learned to take a cosmopolitan view of distant regions. But Virginia could not be entirely forgotten. In 1695, after completing his stud-ies at the Middle Temple, he had made a short visit to his family. He might have settled then in America had the colony not needed a representative in England. Young William Byrd was a natural choice for the business because of his legal training and his familiar-ity with London, and—most likely—because he was glad enough of an excuse to return to the great metropolis. He had arrived back in England in 1697 and argued the colonial side on such questions as whether Virginia should help New York fight an Indian war and whether the colonists should be prevented from planting flax and cotton. For a time he had the title of "agent" of the Virginia Assembly, but in 1702 the position was abolished, leaving him free to return to America in 1705 when he received the news of his father's death.

Upon his return William Byrd took up residence at Westover, a large wood house overlooking the James River and commanding a plantation of six thousand acres. In addition to Westover, he inherited another house on the James and an additional twenty thousand acres. Byrd was immediately occupied with the innumerable details of plantation life. He supervised the planting and harvesting of tobacco and other crops, designed a garden, planted orchards, and experimented with new agricultural techniques. By studying English agricultural tracts he became one of the best farmers in Virginia. He also ran the plantation's many trading enterprises—importing manufactured goods and distributing them to the smaller planters, and exporting furs and tobacco. In addition he had to make frequent trips into the interior to inspect the work on his other plantations.

His early months at Westover must have been lonely. He met other gentry on visits and at church, but he lived in isolation. It was time to find a wife, and Byrd's position as a suitor was now much stronger than it had been in England, where he was easily overshadowed by men of greater wealth and higher rank. In Virginia he was head of one of the colony's foremost families. He was personally attractive as well. His pleasant face, long aristocratic nose, heavy dark brows, and sparkling eyes reflected a captivating good humor. He was a dazzling conversationalist and a charming escort.

He easily won the attention of Lucy Parke, the pretty daughter of Col. Daniel Parke, who would later become governor of the Leeward Islands. Her membership in the colonial aristocracy was a necessary element of their courtship. Conscious of their status, the members of the Virginia elite insisted upon marriage within their own class. Byrd's acceptance of this code was apparent many years later when he met a gentry couple whose daughter had run away with an Irish overseer. He heartily agreed that she should not have married a "dirty plebeian." Certainly Byrd, although only one generation removed from London trade, would mingle with only the bluest blood in Virginia.

But the wedding of William and Lucy was not merely an alliance of social convenience. The marriage roused the passions of both partners. Variety was the hallmark of Byrd's character as well as Lucy's. Their volatile personalities gave off sparks of anger as well as love but never receded into boredom. That we can speak with such confidence about the love affair of a husband and wife who have been dead for more than two centuries is one of the wonders of Byrd's story. Most private emotions are lost with the lives that supported them. A person's house, furniture, or portrait can easily survive. But emotions seldom leave a mark. Even letters between husband and wife most often describe their hours apart rather than their hours together; and a diary is seldom candid about a matrimonial partner, who might glance at its pages at any moment.

It is against all odds, then, that William Byrd should have left an intimate account of his life with Lucy. But he did and solved the problem of privacy by a simple stratagem: he used an obscure form of shorthand that he probably learned in London. Not only did it ensure confidentiality, but it also alleviated a common problem of the diarist, that of finding time for daily longhand entries. After Byrd's death the diaries vanished into obscurity for almost two hundred years. The volumes that are known to have survived were published in the twentieth century when Marion Tinling, a specialist in early forms of shorthand, transcribed Byrd's diary for 1709–1712 at the Huntington Library in California. Two other portions of the diary, covering the years 1717–1721 and 1739–1741, were subsequently transcribed and published. Although they cover only one-seventh of William Byrd's life, they reveal the contours of his personality and experience with remarkable clarity.

It is through the first diary that we come to know the relationship between William Byrd and his wife. In a plantation society, remote from their neighbors, William and Lucy spent many days as one another's only companion. Some of their hours were, of course, spent separately. The husband had to supervise the plantation; the wife ordered household affairs. But they passed many hours entertaining one another, playing cards or billiards or reading books together, especially volumes of sermons by the great English churchman, Archbishop Tillotson. They danced or walked in the garden among William's well-pruned trees or went down to the bay to watch the fishermen. They tended each other in their illnesses and shared meals of beef, venison, pigeon, or turkey. In the evening Lucy sometimes sang to her husband.

William Byrd especially enjoyed these companionable times, but they were often interrupted by periods of violent quarreling. Byrd frequently blamed their disputes on Lucy's feminine "weakness," but it is evident he could be a difficult husband. He enjoyed cheating her at games, amusing himself by provoking Lucy. He teased her by caressing other women and found it difficult to understand her annoyance when he and a houseguest began discoursing in Latin, edifying one another but excluding Lucy from the conversation.

From the diary it is evident that William Byrd expected to govern his wife. Such indeed was the current convention, and it is doubtful that Lucy expected to participate in such "manly" affairs as politics and plantation management. But in some domestic affairs, where she felt she should be respected, her husband seemed unreasonable. He regarded the library as his own province and refused to allow her to take a volume from there without his permission. Intervening in household affairs, he criticized her handling of servants or the family larder. Once when she secretly ordered some personal goods from England, he intercepted them, remarking in his diary that the extra expense was "enough to make a man mad." A few days later he sold most of them, leaving Lucy in tears.

She was not even given free rein in matters of appearance. It was fashionable at that time for women to pluck their eyebrows, but for unknown reasons William Byrd opposed the custom. When he discovered his wife about to remove her brows on the eve of a trip to Williamsburg, the provincial capital, he told her to stop. She protested but finally accepted his judgment. Byrd summarized the incident in telling words: I "got the best of her, and maintained my authority."

Lucy Byrd did not write a diary, but from her husband's notes it appears that she was eager to find some segment of life that she could nourish and control in the way William governed the plantation. She bore four children, but two died in infancy. The other two were reared as much by servants as by their mother. She could of course govern the servants, who looked after the children and did the household work. But William would not give her a free hand even in domestic affairs. In one particularly violent encounter, when Byrd intervened while she was punishing a servant, Lucy was so frustrated that she attacked him with a poker.

The relationship between William and Lucy Byrd was obviously changeable and passionate. It would be inaccurate to describe it as either a wholly "good" or a wholly "bad" marriage. The Byrds experienced periods of mutual tenderness and times of reciprocal hostility. It seems probable, however, that both partners were frequently stimulated and comforted by their companionship and that they enjoyed a satisfying sexual relationship.

Again, it is William Byrd's diary that allows us to make such an observation. In it he recorded not only his discussions and his arguments with his wife, but also their sexual activities. Mingled with the entries on weather, plantation affairs, reading, and politics are dozens of brief notations on lovemaking. William Byrd used two common words of the times, "roger" and "flourish," to denote an act of sexual intercourse. He did not describe these intimate moments explicitly, but even in its stark simplicity the diary indicates the many moods of the couple's love. That range is suggested by these entries:

> About 10 o'clock we went to bed, where I lay in my wife's arms (April 19, 1709).
>
> In the afternoon I took a flourish with my wife and then read a sermon in Tillotson (September 10, 1710).
>
> About 11 o'clock I went to church and heard a sermon from Mr. Anderson. . . . I gave my wife a flourish on the couch in the library (August 3, 1710).
>
> I gave my wife a flourish in which she had a great deal of pleasure (November 4, 1710).
>
> In the evening we drank a bottle of mead, and I ate some toast. . . . I rogered my wife with vigor (May 29, 1711).
>
> In the evening I took a walk about the plantation and found things in good order. . . . I gave my wife a powerful flourish and gave her great ecstasy and refreshment (April 30, 1710).
>
> In the afternoon my wife and I had a little quarrel which I reconciled with a flourish. Then she read a sermon in Dr. Tillotson to me. It is to be observed that the flourish was performed on the billiard table (July 30, 1710).

And so it went. In bedroom, library, and billiard room; with tender pleasure or wild ecstasy; after quarrels, separations, and companionable moments William and Lucy thus consummated their love. There were long periods in which their physical relationship was interrupted by childbirth, sickness, or distance, but sex was there to comfort and thrill them during ordinary times. Byrd continued to have a wandering eye and occasionally allowed himself to fondle one of the chambermaids when he was away in Williamsburg. But if he lusted after other women with his heart and even now and then with his hands, he appears to have confined the ultimate expressions of his ardor to Lucy. He was, in the fashion of the times, a faithful husband.

In his thirties, then, William Byrd discovered the pleasure of commitment to work and marriage. But he sought something more: greater wealth and power. Byrd purchased large tracts of Virginia and Carolina wilderness, and when Lucy's father died, killed in an insurrection in the Leeward Islands, Byrd gained his father-in-law's Virginia lands by assuming his debts.

His desire for power was even greater than his thirst for land. At its most primitive level, power in plantation Virginia meant power over black slaves. At home in Westover, William Byrd had more authority than a medieval baron and treated his slaves with a combination of sensitivity and brutality. He always referred to them as "my people" and was frequently among them, talking with them in the evening, caring for them in sickness. But if a slave seemed lazy, careless, or rebellious, Byrd did not hesitate to administer a beating designed to discourage misbehavior.

He also was a power among the local planters. Soon after his marriage he was assigned the best pew in the local church, much to his pleasure. In his mid-thirties he became commander of the Virginia militia in a two-county area. Occasionally he reviewed his citizen soldiers and supervised training days when the men drilled and held contests at wrestling and marksmanship. He was treated as the great man of the region. As he confided to his diary after one review, "Everybody respected me like a king."

William Byrd enjoyed the deference of slave, pastor, and militiaman. But he knew he was not a king. Power in the world of rural Virginia was a pale imitation of power in London or even in Williamsburg. Byrd could not forget the greater world, even while enjoying preeminence on its fringes. His ambition as well as his sense of duty often took him to Williamsburg. In 1705 he had inherited the position of receiver general from his father, just as an English aristocrat might follow his father in office. The passing on of an office was not as certain as the willing of land, but because property and office were closely associated a man who inherited land frequently acquired a concomitant political role. Byrd had to wait five years after his father's death before he acquired a second family office, a seat on the Governor's Council, but it was assumed from the start that the new squire of Westover would eventually have that position as well as that of receiver general.

Byrd also sought to win the highest office in the colony, the position of lieutenant governor. (The lieutenant governor served in the stead of a titular head, who held the office of governor but resided in England.) Through his London connections Byrd came close to winning the position, but it went instead to Alexander Spotswood in 1710. Thwarted, Byrd became an ardent supporter of the council against the chief executive. He opposed Spotswood's efforts to change the way the receiver general collected taxes, and with his fellow councilors he fought the creation of a new court system that would undermine the judicial functions of the council. Byrd was further annoyed when in 1714 Spotswood established a monopoly over the colony's Indian trade.

Unable to prevail in Virginia, he decided in 1715 to return to England as an agent of the council to seek Spotswood's recall, perhaps even to replace him. He intended to remain in England only a short time, but it was soon apparent that business and politics would keep him longer, and he sent for Lucy. She arrived in summer 1716 and was warmly received by Byrd's old friends, who called her "an honor to Virginia." Lucy's presence in London was a reminder of all the proud Byrd had achieved during the past ten years in Virginia. But, unfortunately, her career there was as brief as it was satisfying. Lucy contracted smallpox and died on November 21, 1716.

Byrd had little time to regret his wife's death. Even as he was burying her, he was engaged in his struggle against Governor Spotswood. He testified to the Board of Trade, the English agency most responsible for colonial government, that Spotswood had threatened colonial liberty by taking upon himself the power to appoint judges. In response, Spotswood wrote from Virginia that the real threat to proper order came from the council itself. Citing the ambitions of Byrd and several of his fellow councilors, he warned that unless such men were thwarted Virginia would soon be ruled by "the haughtiness of a Carter, the hypocrisy of a Blair," and "the malice of a Byrd." He almost succeeded in having Byrd removed from the council. Clearly, the lust for power was not confined to the lord of Westover.

Byrd was able to prevail on one of the specific issues in the conflict but was defeated in a second. In 1717 the Board of Trade repealed the law that had allowed Spotswood to establish a monopoly in Indian trade but upheld the governor's prerogative in the important area of special courts. The council's reaction to this news was so hostile, however, that the board became uneasy about the colony's stability. In 1719 the board asked Byrd to return to Virginia to heal the breach.

He arrived at Westover in 1720, and soon afterward, much to everyone's surprise, he and Spotswood came to an understanding, perhaps because they had much in common. The conflict between the governor and the council had hardly been a democratic protest against royal authority. The councilors sought mainly to protect their elite status. Their cause was neither antiaristocratic nor anti-British; in the fight against the governor, they had appealed to the crown rather than to the people. The road to influence and respectability in 1720, whether for an individual or for an institution, lay in association with British authority.

Certainly this was William Byrd's belief, for after setting his plantation in order he returned once more to England, apparently hoping to use his position in Virginia to gain status in London. In this spirit he courted "Sabina," his pseudonym for Mary Smith, the daughter of a wealthy commissioner of excise. She lived across the street from Byrd in London and had caught his attention shortly after Lucy's death. She was young, lovely, witty, and wealthy—everything Byrd could hope for in a second wife. Their courtship lasted more than a year. At first they courted in secret, even communicating in invisible ink—an awkward arrangement, because sometimes they themselves could not read their messages. Finally Byrd worked up his courage and approached Sabina's father. He tried to impress on this rather forbidding parent that he, Byrd, was a man of great property in Virginia; he owned 43,000 acres, 220 slaves, and prodigious quantities of livestock. But Mary Smith's father was unimpressed with an estate so far from London. He told the crestfallen planter that all his possessions were "little better than an estate in the moon." Never before had Byrd been made to feel more like a provincial, an outsider in London's attractive society.

He was despondent for several months. He tried to persuade Sabina to marry him against her father's will, but she refused. He clung to her in his imagination, seeing her in the window across the street and making "distant love to her." When he received her final note of rejection, he "cried exceedingly." Mary Smith had offered him something more than beauty and wit. She would have brought him great wealth and a fixed place in London society. With her he might have remained permanently in England as an Englishman. Without her he had lost both a woman and a world.

Of course, few such momentous turning points in life are recognizable at the time. Often we are not even aware of our limitations; we reflect that what could not be achieved today might still be gained tomorrow. In this spirit William Byrd continued to seek a wealthy spouse while doing his best to lead the life of a bright London socialite. He met with friends at Will's Coffee House almost daily; played at cards, billiards, and bowls; and gambled at the residence of the Spanish ambassador. He attended plays and went to masked balls, took walks with the fashionable ladies and gentlemen in St. James's Park, and visited friends at fine country estates.

Byrd kept busy with these activities, but his life in London gives an impression of excessive frivolity. He might try to appear lively and gay, but he was a man approaching fifty and yet was exhibiting the rootless passion of a much younger man. He had no spouse and no employment. The Virginia gentleman had become a London gadabout, and his sexual life was a barometer of his condition. The second of his surviving journals covers the years 1717–1721 and is mainly about life in London. With his usual candor he describes an astonishingly intricate love life. Arranged in order of stability, there were three tiers in his relationships. First there were his mistresses. These were usually older women whom he would visit every week or so; sometimes he kept two or three of them simultaneously. Their alliances appear to have been based on mutual affection as well as on monetary compensation. Then there were prostitutes, some of whom he met at a fashionable house run by a Mrs. Smith; others, in the park. Finally, there were contacts with maids, cooks, and women encountered at masked balls.

These companions parade through the pages of Byrd's diary in a seemingly endless procession, reminding the reader of his description of himself in "The Enamored Bird." In that autobiographical sketch Byrd had said, "He would follow a scent with great eagerness for a little while, but then a fresh scent would cross it and carry him violently another way." One evening Byrd might take a prostitute to the Three Tuns Tavern for pheasant and woodcock, then retire with her to an upstairs room. A few days later he would find another woman and make love in a park or a coach. He went to see his friend Lord Orrery; finding him not at home, he kissed Lady Orrery for "half an hour." Another time he kissed Lord Orrery's housekeeper. Apparently never at a loss in such matters, he once visited a mistress and, finding her not at home, caressed the maid; then upon his mistress's return, he retired with her to the bedroom for more serious lovemaking.

Although William Byrd took some satisfaction in his hectic love life, he recognized the disadvantages of these brief encounters. There was always the danger of venereal disease, which he had already contracted at least once. Then, too, his conscience, while permitting him his mistresses, rebelled at his use of prostitutes. He frequently asked God's forgiveness after a furtive meeting with purchased flesh or thanked God for preserving him on evenings when none of the women on the street suited his taste.

Hoping to find stability again in marriage, he continued his quest for a wellborn English lady, proposing three times unsuccessfully to a widow Pierson and once to Lady Elizabeth Lee, an illegitimate granddaughter of King Charles II. Finally in 1724 he won the hand of a woman twenty-five years his junior, Maria Taylor. She was sufficiently wellborn to satisfy his social ambition and attractive and clever enough to win and hold his attention. But although she was an heiress, she was not wealthy enough to allow Byrd to retire in England.

Byrd would have to turn his attention once more to earning a living. His Virginia plantations were in the hands of overseers, who could not be efficiently regulated at a distance of three thousand miles. The lands yielded enough revenue to keep him well as a bachelor, but they would now require his personal attention. Thus, he and Maria went to Virginia in 1726. Byrd probably expected to return shortly to England, for he held on to a fashionable apartment at Lincoln's Inn.

In Virginia, Byrd supervised the management of his main estate at Westover and made frequent inspection tours of the other plantations. Hoping to increase his income, he experimented with new crops such as hemp, grapevines, and ginseng—a medicinal root—and sought new offices in the provincial government.

As the months in America turned into years, William Byrd clearly missed England. In 1727 he wrote a friend telling him that his daughters by his first marriage

Westover. William Byrd was told in London that a Virginia plantation was "little better than an estate in the moon," built this house in America.

had difficulty adjusting to their "retirement" from London. "They can't get the plays, the operas, and the masquerades out of their heads," he said. He did not complain about his own isolation but did his best to carry parts of the great world to Virginia. He continued to build up his library and read almost daily in Latin, Greek, Hebrew, and French; and he surrounded himself with the most cultivated and interesting minds in Virginia, including ministers, professors, sea captains, and English visitors. He kept up a correspondence with his old friends in London and devoted a room at Westover to portraits of English grandees he had known.

Byrd carried his London years with him even on journeys to remote sections of Virginia. On one trip, for example, he was delayed by rain at a plantation house, and finding that his hostess enjoyed plays, he read to her from *The Beggar's Opera* and told her how the play had captivated London a few years before.

In such activities Byrd showed his continuing interest in the wider world that he had known for so many years. Nonetheless, as the years passed, he found himself more and more rooted in American soil. Life with Maria was less exciting than with Lucy, but it brought a domestic tranquility that he now enjoyed. For the first time in his life he was surrounded by a family. His daughters by Lucy had been reared by relatives in England; now they came to live at Westover. In addition, he had three daughters and a son, William Byrd III, by Maria.

He turned his literary genius for the first time to American materials. In England he had written fashionable, witty prose of no great importance, including a poem entitled "Ode to a Fart." His American writings were lighthearted without being frivolous.

They included many fine descriptions of the locales and peoples of the region. The so-called Westover Manuscripts—three books Byrd wrote to circulate privately among his friends—are among the best literary products of colonial America.

The first and best of the manuscripts grew out of his participation in the 1728 expedition to survey the Virginia–North Carolina dividing line. *The History of the Dividing Line* contains witty character sketches of Byrd's fellow commissioners, whose virtues and foibles he revealed perceptively. It also contains engaging portraits of local persons, including the backwoods squatters who made their women do all the work, rising late in the morning "after stretching and yawning for half an hour." He got to know the Indian guide, Bearskin, and wrote a long passage describing the man's religious beliefs.

The other commissioners often chased after women, but Byrd refrained from such activities and did his best to prevent abusive behavior. In an earlier version of the *History* he referred to all the men by pseudonyms; it is symptomatic of his new maturity and self-control that he gave himself the name "Steady."

After returning from the dividing line, Byrd apparently decided to stay in Virginia. In 1729 he sold his London chambers at Lincoln's Inn. A year or two later he began work on a magnificent brick mansion to replace the old wood house at Westover. In many ways the new house was a reminder of England and may have been modeled after the country estate of one of his English friends. A formal garden with gravel paths, gates, fruit trees, cedars, and hedges and rooms crowded with English furniture, ornaments, books, and portraits were reminders of the Old World. But it sat on a Virginia hillside overlooking a Virginia river, an English home in an American setting. If it reflected Byrd's continuing respect for things English, it reflected also his willingness finally to live his English life in an American environment.

A letter written several years before to Lord Orrery suggests that he could take a positive outlook on his Americanization. "Like one of the patriarchs," he said, "I have my flock and my herds, my bondmen and bondwomen, and every sort of trade amongst my own servants, so that I live in a kind of independence of everyone but Providence." Byrd emphasized the simplicity and innocence of plantation life. "Half a crown," he said, "will rest undisturbed in my pockets for many moons together." There was no need to fear "public robbers nor private." Certainly Virginia was not London, but there were compensations. "We are happy in our Canaans," he said, "if we can but forget the onions and fleshpots of Egypt." He wrote in the same vein in a letter to another English friend. "A library, a garden, a grove, and a purling stream," he said, "are the innocent scenes that divert our leisure."

In these letters Byrd struck a note that others would sound again and again in descriptions of America. If Europe could offer great cities, historic buildings, and sophisticated company, America could make a virtue of the absence of these things. Simplicity, innocence, and nature were abundant in the New World. And were they not as attractive as crowded theaters, busy streets, and noisy masquerades? Byrd was still too attracted to the cultural advantages of London to belittle her achievements. But in coming to appreciate American nature and customs, he deepened his attachment to his native habitat.

In one respect, however, these letters are misleading. They suggest that Byrd was able to live a life of endless leisure. In fact, he worked much harder in Virginia than he had in England. As he said in his letter to Lord Orrery, "I must take care to keep all my people to their duty, to set all the springs in motion, and to make everyone draw his equal share to carry the machine forward." Byrd had to supervise the work at Westover and the other plantations. Additionally, his ambition and his debts kept him busy seeking new ways to earn money. These activities led him to become increasingly involved in the government and economy of the region. His thirst for land was inexhaustible; he built up his inherited estate of 26,000 acres to almost 180,000 acres and forged closer ties with other great Virginia landowners. His chief rival for preeminence among the planters was Robert ("King") Carter, who accumulated 300,000 acres before his death in 1732. Two of Byrd's children married Carters.

Byrd's final years had a serene quality. He and Maria governed their beautiful Westover in harmony. He read his Latin and Greek, walked in his garden, visited his people, and entertained his friends. As he approached his seventieth year, he had a wry sense of humor about his own mortality. In 1741 he wrote to a friend in London, "I am alive, and by the help of ginseng, hope to survive some years longer." He was lively enough in his late sixties to "play the fool" now and then with the maids but was not virile enough to give Maria much worry. In 1743 his political career was crowned by his appointment to the presidency of the Virginia Council.

He died a year later and was buried in the garden at Westover. The epitaph on his gravestone called him a "hearty friend to the liberties of his country." In 1776 that description would acquire a meaning that would have been incomprehensible to William Byrd. During Byrd's lifetime, love of America and loyalty to England were part of a single fabric of patriotism. His home was in a place that no longer exists, where colonists in a New World still looked to an Old World to discover who they were.

Bibliography

Brown, Kathleen M. *Good Wives, Nasty Wenches, and Anxious Patriarchs: Gender, Race, and Power in Colonial Virginia* (1996). Explores the roles of gender and race in the genesis of institutions in colonial Virginia.

Lockridge, Kenneth. *The Diary and Life of William Byrd II of Virginia, 1677–1744* (1987). Overview of Byrd's life.

———. *On the Sources of Patriarchal Power* (1992). Uses the commonplace books of Thomas Jefferson and William Byrd to explore the relationship of power and gender in early Virginia.

Marambaud, Marion. *William Byrd of Westover, 1674–1744* (1971). Topical account of Byrd and his world.

Parent, Anthony S., Jr. *Foul Means: The Formation of a Slave Society in Virginia, 1600–1740* (2003). Cogent analysis of enslavement and black resistance to enslavement in colonial Virginia.

Tinling, Marion, Editor. *The Correspondence of the Three William Byrds of Westover, Virginia, 1684–1776* (1977). Fine collection of letters to and from the Byrds.

Woodfin, Maude H., Editor. *Another Secret Diary of William Byrd of Westover, 1739–1741* (1942). Covers later years in Virginia and includes letters and literary exercises.

Wright, Louis B., and Marion Tinling, Editors. *The London Diary (1717–1721) and Other Writings* (1958). Includes the Westover Manuscripts.

———. *The Secret Diary of William Byrd of Westover, 1709–1712* (1941). Covers early years in Virginia and marriage to Lucy.

Identification Topics

William Byrd I, William Byrd II, Byrd's diaries, Bacon's Rebellion, Middle Temple, "The Enamored Bird," Lucy Parke, House of Burgesses, Williamsburg, Alexander Spotswood, "Sabina," Maria Taylor, Westover, *History of the Dividing Line*

Study Questions

1. How did William Byrd's life in Virginia reflect British influences? How did it reflect American characteristics? (Mention pertinent customs, interests, institutions, and objects.)
2. In view of William Byrd's great wealth and influence in Virginia, why didn't he simply stay in America?
3. In what respects was colonial Virginia an aristocratic society? In what respects was it democratic?
4. The author suggests that in England, William Byrd was something of a gadabout, whereas in America his life was more stable and constructive. In what ways do Byrd's vocational, intellectual, and sexual activities support this argument?
5. This chapter describes several levels of authority in colonial Virginia. Describe the distribution of power in each of these relationships: husbands and wives, masters and slaves, local gentry and average colonists, Virginia and England.
6. William Byrd's career reveals both the satisfaction and the frustration of being a British American. In what ways were the two identities compatible? In what ways did they come into conflict?

CHAPTER 4

Reform in Colonial America
John Woolman on Goodness and Greed

During the early eighteenth century, the British colonies in North America were among the most prosperous places on earth. The literacy rate was exceptionally high. Widespread land ownership meant that the average family was well fed and well housed. And yet there were many exceptions to this pattern of abundance. Slaves, of course, were hardly prosperous, nor were Indians and poor whites. Some colonists noted with regret the debased condition of their less-fortunate neighbors, and they lamented also the spiritual cost of rampant materialism. John Woolman, a Quaker reformer, was one such critic. His argument with colonial society in its formative years helped lay the foundation for an enduring American reform tradition.

When he was a child in colonial New Jersey, John Woolman killed a robin with a stone. He was walking to a neighbor's house on an errand when he saw the bird sitting on her nest. As he approached, the robin took flight, but "having young ones, she flew about, and with many cries expressed her concern for them." Woolman began throwing rocks at the bird, struck her, and she fell dead. At first the boy was pleased with his "exploit." But soon afterward he was "seized with horror," as he recalled, "at having, in a sportive way, killed an innocent creature while she was careful for her young." Adding to his "painful consideration" of the robin's death, John realized that without their mother, the babies would surely "pine away and die miserably." So with regret he climbed the tree and killed the chicks. For a long time afterward, he writes, I "could think of little else but the cruelties I had committed, and was much troubled."

This story, as recorded years later in *The Journal of John Woolman*, hints at the personality of one of the most spiritual men in early American history. Many a youngster then and now might kill a bird without a qualm. But Woolman was uncomfortable with his behavior. He summarized the feeling in his journal. God, he said, "hath placed a principle in the human mind, which incites to exercise goodness toward every living creature; and this being singly attended to, people become tender-hearted and sympathizing; but when frequently and totally rejected, the mind becomes shut up in a contrary disposition."

That God-given inclination toward goodness was at work in Woolman when he regretted killing the robins. He devoted his adult life to cultivating and following this impulse. He noted it, for example, when as a young man he suddenly experienced remorse when writing a bill of sale for a slave woman. The owner wanted to sell his human "property"—an act as acceptable in those days as trading a horse. The seller was a shopkeeper for whom Woolman worked, and the purchaser was a respectable, elderly gentleman. Woolman did not want to offend either man. And so "through weakness" he accommodated them both and wrote up the transaction. But he immediately regretted his complicity in the sale and told the men he "believed slave-keeping to be a practice inconsistent with the Christian religion."

Opposition to slavery was an unusual idea at that time. John Woolman's revulsion at helping with the sale was instinctive, like his reaction to killing the bird. In each case, he had believed that he had denied a divine impulse *in himself* to do good to his fellow creatures. This "tenderness" led him to an important critique of American society on the eve of the American Revolution. If Woolman had lived longer—he died in 1772—he might have supported the revolution. But the revolution he advocated was more fundamental than the movement toward American independence. He advocated changes within American society. He was a social reformer and urged men and women to "exercise goodness toward every living creature." That charity, he argued, should extend to women, slaves, Indians, and the poor; in the name of goodness Woolman opposed war, materialism, and economic oppression.

His position on these issues was nurtured by his upbringing as an American Quaker, a member of the Society of Friends, the first religious group in America to oppose slavery. John Woolman was born in 1720 in Northampton, West Jersey, a part of modern-day New Jersey. He was the fourth child and first son among thirteen children. His parents, Samuel Woolman and Elizabeth Burr, were Quaker farmers. On Saturdays John and his parents, brothers, and sisters took turns at home reading aloud passages from the Bible, and on Sundays they attended Quaker worship. Woolman's religiosity came from his own family as well as his Quaker heritage brought to America from England.

Just as Puritans such as John Winthrop had wanted to live a more spiritual life than they found in the Church of England, other religious leaders carried the revolutionary spirit of the Protestant Reformation in other directions based on their religious experiences. Among the most radical of English reformers was a man named George Fox, who led a religious movement that sprang up in northwest England in the mid-seventeenth century. The formative moment in his faith came with a vision he experienced in England in 1652. His description is one of the fundamental documents in Quakerism and an indication of the spiritual tradition John Woolman would inherit in America seventy years later. Describing one of his spiritual journeys in England, George Fox wrote:

> As we traveled we came near a very great hill, called Pendle Hill, and I was
> moved of the Lord to go up to the top of it; which I did with difficulty,
> it was so very steep and high. When I was come to the top, I saw the sea

bordering upon Lancashire. From the top of this hill the Lord let me see in what places he had a great people to be gathered. As I went down, I found a spring of water in the side of the hill, with which I refreshed myself, having eaten or drunk but little for several days before. At night we came to an inn, and declared truth to the man of the house, and wrote a paper to the priests and professors, declaring the day of the Lord, and that Christ was come to teach people Himself.... Here the Lord opened unto me, and let me see a great people in white raiment by a river side, coming to the Lord.

George Fox devoted his life to gathering that pure congregation of the faithful in "white raiment." His followers met in open fields and simple dwellings, and they sought to discover in themselves and each other an "inward light" by which to guide their lives. In Quaker meetings men and women spoke up one by one when they experienced some divine truth. Often such meetings were characterized by long silences, as members waited upon the Lord for spiritual enlightenment. Each man and woman in the congregation was equally entitled to speak out—but only when directed to do so by the experience of an inward call from God. Their personal struggles were sometimes so intense that they led to physical convulsions, and from these movements came the name "Quaker." The followers of George Fox also called themselves "Friends"—members of the Society of Friends.

Quakers embraced an ideal of simplicity that often put them in conflict with English authorities. Believing in the equality of all men and women, they refused to honor notables with such terms as "Doctor" or "Your honor." They addressed themselves and others by the names "thee" and "thou." In court they declined to swear oaths, believing that a simple "yea" or "nay" should be accepted as honest speech. And they refused to pay a tithe, a tax prescribed by law, to support the Anglican Church.

A flash point in their interaction with other English subjects came with the Quaker refusal to do "hat-honor." According to tradition, a man was expected to remove his hat as he passed his "betters" on the street or came before them in a building. But Quakers held that God alone deserved to be honored. This was a "small thing" George Fox admitted, but he wrote that "because I could not put off my hat to them [his "betters"], it set them all into a rage.... Oh, the blows, punchings, beatings, and imprisonments that we underwent for not putting off our hats to men." During the early years of their religion, Friends risked severe punishment for their practices. Roughly 1 percent of the first generation of Quakers died in prison. But the purity of their faith and the courage when persecuted won admiration as well as converts—among them a man named William Penn, the son of a powerful British landowner and admiral.

In 1667 Penn joined the Society of Friends and became a publicist for his new faith. After writing a tract that questioned the Christian doctrine of the Trinity, he was jailed for seven months. While in prison he wrote *No Cross, No Crown*, a pamphlet attacking worldly customs and social inequality. Righteous men and women, he argued, should avoid "gold, silver, plaited hair, fine apparel." They should "adorn" themselves instead with "a meek and quiet spirit." For several years William Penn was in and out of prison. In one case, he was found innocent of the charge of inciting a riot but was imprisoned anyway for keeping his hat on during his trial.

During the 1670s, Penn developed an interest in America, and in 1675 he became a trustee for the Quaker colony of West Jersey, where John Woolman would be born. Within the next few years, hundreds of Quakers immigrated to the colony, worshipping first in tents and then in wooden meeting houses. In 1680 William Penn began work on a new colony, soon to be known as Pennsylvania. His claim to the land came first through a grant from King Charles as payment for a debt the king owed his father and then through a treaty with the Indians. Between 1681 and 1684 Penn sold plots of land, supervised settlement, and with the help of friends and advisors drew up a constitution called the *Frame of Government*. In keeping with the high moral standards of the Quakers, this constitution prohibited cockfights, dice, cards, and stage plays. William Penn spent most of the remainder of his life in England, but traveled twice to America, spending two years in Pennsylvania during each visit.

In Pennsylvania and neighboring West Jersey the Quaker influence was great. In 1723 Benjamin Franklin came to Philadelphia from Boston and left a famous description of the Quaker metropolis. He arrived by boat, early one Sunday morning, bought three rolls for breakfast, and fell in with a crowd of "clean-dressed" people all walking in the same direction. In his biography, written many years later, Franklin described his visit:

> I joined them, and thereby was led into the great meeting-house of the Quakers near the market. I sat down among them, and, after looking round awhile and hearing nothing said, being very drowsy thro' labor and want of rest the preceding night, I fell fast asleep, and continued so till the meeting broke up, when one was kind enough to rouse me.

Where Franklin experienced nothing but a sleep-inducing silence in the meeting house, earnest Quakers experienced that silence as filled with expectation, as they waited individually for an inner enlightenment from the Lord. The challenge for Quakers in the New World was to keep their eyes on God and cultivate that expectation, while living on the earth. In America the Quakers prospered, and with prosperity came the temptation to neglect that "meek and quiet spirit" that William Penn and other Quakers advocated—to become absorbed instead in the pleasures of the world. In his pamphlet *No Cross, No Crown* Penn warned that individuals can easily be drawn from one temptation to the next. The worldly person, he wrote, "*reneweth his Appetite, bestirs himself more than ever, that he may have his share in the* Scramble, *while any thing is to be got: This is as if* Cumber, *not* Retirement; *and* Gain, *not* Content, *were the* Duty *and* Comfort *of a* Christian."

In this passage are several key terms that became fundamental in John Woolman's vocabulary, and in his understanding of the world, its temptations, and its glory. On the side of spirituality were "retirement" and "contentment"—satisfaction in the quiet pleasures of life. And on the side of worldliness was the "scramble"—the "appetite" for "gain" and "cumber." That last word, described in modern dictionaries as an "archaic" term, means "a hindrance, obstacle, or burden." The word indicates something that is desirable such as gold or silver, but a distress nonetheless because it draws a person's attention away from the spiritual life. This sentiment underlies the biblical passage, "It is harder for a rich man to enter the Kingdom of Heaven than for a camel to pass through the eye of a needle." And it underlay the Quaker effort to avoid the "scramble" for worldly possessions.

But as the Quaker settlements in America matured and prospered, "cumber" was always present, always a temptation. Historian Frederick B. Tolles suggests this struggle in the title of his book, one of the classic accounts of the Quaker merchants in colonial America: *Meeting House and Counting House.* As time passed, many Quakers did very well in the "counting houses" of business, and arguably lost some of their original spiritual ardor. When John Woolman was born in 1720 many Quakers, like other colonial Americans North and South, had succumbed to the cumber of various forms of worldliness, including holding slaves.

The Delaware Valley, whose early settlement was shaped largely by the Quakers, was one of the most fertile in America. Wheat harvested in the valley was shipped to the West Indies, where imported grains fed the slaves who harvested the sugar cane. Profiting from this and other trade down the Delaware into the Atlantic, Philadelphia quickly became one of the major ports in British North America. In acquiring the land Quakers had dealt as unscrupulously with Indians as colonists in other provinces, and like colonists elsewhere they had come to hold slaves.

During his late teens, while living with his parents and working on their farm, John Woolman encountered cumbers of a more personal nature. He struggled to cultivate his "inner plantation," but he was often tempted by worldly pleasures. "I began to love wanton company," he writes, "and though I was preserved from profane language or scandalous conduct, yet I perceived a plant in me which produced much wild grapes. . . . To exceed in vanity and to promote mirth was my chief end." Like the young Puritan John Winthrop, Woolman spent long hours contemplating his own inner life and lamented when worldly distractions kept him from a full spiritual life. Like Winthrop, Woolman went through periods of intense spirituality and then, as he writes, "lost ground again." He disciplined himself to read scripture, and he attended Quaker meetings faithfully. Slowly, he became more adept at following sometimes powerful, but often elusive, impulses toward a fuller spiritual life.

Passing through adolescence, John Woolman sensed a change in himself—a new ability to appreciate God's presence in the world around him: "My heart was tender and often contrite, and a universal love to my fellow creatures increased in me." He came to believe that nurturing the love of "God the Creator" meant exercising "true justice and goodness, not only toward all men, but also toward the brute creatures." At age twenty-one he left his parents' farm and moved five miles away to Mount Holly, New Jersey, to work for a shopkeeper.

On the Sabbath, Woolman attended Quaker meetings and waited in silence with his fellow communicants for inspiration from God. He was hard on himself when at one meeting he spoke more than he thought proper. "Not keeping close to the Divine opening," he reported, "I said more than was required of me." The challenge was to open oneself to revelation but not go beyond reporting what seemed to come from God. Woolman learned to embrace "the pure spirit which inwardly moved upon the heart, and which taught me to wait in silence sometimes many weeks together, until I felt that rise which prepares the creature to stand like a trumpet, through which the Lord speaks to his flock."

Watching for the "pure opening" provided by God and then "standing like a trumpet"—these goals describe John Woolman's approach to life. Looking around him at men and women in colonial America, he felt drawn by God to speak out again and again on behalf of charity and justice and against materialism and frivolity. The occasions were many and his account of his pilgrimage provides a window on colonial American society on the eve of the Revolution.

While working for the shop owner in Mount Holly, John Woolman concluded that any business was inevitably "attended with much cumber." Success did not satisfy the "craving" for more gain: "with an increase in wealth, the desire for wealth increased." In contrast "an humble man, with the blessing of the Lord, might live on a little." Acting on this impulse, Woolman left shop-keeping and became a tailor, a craft that provided his living while allowing him to spend more time cultivating his own "inner light" and bearing witness to the truth, as he experienced it.

The Quaker religion was centered in the local congregation, which gathered weekly at a meeting house. Usually one of the members was the minister, but he—or she—was chosen on their personal spirituality rather than formal clerical training. On this basis John Woolman became a minister. There was no hierarchy of bishops in the Friends' churches. To provide organization and unity, the Quakers simply gathered together in monthly, quarterly, and annual meetings to discuss beliefs, behaviors, and policies. These gatherings exchanged information throughout the colonies and across the ocean, weaving Quakers into a coherent, transatlantic community. One form of discourse at these collective meetings was the use of a series of questions to provide guidelines and evaluate Quaker behavior. One such set used in Philadelphia in 1743 included these concerns, reflecting worldly temptations experienced in the late colonial era:

1. Are Friends careful to attend meetings at the time appointed and to refrain from sleeping or chewing tobacco in meetings?
2. Do Friends stay clear of excess in "drinking Drams"?
3. Do young Friends keep company for marriage with non-Friends or marry without parental consent?
4. Are Friends clear from tattling, talebearing, and meddling?
5. Do Friends stay free from music houses, dancing, and gambling?
6. Are Friends careful "to train up their Children in the Nurture and Fear of the Lord, and to restrain them from vice and Evil Company, and keep them to plainness of Speech and Apparel"?
7. Are the poor taken care of, are their children put to school and then apprenticed out to Friends, and do Friends apprentice their children only to Friends?
8. Are Friends cautious not to launch into business beyond what they can do?

Consistency in Quaker doctrine and values came about in part through the journeys of ministers from one meeting to another. During the period from 1691 to 1800, Quakers from Europe made 130 preaching journeys to America, and eighty-nine went from America to England for the same purpose.

Additionally, within the colonies Quakers often traveled from one meeting to another to preach. Typically such a trip began with a Quaker leader experiencing a "calling" to go on a trip to other meetings. Before the proposed journey could begin, the person so moved was required to seek the encouragement of the local congregation and the regional monthly meeting. If the meeting provided a "certificate" granting its approval, the journey could begin. Following this process of personal calling and denominational approval John Woolman made numerous preaching journeys to Quaker communities from the Carolinas to Rhode Island.

Everywhere he traveled in the colonies, Woolman was troubled by the existence of slavery. Visiting Quakers in the South, many of whom owned slaves, Woolman sensed "a dark gloominess hanging over the land." He prophesied that "in the future the consequence will be grievous to posterity." During the 1740s, southern slave-holding Quakers were engaged in what historian Stephen B. Weeks calls the "period of amelioration." In North Carolina, for example, in 1740 the Quaker Yearly Meeting urged Quakers who held slaves "to use them as fellow creatures" and not overwork them. Holding slaves was all right in other words, if the slaves were treated well.

In contrast, John Woolman held that slavery in any form was wrong. In his travels he regretted the necessity of staying with Friends who owned slaves. But often there was no alternative, especially in the South. Not wanting to live free off the labor of enslaved men and women, Woolman sometimes insisted that his host take payment for his lodging and distribute the funds among the slaves; sometimes he gave money directly to the slaves. Describing one journey he made through the South with a companion, he wrote, "We were taught by renewed experience to labor for an inward stillness; at no time to seek for words, but to live in the spirit of truth, and utter that to the people which truth opened in us." That sense of truth often led him to speak against slavery to a host or at a Quaker meeting.

In his late twenties Woolman took a wife. In this as in other decisions, he looked for God's approval. The Lord, he wrote, "was pleased to give me a well-inclined damsel, Sarah Ellis." He likely followed a series of Quaker rules for marriage. A suitor was expected to seek the approval of a woman's parents before beginning courtship. If the couple decided to marry, they also needed the approval of the congregation. The wedding ceremony took place in the meeting house, with the couple sitting at the front. As at other gatherings, the congregation began in silence followed by men and women offering prayers and advice as they felt an inward calling to speak. Then the bride and groom exchanged vows and signed a certificate that served as legal evidence of their marriage.

In Sarah, John Woolman found a woman who would encourage him in his spiritual life and his missionary travels. In his choice Woolman was likely mindful of William Penn's famous words on marriage, written in his pamphlet, *Fruits of an Active Life*: "Never marry but for love; but see that thou lovest what is lovely. He that minds a body and not a soul has not the better part of that relationship, and will consequently lack the noblest comfort of a married life." William Penn's ideal of the good marriage appears also in his *Fruits of Solitude* (1682): "It is the difference betwixt Lust and Love, that this is fixt, that volatile. Love grows, Lust wastes by Enjoyment: And the Reason is, that one springs from an Union of Souls, and the other from an Union of Sense."

Few documents survive to suggest the texture of Sarah and John's marriage, but one, written in 1760 and included in Woolman's *Journal*, reveals John's perception of Sarah as spiritual companion. On a missionary journey he wrote her from Jerico on Long Island, New York. "Dearly beloved wife!" he began, "my mind hath been much in an inward, watchful frame since I left thee." He told Sarah that he regretted being away from his family at a time when sickness was "great amongst you." Home was in his thoughts. "I have often an engaging love and affection towards thee and my daughter," he wrote. But he had work to do among the "widows and fatherless" of the land, those "who have evil examples before them," and men and women whose minds were "in captivity." And so he was traveling to distant places while she was at home. He ended his letter with a description of his sense of mission:

> I feel my mind resigned to leave you for a season, to exercise that gift which
> the Lord hath bestowed on me, which though small compared with some,
> yet in this I rejoice, that I feel love unfeigned towards my fellow-creatures.
> I recommend you to the Almighty, who I trust, cares for you, and under a
> sense of his heavenly love remain, Thy loving husband, J.W.

Sarah sympathized with her husband's challenging and sometimes dangerous calling, including a journey John made among the Indians of frontier Pennsylvania in 1763. Woolman was acutely aware of the plight of the Indians, many of whom had been forced westward by European settlements on the Atlantic seaboard. He declared that he felt "love in my heart towards the Natives of this Land, who dwell far back in the wilderness, whose ancestors were the owners and possessors of the country where we dwell, and who for a very small consideration assigned their Inheritance to us."

In 1761 he happened to "fall in with" a company of the Delaware Indians who were visiting Philadelphia. Through an interpreter he learned that they lived on at Wehaloosing on a branch of the Susquehannah River about two hundred miles to the west. Woolman was impressed by their knowledge of the Christian religion, taught them by Moravian missionaries. During the next two years, he felt "inward drawings" to visit the Delaware in their homes. "I told none (Except my Dear Wife)," he writes, "until it came to some ripeness." As the idea of the journey "ripened" Woolman discussed it with fellow Quakers and won their support. Then in 1763 several Indians who lived just beyond the Delaware village at Wehaloosing visited Philadelphia. Woolman determined to accompany them on their return to the West.

Woolman's account of his preparations for the journey is a classic expression of Quaker religiosity. "This visit felt weighty," he writes, "and was performed at a time when traveling appeared perilous." He was concerned about what lay ahead—and with good reason. He would be traveling into a theater of war, risking captivity, torture, and death.

"My heart," he writes, "was frequently turned to the Lord with inward breathings for his heavenly support."

At a Quaker meeting, on the eve of his departure, Woolman experienced one of those "pure openings of truth," which furnished the spiritual direction for his life. Whatever might befall him in the wilderness, he realized, his life would be in God's hands. "As I spake on this subject," Woolman writes, "my heart was much tendered, and great awfulness came over me." By "awfulness" Woolman did not mean a sense of something terrible, as in the modern sense of the word but rather "awe-full-ness," being full of awe and having a sense of wonder in the presence of God, on whose errand he would be traveling.

At another meeting soon afterward, Woolman sensed that his experience in the wilderness would be like that of the prophet David when threatened by a hostile "band of Syrians." David was unharmed because "The angel of the Lord encampeth round about them that fear him" (Psalm 34:7). On his own journey into the wilderness, among enemies, Woolman sensed that he, like David, would be nurtured by a spiritual presence "encamped" nearby. The service concluded and then, Woolman writes, "in true love and tenderness I parted from Friends, expecting the next morning to proceed on my journey." He returned home, and "Being weary I went early to bed."

Although these passages suggest that Woolman was confident of success in this, the most perilous of his missionary journeys, they can also be read as a measure of his anxiety. He might well need an "angel of the Lord" to protect him on the frontier. That very night the reality underlying his fears came into sharp focus. "I was awoke by a man calling at my door," he writes. The man urged him to come to a nearby "public house" where Quakers from Philadelphia had come to see him. Their urgency was signaled by the hour being "so late that Friends were generally gone to bed." The visitors told Woolman that Indians on the frontier had just recently "slain and scalped some English people."

Woolman returned to bed and "searched his heart" to know what to do. He told his wife about the situation, and she was "deeply concerned." But despite the frontier warfare, Woolman decided that God still wished him to make the journey, and Sarah bore his decision "with a degree of resignation." The next morning he said goodbye to his wife and his neighbors, and in the company of Israel Pemberton, a man known in the region as the "King of the Quakers," he rode away from home. Pemberton was at the opposite end of the Quaker spectrum from Woolman, wealthy and politically influential. But he admired Woolman's spirituality and rode with him for a few miles, leaving just before Indian guides arrived to take the Quaker minister into the backcountry. Benjamin Parvin, a friend of Woolman's, wanted to come along on the journey. Despite worrying that he would blame himself if his friend "should be taken captive," Woolman agreed.

Soon afterward the two men were lodged on the floor of a house near Fort Allen about fifty miles from Philadelphia. Here they met an Indian trader who told them that the white people on the frontier sold rum to the Indians. Woolman made this connection: Indians drank the rum, became intoxicated, and then desperate for more rum they traded their skins and furs, "gotten through much fatigue and hard travels." When they recovered their senses and discovered that they had no furs to trade for such necessities as clothing, they were "angry with those who, for the sake of gain, took advantage of their weakness."

To a moral person, the solution was obvious: Selling liquor to Indians was a crime that demanded the attention of "all true lovers of virtue to suppress." But the problem went beyond the frontiersmen. Woolman characteristically followed the path back to the underlying "scramble" for "cumber," back to landlords in the older settlements, who took advantage of their white tenants. These owners were motivated by an "inordinate desire after wealth" and exploited the poor with high rents, forcing them to migrate to the backcountry, where they in turn exploited the Indians. Woolman could see everywhere the evil effects of greed.

With their Indian guides the two Quakers pressed deeper into the wilderness, crossing the steep, rocky Blue Ridge Mountains, following a narrow trail, crowded in by bushes and hindered by fallen timber. Often they were "wet with traveling in the rain." On a typical night they "kindled a fire, with our tent open to it, then laid some bushes next the ground, and put our blankets upon them for our bed." Sometimes they swam their horses across deep streams; often they were paddled in canoes along rivers while Indians rode their horses along the rough trails to rendezvous points. They encountered rattlesnakes, struggled across patches of fallen trees, waded through swamps, and at least once lost precious hours trying to recover a strayed horse. Woolman wanted to be among the Indians "that I might feel and understand their life and the spirit they live in." And now, day by day, he felt himself drawn further into Indian country, both geographically and spiritually.

At one point along the trail the travelers camped beside trees whose bark had been peeled back to provide a surface for paintings. There they saw "various representations of men going to and returning from the wars, and of some being killed in battle." Looking at these forest images Woolman was moved by the struggles of these people:

> This was a path heretofore used by warriors, and as I walked about viewing those Indian histories, which were painted mostly in red or black, and thinking on the innumerable afflictions which the proud, fierce spirit produceth in the world, also on the toils and fatigues of warriors in traveling over mountains and deserts; on their miseries and distresses when far from home and wounded by their enemies; of the bruises and great weariness in chasing one another over the rocks and mountains; of the restless, unquiet state of mind of those who live in this spirit, and of the hatred which mutually grows up in the minds of their children,—the desire to cherish the spirit of love and peace among these people arose very fresh in me.

John Woolman reckoned that with his hardships on the trail he would better understand the Indians; the journey would "season" his mind, and bring him "into a nearer sympathy with them." In the middle of his expedition, deep in the wilderness, Woolman thought about two societies, the Indian peoples to the west and the colonial settlers to the east, and sensed in a moment the entire sweep of early American history. "As I rode over the barren hills," he writes, "my meditations were on the alterations in the circumstances of the natives of this land since the coming in of the English." The coastal communities had many advantages, fertile land with trade routes made easy by the abundant rivers and the sea. The Indians had given up most of that land, sold for "trifling considerations" or stolen by "superior force."

From the vantage point of the Blue Ridge Mountains, John Woolman thought back to the expanding English settlements on the eastern seaboard, many of which he had visited during his missionary journeys:

> I had a prospect of the English along the coast for upwards of nine hundred miles, where I traveled, and their favorable situation and the difficulties attending the natives as well as the negroes in many places were open to me.... In this lonely journey I did greatly bewail the spreading of a wrong spirit, believing that the prosperous, convenient situation of the English would require a constant attention in us to Divine love and wisdom, in order to their being guided and supported in a way answerable to

the will of that good, gracious, and Almighty Being, who hath an equal regard to all mankind. And here luxury and covetousness, with the numerous oppressions and other evils attending them, appeared very afflicting to me, and I felt in that which is immutable that the seeds of great calamity and desolation are sown and growing fast on this continent. Nor have I words sufficient to set forth the longing I then felt, that we who are placed along the coast, and have tasted the love and growth of these seeds, that they may not ripen to the ruin of our posterity.

At the time, John Woolman had no way of knowing how accurate these prophetic words would prove to be. In retrospect, however, those "seeds of great calamity" would come to fruition in not only the Civil War but also in industrial oppression and environmental degradation. In 1763 Woolman's attention was soon riveted again on the particulars of his missionary journey. As he and his companions moved further toward Wehaloosing, they encountered Indian "runners" with disturbing news. A war party had taken an English fort to the west and "destroyed the people." At that moment the Indians were attacking a second fort, and warriors had come to Wehaloosing, carrying two English scalps, and proclaiming "war with the English."

Further along the trail Woolman came close to being scalped himself—or so it seemed for a moment. He and his Quaker friend were preparing to lodge for the night in a house of a "very ancient" Indian. From another dwelling a native approached Woolman with a tomahawk hidden beneath his coat; as he came closer he revealed the weapon in his hand. This had for Woolman a "disagreeable appearance," but instead of panicking, Woolman walked toward the man and spoke to him "in a friendly way." With the help of the guides, he and the Indian were able to communicate to one another that each meant the other no harm. The Indian with the tomahawk was simply preparing to defend himself if Woolman turned out to be hostile—a real possibility in that region, where Indians had at least as much to fear from whites as whites from Indians.

The Quakers pushed on despite a storm that "beat through our tent and wet both us and our baggage" and in spite of more reports of hostilities ahead. On a particularly difficult day, after a windstorm had blown innumerable trees across their path, Woolman reflected, "I had this day often to consider myself as a sojourner in this world. A belief in the all-sufficiency of God to support his people in their pilgrimage felt comfortable to me." Finally, the travelers reached the outskirts of Wehaloosing. At their guide's instruction, the two Quaker companions sat on a log and waited for further instruction while he went ahead to tell the people who was coming.

Here occurred a small but deeply moving encounter. The first—and so far only—Indian whom Woolman had seen near the village was "a woman of modest countenance, with a Bible, who spake first to our guide, and then with an harmonious voice expressed her gladness at seeing us, having before heard of our coming." As the Quakers sat together on the log "in a deep inward stillness," the woman came and sat near them. With this simple gesture a "great awfulness" (*awe-full-ness*) came over the two men and they "rejoiced in a sense of God's love manifested to our poor souls." Unable to speak the native tongue of these people, Woolman relied as much on gestures as words on his mission among the Wehaloosing. Eventually the Quakers were roused by the sound of a conch calling the Indians and the visitors to a meeting. About sixty Indians had gathered in a lodge when John Woolman arrived. He explained "in a few short sentences" the purpose of his visit: "that a concern for their good had made me willing to come thus far to see them." Some of the Indians understood him and interpreted for the others. A Moravian missionary arrived, a member of a German religious sect already resident among the Indians at Wehaloosing. Unencumbered by denominational jealousy, the Moravian welcomed Woolman and "expressed his goodwill towards my speaking at any time all that I found in my heart to say."

That night Woolman preached to the Indians, where, as he says, "pure gospel love was felt." His preaching was burdened by the challenge of communicating with men and women most of whom knew little or no English. Interpreters did their best but "none of them were quite perfect in the English and Delaware tongues." For a while Woolman spoke slowly, waiting after each few words for the interpreters to translate. Then, encouraged at finding such a receptive audience deep in the forest, after so much hard traveling, and sensing God's presence, he asked the interpreters to remain silent while he offered a prayer. He told them "I found it in my heart to pray to God, and believed, if I prayed aright, he would hear me; and I expressed my willingness for them to omit interpreting." In other words, Woolman hoped that something of his message would reach the Indians, whether or not they understood his words. At the end of the meeting as the Indians were leaving, Woolman saw one of them talking earnestly with an interpreter. Afterward the interpreter told Woolman the man had told him, "I love to feel where the words come from."

No theologian could have described more perfectly the meaning the Quakers gave to religious discourse. In meetings no one was to speak—minister or lay person—except as directed by an inward light. What mattered in worshipping God and discovering his will on earth was "where the words come from."

John Woolman stayed for several days at Wehaloosing. In his *Journal* he provides a brief description of the town, noting that it stood on the banks of the Susquehanna River and consisted of about forty houses "compact together." Their walls were of planks, set in the ground, topped by rafters covered with bark. These dwellings ranged from houses eighteen by thirty feet in size to larger buildings where the meetings could take place. Many residents of Wehaloosing turned out several times to hear Woolman preach, and when Woolman felt that he had accomplished his purpose and decided to return home, one by one they shook his hand in appreciation.

On the homeward journey, a surprising number of Indians, laden with furs, joined the Quakers. Together they struggled across mountains and over swollen rivers. The Indians were more worried about unfriendly whites than harsh nature: that was why so many chose to travel with the Quakers. Given the hostilities on the frontier, the Indians were concerned about "the outside inhabitants [the frontiersmen] being surprised." They would have a better chance of passing safely through the borderland if they traveled with English settlers. And so the Quakers went in advance "to acquaint people on and near the road who these Indians were." The party passed into the English settlements without mishap, and John Woolman returned home safely to the relief of his family and friends. "People who have never been in such places," Woolman wrote, "have but an imperfect idea of them; and I was not only taught patience, but also made thankful to God, who thus led and instructed me, that I might have a quick and lively feeling of the afflictions of my fellow-creatures, whose situation in life is difficult."

John Woolman's journey to Wehaloosing was the most dramatic of his missions, each one aimed at his gaining a "lively feeling" of the real hardships of other men and women. Drawing on his personal observations of oppression, he was able to stand more effectively for an improvement of those conditions. During his lifetime he was the foremost American opponent of slavery. He published a two-part *Essay on Some Considerations on the Keeping of Negroes*, which helped move the Quaker Yearly Meeting to pass measures condemning slavery. His *Plea for the Poor* encouraged readers to consider "the connection of things." For the sake of wealth, for example, landowners gouged poor tenants, who in turn drank too much as an escape, and then abused their wives and children. Those same landowners abused the land itself with harmful agricultural practices.

In addition to these causes, John Woolman was quick to observe other kinds of oppression and recognized how the products of unscrupulous individuals entered everyday life throughout the colonies. Late in life he dressed only in white because the dyes that went into colored cloth were made by slaves, and working with the dyes undermined the health of the slaves. Since taxes went to support the French and Indian War, and Woolman was a pacifist, he refused to pay taxes during the war. And on a voyage to England in 1772 he refused to sleep in a comfortable cabin because the ornate carving on the door was the product, he reckoned, of slave labor. Instead he slept in rough quarters alongside ordinary seamen.

During his lifetime, John Woolman made thirty missionary journeys in the North American colonies from the Carolinas to New England. The trip to England was his first Atlantic crossing, but he was already well known when he arrived in London for an important Quaker gathering. Crowds thronged to see the American in his white clothing.

Quaker founder George Fox might have seen in Woolman one of those "people in white raiment . . . coming to the Lord," whom he had visualized about 120 years before. But many of Woolman's contemporaries accused him of vanity. In his singular simplicity he seemed to be calling attention to himself. Woolman was troubled by this charge, but as in so many other choices, his last resort was to that inner voice—in this case, telling him how to dress.

In England as in America, John Woolman saw oppression and testified against it. Learning that the horses and the boys employed in the stage-coach industry were mistreated, he refused to ride and instead walked all the way from London to York in northern England. There the good fortune that had accompanied him during his many missionary journeys failed him. Woolman fell victim to smallpox in 1772, died quickly, and was buried in York. A few months later the Boston Tea Party in his homeland would lead to the final British-American spiral downward to armed conflict. Even while his homeland was preoccupied with the imperial crisis, American Quakers recognized John Woolman's importance. The Philadelphia Yearly Meeting published his *Journal* and collected works in 1774, and in 1776 the Quakers became the first American denomination to prohibit slavery among its members.

This act, which owed much to John Woolman's persistent antislavery position, seems a fitting tribute to both Woolman and the revolutionary spirit. And yet many of the causes Woolman espoused were neglected by the Revolution, including the complete abolition of slavery itself. If Woolman had read Thomas Jefferson's claim in the Declaration of Independence that all men have a right to "life, liberty, and the pursuit of happiness," he might well have protested that Jefferson's "pursuit" could easily become a greedy "scramble" and that happiness based on materialism alone could easily lead to materialistic "cumber." Other Americans, among them Abraham Lincoln, John Muir, Franklin Roosevelt, and Martin Luther King Jr., would be heirs to the more radical elements of Woolman's critique of American society. They would follow in Woolman's footsteps as advocates for abolition, environmentalism, and social justice.

Most broadly, John Woolman advocated, as he said, "a feeling sense of the condition of others." In his own lifetime, Woolman was accused of being wildly impractical, and yet his vision retains its power and relevance to this day. His spirit is the inclusive spirit expressed in the words of "America the Beautiful": "Crown thy good with brotherhood from sea to shinning sea."

Bibliography

Balfour, Hugh, and J. William Frost. *The Quakers* (1988). History and biographical dictionary of the Quakers; a volume in the authoritative *Denominations in America* series.

Breen, T. H. *The Marketplace of Revolution: How Consumer Politics Shaped American Independence* (2004). John Woolman warned against the "scramble" for "cumber." Breen shows how that scramble helped drive the colonists to revolution.

Cady, Edwin. *John Woolman* (1965). Good narrative of Woolman's life; a volume in the *Great American Thinkers* series.

Hamm, Thomas D. *The Quakers in America* (2003). Traces Quaker social activism from colonial times to the present.

Moretta, John. *The William Penn and the Quaker Legacy* (2006). Valuable brief biography of William Penn.

Rosenblatt, Paul. *John Woolman* (1969). Survey of Woolman's life, focusing on his writing and thought; a volume in the *Twayne United States Authors Series*.

Swift, Ned. *A Finger in the Pye: John Woolman and the Approach of the American Revolution* (Master's Thesis, Eastern Washington University, 2002). Thoughtful and engaging account of John Woolman's "altruistic radicalism."

Tolles, Frederick Barnes. *Meeting House and Counting House: The Quaker Merchants of Colonial Philadelphia, 1682–1763* (1963). A classic history of Quaker efforts to remain true to their spiritual legacy while enjoying wealth in the New World.

West, Jessamyn, Editor. *The Quaker Reader* (1962). Useful anthology of Quaker writings, including works by George Fox, William Penn, and John Woolman.

Woolman, John. *The Journal of John Woolman and a Plea for the Poor* (1961). Two of Woolman's major works, with an introduction by Frederick B. Tolles.

Yannessa, Mary Ann. *Levi Coffin, Quaker: Breaking the Bonds of Slavery in Ohio and Indiana* (2001). Brief biography of Levi Coffin, a Southern Quaker who moved north and became reputedly the "president" of the underground railroad.

Identification Topics

Robin, bill of sale for a slave, John Woolman, George Fox, Quakerism, the Society of Friends, Pendle Hill, the "inward light," swearing oaths, hat-honor, William Penn, *No Cross, No Crown*, West Jersey, Pennsylvania, the *Frame of Government*, Benjamin Franklin, Philadelphia, Sarah Woolman, Wehaloosing, Woolman's *Journal*

Study Questions

1. What were the principal beliefs of the early Quakers, and why were they persecuted?
2. What were the customs and practices in the colonies that John Woolman particularly condemned? What did these behaviors have in common?
3. What did John Woolman mean by the words "scramble" and "cumber," and why did he condemn both? What did he mean by the "inner plantation"?
4. According to William Penn, what is the essence of a good marriage—and what force is most likely to undermine true love?
5. Why did John Woolman write: "the seeds of great calamity and desolation are sown and growing fast on this continent"?

CHAPTER 5

Divided Loyalties
Jonathan Boucher and the Pre-Revolutionary Crisis

In the turbulent years preceding ⋯ ⋯ ⋯ ericans opposed the Revolutionary movement. So⋯ we⋯ ⋯ached to Britain by political, cultural, economic, and religi⋯us tie⋯, ⋯thers feared that independence would produce chaos or oppression. Jonathan Boucher was one of the many Americans who opposed the Revolution. He was a constructive and imaginative citizen, but when he criticized the Patriots, he was forced into exile. His career demonstrates the continuing hold of Old World ties on settlers and suggests the difficulties many colonists faced in choosing between loyalty and rebellion.

On May 4, 1775, George Washington boarded a ferry at Alexandria, Virginia, to cross the Potomac River. The Battles of Lexington and Concord had been fought two weeks before, and he was now on his way to the Continental Congress at Philadelphia. As his boat crossed the river, Washington spied an old friend, Reverend Jonathan Boucher, on board another ferry. The people on Boucher's boat gave Washington three cheers, and he, in turn, beckoned them to stop so that he could come aboard and shake their hands. According to Boucher, "Everybody seemed to be on fire, either with rum, or patriotism, or both."

As Boucher greeted Washington, he was afire with neither rum nor patriotism. Instead, he was worried about the events that threatened to divide Britain and America. In a "few disturbed moments of conversation" he warned Washington that the troubles between England and America would surely lead to civil war and colonial independence. Washington tried to reassure Boucher, telling him that his fears were groundless and that if Boucher "ever heard of him joining in any such measures... [he] had his leave to set him down for everything wicked."

Within a little more than a year George Washington would support both the Revolutionary War and independence. But in 1775 Washington did not know what course the resistance to Britain would take. The War for Independence wrenched American life out of its accustomed patterns. Less violent than many other revolutions, it produced, nonetheless, profound changes in the lives of many Americans. George Washington, a Virginia planter, would become president of a nation that did not even exist in 1775. In contrast, Jonathan Boucher, a Maryland cleric and landholder, would soon become an exile from his American home.

Boucher received a foretaste of this bitter experience a few minutes later when he disembarked at Alexandria. One of the citizens claimed to recognize the minister as a critic of American policy. An angry crowd quickly gathered, and Boucher saved himself only by persuading the mob that the accuser was lying. After this episode he decided never to go to Alexandria again, nor would he venture into any other public place except his own church.

This incident was one of several in which Jonathan Boucher was threatened with violence because of his support of the English government. He was never harmed, but many other, less fortunate opponents of the Revolution, known as Tories or Loyalists, were beaten or tarred and feathered. Moreover, some fifty thousand to one hundred thousand Americans like Boucher were forced to flee the country because of their political beliefs. John Adams estimated that one American in three was in the Loyalist camp at the beginning of the Revolution. Modern historians have revised Adams's figure downward but still conclude that some 25 percent of Americans opposed the Revolution, the ostensible aim of which was "life, liberty, and the pursuit of happiness" for all.

The Tories are frequently ignored in accounts of the Revolution, but they deserve our attention. By studying them we can learn about a numerically significant group of men and women and see the Revolution as a whole with fresh vision. To become a Tory often required more thoughtful deliberation than to become a Patriot; sometimes it even required more courage. For two centuries historians have sought to explain the Loyalists. Patriots vilified them as shortsighted opponents of a noble cause. Twentieth-century historians have tried to understand the Tories better by exploring the socioeconomic sources of their attachment to Britain. We now know that the most important Tories were government officials, merchants, and clerics, whose positions in the colonies depended on royal support. But such members of the colonial elite were relatively few. A much larger group were members of religious and ethnic minorities who feared they would be oppressed by other Americans if English control were removed.

We can generalize about Tory characteristics, but allegiance during the Revolution was also affected by one's ideas. Some of the most interesting Tories shared many qualities with their Patriot opponents. They were Americans who disagreed with other Americans about the proper character of American society. Jonathan Boucher was such a man.

In some ways Boucher was a typical Tory. A minister of the Church of England, he owed his appointment to the royal governor of Maryland. As a historical figure, he is especially serviceable because his opinions and experiences are unusually accessible: he reveals himself in letters, an autobiography, and a volume of published sermons. In these sources we can explore the events, the personal characteristics, and the intellectual commitments underlying his loyalty. Few colonists described in so much detail how they became Tories. Yet after studying Boucher's writings, one is left with the impression that he had much in common with his opponents.

Boucher was born in northern England in the town of Blencogo, Cumberland, on March 12, 1738. His ancestors had lived in this region for many generations and had fought in the border wars with Scotland. War came again seven years after Jonathan's birth when an army marched through Cumberland in an unsuccessful attempt to overthrow King George II. Some of the defeated rebels were executed in nearby Carlisle, their heads hung on display on the city wall.

The short-lived Rebellion of 1745 interrupted an otherwise humdrum existence. Blencogo was a small rural village; its people were poor and worked hard to earn a living. As a youth Boucher had to haul coal, turf, and peat; to drive a plow and work "without intermission" during haying time and harvest. His pleasures were those provided by the rough country environment. Decades later he could still recall places where he had caught a large trout or discovered a bird's nest or fought a "successful battle" against a playmate.

Most of the boys he grew up with would stay in Blencogo and become small farmers. But before Jonathan was twelve he had decided to escape the ceaseless toil of rural life. As a child he had shown an interest in learning. His father taught him to read soon after he learned to talk, and at six he could read and spell almost as well as an adult. Jonathan's parents wanted to encourage him in his studies but were hampered by their own limited means and by the inadequate local schools.

Until he was fourteen Jonathan spent much of his time working for his father. In 1752 he qualified as a teacher in the nearby town of Wigton. During the next few years he taught at several schools while advancing his own education. In 1756 he became assistant to a schoolmaster named John James, an accomplished scholar and teacher, who took an interest in Jonathan and helped him continue his studies. In 1759 Jonathan heard about a good teaching opportunity in Virginia. His parents protested that he would waste his life—and probably feared he would lose it—in America. But Jonathan wanted to travel, and his parents finally agreed. After a tearful farewell, he began the long journey to the New World.

Jonathan's ship sailed on April 27, 1759. Several times it was caught in violent storms and once was chased by an enemy vessel. Jonathan was at sea for two and a half months before reaching the Rappahannock River on Chesapeake Bay in Virginia. Ironically, his ship sailed into the land of opportunity in company with a ship bearing slaves from Africa.

Disembarking at Port Royal, the young man was immediately impressed with the strangeness of his surroundings: "I was now in every sense of the word in a new world," he writes. "The people, in their persons, manners, pursuits, and modes of life were as new and strange to me as their country and climate were." He soon adjusted, however, and felt himself so much at home that he later wondered whether he had not adapted all too well to Port Royal. The social life consisted chiefly of visits and balls, always with plenty of liquor. The people had no literary interests, and so, says he, I "was engaged in many silly frolics with people as silly as myself." Boucher settled into the task of tutoring the four sons of a Virginia planter, but he was dissatisfied with this work and for a while entertained the idea of going into business. But a better opportunity presented itself, one that would pay him well and enable him to pursue his intellectual interests. He was invited to become minister of Hanover, a Church of England parish across the river from Port Royal.

Although he lacked a college education, Boucher's private studies and native intelligence had marked him as a good ministerial prospect. He decided to take the post, but because there were no Anglican bishops in America he had to return to England for his consecration into the Anglican priesthood. He was ordained in London, then traveled by horseback to Blencogo to visit his parents. Now that he was returning to a stable position in America, he realized that he would probably never see his mother and father again. He was twenty-five years old. Many years later he still recalled vividly his last moments with his parents.

Back in Virginia, Jonathan ministered for a time to the congregation at Hanover, then moved to a new position as rector of Saint Mary's Parish a few miles away. Like most other American clerics in the colonial period, Boucher received only a modest salary. To increase his income he purchased cattle, horses, and slaves to establish a plantation, and he also started a boarding school.

Boucher spent seven years at Saint Mary's—years he recalled as "busy and bustling" but not satisfying to a "literary man." The planters were convivial and drank freely, giving little attention to intellectual matters. Naturally inquisitive, Boucher devoted what time he could to solitary studies. For a time he was intrigued by the arguments of contemporary philosophers who questioned the divinity of Christ. He almost became a skeptic himself, but turned to the Scriptures, and having read the Bible in the ancient languages, concluded that the doctrine of the Trinity was a scriptural "fact" that must be taken on faith. His flirtation with heresy persuaded him that complex issues should be confronted with "caution and reverence." He would show the same spirit when he later considered the proper relationship of America to England.

Boucher appears to have been a popular preacher. In other parishes rival denominations, especially Presbyterians and Baptists, were winning Anglicans away from the established church. But Boucher's parish remained orthodox. He advocated treating rival preachers "with well-judged ridicule and contempt, and their followers with gentleness, persuasion and attention." When another minister challenged him to debate the merits of Anglicanism, he refused to dignify the man with a direct reply, sending one of his parishioners, a carpenter with a "voluble tongue," in his stead. Boucher did not oppose religious toleration, but he was convinced that Anglicanism was the one true church and that others fell far short of its excellence.

During his stay at Saint Mary's, Boucher became acquainted with George Washington. The minister's reputation as a schoolmaster was growing, and he was soon boarding thirty pupils. In 1768 Washington wrote asking him to take John Parke ("Jackie") Custis, his wife Martha's son by her first marriage, as a student. Jackie was a somewhat unruly youth who until then had shown no interest in schooling. Washington said that he hoped Boucher could "make him fit for more useful purposes than a horse-racer." Boucher agreed to instruct Jackie, which led to a rather close acquaintance between the minister and the planter. Boucher wrote Washington frequent letters about the boy's progress and made visits to Mount Vernon with his pupil. But Jackie remained an unimpressive student, a fact that Boucher did not try to conceal. He wrote to Washington, "I must confess to you I never did in my life know a youth so exceedingly indolent or so surprisingly voluptuous: one would suppose Nature had intended him [to be] some Asiatic prince." Washington appears to have appreciated Boucher's honesty and left Jackie in the minister's hands for five years.

While Boucher was at Saint Mary's Parish, news of the Stamp Act reached America. This act, placing a tax on newspapers, cards, legal documents, and other paper products, was Britain's first attempt to impose an internal tax on the colonies. In the recent war with France the mother country had acquired a huge national debt and reasoned that the colonists should help pay. The Americans, however, were accustomed to controlling their own internal taxes. They reacted dramatically to the Stamp Act: they drew up petitions, formed mobs, organized a colony-wide congress, and imposed a boycott on trade with Britain. A year later, under pressure from English merchants who were injured by the boycott, Parliament repealed the Stamp Act.

This was the first of several conflicts leading to the American Revolution. How did Boucher react? In a letter to his English friend, John James, in December 1765, he indicates that he was strongly on the side of the colonists. He calls the Stamp Act "oppressive, impolitic, and illegal" and argues that the Americans have a traditional right to tax themselves. Even if they had no such right, he says, Parliament is so ignorant of conditions in America that she might as well try to govern "Kamchatka" (part of Russia). He contends that the British agents in America are "too ignorant, or too knavish" to send back the accurate intelligence required for well-informed administration. Why, he says, a British officer recently sent four or five hundred soldiers to be quartered in a town that had only one house! With so little knowledge of America, how can Britain pretend to have a right to tax the colonists?

Knowing Boucher's later loyalism, these are remarkable sentiments, for he criticized not only the Stamp Act but the very idea of Britain trying to make vital decisions about a land it hardly knew. Other future Tories, including Thomas Hutchinson, who became governor of Massachusetts, shared Boucher's view of the Stamp Act. When presented with a choice between imperfect British rule and complete independence, Boucher and other Tories would rally to the royal standard. But they did not favor the complete subjection of the colonies to the mother country. They preferred an equitable balance of power between Britain and America.

Boucher's sympathy for the colonies in their initial struggles with the crown found a counterpart in his consideration for slaves. During the months when he was complaining about British oppression, Boucher worked to improve the condition of blacks. Finding that they had been ignored by previous ministers, he baptized almost five hundred of them, half the adult slaves in the parish. Some became regular communicants in his church, and Boucher also encouraged their education.

Although Boucher made a success of his ministry in Virginia—the people would pay him an extra six months' salary when he left Saint Mary's—he wanted to live in a more cosmopolitan city, preferably Annapolis, Maryland, which he named the "genteelest town in North America." For several years friends promised that he would be appointed to the next vacant parish in the town, and in 1770 he was offered Saint Anne's Parish in Annapolis.

The new post delighted Boucher. He claimed there was hardly a town in England as desirable. Soon he met other men who shared his love of animated and intelligent conversation, and with three or four of them he founded "The Homony Club," meeting weekly to hold debates and read compositions. It was so successful that even the governor applied for admission.

The boy from Blencogo had come a long way. He was recognized as one of the brightest people in his province, and his friends included many of the most important men in the South. As yet, though, he had no wife. Now he turned to Eleanor Addison, daughter of a wealthy Virginia planter. Boucher describes her as "handsome, sprightly, and a general toast." She was medium in height and had black hair and eyes with "uncommon animation and lustre." She had been courted unsuccessfully several times before Boucher came along. With no great wealth to offer, Boucher, too, might have failed except that Nelly, as she was called, once dreamed that she married a man who looked like him. When Boucher first appeared on her doorstep with her uncle, she hastened from the room and nearly fainted before she could say to her mother, "Yonder is the man I dreamed of that I was to marry!"

Boucher's marriage to Eleanor Addison is one of the most attractive incidents in his life. Both were in their early thirties and ready to settle down. Shortly after they were married Nelly became pregnant but injured herself and miscarried. For the remaining twelve years of her life she was bedridden three days of four. Nonetheless, a deeply satisfying relationship developed between husband and wife. Both were strong personalities, and they frequently argued; but they prided themselves that they never "went to sleep without kissing and being friends." In his autobiography Boucher describes an incident that suggests the vitality in their marriage. They had been arguing, and to clear the air decided each would list the best and worst features of the other. Their remarks, which Jonathan preserved, are very candid. Nelly stated that her husband's manners were "often awkward, but always interesting." He wrote that she was "artless, blushing, bashful." But their fondness for one another survived their frankness. Years later, after Nelly was dead, Jonathan recalled how she had ended the episode: "And now, my dear old man," she said, "prithee end thy catechism; for with all thy romance and eccentricity, all thy foibles and all thy faults, thou art a good and a clever fellow, and I do love thee as much as ever woman loved." Jonathan continues: "And she flung her arms around my neck, finishing the parley in a way of which none but lovers, and I may add, married lovers, can possibly judge."

Boucher remembered the days of courting Nelly as the happiest in his life. In the years after their marriage on June 2, 1772, they would need one another's support. Jonathan was already falling out of favor with the leaders of the Patriot movement in Maryland. Although he had taken the "right" side in the Stamp Act crisis, he found himself on the "wrong" side of two popular issues shortly after coming to the new province.

The first had to do with the appointment of Anglican bishops in America. Boucher believed that the church badly needed an American hierarchy to ordain clergy, help settle disputes, and provide order and stability in the church. Against the Presbyterian opponents of the idea he argued quite simply that those who believed in

Presbyterian government should be allowed to have their presbyters and those who believed in government by bishops should be allowed to have their bishops. The argument was reasonable, but in the tense atmosphere of pre-Revolutionary political discourse any innovation suggesting the least increase in power for the British government looked like a threat to the colonists. Many opponents of the bishoprics believed that an Anglican hierarchy established in America would oppress other denominations. Boucher ridiculed this position—and may well have been correct in doing so—but many Americans disagreed, and no bishops were appointed during the colonial period.

The second conflict concerned payment of salaries to Anglican clergymen in Maryland. Anglicanism was the established faith in the colony. Other religious bodies were tolerated, but the Church of England had the advantage of laws requiring that its ministers be paid. Shortly after Boucher's arrival in Maryland, an argument developed over the proper amount of these payments. Boucher naturally favored the most generous interpretation of the law and published newspaper articles supporting his position. But the opposition appealed to the people's pocketbooks and republicanism. Jonathan realized that the conflict drew on sources deep in Maryland politics. Traditionally one party, which included the Anglican clergymen, had been attached to the governor by royal patronage. The opposition sought to turn "others out that they themselves might come in." Here and elsewhere such clashes between provincial "ins" and "outs" had acquired new urgency. Any increase in royal prerogatives, such as higher clerical salaries, came to be treated as pieces of a British plot to establish tyrannical control over Americans. Because he was an Anglican clergyman, Jonathan Boucher, who had railed against the injustice of the Stamp Act, became identified with a crown interest.

Eleanor Addison Boucher. American by birth she stood beside her husband, Jonathan, as he tried to find his way in the political turmoil of pre-Revolutionary America.

Boucher's problems were compounded by his unwillingness to shrink from a fight when he thought he was right. He saw critics of the Anglican establishment as ignorant and self-serving, and he treated them with contempt. In defending the church he came to defend the authority on which it rested, the monarchy. Between a populace that appeared turbulent and irrational and a crown that represented tradition and order, he chose the latter.

The commitment that made him an exile in 1775 grew from smaller commitments of the previous five years. He published tracts on bishops and ministerial salaries. He became a confidant of the royal governor, Robert Eden. He refused to join associations and sign resolves against British policy or to honor the fast day proclaimed by the Patriots on June 1, 1774, to mark the British closing of the Port of Boston. Above all, he refused to back down from a fight.

The spirit in which he conducted himself stands out in his encounter with a blacksmith who lived on land adjoining his and Nelly's. The man disliked Boucher's political views and also argued with him over property lines. The conflict came to a head when the blacksmith shot and lamed one of Boucher's horses and proclaimed he would deal with the minister in the same way. Boucher realized that his antagonist was much stronger than he, but he knew also that he would weaken his position if he seemed timid. "As I realized we were to come to blows," he writes, "I determined to have the first." One day he took a bare-knuckled swing at the blacksmith and, incredibly, knocked him out with one punch. "No man who has never himself experienced such a state of society as then prevailed in that country," he writes, "can conceive what credit I gained, and I add, what advantage, from this lucky blow." He was now looked up to as a great boxer, which was more advantageous to him "than to have been set down as a Newton."

Boucher stood up boldly for his views on many other occasions. One evening while dining in a "large company of men of differing parties and opinions," an acquaintance proposed this toast: "May the Americans all hang together in accord and concord!" Boucher did not really object to this toast, but he tells us he was prompted by an "evil genius" to remark, "In any cord, Doctor, so it be but a strong cord." A stunned silence must have followed this remark, but most of the guests accepted the minister's quip as a harmless joke. One Patriot, however, was outraged, and to bait Boucher, he proposed: "Damnation to General Gage, the troops under his command, and all who wish well to them." Boucher and several others refused to drink, at which his antagonist, a man named Sprigg, threatened to fight him. Boucher dared the man to come near, but his reputation as a boxer was well known and the man kept his place. Boucher, relieved that no fight ensued, was confirmed in his belief that "the true way to escape a danger is fairly to meet it."

This was the spirit that carried Boucher through his final years in Maryland. Once, while visiting the governor in the capital, he was summoned by a mob to come before the "Provincial Committee" to face charges of disloyalty to the American cause. The governor and his friends urged Boucher to flee, but he felt it would be safer to face his adversaries. He told the mob that he refused to be forced to go anywhere but that if they would withdraw he would go to the meeting on his own. The men agreed, and Boucher followed them to a crowded room, buoyed up by his initial success. As he entered the room he spotted a tough militiaman, one of the town's meanest characters. To Boucher's surprise, the man whispered to him that if he came through the interrogation well, he had friends in the room who would fight for him. This unexpected support further encouraged Boucher, and he went to the front of the room. There the committee "president" read a list of charges against him. In this tense atmosphere several committeemen argued that a man of Boucher's views should not be allowed to communicate with the public. Then Boucher's turn came. He could not later recall what he said but wrote that "necessity may perhaps be the parent of eloquence." He addressed the crowd rather than the committeemen and, at the end, had many shouting for his acquittal. The "judges," who depended on the people for their positions, went along.

It was a measure of Boucher's unusual strength of personality that he could win popular support even while criticizing the principles the populace now seemed to uphold. But once the war had begun at Lexington and Concord, it grew more difficult to continue preaching. He received so many threats that during spring and summer 1775 each time he preached he would carry two loaded pistols into the pulpit.

The final crisis came in summer 1775. A fast day had been ordered by the Provincial Congress to implore divine help in the confrontation with Britain. Boucher composed a sermon urging his people not to take part in the Revolutionary conflicts. When he arrived at the church, however, he found that his assistant, a man popular with the Patriots, was preparing to preach. Soon a large body of armed men—Boucher says two hundred—entered the building. They were led by his old adversary, Sprigg. As in the previous confrontations, Boucher decided it would be best to stand his ground and declared that they would not take him from his church alive.

But as he began to preach, one of his friends grabbed him from behind and told him that twenty men had been instructed to shoot him if he entered the pulpit. Boucher still attempted to deliver his sermon, but supporters and opponents began to throng around him, and Boucher had to conclude that the situation was becoming dangerous. He grabbed Sprigg by the collar and put a loaded pistol to his head, saying that if anyone tried to harm him he would blow out Sprigg's brains. He then walked with his captive through the hostile crowd, mounted his horse, and rode away.

Boucher now faced a distasteful choice. He liked America and thought of the new land as his home. Here were his friends, his wife, and his property. If he left, his estate might well be confiscated, but if he stayed he could lose life as well as property. After September 10 there would be no more commerce between the colonies and England. If Boucher was to flee, this was the time.

And so, reluctantly, he decided to return to England. Nelly, who could not bear the thought of separation from her husband, insisted on joining him. Her uncle and cousin also decided to go along. Time was short; they had less than a week to prepare for the journey. The estate would be left in the hands of Nelly's brother-in-law. The Bouchers decided to take only a few possessions, hoping they could soon return. On their last night at home the house was crowded with friends. Boucher had many admirers, even among moderate supporters of the Revolution. He later reflected that all this activity had dispelled his pain "on thus leaving a country where now almost all my attachments were, to go to another now become foreign to me."

On Sunday morning, "amidst the tears and cries" of their slaves, they boarded a small schooner that would carry them to their ship. Exhausted after a night without sleep, they retired to a "miserable cabin," where they lay down with an old sail for a cover and a bag of hominy for a pillow. They spent a day and night on this boat, then reached Quantico, where they boarded the ship that would take them across the Atlantic. Years later Boucher described their departure: "At length the wind came fair, and we sailed with a fine fresh breeze down the Chesapeake; and on the 20th of the month, just about sunset, in a charmingly fine evening, we lost sight of the capes of Virginia, never to see them more."

Thus Jonathan Boucher left America, never to return. As he sailed across the Atlantic, George Washington was organizing the Continental army outside Boston; battles had already been fought at Lexington and Concord and Bunker Hill. In less than a year the American colonies would declare themselves an independent nation. By moderating his views Boucher could easily have retained his church and plantation in Maryland as a citizen of the new country, but, ironically, he believed that his freedom would be diminished by joining America's fight for "freedom." To stay, he reflected, would have made "shipwreck of my conscience."

But why? Surely many conscientious men and women favored the Revolution. Boucher had been on their side during the Stamp Act crisis. He certainly had the idealism, independent-mindedness, and courage that Americans like to associate with the Revolution. Imagine the hero he would have been on that fast day in 1775 if he had been a Patriot seeking to preach to two hundred armed redcoats. What, then, were the roots of his loyalty? Was it personality or philosophy or circumstances that drove him inexorably into the Loyalist camp?

Boucher's character furnishes one clue. One of his greatest singularities was his yearning for respectability. He had always been drawn to people of wealth and culture. His parents were poor, but to him their background associated them with a more elevated life. Jonathan's grandfather was a gentleman farmer with an estate worth some £60 a year, a respectable sum at the time. The man had married a wealthy girl and doubled his estate with her dowry. But the Bouchers' fortunes were reversed a few years later when Jonathan's grandfather died before his twenty-fifth year, leaving a young widow and three children, including Jonathan's father, James. The mother married a man who took her and the children to Dublin. Lacking affection for his wife's children, he put them out as apprentices, James to a shoemaker.

James became economically independent by marrying a wealthy young widow and going into business. For a time he prospered, but then the business went bad. He returned to Blencogo where the family lived in "a state of penury and hardship." Foreseeing bankruptcy, he had to sell part of the family estate. Jonathan suggests that his father's personality kept him from success in business: "He was a lively facetious man, sung a good song, and was fond of company, and of course was almost always in company." Jonathan loved his father but could not respect him, and he seems to have sought a father figure in other men, such as John James, his English mentor.

Blencogo too was discouraging. Jonathan called it a "wretched," "obscure," and "unpolished" place. The townspeople respected hard physical work, and Jonathan despised it. An "ill end" was predicted for him.

Jonathan was able to escape the sordid circumstances of his home and village on periodic visits to a wealthy neighbor who befriended him. The lady of the estate, a Mrs. Thomlinson, took an interest in the bright boy. The contrast between the world in which Jonathan was raised and the world to which he aspired was laid out in miniature before each visit when he entered the Thomlinsons' barn to change from his dirty wood clogs into clean shoes to wear into the parlor. The Thomlinsons' house was Jonathan's introduction to polite society. He recalled that the house made him long for a more genteel life.

As a very young man, then, Jonathan had decided to separate himself from the world in which he lived. For the sake of more wealth, elegance, and culture he would leave Blencogo. In America, too, Boucher was attracted to wealth and culture. As a tutor and a minister he had access to some of the best plantations in Virginia, including George Washington's. He attended balls and dinners with the finest Virginia gentry. He went into debt to be able to make the right appearance on these occasions. "I had not the patience to wait for the slow savings of a humble station," he writes, "and I fancied I could get into a higher, only by my being taken notice of by people of condition; which was not to be done without my making a certain appearance." He borrowed money, purchased fine clothes, and associated with aristocrats.

The pattern was the same in Maryland, where both his intelligence and his appearance won him a place in the governor's circle. The Homony Club, of which he was president, attracted the most socially prominent as well as the most culturally refined people in Maryland. In marriage also Boucher elevated his social station. Although none can doubt that his marriage to Nelly brought about a close personal relationship, it was also socially advantageous. Nelly had a large dowry and helped him purchase the plantation into which they settled after their marriage.

Could it be that Boucher's aristocratic temperament, his attraction to people with wealth and elegance, ultimately led him back to England? Certainly he seems at times to see America as a larger version of Blencogo. There lived the people he mentions who drank too much and had no literary interests, and there we see his bemusement with the people who admired him for his victory over the blacksmith. Even George Washington, one of the wealthiest planters in the South, did not particularly impress Boucher. Washington, he says, had "no quickness of parts, extraordinary penetration, nor an elevated style of thinking."

Set beside Britain, America was backward and raw. Both he and Nelly were impressed with the grandeur of the mother country when they arrived there in 1775. When he took his wife to the cathedral at Canterbury, "whilst the organ was playing and the choristers singing" she was almost overwhelmed by "the magnificence of the building, the venerableness of its history... and the solemnity of the worship."

His love of elegance and culture suggests that Boucher was by temperament better suited to England than to America. But this conclusion overlooks the fact that the same attraction was shared by many American Patriots. Southern planters and northern merchants mimicked the British in their dress, speech, furniture, architecture, literary tastes, and in other ways. So too, Jonathan's ambition, his effort to climb above his poverty-darkened background, was matched by that of many Patriots. Benjamin Franklin, for one, had many of Boucher's characteristics: independent-mindedness, intellectual curiosity, and personal resilience. Thus, it was not Boucher's temperament that clearly separated him from other Americans.

What, then, of his ideas? Did they differ radically from those of the Patriots? The prevailing political ideology among the Whigs was the "libertarian philosophy" that they inherited from John Locke and his eighteenth-century successors. Locke had set forth principles of government in a theoretical model describing how politics had begun. According to Locke, people initially lived in a condition of complete freedom, a "state of nature." This was an inherently good condition, but it involved a crucial problem—some people used their freedom to oppress others. To prevent such abuses men established government. But sometimes governments themselves became oppressive. Revolution was therefore justifiable and could return the government to a condition in which it would defend, not curtail, individual liberty.

The libertarian ideology, emphasizing the government's responsibility to the people, appeared in the colonies in a number of circumstances. Essays by Locke and by such eighteenth-century thinkers as John Trenchard and Thomas Gordon were read widely. The colonists themselves articulated the libertarian philosophy during scores of conflicts with the royal governors, and they used libertarian philosophical reasoning in opposing the Stamp Act and subsequent oppressive British acts.

Boucher's ideas on government are surprisingly compatible with the libertarian ideology. In fact, he carried belief in the rights of the people further than many Patriots. As we have seen, he cared about the welfare of slaves. He proclaimed slavery to be the worst form of tyranny and encouraged the education, Christianization, and fair treatment of blacks. Like many other southern opponents of slavery, he did own Africans—no doubt his desire for status led him to follow colonial practice in acquiring land and servants—but he was thought one of the most humane of masters. A neighbor asked one of his slaves to whom he belonged, and the man answered, "To Parson Boucher, thank God."

He then agreed with the Patriots that governments should respect the rights of individuals, frequently making statements on behalf of these ideas in the 1760s. In the 1770s, however, he began to stress respect for current political institutions. His position as a beleaguered Anglican minister in a region that had cut ministerial salaries undoubtedly contributed to his sympathy for the status quo. But his posture was not merely a defensive one. Admitting that some British policies were bad, he argued that the colonial response was more "wicked" than the policies themselves.

Boucher believed that the average person is naturally fickle and can be led away from allegiance to good government by ambitious and designing demagogues. He believed that the South was full of empty-headed orators who loved to sway people's minds for their personal gratification. Some of them had used the salary question in Maryland to "train and habituate the people to opposition." He asserted: "Kingdoms are shaken and overturned, to gratify these perturbed spirits, whose natural element is a storm."

The conclusion Boucher drew from such observations was that individuals are more inclined to error than their governments. Political institutions were initially formed to curtail the activities of "perturbed spirits" who disturbed the welfare of others. Opposing those who argued that people are sacred and governments are merely their instruments, Boucher argued that humans are prone to error and that governments, embodying inherited wisdom, should be respected.

During the turbulent days preceding the Revolution, Boucher frequently preached on the idea of "obedience for conscience' sake." At all levels of society—in relations between parents and children, employers and employed, and upper class and lower class—the principle of obedience should prevail. "The manners of a community," he declared, "may be regarded as one great chain." He admitted that governments may make errors and stand in need of correction but declared that current notions, such as the idea that "all government is the mere creation of the people" or that liberty must be protected by a permanent and systematic opposition to government, could lead only to chaos.

As early as 1773 Boucher asserted that a revolution had already taken place in America. The opponents of England had gained effective control of the government. "To public speakers alone," he declared, "is the government of our country now completely committed: it is cantoned out into new districts, and subjected to the jurisdiction of these [revolutionary] committees.... An empire is thus completely established within an empire." Boucher believed that in revolutionary gatherings people's worst tendencies come to the fore: "It matters not that in our individual capacities we are wise, temperate, and just." He said, "Collected together in a mob, we inevitably become irrational, violent, tyrannical." In short, the greatest threat to liberty comes, not from the state, but from demagogues. Popular orators are especially dangerous because they obscure the real virtues of a political state and set before the people an imaginary creation. The people, he said, are "amused, bewildered, and enflamed, by certain words and sounds of almost magical potency, to attempt the reformation of some imaginary abuses." The most magical and misleading word of the time, he added, was "an undefinable something, which we call Liberty."

Boucher thus treated the current idea of liberty as a phantom. No wonder he was out of favor with the Revolutionaries and needed to carry pistols into his pulpit! But even in his apparent conservatism we may wonder whether his ideas were actually so distinct from those of the founding fathers, none of whom advocated a continual state of anarchy. The Declaration of Independence declares that "prudence indeed will dictate that governments long established should not be overthrown for light and transient causes." The Constitution was drafted under the influence of men who desired to create an authoritative government that would command the people's respect. During the administrations of the first two presidents political parties were looked upon by many Americans as treasonous, and under the Alien and Sedition Acts of 1798, President Adams sent Americans to prison for criticizing his administration. In such ways the Patriots indicated their own hunger for stable government.

The difference then between the philosophy of a Jonathan Boucher and that of many Revolutionary leaders was one of degree. Both believed in a blend of freedom and authority. Circumstances, particularly his position as an Anglican clergyman, forced Boucher to look to England for political and cultural standards; other colonists found them in America. He was vilified by the radicals, but we have the perspective of two centuries: his similarity to other Americans is more impressive now than his difference from them.

Bibliography

Bailyn, Bernard. *The Ordeal of Thomas Hutchinson* (1974). Fine biography of the best-known American Tory.

Boucher, Jonathan. *Reminiscences of an American Loyalist, 1738–1789* (1925). Boucher's lively and well-written autobiography.

———. *A View of the Causes and Consequences of the American Revolution* (1797, 1967). Contains texts of Boucher's sermons, mainly on political affairs.

———. *Letters of Jonathan Boucher to George Washington* (1899, 2009). Their letters with commentary—also available online at www.archive.org.

Calhoon, Robert M. *The Loyalists in Revolutionary America, 1760–1781* (1973). Extensive survey of Tory history.

Hodges, Graham Russell, Editor. *The Black Loyalist Dictionary* (1995). Resource on African Americans who went into exile during the Revolution.

Nelson, William H. *The American Tory* (1961). Brief, thoughtful survey of Loyalist history.

Potter-Mackinnon, Janice. *While the Women Only Wept: Loyalist Refugee Women* (1993). The experience of a group of Loyalist women who fled to Canada.

Roberts, Kenneth. *Oliver Wiswell* (1940). Sensitive and beautifully written fictional account of a Loyalist.

Van Buskirk, Judith L. *Generous Enemies: Patriots and Loyalists in Revolutionary New York* (2002). Detailed account of the Loyalist experience in New York.

Zimmer, Anne Y. *Jonathan Boucher: Loyalist in Exile* (1978). Thorough biographical account.

Identification Topics

Jonathan Boucher, Blencogo, Church of England, John Parke ("Jackie") Custis, Stamp Act, Homony Club, Eleanor Addison, Maryland "Provincial Committee," Anglican clerical salaries, John Locke, libertarian ideology, "Liberty"

Study Questions

1. What were Jonathan Boucher's main criticisms of America in his early years as a colonist? What did he like about America?
2. In what ways did Boucher contribute to colonial society and education while he was in America?
3. Like the Patriots, Jonathan Boucher opposed the Stamp Act—why?
4. What was Boucher's position on the questions of bishops and clerical salaries? How did his thinking on these issues influence his relationship to the Revolutionary movement?
5. Why did Jonathan Boucher leave America? How did other people treat him in his final months in the colonies?
6. What was the Lockean view of government? In what ways did Boucher support it? What was the philosophical basis of his opposition to the Revolution?
7. What did Jonathan Boucher mean when he argued that liberty is merely a "phantom"—a "magical and misleading word"?
8. Were the Patriots justified in driving Jonathan Boucher into exile? Should they have allowed Tories the same liberty they demanded for themselves?

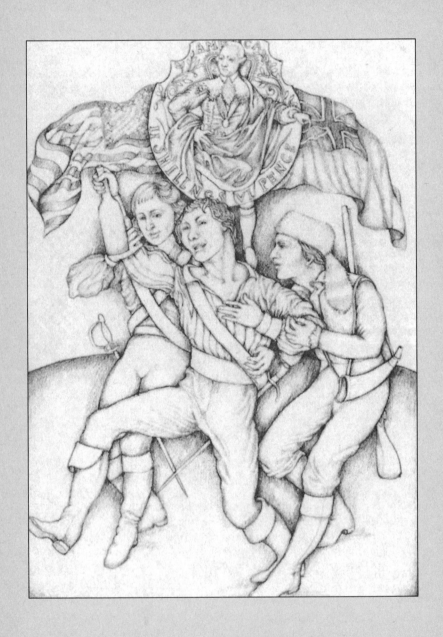

CHAPTER 6

The American Revolution

1776: The Continental Army in the Year of Independence

The United States declared its independence from Great Britain in 1776, becoming the first Euro-American community to attempt to break away from Old World control. The colonists had taken a century and a half to gain the power and confidence to seek independence, but even now success was uncertain. Britain was unwilling to give up the colonies and sent huge armies and navies to suppress the rebellion. The dream of American independence would become a reality only if the United States could create an effective military force. In 1776 hope for independence grew and faded with the Continental army's halting progress.

In his first meeting with Gen. George Washington, commander of the Continental army, Lt. Col. James Paterson was unnerved. Paterson, a high-ranking aide of Adm. Lord Richard Howe, had come to meet Washington at Kennedy House, an elegant mansion in New York City. The day was July 20, 1776, and America had been independent sixteen days—or so the Americans claimed. But neither Lord Howe, with more than four hundred ships under his command, nor his brother, Gen. Sir William Howe, with an army of 32,000 British and Hessian soldiers at his disposal, took the claim seriously. They regarded Washington as an upstart, a misguided British subject rather than a military commander. Accordingly, they had addressed a letter to him a few days previously as "George Washington, Esq.," omitting his American titles of general and commander in chief. Washington refused to accept any note that did not recognize his official position. To break this impasse Paterson came as an emissary from Admiral Howe, whose ship was anchored off Staten Island. As he approached Kennedy House, an American honor guard posted at the door stepped smartly aside.

Paterson was greeted by Gen. Henry Knox, one of Washington's most trusted advisers, and was then introduced to the American commander. The British officer was immediately disarmed by the general's appearance. Washington, he knew, was a former Virginia militia officer who had sought unsuccessfully to obtain a commission in the British army. He was a planter in a remote corner of the British Empire and a former representative in an obscure colonial legislature. The royal officer had expected to meet someone who would reflect the mediocrity of this provincial background.

Instead he was greeted by a man who had the bearing and looks of a European monarch. Standing six feet two inches tall and weighing 210 pounds, Washington was one of the largest men Paterson had ever met. He wore a fine blue coat with wide buff lapels and gold epaulets; his well-tailored buff trousers were tucked neatly into high black riding boots. A wide light-blue ribbon ran diagonally across his broad chest. His solid chin, firm mouth, long, straight nose, and lightly powdered brown hair tied back in a queue at his neck completed his fine appearance.

Washington seemed to melt the smaller man with his massive dignity and direct, penetrating stare. The British officer prefaced every statement with "Your Excellency," and he came cautiously to his main topic, the pardon offered by His Majesty to "rebels" who would lay down their arms and submit to British authority.

The commander bluntly dismissed the subject. "The Americans have not offended," he said, "therefore, they need no pardon." There was nothing more to say. The ruffled Paterson excused himself and hurried back to the familiar world of a British man of war, while Washington, Knox, and other members of the commander's official "family" sat down to a lunch of wine, cold meats, cheese, and bread. Knox later wrote to his wife that "Colonel Paterson appeared awestruck. . . . He was before a very great man indeed."

The minor triumph of that day is all but forgotten while the events at Lexington and Concord, Saratoga, and Yorktown live on in legendary splendor. But the winning of American independence was as dependent on matters of ceremony, appearance, and confidence as on larger events. On July 20 Washington had given the impression of a victorious general and had thus lent substance to the paper pretenses of the Declaration of Independence. Two centuries later Americans would celebrate a single day, July 4, as the anniversary of their national freedom, but in fact, independence came through a long series of tribulations rather than in a moment of transformation. To participate in the Revolutionary War in the year of independence was to be at one moment a soldier in a victorious army of well-disciplined soldiers, at another a refugee in a disorderly rout of farmers and artisans. Sometimes independence was as real as the stone walls of New England or the orderly plantations of the South. At other times it was as insubstantial as a dimly remembered dream.

The Continental army was both the symbol and the agent of that dream. The vision of national independence, of an "equal station" in the world, became a reality when the army worked. And "working" involved creating confidence as well as winning battles. It was largely because of his dignified presence—of his ability, that is, to inspire confidence—that George Washington had been chosen commander in chief. When in 1775 the Continental Congress determined that there should be a national army to fight the British, the tall, distinguished southerner was an obvious choice. As an aristocratic planter, his social standing would dignify the Revolution. His Virginia background accentuated the continental character of the Revolution that had begun in Massachusetts. Washington's political moderation made him acceptable to a broad spectrum of political opinion. And his forty-three years gave him the experience to lead the new Revolutiona   army and the vigor to stay on the job. Additionally, he impressed his colleagues i . the Congress as a man with "an easy soldierlike air." The impression was no doubt encouraged by his garb: he came to the Congress dressed in an ill-fitting uniform he had worn more than two decades before in the Virginia militia. Thus George Washington became commander in chief. He accepted the appointment with characteristic modesty, protesting his limitations and offering to serve without pay. He wrote his wife, Martha, that he hoped to be home soon, having no way of knowing that the war would drag on for almost a decade or that he would see Mount Vernon only twice in the next eight years.

On June 23 he left Philadelphia, escorted to the city limits with all the pomp the Patriots could muster, including a troop of light horse and a military band. Nine days later he rode through a heavy rainstorm to his new headquarters in Cambridge, Massachusetts, and began at once to assume the responsibilities of his command. Conscious of the need to establish his authority, he toured the colonial lines with a ceremonial accompaniment of twenty-one drummers and twenty-one fifers. He found the men in good spirits, encamped in a long line around the besieged town of Boston. They had bloodied the British at Lexington and Concord and then on June 17 had killed and wounded a thousand redcoats in the Battle of Bunker Hill. Although they had lost the hill, they had mauled the enemy, leaving the enemy troops isolated in Boston.

As Washington toured the lines, however, he did not see a victorious army but an unruly tangle of men, looking more like the colorful denizens of a county fair than the orderly soldiers of a well-regulated army. Most wore farm clothing or hunting jackets and identified themselves in battle with a slip of paper worn in their caps. They were inadequately quartered in college dormitories, private homes, tents made of boards and sailcloth, or crude shelters of stone, turf, and brush; and they lacked medicine, blankets, powder, cannon, and food. Worse still, they were unorganized and poorly disciplined. Many militia units elected their own officers and treated them as comrades rather than as superiors. Washington referred to the men rather disdainfully as "a mixed multitude of people."

Under the best of circumstances, organizing the scores of local militia companies outside Boston into a unified command would be difficult. But Washington, a new, untried leader, could not be certain of support even from his fellow officers. Many had fought in recent battles and might question why Washington had received the top position. Israel Putnam, for example, was Washington's senior by fourteen years. Known affectionately as "Old Put," he had already won immortality for his stirring words at Bunker Hill: "Don't fire, boys, until you see the whites of their eyes." Artemas Ward was an experienced soldier, five years older than Washington, and had commanded the Boston siege quite to his own satisfaction before Washington's arrival. Others were British veterans, among them Charles Lee, a proud and eccentric officer who paraded about with a large retinue of dogs.

If Washington was untested and the army disorganized, there were, at least, many good soldiers in his army. Nathanael Greene, a Quaker's son who left his church to fight for the colonies, commanded an orderly, well-supplied group of Rhode Island volunteers. John Glover of Marblehead, Massachusetts, led a colorful regiment of seamen-soldiers, smartly dressed in cocked hats, blue sailcloth jackets, and loose white navy trousers. During the siege of Boston they captured twenty-three enemy vessels, including the brig *Nancy* with two thousand muskets and a huge 2,700-pound brass mortar that Old Put, rum bottle in hand, christened with the name "Congress."

Glover's oarsmen would later prove indispensable when Washington's army had to retreat over the East River and attack across the Delaware.

Equally colorful were the new Continental recruits from the middle colonies. During the summer the first regiments of riflemen began to arrive from Virginia and Pennsylvania. The most famous were Daniel Morgan's ninety-six frontiersmen, who marched six hundred miles from Virginia in twenty-one days with the loss of only one man. The frontiersmen were crack shots and loved to show off by shooting boards from one another's hands. Unfortunately, their boisterous enthusiasm was combined with a dislike of discipline, and they often were the most ungovernable soldiers in an ill-governed army.

Washington's first job was to create a well-disciplined army from the materials of this "mixed multitude." He began by securing supplies; drilling and disciplining the men; and weeding out bad officers, including some who drew pay for absent or nonexistent soldiers. He gave thirty lashes and drummed men out of the army for insulting an officer or punished men absent without leave with extra latrine duty.

Still, an atmosphere of informality and spontaneity continued. Bored by lack of action, soldiers drank heavily. One ill-advised trooper gave a toast to Gen. Thomas Gage, commander of the British forces, and was forthwith ridden around the camp in a cart with a rope around his neck. Some soldiers diverted themselves with competitions to catch cannonballs, shot down from Bunker Hill, as they rolled along the ground: several lost their lives in this entertainment. Other men bathed nude in the Charles River at Cambridge and paraded naked on the bridge, much to the chagrin of Washington, who remarked that these exhibitionists appeared to "glory in their shame." In a fit of exasperation at these and other misdemeanors he called his men "exceeding dirty and nasty."

But he persevered, and his troops slowly began to look more like an army. He was on the lines every day, ordering, observing, and inspecting. The men were drilled twice a day and kept busy digging new trenches. As time passed, the distinctions between officers and men became plainer. Washington wore a light blue ribbon across his chest; his major generals wore a purple sash; and the brigadiers wore pink. Unfortunately, Washington's army dwindled while it improved. As autumn came to Massachusetts and the wind blew cold over sea, forest, and encampment, men began to think of home, and many a soldier on short-term enlistment walked away from the army for the sake of a fire and a warm bed. Washington wanted to replace this "Eight Month Army" with Continentals, recruited for longer terms of service. He was authorized to raise twenty-eight regiments totaling twenty thousand men, led by officers appointed from the top down, in conventional military fashion.

But progress was slow. Before long General Washington was complaining of "a dearth of public spirit and a want of virtue" among the citizenry. The recruits signed up at a disappointingly slow rate, many refusing to join because colonial militia units gave better bonuses. Others signed on but drifted away when rain put out their campfires and cold winds blew through their tents. Those who stayed through the first winter demonstrated patriotism both fine and rare. One was Joseph Hodgkins, an Ipswich, Massachusetts, shoemaker who supplemented his meager officer's pay by serving as army cobbler. In late November many of Hodgkins's Ipswich comrades had already left for home. But he wrote his devoted wife that he meant to stay on. "Our all is at stake," he wrote, "and if we do not exert ourselves in this glorious cause, all i   e and we made slaves of forever."

There were too few Joseph Hodgkinses in the encampments around Boston. At the end of the year Washington had raised fewer than ten thousand Continentals. These men, inadequately supported by small contingents of militia, possessed an average of only thirty cartridges apiece. On New Year's Day the siege lines were so ill manned that Washington feared an attack. He wrote a friend despairingly that rather than take command of the Continental army he wished he had retired to the West to live "in a wigwam."

Fortunately for the Americans, the British were suffering their own kind of discomfort in Boston. Since the disastrous Battle of Bunker Hill the city had been an increasingly unpleasant place; the town nursed scores of horribly wounded soldiers, many of whom died during the summer. The frequent street auctions of the dead men's belongings led one British soldier to write home that Boston was the "slaughter house of America."

The town festered with animosities. British officers disputed among themselves about matters of policy. Tories cursed their supposed deliverers for failing to take decisive action. And Patriots, living awkwardly in a hostile town, suffered persecution from British and Tories alike. As the snow fell, the privation grew worse, with little food and less firewood. Desperate men pulled down fences and houses to burn for warmth. In their frustration the British soldiers sometimes vented their rage on Boston itself. Needing a place to exercise their horses in the crowded town, they stripped the fine wood pews out of Old South Church and turned the gutted edifice into a riding ring.

The fate of the British in Boston was sealed in late February when Henry Knox, a former Boston bookseller, arrived from Fort Ticonderoga with fifty-seven cannon and mortars. His men and oxen had dragged their cargo for many days, crossing the Hudson, where he lost several cannon through the ice, and continuing on crude roads through the steep Berkshires, where fascinated countryfolk gathered to touch the precious weapons. On the night of March 4–5 three thousand colonial soldiers worked in the darkness to place these guns on Dorchester Heights above Boston. The ground was so hard they could not dig breastworks; so they hauled barrels, posts, and bundles of sticks to the hilltop. The next morning the British saw above them a makeshift fort.

They considered attacking the American position, but a great storm swept down from the north, scattering their boats and dampening their ardor. General Howe, who had replaced General Gage as commander, recognized that their position was untenable and elected to abandon Boston to the Patriots. By mutual agreement the British did not destroy the city and the Patriots did not molest the British retreat. The vanquished army spiked their cannon and pushed them, along with General Howe's stately coach, into Massachusetts Bay. They embarked, taking with them one thousand Loyalists, the first of almost one hundred thousand such exiles, many of whom would never see their American homes again. On April 17 the British fleet sailed to Nantasket Roads, ten miles away, where they spent ten miserable days at anchor under mist, rain, and a perpetual cloud of cookfire smoke, trying to decide where to go.

It was fitting that the first great American victory should come in Boston, the city whose Tea Party had provoked Britain into passing the Coercive Acts, hastening the outbreak of the Revolution. For a decade Boston had been a center of

Revolutionary activity: the scene of a bloody "massacre," the birthplace of the Committees of Correspondence, and the victim of economic and political punishment. In its environs the Revolutionary War had begun, and now the last British soldier had been driven from its streets.

But Washington did not celebrate. He entered the city without ceremony, asking only that a Boston minister preach a sermon of thanksgiving. He recognized that the British army in Boston had been a mere fraction of the mother country's strength. Frustrated in Massachusetts by the rebellious colonists, she would certainly strike at some other point. Washington believed that place would be New York City, for several reasons: it was America's largest city and would thus provide ample accommodation for the army; it was surrounded by water, making it easily defensible; it commanded the Hudson River, providing easy access to Canada; and it was centrally located, making it a potential barrier to communication between New England and the other colonies. Recognizing the British interest in New York, Washington said, "It is the object worthy their attention; and it is the place that we must use every endeavor to keep them from."

To do so would put his army to a test. The Continental army in Boston was primarily the creature of local circumstances, drawn in large measure from men who had come out to help their neighbors at Lexington and Concord. In colonial times the provincial armies had been notoriously reluctant to fight battles beyond their own boundaries, and it was not yet clear whether local troops would travel farther in the new war. Thus far, the Revolutionary War had been fought mainly by men near their own homes. A notable exception occurred during the previous fall when Richard Montgomery and Benedict Arnold led a two-pronged attack on Canada. But barely two thousand men had been with them, and even this select force had been plagued by desertions.

Now Washington must try to move almost ten times as many men from Boston to New York. Some would follow for pay; some for adventure; some, like Joseph Hodgkins, because they genuinely believed in American rectitude. When he learned that he was going away, the Ipswich shoemaker wrote his wife, "I would not be understood that I should choose to march, but as I am engaged in this glorious cause, I am willing to go where I am called."

Between late March and early April 1776 the bulk of the Continental army, along with many state militia units, made their way south. Washington left five regiments in Boston under the command of Gen. Artemas Ward and went ahead to New York to set up his headquarters. The soldiers marched three abreast through New England, led and followed by mounted dragoons, their movements coordinated across thousands of yards by drum cadences. They camped each night in fields staked out by an advance party.

After twelve days of marching, the men came to Manhattan, a lovely island located at the mouth of the Hudson River. They crossed onto it in the north and marched through woods, fields, and pastures to New York City at the southern tip of the island. Still a town by modern standards, it was by far the largest one most of the young soldiers had ever seen. Before them lay a cosmopolitan city of twenty thousand inhabitants, a place of solid brick houses, proud spired churches, and row upon row of shops and warehouses.

When George Washington arrived in New York, he occupied an old mansion and supplied it with a new feather bed, pillows, crockery, and glasses; to complete this comfortable lodging he persuaded Martha to join him. In less style, but with considerable enthusiasm, the men adapted to the new environment, soon discovering the "Holy Ground," a seedy but alluring cluster of whorehouses, where many contracted venereal disease and a few were murdered. Others entertained themselves by stealing melons or digging for oysters.

There were other activities that soon consumed their energy. They would have to defend Manhattan against an enemy that could easily command the surrounding waters. With shovel and pick they fortified Brooklyn Heights and both banks of the Hudson. They sank a row of boats to form a blockade across the Hudson halfway up the island and farther north stretched a chain across the river. They did not always build wisely. Some of the earthen walls contained fragments of rock and glass that became secondary missiles when struck by British shells; others, especially those on Long Island, were poorly designed and offered scant protection against a well-planned attack.

Nonetheless, American morale was high in early summer 1776. Washington had at his disposal twenty thousand confident troops. He had even turned an attempt on his life into an American triumph. New York was a stronghold of loyalism, and after Washington's arrival a network of Tories plotted against him. The conspirators bragged of their plans so openly that they were easily discovered. Among the conspirators was Thomas Hickey, one-time British soldier, now a member of Washington's lifeguard, who was hanged on June 28 before an appreciative audience of thousands of soldiers and civilians. One witness was Joseph Hodgkins, who wrote to his wife, "I wish twenty more were served the same."

Those who had enjoyed the spectacle of a conspirator at the gallows looked on a less welcome scene next morning. In the lower bay off the tip of Manhattan was a forest of ships' masts flying the British flag. Sir William Howe's fleet had arrived with more than 130 ships. A few days later Howe's brother, Adm. Richard Howe, arrived with an additional 150 ships. Together their fleets constituted 45 percent of the British navy and carried 42,000 soldiers and sailors, the largest military force yet assembled in America. As a land base they chose Staten Island off the southwestern tip of Manhattan, occupying it without opposition.

Perhaps more disconcerting than the fleet was the casual, even contemptuous manner in which the ships treated the American fortifications. When a shore battery fired, they responded with a short bombardment of the city, as if to suggest they could destroy it at will. In mid-July two British ships, the *Phoenix* and the *Rose,* easily sailed past the blockade and fortifications on the Hudson River and came to anchor forty miles to the north. With little difficulty they beat off an attack by American fireships and, after several days in the interior, sailed unharmed back to the fleet.

By such gestures the British demonstrated their intent to rule the American colonies. But the Americans had simultaneously formalized their claim to independence. On July 9, by the order of the Continental Congress, officers read a new document, entitled the "Declaration of Independence," to the soldiers at New York. In 1775 many Americans, including George Washington, had anticipated that the Revolutionary War would result in a new status for the colonies within the British Empire. But the past year had shown that Americans could erect governments, pass legislation, and wage war without British help. Thomas Paine's pamphlet, *Common Sense,* urging American independence, had impressed many moderates, including

Washington, that independence was the logical goal of the Revolution. The Patriots were cheered by the news of the Declaration and celebrated in New York by putting ropes around a statue of George III, pulling it from its pedestal, and melting the four-thousand-pound figure to make bullets and cannonballs.

The hostile armies spent the midsummer of 1776 preparing for battle. Still low on men, Washington sent out an urgent request to neighboring states for help. By now a pattern of recruitment had been established that would last through the war. Each state was called upon to raise a quota of men, determined by the Congress, to serve in the Continental army as state units or "lines." In addition, each state had its own militia units that would supplement the Continental forces if fighting took place in their area. It was always difficult to raise troops. Although bounties of land and money were offered to volunteers, potential enlistees held back, reluctant to be shot or desiring to maintain their trade or farm. Although the Congress stipulated that men should be healthy, more than five feet two inches in height, and sixteen years of age or older, exceptions were necessary. The Pennsylvania Continentals included David Hamilton Morris, age eleven, and Jeremiah Levering, age twelve. One Massachusetts soldier stood a full seven inches under the height standard. Many were beyond their physical prime—10 percent over forty, and a few were well into their fifties.

Young and old, short and tall, Washington did all he could to mold them into an orderly force. The early months in Massachusetts had strengthened his belief in the value of discipline and work. When men were not busy digging trenches, he put them through drills and parades. Finding that the customary punishment of up to thirty-nine lashes for misdemeanors was not a sufficient deterrent, he increased the limit to one hundred lashes (and would have raised it to five hundred had not the Congress objected).

To compensate for the rigors of camp life and the dangers of battle, the Continental Congress stipulated that the men should be provided with abundant daily rations. Its November 4, 1775, orders read as follows:

> Resolved, That a ration consist of the following kind and quantity of provisions: 1 lb. beef or 3/4 lb. pork or 1 lb. salt fish per day; 1 lb. bread or flour per day; 3 pints of peas or beans per week, or vegetables equivalent, at one dollar per bushel for peas or beans; 1 pint of milk per man per day, ... 1 half pint of rice, or one pint of Indian meal, per man per week; 1 quart of spruce beer or cider per man per day, or nine gallons of molasses, per company of 100 men per week.

Such provisions would have more than supplied the needs of men if they had been available, but often there was an aching chasm of hunger between prescription and reality. The men probably spent more time foraging for food than fighting the British. Often what they had was inadequate, like the bread, which one soldier complained was "hard enough to break the teeth of a rat."

Despite such disadvantages, thousands of men joined Washington's forces in New York. Typical in motivation was Pvt. Joseph Plumb Martin, who is remembered today as the author of the finest account of the war by a common soldier. Martin was a Connecticut farm boy who was sixteen years old at the outbreak of the war, barely old enough to remember the Stamp Act crisis. At first he had no inclination to be caught "in the toils of an army," and he played no part in the events around Boston. But as the months of war passed, he grew hostile to the British and wanted "to be called a defender of my country." In spring 1776, watching as friends marched out of town on their way to New York, he could wait no longer and enlisted in the state militia. His family supplied him with arms, clothing, a piece of cake, and a pocket Bible. Thus equipped, he set out for New York.

While Washington was busy with fortifications, drills, and discipline, the Howe brothers planned their attack. They were already at an advantage but expected additional reinforcements from Adm. Peter Parker, who would soon arrive in New York with armies commanded by Sir Henry Clinton and Lord Charles Cornwallis. The British delay was occasioned in part by the desire to attack the Americans with as much force as possible and to end the war immediately with an overwhelming victory.

Additionally, the Howes attempted a diplomatic mission, having been empowered not only to wage war against the Americans but also to negotiate with them. Their dual role reflected an awkward compromise between British factions led by the colonial secretary, Lord George Germain, who favored the maximum use of force, and others who followed the prime minister, Lord North, in favoring a political solution. Germain's influence was evident in the huge British force at New York. North's resulted in the Howes having authority to pardon penitent rebels and colonies.

As we have seen, the attempts at negotiation fell upon an impasse when the Howes addressed an invitation to parley to "Mr." George Washington and Washington refused to receive any communication that failed to address him as "General." There in microcosm was the whole issue of American independence. The "Mr." implied that the Continental Congress had no authority; the "General" implied that the colonies were independent. Neither side would accept the other's view, and Colonel Paterson's visit failed to establish a basis for negotiation. The Howes would be warriors rather than diplomats.

On August 22 British troops began to move in barges across the Narrows between Staten Island and Long Island to occupy unprotected beaches near the town of Gravesend. In the evening General Howe had fifteen thousand troops ready to challenge Washington's positions in Brooklyn. Three days later Hessian mercenaries were ferried across, standing at attention in the barges in an impressive display of discipline.

Even before the Battle of Long Island began, Washington was at a disadvantage. His outnumbered army was divided into two forces, and those in Manhattan would be unable to help their comrades in Brooklyn. Moreover, an important segment of the Long Island force was placed in advance of the well-fortified Brooklyn base, an unwise decision, because it stretched out the force in a thin, indefensible line, with a road around their right flank covered by only five men. The error was primarily the result of poor planning by Gen. Israel Putnam; but Washington also was to blame, having surveyed the positions and left them unchanged.

The battle began on August 26 when British and Hessian troops made a frontal assault against 3,500 forward troops under Gen. John Sullivan and Gen. William Alexander. The Americans were holding their own when they heard gunfire on their left flank. During the night Generals Howe and Clinton had marched behind the Americans along the poorly defended road and threatened to encircle them. British and Hessian soldiers plunged into the American ranks, using their superior training in hand-to-hand fighting to overwhelm the Patriots, most of whom used rifle butts against fixed bayonets.

The Americans fled from the carnage toward their fortifications on Brooklyn Heights. George Washington, who had rushed over from Manhattan to be near the battle, tried to rally them, calling out, "Remember what you are contending for." At that moment, however, self-preservation seemed to most of the men the main object to "contend for." Private Martin, who watched the approach of these wounded and dispirited men, found himself "a little daunted" and began thinking wistfully of home.

A few of the Continentals' lines had fought bravely even after the collapse of their positions, but most ran. In all, more than one thousand Americans were killed or captured. Among the prisoners were Generals Sullivan and Alexander. Fortunately, Howe did not pursue the confused Americans into Brooklyn; had he done so, he might have easily crushed them with his superior force. But rather than attacking Brooklyn Heights and running the risk of another disaster like that at Bunker Hill, he decided to take the safer course of building protective trenches and laying siege to Washington's position.

In the Brooklyn encampment the defeated Americans were confused and discouraged. The first year of the war had been so easy: they had defeated the British at Lexington and Concord, killed them by the hundreds at Bunker Hill, and forced them out of Boston. Now, in their first major battle since the Declaration of Independence, they had broken and run. No jaunty sounds of fifes and drums, no talk about invincibility circulated in camp; ominous doubts gripped the soldiers. Joseph Hodgkins realized that the ability of America to win her independence was in doubt. "The day is come . . . ," he wrote to his wife, "on which depends the salvation of this country."

There was no question of defeating the British on Long Island, only of keeping the hope of future victory alive through the difficult maneuver of evacuating the army from Brooklyn Heights across the East River to Manhattan. On the night of August 29–30 a cold wind blew from the northeast. Rain fell on the solid wood decks of the British men of war anchored off the tip of Manhattan and ran down the sides of canvas tents and along the muddy paths in the Brooklyn encampment. It sent thousands of British seamen and soldiers scurrying for the cover of ships' cabins and army tents. It left Washington's army free to attempt an audacious maneuver in the wet, blackened world.

Throughout the night a fleet of flat-bottomed boats under the command of Marblehead's John Glover ferried men across the river. Hour after hour the fishermen-sailors worked at muffled oars; Washington stood on the shore supervising the loading. Only after ten thousand men with their arms, horses, and supplies had made their escape did the commander allow himself to be rowed to safety. When the fog cleared in the morning, the British occupied an empty fort.

The evacuation boosted American morale. On Long Island an Anglican parson's daughter, Lydia Minturn Post, began a secret diary she would keep for her husband, an officer in the Continental army. Although Washington's retreat left her in enemy territory, she regarded the escape as a commendable achievement. "What a skillful movement was that of George Washington," she wrote, "a wonderful retreat!—the enemy so near that the sound of their pickaxes and shovels could be heard! It is new proof of his cool forethought and judgment."

On Manhattan, however, the Americans had little time to congratulate themselves. The fall of New York was now inevitable owing to the superiority of the British fleet and their command of Brooklyn Heights, from which they could fire at the American positions in the city. Some of Washington's advisers wisely suggested burning the city to reduce its usefulness to the invader. But the Congress was unwilling to approve such a stern measure, and Washington was unwilling to conduct a hasty retreat. He badly needed to defeat the British, even if only in a skirmish, to bolster American morale. He stationed his main force behind fortifications on Harlem Heights in the northern part of the island but left five thousand men in the city under General Putnam.

The Howes were in no hurry to pursue the war. Anticipating that Washington's recent defeat might make the Americans more willing to negotiate, they dispatched a message to the Continental Congress requesting a parley. A few days later the Congress sent John Adams, Benjamin Franklin, and Edward Rutledge to meet with the Howes aboard the British flagship off Staten Island. The conference was a civil affair accompanied by good wine and a pleasant meal. But there was no real chance for a settlement. The Americans demanded recognition of independence as the basis for negotiation, and the Howes declared that they could merely pardon those who denounced the rebellion. Admiral Howe professed to regret the necessity for the war, saying that if America should be defeated he would "lament it like the loss of a brother." Franklin answered wryly, "My Lord, we will do our utmost endeavors to save your lordship that mortification."

The conference ended in a stalemate, and the rival forces continued to prepare for the next battle. The two weeks following the defeat on Long Island had done nothing to restore the shattered American morale. Food and blankets were in short supply, and militiamen, sensing defeat, deserted by the thousands. Still there were many who stayed, watching anxiously for some indication of the enemy's next move. One of the faithful was the young Connecticut militiaman, Pvt. Joseph Plumb Martin, who was one of the soldiers assigned to guard Manhattan's east shore.

On September 14 four British warships sailed up the East River and anchored opposite Martin's position. They were so close that when the sentries standing watch along the blackened shore shouted the watchword "All is well," a voice from one of the ships boomed out, "We will alter your tune before tomorrow night." And indeed they did.

The next morning Private Martin saw the British ship, *Phoenix,* anchored so close to shore that he could read her name as if he "had been directly under her stern." The large ship and her companions were ominous enough, but now a more threatening sight appeared. Scores of small boats packed with British and Hessian soldiers began to make their way toward the Manhattan shore. Soon there were so many that they "appeared like a large clover field in full bloom." The ships opened fire, and "there came such a peal of thunder from the British shipping," says Martin, "that I thought my head would go with the sound." He jumped into a ditch and began to wonder "which part of my carcass was to go first."

Martin's fellow militiamen and their officers were equally impressed and withdrew from the exposed position. When the British landed at Kip's Bay on Manhattan they found a quiet farmhouse and a pleasant field but no Americans. Panic had struck the Patriots all across the island. The most endangered were five thousand men in New York who might easily be cut off from Washington's main force on Harlem Heights if Howe had swept across the island. They and the other troops along the East River swelled the country roads leading north from the city.

Soon after leaving their positions at Kip's Bay, the men in Martin's regiment were scattered by British grapeshot. Martin found himself alone with two other militiamen as frightened as himself. Hoping to fortify their spirits, they stopped at a house and asked for a drink. The residents, two women and several children, were in tears, frightened by the proximity of battle, but one managed to place a bottle of rum and some glasses on the table for the soldiers, who refreshed themselves and left.

The highways, fields, and woods of Manhattan were alive with movement. Martin came upon men he thought were friends only to find that they were Hessians. He barely escaped and overtook a party of militiamen just as a British force opened fire. The Patriots fled in abject confusion, littering the ground with their weapons and knapsacks, coats, and hats. Martin admitted that he and others were dreadfully afraid. "Every man that I saw," he writes, "was endeavoring by all sober means to escape from death or captivity."

No man suffered more on that day than George Washington. He realized that he could not hold New York but wanted to maintain order in retreat. When he heard the guns on the morning of September 15, he hurried toward Kip's Bay, discovering to his "surprise and mortification" that his sometime army had been reduced to a pathetic mob. Again and again he tried to rally the troops who surged past him. Finally Washington came upon two brigades, less terrified than the others, and stationed them behind a stone wall to oppose a British advance. But as soon as a handful of the enemy appeared, these also fled. Now Washington completely lost control of himself. Throwing his hat on the ground and lashing out with his riding crop at men and officers, he cursed and exclaimed: "Are these the men with whom I am to defend America? Good God! Have I got such troops as these?"

But the men continued to run, and Washington slumped in his saddle, exhausted from anger and despair. His aides stayed by their chief, watching anxiously as the last of the soldiers made their escape. Across the Weld, some fifty British soldiers came toward the paralyzed leader. Washington was too hurt to care what happened. Finally, the aides, realizing that they must act, took his bridle and led their dazed commander to safety. It was the saddest moment in Washington's military career—and it was nearly the last.

The day was as glorious for the British as it was tragic for the Americans. With their men spread across Manhattan, General Howe and his subordinates, Generals Clinton and Cornwallis, stopped for an afternoon respite at Murray Hill, a fine country estate overlooking Kip's Bay. While the pathetic Americans struggled northward through the hot, humid afternoon, the British officers sipped Madeira and ate cakes. New York was theirs. Soon, it seemed, Washington must be theirs, and with his fall the little American rebellion would be ended.

A few miles away the remnants of the American army spent a miserable night at Harlem Heights. Their hasty retreat had prevented Howe from dividing the army and cutting off Putnam in New York. But valuable stores and arms had been abandoned to the foe, and there was not enough food to feed the bedraggled refugees. Militiamen by the hundreds were again deserting the apparently doomed army. Worse still, men and officers bore the shame of having fled without testing the enemy.

The soldiers found some solace next day in an engagement near Harlem Heights when two small parties of American and British soldiers ran into each other in no-man's-land between the two armies. As the Americans retreated, a British bugler insulted them with a disparaging air, the signal to end a fox hunt. But the Americans were not finished. Washington sent more men down from the Heights into the engagement and forced the British to abandon their advance position.

This minor triumph afforded some comfort, but the commander in chief could not ignore the dismal state of his army. In the last month of fighting he had lost men, supplies, territory, and pride. It was bad enough to lose the battles, but it was worse to watch the progressive deterioration of the army. For every man killed or captured, four or five soldiers had deserted and gone home, reckoning the Revolutionary War was over.

Washington wondered if it was not over for him also. In a letter to his cousin, Lund Washington, he declared that "the bitterest curse to an enemy" would be to occupy his place. There appeared to be no way to win the war, and yet his associates insisted that he must not quit his position. None of the apparent alternatives was satisfactory. "In confidence," he wrote, "I tell you that I never was in such an unhappy, divided state since I was born."

What most troubled Washington was the volatile condition of his army. Most soldiers were short-term militiamen who retreated and deserted with disturbing regularity in times of trial. Their influence upset the Continentals, who themselves enlisted for only one year at a time. Washington tried to persuade the Continental Congress to provide for an army of soldiers bound to the cause by long-term enlistments. But the Congress balked: such a force would be expensive and might become too independent for the welfare of the young republic. America had revolted against a strong military power and did not want to become overly centralized herself. For the moment, Washington would have to make do with what he had.

British and American forces in New York were now in tenuous balance. Washington occupied the northern part of Manhattan, and Howe occupied the southern. The British could easily land their troops above Washington in Westchester County, thus isolating him in Manhattan, but for the time being they appeared content to occupy themselves with establishing their headquarters in New York City. Their comfort was greatly diminished on September 21 when a great fire of undetermined origin destroyed three hundred buildings. Washington, who had wanted to destroy the city himself, concluded that "Providence, or some good honest fellow," had done the job.

But even after the burning of New York City the British forces were well housed and supplied. Not so the Americans, who continued to have problems in providing themselves with blankets, clothing, and food. Pvt. Joseph Plumb Martin says he was so hungry that he liked to go on patrols because it improved the chance of finding food. He considered himself fortunate when he could steal a few turnips or beg a sheep's head from the officers' mess. Despite such hardships, hunger was only a "secondary matter" in comparison with exposure to the elements. It was now autumn, but Martin and many of his comrades had only summer clothes and no blankets. They had to spend the night "freezing and thawing" alternate sides of their bodies. "I have often while on guard," Martin writes, "lain on one side until the upper side smarted with cold, then turned that side down to the place warmed by my body and let the other take its turn at smarting, while the one on the ground warmed." On some mornings he awoke to find the ground "as white as snow with hoar frost."

The most memorable event in days of cold, hunger, and desertion was a single act of heroism that became one of the great mythic legacies of the Revolution. After losing Brooklyn and New York, Washington needed good intelligence reports on British movements and commissioned a young captain named Nathan Hale to enter New York as a spy. Clothed in a brown broadcloth suit and a wide-brimmed hat and posing as a schoolmaster, Hale wandered unmolested through the British lines gathering intelligence. He was waiting for a boat to carry him back to safety when he was apprehended, searched, and proved a spy. In short order he was condemned to be hanged. At the gallows on September 22 he uttered words that would recall the spirit of American resistance to British tyranny long after the disgrace at Kip's Bay was forgotten. "I only regret," he said, "that I have but one life to lose for my country." Hale's heroic death typified the stoic patriotism of the New York campaign. Denied victories, the expression of American resourcefulness was limited to orderly retreat, uncomplaining privation, and resolute self-sacrifice.

On October 12 the Howes sought to outflank Washington by landing four thousand men at Throgs Neck, a peninsula north of his Harlem Heights headquarters. As they approached a bridge to the mainland, they encountered stiff rifle fire from behind a well-designed fortification. Not realizing that the position was held by only twenty-five Americans, the attackers withdrew and sailed on a few miles to New Rochelle where they made a second landing. Here, on October 18, they overcame spirited resistance from four battalions of Massachusetts troops, well protected behind stone walls.

In the meantime, Washington had realized that his Manhattan position was untenable and began retreating to the north, leaving five thousand men under Gen. Nathanael Greene divided between Fort Washington on the Manhattan side of the Hudson and Fort Lee in New Jersey on the opposite shore. Washington fortified himself on high ground near White Plains, where Howe attacked him on October 28. Howe managed to take one of the hills on Washington's right flank, forcing the American commander to supervise another night retreat. Washington reassembled his army five miles away at North Castle, and Howe, seeing that he could not lure Washington into an engagement, turned south toward Fort Washington. Washington was now forced to make one of the most difficult and, as it turned out, unfortunate decisions of his career.

Fort Washington, the last American stronghold on Manhattan, was on a high cliff over the Hudson, surrounded on all but the river side by the British. Washington believed that the position was indefensible but was persuaded by his subordinate, Nathanael Greene, that it could be held. On November 16 he watched in despair from the opposite shore as his fears were realized. The outerworks of the fort were too extensive to be held by the 2,800 men left in Manhattan. They were easily overwhelmed, and the defenders retreated into the fort itself. But it was small and impossibly crowded, and at the day's end the situation was hopeless, and the garrison surrendered. It was the worst defeat of Washington's career. In addition to losing almost three thousand men, he lost guns, cannon, munitions, and supplies.

Additionally, the loss of Fort Washington was a uniquely personal loss for the general. The episode was not merely a news item he studied in a field report or a remote event on a battlefield he commanded. As the fort was overwhelmed, Washington was on the opposite side of the Hudson River, on the New Jersey Palisades, watching through a telescope. In painful detail he could see Americans overwhelmed, finally surrendering or falling to the sword. Following the losses of the previous months, this was simply too much. Washington turned away and began to weep, in the words of one historian, "with the tenderness of a child." This was no weakness on the commander's part; rather it indicates one of his strengths. Washington could care deeply, intimately, about his men, even while dealing with larger, impersonal questions of conducting the war.

Two days later Cornwallis crossed the Hudson and moved toward Fort Lee. Joseph Hodgkins, then garrisoned at Fort Lee, had built himself a comfortable log cabin and hoped to spend the winter. But in the face of the British advance the Americans had to make a hasty retreat, leaving behind tents, cannon, ammunition—and Hodgkins's homey cabin. After losing New York the disheartened Washington must have hoped for some respite, having retreated from Brooklyn to New York, to Harlem Heights, to White Plains, to North Castle, and to Fort Lee. But now he must abandon Fort Lee and cross New Jersey, hoping to station his army between Howe and Philadelphia.

As he and his men fell back through New Jersey his situation grew worse. They lacked food, clothing, and shelter; and the New Jersey militiamen who were expected to muster with his arrival did not materialize. Howe, moving slowly after Washington, offered to pardon those who renounced the Revolution and found thousands of luke-warm Patriots willing to accept the offer. Washington's humiliation was completed by disaffection among his officers. General Lee, still commanding seven thousand troops at North Castle, refused to come to Washington's aid and plotted to increase his own power. After the fall of the two Hudson River forts, he wrote to a friend in the Continental Congress, saying, "Had I the powers, I could do you much good." Washington's adjutant general, Joseph Reed, wrote to Lee encouraging him to supplant the discouraged chief.

The trials of autumn 1776 extended well beyond Washington's camp. To the north the Continental army had been pushed out of Canada and barely held on to Fort Ticonderoga. Thousands of Americans in the environs of New York City experienced the hardships of British occupation. The end of America's first year of self-styled independence was drawing near, but many Americans professed doubts about the "glorious cause." Some were ardent Tories like the old woman who while selling milk to Pvt. Joseph Plumb Martin lectured him on his opposition to "our good King George" and warned him that "the regulars would make us fly like pigeons." Others were Patriots who genuinely desired American independence but doubted that it was attainable.

The conflicting sentiments of patriotism and fear are set out clearly in an account by Lydia Minturn Post, the woman who had been so impressed with Washington's "wonderful retreat" from Brooklyn. The retreat may have saved the Continental army, but it left families like hers to a precarious existence under British occupation. Separated from her husband, a Continental officer, she went with her three children to live with her father in a pleasant Dutch-style house. The location itself hardly suggested a war. The whitewashed house with its low gabled roof was covered with sweetbrier and creeping vines. Her father, a Church of England minister, had planted ivy and sweet clover in the yard.

This fine pastoral scene had become a place of privation and fear. The army requisitioned men, horses, and wagons for work details and billeted Hessian and British soldiers in American houses. Soldiers carted away trees and fences to provide fuel. Lydia Post spoke with contempt of the German mercenaries quartered in the neighborhood, as many as six in a house. These invaders strung up hammocks in the kitchens and spent the days drinking and smoking. British officers could be even more obtrusive. The Posts had to share their home with a wounded British officer and his two servants. A neighbor endured the presence of an officer and his silly mistress, a woman who knocked holes in their walls to mount a collection of stuffed parrots.

Lydia Post recounts many incidents where neighbors were punished for refusing to flatter the British soldiers. One man was killed on the spot by a bully who tried unsuccessfully to make him say "God save the King." Her neighbors were ravaged also by outlaws who used the disorder of war to facilitate their activities. They came at night, forcing their way into houses and stealing whatever valuables they could find.

Thus, life for conquered Americans was a combination of hardship, annoyance, fear, and outrage. For those like Lydia Post the price of liberty was high indeed. She watched with pathetic interest the course of the Revolutionary War after Washington's departure from Long Island. Certainly she was a Patriot. "We love this our native land," she wrote her husband, "She is over-taxed, oppressed, insulted." But she was also a realist and knew that the war was going badly. After hearing of Washington's loss at White Plains, she wrote, "Who can look without trembling at the failure of this struggle to throw off our yoke?" When she heard of Washington's forlorn retreat through New Jersey, she felt the American cause was hopeless. "The disparity between the two contending parties," she reflected despairingly, "is so immense." In late December she wrote, "The year has closed disastrous, gloomy."

Lydia Post's account serves as a barometer of public sentiment. Living close to the war, she found her patriotic feelings challenged by personal observations of British power. Her concerns were matched by Washington's own. In mid-December he found himself on the Pennsylvania side of the Delaware River, having been forced out of New Jersey as well as New York in less than two months. The proud soldier who had faced down General Howe's adjutant in New York a few months before had lost confidence in himself and his cause. He contemplated going south to Virginia and crossing the Appalachian Mountains into the interior to escape the British army. Independence seemed an empty hope. "I think the game is pretty near up," he wrote. "I am wearied to death."

Thousands of Americans shared Washington's discouragement, but it was an Englishman recently migrated to Philadelphia who coined an immortal phrase to describe the feeling in those dark days. A year earlier Thomas Paine had caught the American imagination with his plea for independence in *Common Sense*; now in an essay called "The American Crisis" he called for renewed dedication to the cause. "These are the times that try men's souls," he wrote. "The summer soldier and the sunshine patriot will in this crisis shrink from the service of his country: but he that stands it now, deserves the love and thanks of man and woman." The essay made popular reading in Washington's camp. The commander had seen an army of "summer soldiers" evaporate after the debacle in Brooklyn and Manhattan. But the men who were still with him had "stood," having resisted the temptation to desert.

Still, it would take more than patriotism to keep the army together and win the war. For that there must be victories. Across the Delaware there were British encampments in nearby Trenton, Princeton, and Brunswick. If Washington could cross the river and take them by surprise, he could capture several thousand enemy soldiers along with their valuable stores. But the risk was great; if discovered, the war might be ended in a single battle. It was a desperate gamble but one made necessary by the disasters of the previous months. The Americans had not won a significant victory since declaring their independence.

On the night of December 25 Washington began to prepare 2,400 men for the crossing of the Delaware. He had assembled a fleet of long, shallow-draft Durham boats, normally used as trading vessels. These were manned by Col. John Glover's Marbleheaders. During the night the temperature dropped and the wind came howling down the valley. Snow fell on the small transports as they made the three-hundred-yard trip across the cold water between hard blocks of ice. But in the early morning of December 26 the army was across and marched over frozen roads to Trenton.

There they surprised the Hessian garrison, sleeping off a Christmas celebration. The enemy tried without success to organize themselves to fend off Washington's attack, but they surrendered after forty-five minutes. It was a stunning victory. Washington captured a thousand enemy troops and their supplies at the cost of only twelve casualties.

Fearing a British counterattack, Washington took his men and their prisoners back across the Delaware. In a few days his soldiers would complete their one-year enlistments, but Washington persuaded most to stay another six weeks. On December 30 he recrossed the Delaware. This time the British were prepared. General Cornwallis was in the vicinity with six thousand troops. On the night of January 2 the British general camped his men near Washington's position on Assumpink Creek. Expecting to attack Washington the next day, Cornwallis remarked, "At last we have run down the old fox and will bag him in the morning." But his prediction was wrong, for Washington once more eluded the British with a night march. Leaving a few men behind to tend the campfires, the Americans marched past Cornwallis deep into enemy-held territory. On the morning of January 3 they routed the British at Princeton, and Washington watched the retreat with childlike enthusiasm. Sitting astride his horse, he waved his sword and shouted, "It's a fine fox chase, my boys."

Cornwallis, who had expected the day to be his, had heard gunfire behind his lines. Afraid that Washington would go on to capture the main British supply depot at Brunswick, he hurried his men back to defend his stores, leaving Washington in control of Princeton. The Americans soon marched on to Morristown, where they established winter quarters deep in the heart of British territory.

The victories at Trenton and Princeton gave an enormous boost to American morale. In Europe the New Jersey counterthrust was described by such eminent military experts as Frederick of Prussia as one of the great campaigns of the century. At home in New York, Lydia Minturn Post credited the American success to divine Providence; to "the judgment, skill, and intrepidity" of George Washington; and to the "deep-rooted indignation" of the Patriots who would "do and dare for liberty, or death." Even an old English observer had to admit that Washington's successes restored American confidence. "A few days ago," he said, "they had given up their cause for lost. . . . Now they are all liberty mad again."

The ceremonial dignity of the commander in chief, which had so impressed Col. James Paterson during his meeting with Washington six months before, was now reinforced by Washington's imaginative military leadership. But in the interim he had almost failed. The independence that had been declared so confidently in 1776 was in reality an elusive goal. The Washington who would one day accept a British surrender at Yorktown was also the Washington who was "wearied to death" time and again the first year of the struggle. America was able to persevere beyond the year of independence only because of small triumphs salvaged from great disasters: a Patriot spy who died well at the gallows; a general whose bearing encouraged respect despite his inexperience; a few thousand soldiers who stayed with Washington when other thousands deserted; an army that avoided annihilation while suffering defeat; an impassioned publicist who understood "the times that try men's souls."

Bibliography

Carp, E. Wayne. *To Starve the Army at Pleasure: Continental Army Administration and American Political Culture, 1775–1783* (1990). Helps explain why Joseph Plumb Martin and other soldiers were so poorly fed and clothed.

Fischer, David Hackett. *Washington's Crossing* (2004). Thorough and superbly written, this is a Pulitzer Prize–winning narrative of the events surrounding the two Battles of Trenton.

Lengel, Edward G., Editor. *This Glorious Struggle: George Washington's Revolutionary War Letters* (2008). Thoughtful compilation of some of Washington's most interesting and colorful letters from the Revolution.

Martin, James Kirby, Editor. *Ordinary Courage: The Revolutionary War Adventures of Joseph Plumb Martin* (1999). Excellent edition of the best account of the Revolutionary War by a common soldier.

Middlekauff, Robert. *The American Revolution, 1783–1789* (2005). Beautifully written and carefully researched narrative of the entire sweep of the American Revolution.

Post, Lydia Minturn. *Personal Recollections of the American Revolution* (1859). Long Island woman's account of British and Hessian occupation.

Royster, Charles. *A Revolutionary People at War* (1979). Sensitive analysis of the relationship between the Revolutionary War and the American character.

Scheer, George F., and Hugh F. Rankin, Editors. *Rebels and Redcoats* (1957). Fine anthology of letters and diary accounts of the Revolution.

Smith, Page. *A New Age Now Begins* (2 vols., 1976). Lively narrative survey of the Revolutionary War.

Wade, Herbert T., and Robert A. Lively. *This Glorious Cause* (1958). Story of two officers, Joseph Hodgkins and Nathaniel Wade; includes Hodgkins's letters.

Identification Topics

Joseph Hodgkins, *Common Sense*, Joseph Plumb Martin, "Mr." George Washington, Battle of Long Island, John Glover, Hessians, Lydia Minturn Post, Kip's Bay, Nathan Hale, Fort Washington, Trenton, Princeton

Study Questions

1. The author claims that American independence did not become a reality on July 4, 1776. In what ways was America still subordinate to Britain after Independence Day?

2. For what reasons did people join and desert the Continental army?
3. What were George Washington's principal accomplishments and weaknesses as a military leader in 1775–1776?
4. Why was Washington "wearied to death" in 1776?
5. Describe the contribution of each of these persons to the Revolutionary War: Nathanael Greene, Joseph Hodgkins, Joseph Plumb Martin, Nathan Hale, Lydia Minturn Post, and Thomas Paine.
6. How did each of the following contribute to American independence: the rhetoric of Nathan Hale and Thomas Paine and the victories of the Continental army at Trenton and Princeton?
7. In 1776 Americans took pride in being a small nation that fought bravely against a larger nation. America is now one of the most powerful nations in the world, but can you see evidence in our statesmanship of a tendency to associate ourselves with smaller, "oppressed" nations?

CHAPTER 7

Testing the Constitution
The Alien and Sedition Acts

By 1798 the United States had been independent for two decades, but the nation's character was not yet fully defined. The Constitution, although creating a republican instrument of government, could not anticipate every historical circumstance. The political crisis resulting in the Alien and Sedition Acts was one of many episodes in which Americans were torn between conflicting political values. In this case it seemed that they must sacrifice either free speech or political unity. The Adams's administration chose the latter, provoking a nationwide debate about American institutions and inadvertently encouraging the growth of free speech and two-party government.

When the carriage bearing President John Adams came into view on the morning of July 27, 1797, Newark, New Jersey, was alive with a holiday atmosphere. Flags flew above the streets; church bells rang; young men fired a cannon salute; and local dignitaries stood ready to greet the president. Those without official business crowded the taverns, drinking freely.

President Adams was both pleased and vexed with this display. The country was ablaze with patriotism because France had recently insulted three American negotiators. For the past four months the president had found himself delightfully and disturbingly popular. The delight lay in the compliment to his ego, one of the largest in the land; the disturbance, however, grew out of his belief that such adoration was fickle. His Puritan reserve led him to distrust, even while he enjoyed, the momentary cheers of the crowd.

He had hoped to travel quietly from Philadelphia, the national capital, to Quincy, Massachusetts, where he and his wife, Abigail, would spend the summer. The business of preparing for war—expanding the army, building new ships, appointing officers—had left him exhausted. Abigail, too, needed rest, having followed every turn of national affairs almost as closely as her husband. She found Philadelphia's summer air so hot and close that "you had as good be in an oven." She missed her friends at home and now wanted to "slide along to them, unnoticed and without parade."

As the carriage entered Newark, then, the good citizens of that place were more pleased to see the president than he was to see them. Undoubtedly he waved and smiled politely, but he did not stop to greet the notables who had hoped to kiss his hand. As he drove past the young men at the cannon, they chanted in unison, "Behold the chief who now commands." The president probably acknowledged their greeting, but his carriage rattled on, leaving the youths to fire a sixteen-gun salute after their departing commander in chief.

At the doorway of John Burnet's tavern a well-liquored crowd watched the coach as it disappeared down the road. The town's moment of glory had ended abruptly, and there remained only the anticlimax of the day ahead. Perhaps to enliven the atmosphere, one of the men remarked, "There goes the President, and they are firing at his ass."

In response another fellow, one Luther Baldwin, who was said to be "a little merry," expressed his political sensibilities in a few pithy words: "I do not care," said he, "if they fire through his ass."

Suddenly the town had a new event at which to marvel. Here in their midst was a traitor, a speaker of forbidden words. Such, at least, was the conclusion of the tavern owner. "This is sedition," he said. A group of Federalists who had gathered around expressed their agreement. Luther Baldwin had broken the law, and he must pay the penalty.

In due course the tavern wit, known to history only for the ten words he spoke that day, was indicted for speaking "seditious words tending to defame the President and government of the United States." He was tried by a court presided over by Associate Justice Bushrod Washington of the U.S. Supreme Court. Found guilty, he was fined $150 and committed to federal prison until the fine was paid.

Luther Baldwin was apparently punished for his querulous wit. But in truth he was less the victim of his tongue than of his times. His remark was sedition only because in 1798 it was regarded as sedition; in other periods it would never have attracted the attention of the law. It is less significant, then, that Baldwin joked about cannonballs and presidential anatomy than that such behavior was regarded as a crime. The immediate occasion for Baldwin's trial was the passage in 1798 of the Alien and Sedition Acts, four statutes aimed at discouraging opposition to the government. The acts, in turn, reveal current thinking about freedom of speech, the legitimacy of political parties, and dissent in wartime.

In 1798 the Bill of Rights was only seven years old. The First Amendment declared that "Congress shall make no law. . . abridging the freedom of speech, or of the press." But America lacked a tradition of political and judicial experience to draw out the meaning of that clause. It was generally agreed that certain kinds of speech could be so malicious, so crude, or so harmful as to fall outside the scope of legitimate discourse. Even today such speech-related issues as pornography, wartime dissent, and the sanctity of a reporter's sources have eluded definitive boundaries. It should not surprise us to learn that the early republic had not fully defined the First Amendment.

The issue of free speech was complicated in 1798 not only by the newness of the Constitution but also by the hostility of early Americans to political parties. Eventually parties would seem as right, natural, and patriotic as the Constitution itself. But in the 1790s they were viewed as a cancer in the body politic. In a good republic, it was thought, no person would need to criticize the government or form an opposition faction. The Constitution did not provide for parties, and eighteenth-century statesmen generally denounced them as destructive—even treasonous—threats to the nation's unity and welfare. When George Washington became president in 1789, Americans did not expect to be troubled with internal dissent. The Constitution provided an apparently stable government, and Washington had been elected by a unanimous vote in the electoral college. Seemingly any right-thinking individual would now support the government and the administration.

Despite such optimism, however, discord soon emerged, encouraging the formation of two rival political organizations. Alexander Hamilton, Washington's able and ambitious secretary of the treasury, served as the catalyst for the divisions of the 1790s. Hamilton wanted to attach wealthy Americans to the government by skillful management of the national debt and the tariff and by creating a national bank. His financial program aimed to establish a strong central government allied with a progressive business community. No admirer of the people—he once called the public a "great beast"—Hamilton was distrustful of human nature and felt that America was best governed by a political and economic elite.

The Hamiltonian program led to the formation of the first American party system. Opposition to Hamilton's program centered on Secretary of State Thomas Jefferson. Hamilton despised the common man; Jefferson exalted him. Hamilton wanted a strong federal government; Jefferson favored a modest national establishment. Hamilton felt that America's future lay in the factory. Jefferson believed that the real source of national virtue was the farmer.

The Hamilton–Jefferson opposition evolved into a system of political parties during the next five years. At first these consisted of loose divisions within Congress in 1792. In that year no one opposed George Washington as president, but Hamilton's opponents offered George Clinton as a vice-presidential candidate against John Adams and acquired a party organ in Philip Freneau's *National Gazette*.

In the course of Washington's second administration the breach between Hamiltonians and Jeffersonians—soon to be known as Federalists and Republicans—was further widened by divisions on foreign policy. In 1789 when French patriots stormed the Bastille, a symbol of monarchic tyranny, most Americans rejoiced. The American principle of liberty was apparently gaining ground in Europe, and several of the new revolutionary leaders—notably the Marquis de Lafayette, who sent Washington the key to the Bastille—had helped America win her own revolution. But each year the French Revolution grew more radical. The king and many of his supporters were guillotined, and revolutionaries began to attack the church. In 1793 France and England went to war. Many Americans favored England because of trade relations and hostility to radicalism. Others supported France in the belief that France represented the libertarian principles of the American Revolution. England's supporters were mainly those who had favored the Hamiltonian economic program, and France's were by and large Jefferson's colleagues.

The conflict came to a head in 1795 with the debate over ratification of Jay's Treaty, a document designed to resolve outstanding conflicts between England and America. Jeffersonians believed the treaty conceded too much. The United States accepted Britain's wartime limitations on trade with France, agreed to deny French privateers the use of American ports, promised not to carry French goods as a neutral, and agreed to settle outstanding British claims against American citizens. In return, Britain promised only to withdraw from several western posts on American territory and to pay for American ships confiscated by the British navy. Nothing was said about Britain's unpopular policy of searching American ships and impressing alleged deserters into its navy.

The treaty was so unpopular that John Jay claimed he could have made his way across the country at night by the light of burning effigies. But the Federalists wanted to avoid war with England, and Hamilton had even undercut Jay's negotiating position by secretly assuring the British ambassador that America would not go to war against his country.

The treaty debate in the Senate, which resulted in a narrow victory, crystallized the Federalist–Republican division. In the 1796 presidential election the two parties operated as fully developed political organizations with supportive newspapers, local machines, and presidential candidates. The contest between John Adams and Thomas Jefferson was the first electoral race for the presidency, and Adams's narrow margin of victory in the electoral college, seventy-one to sixty-eight, revealed the close division of strength between the two parties.

The rivalry between Federalists and Republicans was surprisingly shrill in a nation that abhorred party discord. But the expectation of unity made the discovery of disagreement all the more alarming. Each side could accuse the other of disloyalty and corruption because it seemed that its own ideas should prevail. Was not each, after all, the spokesman for the ideal nation? In his Farewell Address, George Washington warned against the "baneful effects of the spirit of party" and the "insidious wiles of foreign influence," but to no avail. Party conflict and fears of foreign intrigue marked the presidency of John Adams and had their apotheosis in the Alien and Sedition Acts.

John Adams was inaugurated president on March 4, 1797. He later said he could imagine George Washington saying to him: "Ay, I'm fairly out, and you're fairly in. See which of us will be happiest!" The new president had good reason to be apprehensive. As soon as he moved into the large stone house in Philadelphia that served as the Executive Mansion, Adams began to receive discouraging news from abroad. France was angered by America's recent treaty with England. In the past year France had captured or sunk more than three hundred American merchant vessels on the ground that they carried contraband to England; refused to receive America's new ambassador, Charles Cotesworth Pinckney; and decreed that any American sailor found aboard a captured British warship would be executed.

These affronts seemed consistent with grisly tales of domestic turmoil in the self-proclaimed land of "Liberty, Equality, and Fraternity." The Reign of Terror against supposed enemies of the French Revolution was now in full force. Aristocrats by the hundreds were tied onto barges and drowned; priests were cut to pieces at their altars; and public guillotine executions were common. The French army was occupying neighboring countries, including the republics of Holland and Switzerland. Many Americans regarded the French Revolution as an obscene perversion of republican principles.

On May 15 President Adams addressed a special joint session of Congress, summarizing French affronts and calling on the legislators to "convince France and the world that we are not a degraded people, humiliated under a colonial spirit of fear and a sense of inferiority." He urged Congress to provide for expansion of the army and the navy.

The request was reasonable, for at that time the military establishment consisted of only two thousand soldiers and a few vessels—hardly enough to convince France of anything. But many Americans, especially those associated with Thomas Jefferson, believed that France's naval policy was no more repressive than England's and preferred the republicanism of France, misguided though it might be, to the obdurate monarchism of England. After the May 15 address Adams became, for the first time in his presidency, the object of attack from the Republican press.

Adams was, nonetheless, as eager to avoid war as the Republicans. Although he might prefer England to France, he realized that in her comparatively defenseless condition America was not a match for France. And so while he urged the nation to prepare for war, in summer 1797 he pressed forward with another attempt at negotiation. With the acquiescence of Congress he sent Elbridge Gerry and John Marshall to join Charles Cotesworth Pinckney in Paris as special envoys.

No word of their progress arrived until March 1798, when secret dispatches from Paris informed him that the negotiators had been insulted by the French government. Three emissaries, called X, Y, and Z in the report, had come with the message that the French foreign minister, Talleyrand, would be willing to negotiate if he were given a $250,000 bribe and France was granted a $12 million loan. Such demands were not uncommon. America was already paying bribes to the Barbary pirates on the northern coast of Africa to protect American shipping. But in the atmosphere of distrust and hostility between the two nations, Talleyrand's demand seemed degrading. The envoys' response to this demand was: "No, no. Not a sixpence!"

Adams notified Congress that the mission had failed and called upon the lawmakers to enact defensive measures. In the meantime, he would permit American merchant ships to arm for their own safety. The initial response to his message was lukewarm because Adams had not yet released the text of the dispatches from Paris. Vice President Thomas Jefferson called the speech an "insane message," and Republican publicists denounced the president. Expecting to prove that he had exaggerated the crisis, they demanded full disclosure of the envoys' communications.

But the dispatches supported Adams's characterization. They described the so-called XYZ Affair and also revealed that Talleyrand expected America to assume France's debts to United States citizens, including those for ships France had confiscated, and wanted President Adams to apologize for remarks he had made about France.

The news swept across the nation, and the envoys' reply to the bribery demand was embellished by a Federalist journalist into a strident and highly quotable phrase. Charles Pinckney supposedly told the insidious French negotiators: "Millions for defense, but not one cent for tribute." The phrase neatly captured America's belief in its own strength and rectitude.

A wave of patriotic fervor swept across the land. A new song, "Adams and Liberty," was set to a tune that later became "The Star-Spangled Banner." Another patriotic song, "Hail Columbia" by Joseph Hopkinson, received thunderous applause at its first performance in a Philadelphia theater: the audience demanded four encores, joined in the choruses, and shouted their approval. Three cavalry units welcomed

John Marshall on his return to Philadelphia and escorted him through an immense cheering throng. From all over the country petitions of support came to President Adams. When, finally, a group of drunken patriots gathered outside the Executive Mansion late one night and serenaded the president with "Hail Columbia," he and Abigail may have longed for more settled times. But the national spirit was aflame, and his was the job of accommodating it.

A deep fear of French aggression underlay the enthusiastic nationalism of such displays. The French Revolution had become turbulent and cruel; French armies had overwhelmed neighboring states and were preparing to invade England; the French navy thwarted American commerce. Many Americans feared that France would dominate both Europe and America. Abigail Adams believed that France aimed "not only at our independence and liberty" but sought also "a total annihilation of the Christian religion." The Massachusetts Federalist Fisher Ames characterized France as "an open hell, still ringing with agonies and blasphemies" and speculated that such might be America's "future state." In his July Fourth oration the president of Yale predicted that if Jefferson and the supporters of France prevailed, Americans would "see the Bible cast into a bonfire . . . our wives and daughters the victims of legal prostitution."

Fear of invasion from France was intensified by belief that the enemy had supporters throughout the United States. Talleyrand himself had belittled the pretensions of the American negotiators by insisting that he had support of a "French Party" in the United States. During spring 1798, alarms of war circulated through the country. French privateers continued their raids along the American coastline, and one even had the temerity to sail into the harbor at Charleston, South Carolina, and burn a British vessel in American waters. Letters were discovered in Philadelphia revealing a plot to set fire to the city while citizens were attending religious services on May 9, a national day of fasting. A Francophile mob in Philadelphia, wearing French tricolor cockades, attacked a group of Adams's supporters. More disturbing still, French supporters in one city talked about forming a separate volunteer army, to be known as the Republican Blues. And always there were the Republican newspapers, sniping at the administration, belittling the French threat, and destroying the American effort to present a united front to the foreign foe.

Among the Republican publicists the foremost was Benjamin Franklin Bache, young editor of the *Philadelphia Aurora*. The grandson of Benjamin Franklin, he was sometimes known as "Lightning Rod, Junior," perhaps as much for his shocking invective as for his prestigious ancestry. He was impetuous, harsh, narrow-minded, and totally devoted to the belief that the sins of the mighty must be exposed. His unremitting hostility led him to make fun of Abigail for crying when her husband was honored with the first singing of "Hail Columbia." He accused her husband of nepotism, misuse of public funds, and monarchic ambitions and called him "old, querulous, bald, blind, crippled, toothless Adams." In return, Abigail described him as "that lying wretch of a Bache."

The *Aurora* and other Republican newspapers, such as John Daly Burk's *New York Timepiece* and Thomas Adams's *Boston Independent Chronicle*, continued to attack Federalist foreign policy despite the revelation of the XYZ Affair. They demanded that America try again to negotiate a settlement with France and accused the Federalists of using the war scare to gain support for their party.

Such charges were galling to Adams during these, the most difficult days in his public career. Abigail wrote to her sister that she had never seen him look so tired and pale. Adams wanted to build up the nation's defenses but hoped, through a display of patriotic resolve, to persuade France to adopt a more conciliatory stand. The administration sought to walk the thin line between a declaration of war and humble acceptance of French attacks. The Republican attitude made his position all the more difficult, because he believed the nation could avoid a potentially catastrophic war only if it appeared united. The Republicans were destroying that chance with their criticisms. They were so pigheaded, so unreasonable, and—Adams must sometimes have thought—so treasonous.

Ever vigilant in support of her husband, Abigail Adams came to regard the opposition as plotting to overthrow the government. "French emissaries are in every corner of the union," she wrote on March 20, "sowing and spreading their Sedition. We have *renewed information* that their system is, to calumniate the President, his family, his administration, until they oblige him to resign, and then they will reign triumphant." Other Federalists declared more bluntly that in the current situation dissent equaled treason. One Federalist editor concluded that any American who "opposed the administration is an anarchist, a Jacobin, and a traitor."

By the middle of 1798 many Federalists believed that if the country were to avoid foreign domination and civil strife, the shrill denunciations of the opposition press must be put down. Certainly full discussion of important issues was important in a free society. But when power-mad publicists misused that freedom and printed lies to stir up sedition at home and encourage enemies abroad, they could destroy the republic. Again Abigail Adams caught the spirit of this reasoning when she wrote to her sister on May 26: "I wish the Laws of our Country were competent to punish the

Abigail Adams. Ardent supporter of her husband and herself resourceful, she believed the president should be spared criticism in times of crisis.

stirrer up of sedition, the writer and printer of base and unfounded calumny. This would contribute as much to the peace and harmony of our Country as any measure."

The Federalists developed a two-pronged approach to their domestic and foreign problems. First they made plans for military defense. Adams had already decreed that American merchant vessels could arm themselves to stave off French attacks. In April he created the Department of the Navy and appointed Benjamin Stoddert of Virginia its first secretary. During the next three months his supporters in Congress passed acts providing for coastal fortifications, military supplies, and expansion of the army and the navy. Three new frigates, the *Constellation*, the *Constitution*, and the *United States*, would be made seaworthy along with other ships. For the first time since the Revolution, the United States would have an active navy.

A new force of ten thousand men and a provisional army of another fifty thousand would strengthen the army. George Washington, nearing the end of his life in retirement in Mount Vernon, reluctantly agreed to serve as nominal commander but insisted that his old military aide, Alexander Hamilton, be appointed second in command of the force and its actual leader.

Adams completed the rupture between the two nations by suspending all commerce with France and declaring that the old treaties of 1778 were void because of French violations. On July 21 he told Congress: "I will never send another minister to France without assurances that he will be received, respected, and honored as the representative of a great, free, powerful, and independent nation." Adams also considered a declaration of war. Many of his more extreme supporters, called "High" or "Ultra" Federalists, favored the commencement of hostilities. Once he had been appointed to lead the army, Hamilton, in particular, grew excited at the prospect of attacking France's ally, Spain, and taking Florida, Louisiana, and Mexico, at that time Spanish territory.

But Adams was reluctant to declare war. He realized that the country was not yet ready to fight a major European power and surmised that the people's mood was exuberant but not warlike. If the nation must bear the burdens of war, he reasoned, let France rather than America be the first to announce hostilities. In the interim the country could prepare her defenses and wage a "quasi-war" against French privateers.

The Quasi War, as it came to be known, was waged with France from 1798 to 1800. It was a naval war fought first along the Atlantic Coast and then in the Caribbean. Despite the tentativeness of the name "quasi," real ships were captured on the high seas during battles with the French, and real seamen were killed and injured in the encounters. In July 1798 the United States won its first victory at sea under the newly organized Navy department. A French privateer, *Croyable*, had been attacking American shipping off the New Jersey coast. Stephen Decatur Sr., captain of the *Delaware*, caught the French vessel off guard, pretending to be a slow merchantman, and luring the enemy into attacking his ship, revealing at the last moment that the *Delaware* was, in fact, a war sloop with sixteen guns. Overwhelmed, the *Croyable* surrendered and Decatur took his prize triumphantly into port. The captured ship was soon sailing for the United States, renamed *Retaliation*. Despite this encouraging beginning to the Quasi War, the United States lost several hundred merchant ships to the French, mainly in the West Indies during the next two years. The existence of this war at sea helped stir up anti-French passions in the United States. And along with military preparedness and naval action came support for a crackdown on civil liberties at home.

The second level of administrative policy covered the domestic situation and consisted of the four bills known collectively as the Alien and Sedition Acts. The first three, passed in June and July 1798, dealt with aliens residing in the United States. There were several reasons for the Federalist mistrust of recent immigrants. The first was plain, simple nativism—the belief that the only good American was a native-born American—an idea common among the Federalists of that time. Harrison Gray Otis said that "the native American germ" was sufficient to produce such individuals as are "worth cultivation." In 1798 the Massachusetts legislature proposed a constitutional amendment that would allow only citizens born in the United States to hold public office. Some Federalists wanted to go one step further and end all immigration to the United States. Their nativistic prejudices were heightened because many recent immigrants had come from France and Ireland, where anti-British sentiment and revolutionary radicalism were common. Aliens, once naturalized, tended to support the Republican party, another black mark against each group.

The first of the bills, the Naturalization Act, extended the period of probationary residence prior to citizenship from five to fourteen years, delaying the immigrants' entry into the electorate; the second, the Alien Act, allowed the president to expel any alien suspected of dangerous or treasonous acts; the third, the Alien Enemies Act, empowered the president to imprison or expel citizens of enemy states in time of war. The administration never had occasion to use the last two acts, but their existence on the statute books may have frightened some immigrants into exile and dissuaded other Europeans from coming to America.

The idea underlying these three acts was phrased most explicitly in the Alien Act, which spoke of preventing behavior "dangerous to the peace and safety of the United States." The Sedition Act suggested that Americans as well as foreigners could threaten domestic peace through unbridled dissent. The proponents of the Sedition Act regarded speech as a dangerous weapon. Robert Goodloe Harper, South Carolina Federalist and chairman of the House Ways and Means Committee, warned his colleagues that visionary radicals could shake "the foundations of order" by spreading unfounded discontent among the populace. Joseph Hopkinson, the Federalist lawyer who wrote "Hail Columbia," claimed that an "INTERNAL FACTION" was spreading "groundless jealousies" against the government in order to deliver the country to France.

The consistent theme in these and other Federalist discussions of Republican rhetoric was the charge that their opponents criticized the administration with malice, falsehood, and treasonous intent. The administration's critics did not simply disagree about matters that reasonable people might properly debate; they sought rather to destroy the republic itself for their own greedy ends. They lacked the commonality of interest with their fellow citizens upon which free speech must be based, and in misusing speech they were as guilty of misconduct as an assassin who shot his gun at the president's breast.

Reasoning in this fashion, the Federalists concluded that a sedition bill was a proper measure for protecting the national welfare. The Senate sponsor of the bill, James Lloyd of Maryland, expressed the Federalist view frankly when he remarked that the act would muzzle the administration's opponents. He regretted only that it was not reinforced by a declaration of war to make it easier to "lay our hands on traitors." In a letter to a group of Braintree, Massachusetts, supporters, President Adams declared that seditious speech was the instrument "with which our enemies expect to subdue our country." Or as one of the Federalist newspapers summarized the issue, "It is *Patriotism* to write in favor of our government—it is Sedition to write against it." Political dissent and party activity had come to be identified with treason.

The Republicans, recognizing that they would be its principal victims, opposed the Sedition Act. They complained that it was tyrannical and would undermine the Constitution, and they asserted that there was no evidence that sedition even existed. Upon hearing of the proposed bill, Thomas Jefferson declared that it flew "in the teeth of the Constitution." On June 6 Benjamin Bache claimed it was contrary to the First Amendment. Representative Albert Gallatin of Pennsylvania remarked on the obvious political implications of the act—it was "a weapon used by the party now in power in order to perpetuate their authority and preserve their present places."

Lacking control of either branch of the Congress, however, the Republicans were unable to block the sedition bill. It cleared the Senate on July 4, 1798. On that day a group of Federalists in a New York militia company drank a toast to "One and but one party in the United States," thereby expressing the spirit of the act. Republicans were less in evidence that day, but one group in Easton, Pennsylvania, greeted the bill with this toast: "May the friends of the gag-bill sleep in oblivion until the angel Gabriel sounds his last trumpet." Ten days later the bill was law.

The Sedition Act declared it unlawful to "combine or conspire" to impede the operation of the federal government by insurrection, riot, or unlawful assembly. It was now illegal to write, publish, or utter any "false, scandalous, and malicious" statement against the president or Congress or to excite "the hatred of the good people of the United States" against the government.

The act was broad enough to encompass most forms of political dissent, but for its time it was not a particularly restrictive measure; similar limitations on freedom of speech existed throughout the world. The British Treasonable Practices Act of 1795 was harsher than the Sedition Act, and the common law—the body of legal tradition deriving from previous judicial decisions in England and America—was more severe in several respects. Unlike the existing law, the Sedition Act required proof of malice, allowed truth as a defense, required the jury (rather than the judge) to determine whether libel had been committed, and stated maximum penalties.

The act did, however, publicize limitations on speech and encourage enforcement, and it inaugurated an era that Thomas Jefferson referred to as the American "Reign of Terror." Charges were brought against twenty-five Republicans, twelve of whom were tried and convicted. Luther Baldwin, our tavern wit, was the most obscure. Many were important Republican newspaper editors, and one was a member of the U.S. House of Representatives. Because of his political position, Matthew Lyon, a congressman, attracted special interest.

Lyon had come in his youth to America as an indentured servant from Ireland. He worked hard, purchased his freedom, and fought in the American Revolution. After the war he became one of the most successful businessmen in Vermont, founded the town of Fairhaven, and established a sawmill and an ironworks. An outspoken Republican, he campaigned successfully for a congressional seat in 1796.

When he took his House seat in 1797, Federalists immediately ridiculed him because of his republicanism and his Irish background. When John Allen, one of the extreme nativists in the House, disparaged Lyon's ancestry, the new representative eloquently defended his character. This was his country, he said, because he had "no other" and had fought for her during the Revolution; he had earned everything he owned "by means of honest industry."

Lyon's strident self-confidence only further enraged nativist sentiment against him. One Federalist editor compared him to a wild beast and claimed that he was violent but cowardly. On January 30, 1798, Roger Griswold of Connecticut disparaged Lyon's Revolutionary War record, and in response Lyon spat in Griswold's face. A few days later Griswold attacked Lyon on the House floor, beating him with a cane while Lyon fought back with fire tongs. They rolled on the floor in violent combat until other congressmen finally pulled them apart. The Federalists, outraged that an Irishman's spittle should have touched a native New Englander's face, sought to expel Matthew Lyon from the House of Representatives. After fourteen days of debate the congressmen voted fifty-two to forty-four for expulsion, twelve votes short of the necessary two-thirds margin. For the remainder of the session Lyon was one of the most vigorous Republican spokesmen in Congress, opposing the military defense measures and the Alien and Sedition Acts. He told a friend he expected to be one of the Sedition Act's first targets.

When Congress adjourned in July, Lyon went home to plan his reelection campaign. Federalists throughout the nation were seeking his defeat. Lyon lashed out at them in a letter to his constituents, claiming that under their rule public welfare was "swallowed up in a continual grasp for power, in an unbounded thirst for ridiculous pomp, foolish adulation, and selfish avarice." When a leading Federalist paper in Vermont refused to print his ideas, he began a new journal called *The Scourge of Aristocracy and Repository of Important Political Truths.*

The first issue appeared on October 1, 1798. Four days later Matthew Lyon was indicted for treason by a grand jury convened at Rutland, Vermont. He was charged with bringing the government into disrepute in his letter to the voters. On October 8 Lyon was tried before fourteen local jurors with Justice William Paterson of the U.S. Supreme Court presiding. Because no lawyers were available, he elected to plead his own case before a jury that included many of his political enemies. In his defense he claimed that the Sedition Act was unconstitutional, and, in any event, his statements were neither malicious nor seditious—they were simply legitimate statements of political opinion. The jury brought in a verdict of guilty after deliberating for only one hour. The next day, October 9, Justice Paterson sentenced Lyon to four months in jail and a $1,000 fine, declaring that he was making an example of Lyon because, he told the prisoner, "as a member of the federal legislature, you must be well acquainted with the mischiefs which flow from an unlicensed abuse of government."

Local officials took Lyon from the courtroom to the neighboring town of Vergennes, not even giving him time to visit his apartment in Rutland to gather his papers, and locked him in a common jail cell. The bright colors and crisp air of a Vermont autumn gave way to the sharp, white cold of winter while Lyon languished in prison. A single window barely lighted the dark cell; the privy consisted of a stinking receptacle in the corner of the chamber; and the cold room had no fire.

Fortunately for Lyon, his constitution was strong and he was invigorated by a sense of outrage. He wrote to fellow Republicans describing his situation, the squalor of the prison, the injustice of the law. "It is quite a new kind of jargon," he said, "to call a Representative of the people an opposer of government because he does not, as a legislator, advocate and acquiesce in every proposition that comes from the executive." In a short time Lyon was regarded as a martyr. He ran a successful reelection campaign from prison and was returned to Congress by a great majority. On February 9 he was released from jail. As he left the building and stood once more among the open hills of Vermont, he found himself surrounded by a welcoming crowd. Embraced by their support, he walked twelve miles to Middlebury. At the head of the parade his supporters carried American flags that waved triumphantly in the air of Matthew Lyon's adopted homeland.

The Lyon case was especially important because of the victim's political status and the severity of his punishment. But other cases contained the same ingredients: harsh penalties and public sympathy. The accused included editor Benjamin Franklin Bache; Thomas Adams, of the *Boston Independent Chronicle*; Thomas Cooper, a lawyer and later president of the University of South Carolina; and David Brown, an itinerant Republican publicist, who offended the Federalists by constructing a liberty pole in Dedham, Massachusetts. The law's critics claimed that these men had merely exercised their American right of free speech. Republican spokesmen took particular delight in chiding the Federalists for the Luther Baldwin case. Was the government so defensive, they asked, that it could not withstand a harmless joke?

In some areas opposition to the Alien and Sedition Acts was so strong that Thomas Jefferson and James Madison were able to persuade two states to adopt bills condemning the acts. The Virginia and Kentucky Resolves of 1798–1799 declared that the laws were unconstitutional and advanced the novel claim that individual states could invalidate improper federal legislation. These resolutions furnished precedents later for the doctrine of nullification, a theory that states did not have to honor legislation they considered invalid.

Support for Adams remained strong, however, and other states condemned the Virginia and Kentucky Resolves. But on the whole the Alien and Sedition Acts did more to harm than to help the Adams administration. During 1798 most Americans had feared threats to their liberty from France and from a "French Party" in America. By 1799 the war had not materialized, and Americans began to question the legitimacy of bills that protected them by eliminating dissent. Perhaps the Republicans had been right in holding that the administration wanted to establish a monarchic and tyrannical regime.

Such charges hurt Adams, but ironically he was damaged more by his effort to reduce tensions than by his desire to eliminate sedition. Late in 1798 he learned that Talleyrand, wanting to avoid war, hoped to resume negotiations. The High Federalists sought to prevent Adams from sending a negotiator, but Adams threatened to resign and turn his office over to Republican Thomas Jefferson if they blocked his effort to negotiate. Adams sent a peace mission across the Atlantic in 1799, and a few months later America and France signed the Convention of 1800, calling off the undeclared naval war.

If Adams had cared only for his own political future, he might have fought France and ridden a wave of popular support to a second term. Instead, he allowed the patriotism of 1798 to end in a frustrating anticlimax, making the repressive acts passed in the name of national defense seem unjustified. The Republicans castigated Adams as a tyrant, while war enthusiasts in his own party regarded him as too mild.

In this situation Thomas Jefferson was elected president in 1800 by a narrow margin. He pardoned the remaining prisoners jailed under the Sedition Act and allowed the offending bills to expire in 1801 and 1802. The reaction against the Alien and Sedition Acts facilitated a more liberal interpretation of free speech. Criticism might be galling to an administration, but Thomas Jefferson, James Madison, Matthew Lyon, and others had argued forcefully that a free government could not exist without diversity of opinion. This liberal view of the right to dissent has endured for two centuries despite periodic challenges.

Political invective was especially virulent in the late 1790s because both sides felt there should be just one party and one truth. Thomas Jefferson was probably the last vice president to accuse his chief executive of "insanity" after hearing a presidential address. Had the Republicans been in control, they might have sponsored their own Alien and Sedition Acts—certainly Jefferson's record with respect to civil liberties was not unblemished. The acts, however, reinforced freedom of speech by creating a backlash of support for the administration's critics. Once it was admitted that the state could contain several legitimate but competing philosophies, an opposition party could criticize the government without accusing it of tyranny, and the administration could resist opposition without characterizing it as sedition. In such a time the merry wit of a Luther Baldwin can find expression without ever coming to the attention of a federal court.

Bibliography

Akers, Charles W. *Abigail Adams* (1980). Lively account of John Adams's foremost supporter.

Deconde, Alexander. *Quasi-War: Undeclared War with France, 1797–1801* (1966). History of the naval war with France.

Elkins, Stanley M., and Eric L. McKitrick. *The Age of Federalism* (1993). An insightful analysis of the ideologies and personalities of the era.

Gelles, Edith B. *Portia: The World of Abigail Adams* (1992). Beautifully written, prize-winning account of Abigail Adams.

Hofstadter, Richard. *Idea of a Party System* (1969). Classic description of early American opposition to parties.

McCullough, David. *John Adams* (2002). Pulitzer Prize–winning biography.

Smith, James M. *Freedom's Fetters* (1956). An extensive account of the Alien and Sedition Acts written during the McCarthy era, when free speech was again threatened by the government.

Stone, Geoffrey R. *Perilous Times: Free Speech in Wartime from the Sedition Act of 1798 to the War on Terrorism* (2004). Stone contends that America upholds the First Amendment about 80 percent of the time but often ignores it in times of war and civil disorder.

Thompson, C. Bradley. *John Adams and the Spirit of Liberty* (1998). Argues that Adams was one of the most influential political thinkers of the Revolutionary generation.

Withey, Lynne. *Dearest Friend: A Life of Abigail Adams* (1981). The personal and public life of Abigail Adams.

Identification Topics

John Adams, Luther Baldwin, First Amendment, Alexander Hamilton, Thomas Jefferson, Jay's Treaty, XYZ Affair, Federalists, Republicans, "Hail Columbia," Talleyrand, Abigail Adams, the "Quasi War," Alien and Sedition Acts, Matthew Lyon, Virginia and Kentucky Resolves, American "Reign of Terror"

Study Questions

1. What were the principal issues leading to party formation in the 1790s? How did the "expectation of unity" worsen party divisions?
2. The political rhetoric of both parties was especially heated in the 1790s. Give examples of extreme statements by Federalists and Republicans.
3. Why were some Americans hostile to France in 1798? Why did other Americans support France?
4. How did Federalists justify the Alien and Sedition Acts, and on what basis did Republicans oppose them?
5. What is the significance of the Federalist toast: "One and but one party in the United States"?
6. Why does freedom of speech tend to be curtailed in wartime? Were the Alien and Sedition Acts needed to strengthen America in the face of war, or were they brought on by hysteria and paranoia?
7. The doctrine of nullification, first suggested in the Virginia and Kentucky Resolves, has never been an accepted constitutional principle in the United States. Why not?
8. Why was Matthew Lyon singled out as the only congressman imprisoned under the Alien and Sedition Acts?
9. How did the persecution of Matthew Lyon, Luther Baldwin, and other Republicans ultimately strengthen the American tradition of free speech?

CHAPTER 8

Republican Nationalism
The Lewis and Clark Expedition

The possibilities for American growth seemed limitless early in the nineteenth century. The nation's experiment in representative government captured the imagination of other peoples, and Americans watched with approval as Spanish Americans, emulating the "Spirit of '76," fought for independence from European control. They congratulated themselves for whipping the British army in 1815 at the Battle of New Orleans and declared their preeminence in the Western Hemisphere with the Monroe Doctrine in 1823. Americans, it seemed, could do anything. The Lewis and Clark Expedition of 1803–1806 provided the country with its first western heroes and revealed a land so bounteous and alluring that nature itself appeared to have smiled upon the American republic.

In 1803, the year of the Louisiana Purchase, the United States was a strong, confident nation with a population of six million. Americans were building canals, bridges, factories, and highways and experimenting with steamboats and gaslamps. Along the Atlantic seaboard the wilderness had long since vanished, and the land was familiar, lived upon, and subdued.

But there was another America, totally unknown to the people of the East. When Thomas Jefferson was elected president in 1800, tens of thousands of Native Americans living within the boundaries of the future United States had never seen a white person. In reality, America was not one country but many. Its nations included Mandans, Sioux, Shoshones, and Nez Percés, as well as the polyglot population of Europeans and Africans that knew itself as the United States. Few easterners had traveled among the western Indians or seen the Rockies. The United States was bordered by a mystery.

The existence of this unknown land fascinated and challenged President Thomas Jefferson. Although he was best known as a statesman, Jefferson was a deeply contemplative man and an accomplished astronomer, archaeologist, geologist, and naturalist. As a young man, he wrote *Notes on Virginia*, a natural history of his native region. While in Paris in 1786 he encouraged the American adventurer, John Ledyard, to walk across Siberia and western America to the headwaters of the Missouri. Ledyard, accompanied by two dogs, actually covered three thousand miles across Russia before authorities, suspecting that he was a spy, shipped him back to Poland. In 1792, as secretary of state, Jefferson supported another abortive expedition to the West.

As president, Jefferson was determined to try again. He delivered a message to Congress on January 18, 1803, advocating a secret expedition to explore the West. Anticipating that his proposal would be accepted if he offered economic reasons, he suggested that contact would lead to "commercial intercourse." The fur trade of the upper Mississippi Basin was already being siphoned off into Canada, and for a cost of only $2,500 the United States could open up the region to Americans. Impressed by his argument, Congress approved the proposal, and Jefferson began to make plans.

In the meantime, history had radically altered the character of the proposed expedition. The land Jefferson intended to explore was owned by France, and in 1802 Napoleon contemplated posting a large military force in the area. But his army in America was decimated in Hispaniola while fighting a black insurrection led by Toussaint L'Ouverture. Needing funds, and having lost interest in America, Napoleon offered to sell all of Louisiana, then reckoned at about nine hundred thousand square miles, for $15 million. Jefferson's opponents doubted the constitutionality of the transaction and characterized the purchase of these remote, unknown lands as the "wildest chimera of a moonstruck brain." But the measure won congressional approval, and suddenly the expedition to a foreign land became the exploration of American territory.

The spring and summer of 1803 were given over to preparations. Jefferson chose as leader a man named Meriwether Lewis, whom he described as "brave, prudent, habituated to the woods, and familiar with Indian manners and character." Lewis was born on a plantation in 1774 in Albemarle County, Virginia, in a wood-frame house near Jefferson's Monticello. His father died while he was a boy, and he went with his mother to live on the Georgia frontier, returning in his teens to manage the Virginia estate. Lewis soon became one of Jefferson's closest friends, often visiting him to talk about natural science and exploration. Both were interested in the West.

Lewis joined the army in 1794 during the Whiskey Rebellion; he was a captain in 1801, when Jefferson was inaugurated president. Jefferson chose his old friend as his personal secretary, and the two men worked together in developing the proposal for a western expedition. Jefferson was determined that the expedition would not only blaze a trail to the West but would also gather scientific information about the country through which it passed. At that time there were few professional scientists in the United States, and a bright, interested person could become something of an expert in botany, zoology, or anthropology with little training. Undoubtedly, Jefferson, as an amateur scientist, would have liked to accompany the expedition himself. That being impossible, he planned to provide Lewis with a "cram course" in natural history.

At the president's request, Lewis spent April and May 1803 in Philadelphia studying under the direction of several of the nation's leading scientists at the American Philosophical Society and the University of Pennsylvania. His instructors included Dr. Benjamin Rush, the preeminent American physician of the time. At

Jefferson's suggestion, Rush prepared a list of questions for Lewis to ask the Native Americans. He should study their physical history and learn about Indian diseases, longevity, marriage, menstruation, breast-feeding, weaning, heartbeat, diet, medicine, and morals. What were their vices? Were suicide and murder common? Did they "employ any substitute for ardent spirits to promote intoxication"? Finally, Lewis should learn about their religion—sacrifices, burial ceremonies, and affinity (if any) to the Jews. The last question grew out of the belief that the ten Lost Tribes of Israel might have mingled with the natives.

Lewis would not be able to explore all these topics. But the list indicates Jefferson's and Rush's desire to learn as much as possible about the unknown land and its peoples. Underlying the whole expedition was profound curiosity about the American continent. Jefferson anticipated that American farmers would one day settle the West. The expedition would prepare the way for expansion, but it would also compile a record of what the country was like in its own right.

Jefferson and Lewis agreed that it was essential to recruit good men to accompany the expedition because the explorers would depend on one another for survival. They must screen out unstable adventurers who would resist authority or quit at the first obstacle. "Their qualifications," Lewis wrote the president, "should be such as perfectly fit them for the service, otherwise they will rather clog than further the objects of the cause." He wanted good boatmen, hunters, and craftsmen, men who were strong and steady but willing to accept discipline.

Lewis's most important staffing decision was the choice of an old friend, William Clark, to share the leadership of the expedition. Clark was a tall, redheaded Kentuckian who had served with Lewis in the frontier Indian wars of the 1790s. Born on August 1, 1770, in Caroline County, Virginia, he was a younger brother of Revolutionary War hero Gen. George Rogers Clark, who led the American troops fighting in the old Northwest. In 1784 the whole family moved to the lands George Rogers Clark had known as a soldier. With livestock, slaves, and furniture they boarded a flatboat and floated down the Ohio to Louisville, Kentucky, where they settled into a large log plantation house. In the late 1780s and early 1790s William Clark fought under Gen. Anthony Wayne in a rash of local Indian wars.

Lewis believed his old friend was the perfect choice for a shared command. In addition to being daring and resourceful, he was, like Lewis, an amateur naturalist and could draw birds, fish, and animals during the expedition. Lewis's letter of invitation summarized his view of the expedition. The explorers would develop "an early, friendly, and intimate acquaintance" with the western tribes to foster trade and impress them "with the rising importance of the United States." They would study native culture, wildlife, soil, and plants of the new country. "Believe me," he told Clark, "there is no man on earth with whom I should feel equal pleasure in sharing them as with yourself." Clark's response was immediate and enthusiastic. "My friend," he wrote, "I join you with hand and heart." The close and effective cooperation of the two men would be one of the great assets of the expedition.

Lewis spent the early part of the summer choosing equipment. He showed his ability to anticipate problems by his choice of guns. He was impressed with the accuracy of the Kentucky rifle, but he felt it was too frail to hold up on the long journey. So he redesigned the gun, creating the Harpers Ferry rifle, which was used on the expedition and became a standard army weapon, the first to be turned out in mass production.

Careful planning was also apparent in his provision for ammunition. Because powder could not be replaced in the middle of the wilderness, Lewis stored it in waterproof lead kegs. After each keg was emptied, it could be melted down for bullets. Lewis rounded out his weapons with a new-fangled device, an air rifle.

Scientific tools included a microscope, a quadrant, compasses, and thermometers, as well as a two-volume work explaining Linnaeus's system of animal classification. The anticipated negotiations with Native Americans would be facilitated by gifts including calico shirts, glass beads, handkerchiefs, magnifying glasses, scissors, needles, thread, knives, tobacco, fishhooks, combs, and peace medals bearing the image of Thomas Jefferson.

The men in what would be called the Corps of Discovery were provided with hunting shirts, greatcoats, and blankets and given copper kettles and an iron mill for preparing food. Dr. Rush supervised the accumulation of medical supplies including epsom salts, opium, and his own invention, Rush's constipation pills. The equipment included many items that were surprisingly modern. The explorers carried a forty-foot-long collapsible canoe with an iron frame and phosphorous matches, which proved a convenience to the explorers and a marvel to the Indians. They brought 193 pounds of powdered soup, which the men soon came to hate, but on at least one occasion it sustained them when other food supplies ran out. Finally, there was a simple but useful device that was so innovative Lewis did not even have a name for it. He entered it in his list with the following description:

> Instrument for measuring made of tape with feet & inches mark'd on it, contained within a circular lethern box of sufficient thickness to admit the width of the tape which has one of its ends confined to an axis of metal passing through the center of the box, around which and within the box it is readily wound by means of a small crank on the outer side of the box which forms a part of the axis, the tape when necessary is drawn out with the same facility & ease with which it is wound up.

This instrument would soon be known more simply as a tape measure.

The most important item prepared for the expedition was a sturdy barge built in Pittsburgh, nearly sixty feet long with a raised deckhouse at the rear. Depending on the weather and river conditions, it would be propelled by oars, poles, or sail. On July 5, 1803, Lewis left Washington and went to Pittsburgh, where the boat was being constructed, to assemble supplies and begin the voyage down the Ohio to the Mississippi. Finding that the barge was not ready owing to the builder's frequent drunkenness and quarrels with his men, Lewis decided to stay on the spot and supervise, "alternately persuading and threatening," to keep the work going.

The boat was finally ready on the last day of August at 7:00 A.M. Within three hours Lewis had the craft loaded and was floating downstream on the Ohio, planning to meet Clark in Louisville and take the expedition up the Missouri River for a winter encampment. The large, shallow-draft barge drew only three feet, but at places the river was a mere six inches deep, and it menaced travelers with treacherous gravel bars and snags laid bare by the season's low water. Anticipating these obstacles, Lewis had written Jefferson a month before, saying, "I am determined to proceed though I should not be able to make greater speed than a boat's length per day."

At times he barely made that. The voyage proved a good testing ground for his men. If they had given out on this trip through settled country, they could hardly have persevered through the long months ahead. The boat ran into its first obstacles shortly after leaving Pittsburgh, and in the following days the men spent as much time walking along the river bottom as floating downstream. They often had to lighten the barge by disembarking, and sometimes they had to dig through gravel shoals. The worst obstructions were snags of timber and brush that blocked the river from bank to bank, requiring the men to unload the cargo and haul the all-too-solid barge. When they could no longer budge their craft, they scoured the riverbank to find help. Lewis reported to Jefferson that in such cases "horses or oxen are the last resort: I find them the most efficient sailors in the present state of navigation of this river, although they may be considered somewhat clumsy."

Through it all the men maintained good spirits and quickly learned to like the simple pleasures of the voyage. At Wheeling they had a watermelon feast aboard the barge. Farther downstream they enjoyed passing beneath leafy sycamore trees and watching hordes of squirrels swimming to the southern shore. Lewis's big Newfoundland dog, Shannon, who accompanied the expedition to the Pacific, plunged into the water after the swimmers, caught many, and brought them back to the barge. In the evening the men feasted on fried squirrel.

In Louisville, Clark joined the expedition with some additional men. In these early stages, though the expedition passed through lands that were extensively settled by Americans, Lewis was already beginning his scientific observations. Near Cincinnati he visited Big Bone Lick and sent Jefferson a report on a collection of mammoth bones. When the boats reached the Mississippi, Lewis visited the Shawnee and Delaware who lived along the shore and made notes on plants and animals, including a 138-pound catfish the voyagers caught for dinner.

The expedition then began to move north toward Saint Louis, and the men entered a new world. The French had explored and settled it more than a century before, but it was still a frontier, controlled largely by Native Americans. Many of the old settlers were of French-Canadian and Indian descent and had themselves taken Indian wives. Lewis and Clark encountered one of these rough, lively men, Louis Lorimer, at Cape Girardeau. The commander of the fort, he had come west after the American Revolution. His long hair, worn in a queue, had once extended to the floor, but finding it inconvenient at that length, he now wore it at knee length held discreetly to his back by a belt. Lorimer presided over a rough frontier community of a thousand residents, many of whom had migrated from Kentucky and Tennessee. He and his Shawnee wife provided dinner for the explorers and discussed the country.

The expedition reached Saint Louis on December 5. At this time the city was not yet in American hands, and it would be several months before the Louisiana Purchase and American sovereignty would take effect. To avoid offending the existing regime, the party set up a winter camp on the eastern, or American, side of the Mississippi at Wood River, opposite the confluence of the Missouri. Here they constructed cabins, collected stores, and recruited the last of their party. By the following spring the expedition would consist of twenty-nine permanent members, plus sixteen soldiers and rivermen to assist the expedition in its first season of travel up the Missouri.

Lewis and Clark assembled a remarkable group of men, most of whom would work well together for the next two years. The most important next to the two leaders was George Drouillard; the son of a Shawnee mother and a French-Canadian father, he was an experienced hunter, scout, and interpreter. Another man of French and Indian descent, Pierre Cruzette, was the foremost boatman on the expedition and entertained the Corps of Discovery and fascinated the Native Americans with his skill as a fiddler. Patrick Gass was the chief carpenter; in lands where wood houses and boats had to be fashioned from the forests, he provided the means of shelter and transportation. Although Gass had had only nineteen days of formal schooling, he wrote a lively journal of the expedition. Other men rounded out the corps' reservoir of skills: William Warner was a fine cook; William Bratton served as gunsmith; Silas Goodrich was an expert fisherman. One of the most remarkable men on the expedition was William Clark's slave, Black York. Tremendously strong and a good dancer, he impressed the Indians, who had never seen a black man. There was a fine spirit of anticipation among the men; as one of the soldiers, John Ordway, wrote to his parents, "I am so happy as to be one of them picked men."

While Clark supervised the preparations at Wood River, Lewis spent time in Saint Louis gathering information about the Missouri country they would be visiting. Approximately eight thousand French-Canadian and American settlers as well as some two thousand black slaves lived in upper Louisiana. Because Napoleon had never sent a French governor, the nominal chief of the region was still Spain's agent, Governor Don Carlos Dunhault Delassus. Lewis quickly befriended him and other civic leaders and traders. There were no major settlements north of Saint Louis, but traders had frequently penetrated a thousand miles up the Missouri. With their help Lewis was able to construct a rough picture of Indian tribes and terrain to the north. Early in 1804 he sent Thomas Jefferson the first of his samples of western flora and fauna, including a horned toad and a slip of Osage plum.

Despite Lewis's friendly manner and his promise that America had no designs on Spanish territory, the expedition inevitably excited suspicion among white settlers who had already grown accustomed to regarding the West as their own. Many traders on the Missouri were Englishmen associated with the North West Company and had no interest in seeing the United States establish a rival trade. One English trader had already sown seeds of mistrust by intercepting and mistranslating a message from Lewis to the Sauk and Fox tribes. The Spanish, too, were apprehensive about American penetration into the West. Governor Don Carlos was friendly enough, but his superiors opposed the expedition. The boundaries between the new American territory and Spanish-held New Mexico were but vaguely understood, and in Santa Fe there was some worry lest the American party should find the headwaters of the Missouri in the mountains just north of their city. In actuality, Lewis and Clark were never within a thousand miles of Santa Fe, but a Spanish expedition left New Mexico in 1804 hoping to intercept the explorers—a well-nigh impossible goal in a region of almost one million square miles. The abortive Spanish expedition was attacked by Indians and retreated to Santa Fe before the end of 1804.

Unaware of the Spanish plan, Lewis and Clark continued their preparations in spring 1804. Their supplies now included two thousand pounds of pork, two thousand pounds of flour, five barrels of whiskey, and sixteen "Musquito nets." After a year of preparation everyone wanted to start. From the capital, Jefferson reported with annoyance that his Federalist opponents were still belittling the expedition and would rejoice in its failure. "I hope you will take care of yourself," he wrote Lewis, "and be the living witness of their malice and folly."

On May 14 the expedition was finally ready, and that afternoon Clark ordered the boats to row across the Mississippi and begin the long journey up the Missouri. They reached Saint Charles, a small French-Canadian community a few miles upriver, and waited for Lewis while he completed the expedition's business in Saint Louis. He came to Saint Charles on horseback, accompanied by friends from the town who made a picnic outing of the occasion.

Then with his men he set forth on the Missouri. In ten days the expedition passed La Charette, the last white community on the Missouri, a place where the great eighteenth-century frontiersman Daniel Boone, now in his seventieth year, still lived. The men soon fell into a routine that would prevail through the next five months of travel to the Mandan country, sixteen hundred miles away. The keelboat *Discovery*, with Pierre Cruzette standing at the bow, led the small fleet up the river. A sergeant standing amidships gave instructions to the oarsmen, and Lewis and Clark took turns overseeing the fleet from the stern. Two small pirogues, or rowboats, one red and one white, followed the barge.

Clark soon proved himself the company's best navigator and geographer and was most often at the helm, compiling a record of the boat's location, the course of the river, and the appearance of tributaries. Cruzette, having traveled on the Missouri many times before, made moment-to-moment decisions in negotiating the more difficult sections of the river. When their course along the wide river lay through deep water and they were aided by a following wind, the fleet could cover twenty miles or more in a day. But the river often challenged their resources.

Shallows forced the men to disembark and pull the barge with towropes; fierce winds swept down the river causing the boats' crews to seek shelter behind islands; low branches could, and once did, break the *Discovery*'s mast. The boats were frequently more troubled by the land than the water. The Missouri was a powerful river, often a half mile from shore to shore. Known as the "Big Muddy" because of the dirt swept along in its current, it continually ate into the shores. Once the men had to flee when a riverbank suddenly collapsed into the water; on another occasion they had to evacuate an island as it washed away from under them during the night. They often came upon traveling sandbars that swirled under the boats, threatening to overturn them.

Hidden logjams were common, too, and thick fogs sometimes obscured the route. The men suffered from the ravages of mosquitoes, boils, and intestinal disorders; one was bitten by a poisonous snake and others collapsed from sunstroke. Despite such hardships, however, the men were excited by their journey. They had joined Lewis and Clark because they liked the idea of exploring a new territory. Journals kept by nine of the men reflect the excitement of voyagers seeing a new land. In the early weeks they passed through flat country covered with cottonwood, oak, hickory, sycamore, walnut, mulberry, and linden trees. As they traveled farther north they entered the Great Plains, one of the largest grasslands in the world, and beheld tall bluestem grasses that undulated like the waves of the sea over rows of gently sloping hills. The grasses were dotted with wild apples, grapes, and plums, exuding a rich, sweet smell. The explorers awoke to fine warm mornings when a light mist hung on the river and great flocks of geese wheeled past overhead; and they enjoyed evenings when the sun, setting over the vast prairie, illuminated the clear sky and wisps of cloud "in the most beautiful manner."

Meriwether Lewis and William Clark recorded their observations of this country. They listed the names of landmarks already seen by French trappers—Turkey Creek, Bear Medicine Island, Cow Island, Reevey's Prairie—and they bestowed new names, which reflected their own perceptions or experience. A creek flowing into the Missouri past a bluff that looked like a cupboard became Cupboard Creek. A rivulet near which they believed a nightingale had sung during the night became Nightingale Creek.

Lewis was particularly active in locating and identifying new plants and animals. He often left the fleet and walked along the riverbank. A somewhat solitary man by nature, Lewis loved being alone on the prairie. He became a great walker, outdistancing the scouts and hunters, getting so far ahead of the fleet that he sometimes spent the night alone deep in the wilderness.

What did Lewis think about during these solitary travels? He was a pensive man, so introspective and melancholy at times that when he died of a gunshot wound a few years later some of his friends, including Jefferson, assumed he had taken his own life. Separated on his walks from the immediate cares of the expedition—moving boats, mending oars, and cooking meals—the captain may have reflected on the strange course of history. The land around him was so pristine it seemed it could never change. Here was a vast wilderness, barely touched by man. Its hills stretched endlessly westward; its pure odors alerted the senses; its grasses swayed with a soft rustle in the wind. It had been neither improved nor degraded by white settlers. No surly squatters lived along its banks, ready to overcharge his men for helping them over snags. No toll roads or bridges or cities scarred the landscape. If Lewis thought about history, he must have known that he and his men would change the land simply by visiting and describing it.

But if such thoughts crossed his mind, the country's vastness reassured him. It was a large land and his was a small fleet. After a day of walking alone, he could come down from a hill in the evening and hear the sound of axes, the rattle of kettles, and the voices of men, a tiny encampment in the wilderness.

At mealtime the men were well served by the land. The expedition's diet was planned around a three-day sequence beginning with hominy and grease, followed by pork and flour, then by pork and cornmeal. Fortunately, this dreary fare was soon varied by the products of forest and plain. The men frequently ate deer, bear, beaver, and, later, buffalo, as well as gooseberries, raspberries, and wild plums and apples. On August 1, Clark's birthday, he could celebrate over venison and beavertail, followed by cherries, plums, raspberries, and grapes.

As the expedition made its way northwest through the present states of Missouri, Kansas, Nebraska, and Iowa, the work of describing the plants and animals became more exacting. Lewis and Clark were the first American explorers to report the mule deer, the white-tailed jackrabbit, the prairie grouse, and the pronghorn—a distant cousin of the antelope. Whenever possible, they obtained a living specimen or the skin of a new animal. In one pursuit they diverted themselves for a whole day by pouring water into a prairie dog hole in an attempt to capture one of these hitherto unknown creatures.

The explorers were equally interested in making contact with the human inhabitants of the region. All the local Native Americans were nomadic, living in buffalo-hide tents and traveling across the country. Shortly after the departure from Wood River, Lewis and Clark began to encounter Indian and French-Canadian trading parties bound for Saint Louis with cargoes of fur. They persuaded one of these traders, a French-Canadian named Pierre Dorien, who had lived among the Sioux for twenty years, to accompany them upriver as a translator. Despite this promising start, they pushed on for day after day without meeting Indians. They placed guards around their camps or stayed on islands to avoid surprise by hostile natives, but no Indians, hostile or otherwise, appeared. Finally Drouillard, the hunter and scout, came across a party of Oto and Missouri Indians and persuaded a delegation from each tribe to come and talk with Lewis and Clark. The place they chose was near a prairie that stood high over the Missouri. They called it Council Bluffs.

On August 2 the Indians arrived, announcing their coming by firing their rifles, indicating by their possession of such weapons that even in this remote land the fur trade was already well established. The Indians and whites spent the first evening entertaining each other with a feast, the Americans supplying pork and cornmeal and the natives contributing watermelon. The next morning they met on a beach beside the river beneath an awning fashioned from the barge's sail. Lewis delivered a speech announcing that white men in the region were now under the authority of the "Great Chief of the Seventeen Nations." Without claiming that the seventeen United States owned the Indian lands, he laid down terms for the Native Americans. They should regard his country as their friend, make peace with one another, and not obstruct American travel on the Missouri. If they behaved properly, they could anticipate a profitable trade with the United States. Lewis and Clark gave the Indians medals, powder, and whiskey and treated them to a demonstration of the air rifle. The groups parted in good humor.

The explorers met delegations from many other tribes during the following weeks. Usually these meetings progressed as smoothly as had the first. Indians occasionally opposed their progress, but Clark was adept at choosing the proper words and addressing them to the right chief to overcome suspicions, and the expedition continued without delivering or receiving hostile blows. In addition to serving a political function, these conferences enabled the explorers to investigate Indian customs and beliefs. They compiled data on language, religion, society, and population. Later Jefferson would take the observations and publish them under the austere title, *A Statistical View of the Indian Nations Inhabiting the Territory of Louisiana and the Countries Adjacent to Its Northern and Western Boundaries.*

In September and October the expedition still pressed northward through the Dakotas. Leaves were turning to yellows and reds; nights were cold; flocks of migrating geese flew overhead. The men wore extra flannel shirts and huddled closer to the campfires at night. On October 17, Clark wrote, "The leaves are falling fast."

It was time to build a winter encampment. In late October the Corps of Discovery reached Mandan country, in today's North Dakota, where natives stood on the roofs of their conical earthen houses and waved at the explorers as they rowed by. The region was richly forested, promising good shelter for the winter, and the Mandans and their neighbors, the Hidatsas, were friendly. The travelers went to work felling cottonwood trees and building a fort. In a few weeks they fashioned a sturdy stockade of high spiked timbers and eight log huts daubed with mud. Each hut had a large fireplace and tables, shelves, beds, and benches crafted by the skillful carpenters.

Route of Lewis and Clark westward to the pacific.

They called the place Fort Mandan and spent the winter here, Lewis and Clark sharing one hut, and the rest of the men sleeping in the other seven. Temperatures soon fell far below freezing. On nights when the thermometer dropped to 30 and 40 degrees below zero, the sentries could stand guard only in half-hour shifts. The sharp winter was eerie and fascinating, and one night the sergeant on guard awakened all the men to show them a new sight, "the beautiful phenomenon called the northern lights." They watched, amazed, as the colors played along the horizon in "floating columns sometimes advancing, sometimes retreating and shaping into infinite forms."

The men had never seen or felt a winter like this, but they lived well. They wore thick clothes, and fires blazed day and night in their sturdy cabins. When the temperatures were comparatively mild they could easily shoot enough game to feed themselves. Music and dance broke the monotony of the winter encampment. On Christmas Day they fired their cannon and muskets and then drank a heady concoction of rum and brandy. Pierre Cruzette produced the fiddle that he had carried so carefully up the Missouri and played while the men clapped and danced.

Throughout the winter Lewis and Clark continued to gather information on local Indians and on the route ahead. The four thousand Mandans and Hidatsas were quite willing to help. The only chieftain who could not be won by gift of peace medal or display of air gun, a man known to the French traders as Le Borgne (One Eye), finally came to admire the strangers when he met Black York. Clark's slave was always an attraction among the Native Americans, who had seen whites but no blacks. York enjoyed the attention, sometimes pretending to be a tamed beast, sometimes displaying his enormous strength. But it was the color of his skin that most impressed Le Borgne. Suspecting that it was dyed, he tried to remove the black color and was fascinated when it proved to be real. The Indians were further amazed by the skills of John Shields, the company's best blacksmith. They owned metal tools and weapons that needed repair, and Shields spent many hours fixing Indian implements. Lewis and Clark asked the Indians about the lands up the Missouri, and with Indian help they pieced together a reasonably accurate map of the country between Fort Mandan and the Rockies.

In establishing relations with the Indians, Lewis and Clark met with hostility from local French-Canadian and Scottish traders, who regarded the American presence as a threat to their accustomed control of the Mandan fur trade. One of these men represented the British North West Company, an organization whose best-known explorer, Alexander MacKenzie, had anticipated Lewis and Clark by a decade in making the first overland journey to the Pacific in 1793 on a route through present-day Canada. This English trader was alone, however, and could not dissuade the Mandans from befriending the Americans.

At Fort Mandan the Americans found a fine ally in the person of the young Indian woman, Sacajawea. She was a member of the Shoshone tribe, whose lands lay in the Rockies along the expedition route. Captured as a child by an enemy tribe, she had been brought to the Mandan country where a French-Canadian trapper, Touissant-Charbonneau, had purchased her. Lewis and Clark hired Charbonneau as a guide and translator and got Sacajawea in the bargain. At first this did not seem a promising arrangement. On February 11 she gave birth to a son, Baptiste; the expedition would be doubly encumbered by an infant and a woman—or so it seemed—but within a few months Sacajawea would prove to be one of the most useful members of the party.

When spring arrived at Fort Mandan and the Missouri River was clear of ice, the Corps of Discovery made ready to set forth on another season of exploration. Because the barge would be useless in the mountains, Lewis and Clark sent it downriver with a few men and a wide assortment of reports and artifacts, including animal hides; Indian tools and weapons; plants; and two living creatures, a squirrel and a magpie. These items arrived in Washington a few months later. The capital had no Smithsonian Museum in those days, so the animals and hides were unpacked in the White House. The magpie and the squirrel took residence in the president's reception hall, and the skins were aired in the cabinet room. Unable to visit the West in person, Jefferson surrounded himself with its exotic fruits.

On April 7 William Clark went upstream with the two pirogues and six new canoes. Meriwether Lewis watched from the shore as the men parted company. On the excuse that he needed exercise, he walked upriver to join the expedition at nightfall. He probably wanted to withdraw from the corps for a moment and contemplate their achievements and goals. He committed some of his thoughts to his journal: "This little fleet, although not quite so respectable as those of Columbus or Captain Cook, were still viewed by us with as much pleasure as those deservedly famed adventurers ever beheld theirs; and I dare say with quite as much anxiety for their safety and preservation." He calculated that two thousand miles of wilderness lay ahead. Unlike the country they had traversed in the previous year, the western land had not been explored. Lewis was uncertain about what dangers lay ahead, but he was proud of the spirit of his party. The men were "zealously attached to the enterprise" and joined together "with the most perfect harmony." All in all, he was pleased with the thought of the journey, which would surely take them to the Pacific. "The picture which now presented itself to me was a most pleasing one," he wrote, "entertaining as I do, the most confident hope of succeeding in a voyage which had formed a darling project of mine for the last ten years, I could but esteem this moment of my departure as among the most happy of my life." Buoyed up with such thoughts, Lewis walked among the trees along the banks of the Missouri and rejoined the fleet at nightfall.

For the next few weeks the expedition passed through rich country where buffalo, deer, bear, and beaver were abundant. On April 26 they passed the Yellowstone River, which flowed into the Missouri through banks shaded by cottonwood, elm, and willow trees. Early in May they came upon their first grizzly bears. They had heard of these giant beasts from Indians and trappers but concluded that descriptions of their awesome size were exaggerated. The first bear tracks they saw were huge and caused some worry, but they managed to kill two grizzlies with relative ease. Apparently, Harpers Ferry rifles could easily accomplish what bow and arrow could not. On May 11, however, William Bratton shot a grizzly that refused to die; it pursued him for a half mile and required two balls through the head before it succumbed. The men were impressed to discover that Bratton's initial shot had lodged in the bear's lungs.

A few days later six explorers came upon another grizzly. Four shot and hit him, but the bear charged at them. The other two men fired, only further enraging the bear. The men fled behind bushes and trees and into the river, desperately trying to escape and reload. A marksman shot the bear through the head, and it finally collapsed. Eight balls had struck the grizzly before it fell. Lewis summed up the party's new-found respect for this giant of the West: "These bear being so hard to die rather intimidates us all," he wrote. "I must confess that I do not like the gentlemen and had rather fight two Indians than one bear."

The upper Missouri provided other challenges as well. The river was not running clear, but rocks had replaced silt as the prime obstacle. The water flowed swiftly over a stony bed that tore at canoes and feet. On May 14 the boat carrying most of the important scientific equipment and journals was swamped, and only Sacajawea's quick action saved several important records.

On May 26 Lewis caught his first glimpse of the Rocky Mountains. When he was planning the expedition, he and others had hoped that the only thing between the Missouri and the Columbia might be a short span—say, a half-day's march—of hilly plain. But Lewis had learned at Fort Mandan that a range of high mountains lay between the two rivers. He now saw clearly both the beauty and the danger of the Rockies. The "mountains were covered with snow, and the sun shone on it in such a manner as to give me the most plain and satisfactory view," he wrote; but "I reflected on the difficulties which this snowy barrier would most probably throw in my way to the Pacific, and the sufferings and hardships of myself and party in them."

With each day the country presented new difficulties. Unlike the voyage on the lower Missouri, this was not a trip along a well-traveled route. Even Sacajawea, who had grown up in the mountainous Shoshone country, had traveled the route only once before, and then as a twelve-year-old girl and a captive. She is sometimes mistakenly credited with having "guided" the expedition; but although she was a valuable member of the party, she knew little more about the route than Lewis or Clark.

A crucial test came on June 2 when the navigators had to choose between two forks in the river. To determine which was the true Missouri, Lewis and Clark spent a day studying the topography of the country and the speed and clarity of the water. They finally concluded correctly that the south branch was the main river.

A few days later the expedition reached Great Falls, in present-day Montana, a beautiful and formidable series of five waterfalls, up to ninety feet high. Lewis was again ahead of the corps and enjoyed contemplating the sight, which he described in one of the more rhapsodic entries in his journal: "The water descends in one even and uninterrupted sheet to the bottom where, dashing against the rocky bottom, it rises into foaming billows of great height and rapidly glides away, hissing, flashing, and sparkling as it departs."

The "foaming billows" might be pleasant to contemplate, but they were difficult to ascend. The explorers must make a hard portage across rough ground and ravines, hauling heavy gear in crude carts fashioned from a cottonwood tree and a boat's mast. Already exhausted from the long upriver journey, many fell asleep instantly every time the portage work came to a halt. A bruising hailstorm fell upon the party, cutting the men, and grizzly bears sought to intimidate these invaders of their territory. The party's morale, however, was equal to the difficulties. "No one complains," wrote Lewis, "all go with cheerfulness."

At the head of the falls, Lewis attempted to float his portable canoe, whose heavy iron frame had lain inert in other boats. He assembled the frame and covered it with hides but could not stop leaks where the hides were sewn together. He tried to caulk the seams and save the craft, which could carry eight thousand pounds of cargo. When he launched the canoe he watched hopefully as it floated tentatively on the current, but its hides soon opened up and the boat sank precipitously to the bottom. The age of the portable canoe had not yet arrived.

On July 25 they came to a confluence where the Missouri divided into three forks, which they named the Jefferson, the Madison, and the Gallatin. They followed the Jefferson because it had the most westerly course. As they traveled westward the explorers entered a rocky land where steep cliffs fell directly into the river. The leaders became increasingly apprehensive with each day's travel. Ahead lay great mountains with sheer stone faces and snow-clad peaks. If they could find Indians, they might hire horses and guides to help them through the barrier. The landscape was familiar to Sacajawea: here she had gathered berries as a child; there the warriors had collected pigment. But these places were now deserted.

On August 13 Lewis came upon three Indian women. Unable to speak their language, he rolled up his sleeves to show that he was a white man. As they were talking, the Shoshone chief, named Cameahwait, rode up with sixty warriors. When they understood that Lewis and his companions were not from a rival tribe, that they were indeed a new kind of man, and that they came in friendship with gifts, the warriors welcomed and embraced them. As Lewis describes the scene, "We were all caressed and besmeared with their grease and paint till I was heartily tired of the national hug."

Lewis and his advance party spent three days with the Indians. He had made a great beginning with the Shoshones, but he wanted them to meet his main party, still working its way upriver. The Indians grew suspicious. Was Lewis, after all, an enemy, and would he lead them into a trap? With difficulty the captain coaxed the Indians down to the river, giving them his rifles and dressing his own party in Shoshone garb to assure the Indians that no ambush lay ahead.

On August 16 the explorers must have felt that their mission was blessed. As the main party caught sight of the Shoshones, Sacajawea was speechless with joy; she ran and laughed and sucked her fingers in a gesture indicating a close relationship. By a remarkable chance, the Indians were members of her nation and of the very family from which she had been stolen. Moreover, Chief Cameahwait was her brother. The explorers could not have asked for better entree into the Indians' good graces.

The explorers made camp with the Shoshones and began to contemplate the next stage of their journey. They knew they were near a river that flowed to the Pacific but did not know whether they could travel safely on its waters. Clark set out to reconnoiter the westward-flowing Lemhi and Salmon Rivers and found the route impossibly difficult: the rivers bristled with rapids and their banks were too steep to allow portage or even encampment. They must find some other route, and the explorers decided to go by horseback across the Bitterroot Mountains. They purchased horses from the Shoshones, fashioned packsaddles out of hides, and began their first long overland trek.

They crossed the first range of mountains without difficulty and descended into the Bitterroot Valley, where they encountered a party of Flathead Indians and bargained for horses. Because none of Lewis and Clark's party spoke the Flathead language, business was conducted by means of three translators. Clark spoke English; one of the privates translated into French; Sacajawea translated into Shoshone; and a Shoshone boy who lived with the Flatheads translated into their language. In this circuitous manner the party obtained a few more horses and set out across the mountains again.

The second range was more difficult. The travelers followed a steep route where the land dropped away into deep valleys and ravines. Two horses slipped off the trail to their deaths. The weather grew colder, and one night four inches of snow fell on the camp. Short of food, the explorers had to eat tallow candles and their two colts. Worst of all, they did not know when they would clear the rugged mountains.

Clark went ahead with a scouting party, finally reaching a place where the plains were clearly visible. He descended and found a party of Nez Percés. Suddenly the ordeal was over. They sold him all the food a horse could carry, and Clark sent one of the men back to relieve Lewis and the main party. With this help they made their way out of the mountains. In a few days the men recovered their strength and were able to build new boats from a grove of ponderosa pines along the Clearwater River.

On October 7, leaving their horses in the care of the Nez Percés, the explorers began the trip down the Clearwater. For the first time on the long voyage they were traveling downstream. Because the season was late, they took chances on the rapids, preferring a hasty to a safe route. Canoes were frequently overturned, but never with much damage to men or equipment. As the party followed the Clearwater into the Snake, they left the Rockies and entered a dry, steep brushland where they traded with Indians for horsemeat and dogmeat and shot prairie cocks. At last they reached the Columbia and saw the Cascade Mountains ahead, the last great range before the Pacific Ocean. The ample waters of the Columbia bore them through the Cascades, and they found signs that they were nearing the ocean: Indian trinkets from the Pacific trade, rain and fog coming from the ocean, and white sea gulls flying above. On November 2 they felt the swell of the tide in the river.

On Wednesday, November 6, the Corps of Discovery camped near the mouth of the river. They built large fires to dry their bedding and settled down for the last night of the westward journey. The next morning rain and a thick fog darkened the land.

The corps continued along the river, stopping at a small Indian village where they traded fishhooks for food and took on a native, dressed in a European sailor's jacket, as a guide. In a few miles the river widened, and as the fog lifted, opening out before them they beheld the waters of the Pacific Ocean. That night they spread their mats on the shore of Gray's Bay with the sound of the ocean in their ears. In his journal Clark wrote, "Ocean in view. O, the joy!"

The corps had still to find their way back east, but now that seemed comparatively simple. They built a winter camp called Fort Clatsop at the mouth of the Columbia, explored the countryside, hunted elk, and took notes on the local Indians. Oregon's winter rain and mist were far less trying than the extreme cold of the previous winter at Fort Mandan.

Lewis and Clark had hoped to encounter a ship that might take them back to the eastern United States, but the seaborne trade to the Northwest was still in its infancy, and no vessel appeared. When spring arrived, the explorers retraced their steps to the Missouri, leaving Fort Clatsop on March 23 and arriving in Nez Percé country seven weeks later. The Indians had cared well for their horses and flew an American flag over their encampment. After waiting for the snow to melt on the high passes in the Rockies, Lewis and Clark explored different routes to the Missouri and then regrouped. They left Sacajawea and Charbonneau in the Mandan country and continued downriver, arriving in Saint Louis on September 23. Lewis immediately wrote to the president announcing their return.

The country was excited to learn that the corps had come back safely from the West. Lewis and Clark captured national attention for weeks. Jefferson welcomed Lewis to the White House—Clark, too, could have visited the president but was busy courting Judith Hancock, for whom he had named the Judith River in Montana. Jefferson had little difficulty in persuading Congress to vote a special bonus in land and money to the veterans of the expedition and appointed Lewis governor of the Louisiana Territory.

The Lewis and Clark Expedition is generally regarded as one of the most successful in history. The explorers had covered more than seven thousand miles from Saint Louis to the Pacific and back and lost only one man—from an unknown disease. They were the first men to cross the continent within the boundaries of what became the forty-eight contiguous states, establishing that there is no convenient water route from the Atlantic to the Pacific. The explorers initiated friendly relations with dozens of Indian nations and compiled extensive records on the character of each. They were the first to discover or describe 178 plants, 15 reptiles and amphibians, 44 mammals, 51 birds, and 12 fishes. Among these plants and animals were the ponderosa pine, the sagebrush, the prairie rattler, the steelhead trout, the coyote, and the grizzly bear.

Many veterans of the expedition would go west again. John Colter became a famous frontiersman and trapper, and William Clark settled in Saint Louis, serving as an Indian agent and territorial governor. The territory they had explored caught the imagination of other Americans. The West was now perceived as a reality—and an American reality at that. The United States was blessed with an embarrassment of riches. America had the lands of her original boundaries and almost as much country again in the West. The land would offer opportunities for trade, settlement, and adventure to millions of Americans yet unborn. Such was the glorious prospect that lay before Jeffersonian America.

Unfortunately, the conquest would have its sordid side, for the land would change as millions of settlers overwhelmed Native American cultures and killed wild animals. Even the sweet-smelling wild grasses of the prairies would give way to less romantic, if more profitable, wheat crops. But the Corps of Discovery had been able to see the West without subduing it, and in the young republic there appeared to be no limit to America's resources.

Bibliography

Ambrose, Stephen. *Undaunted Courage: Meriwether Lewis, Thomas Jefferson, and the Opening of the American West* (1996). Narrative history of the expedition.

Christian, Shirley. *Before Lewis and Clark: The Story of the Chouteaus, the French Dynasty That Ruled America's Frontier* (2004). The Chouteaus pioneered the Indian trade from Saint Louis long before the arrival of Lewis and Clark.

Cutright, Paul Russell. *Lewis and Clark: Pioneering Naturalists* (1969). Favorable assessment of the expedition's scientific role.

Mann, John W. W. *Sacajawea's People: The Lemhi Shoshones and the Salmon River Country* (2004). Valuable account of one of the key Indian groups on the route of the Lewis and Clark Expedition.

Morris, Larry E. *The Fate of the Corps: What Became of the Lewis and Clark Explorers After the Expedition* (2004). The varied activities of the explorers included fur-trapping, merchandizing, writing, and governing.

Ronda, James. *Lewis and Clark Among the Indians* (1984). Lewis and Clark as diplomats and ethnographers.

———. *Finding the West: Explorations with Lewis and Clark* (2001). A critical examination of the expedition and its journals by the foremost Lewis and Clark scholar.

Sheehan, Bernard. *Seeds of Extinction: Jeffersonian Philanthropy and the American Indian* (1973). Chronicles the destructive influence of Jeffersonian policy on eastern Indians.

Thwaites, Reuben G., Editor. *Original Journals of the Lewis and Clark Expedition* (8 vols., 1904–1905). Extensive collection of expedition journals.

Woods, Willis F., et al. *Lewis and Clark's America: A Voyage of Discovery* (1976). Nineteenth-century paintings and sketches of the expedition.

Identification Topics

Louisiana Purchase, Thomas Jefferson, Meriwether Lewis, Benjamin Rush, William Clark, Harpers Ferry rifle, *Discovery*, Missouri River, Mandans, Pierre Cruzette, Black York, Sacajawea, Shoshones, Columbia River, Fort Clatsop, Missouri River

Study Questions

1. How did the planning and course of the Lewis and Clark Expedition reflect its scientific intent?
2. Did the Constitution give President Jefferson the specific right to purchase the Louisiana Territory from France? If not, how did Jefferson justify such an action?

3. Would the Lewis and Clark Expedition have occurred if the United States had not purchased Louisiana?
4. How did the following nations or groups of people facilitate or react to the Lewis and Clark Expedition: the French, the Spanish, the trappers and traders, Indians, and the American government?
5. Summarize the reception given to Lewis and Clark by various Native American tribes and individuals.
6. The United States was so large in 1803 that it was difficult to imagine a time when it would be highly settled. How does the experience of Lewis and Clark support this statement?
7. In what ways did the Lewis and Clark Expedition embody the optimism of the early republic?
8. Compare and contrast the characters and achievements of Lewis and Clark. Which man (if either) contributed more to the expedition?

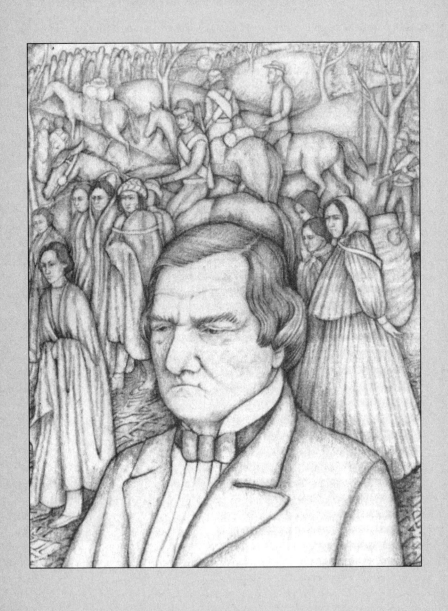

CHAPTER 9

The Limits of Jacksonian Democracy
The Cherokee Removal

Andrew Jackson's election to the presidency in 1828 symbolized an age of new opportunity for the common man. The first chief executive born in a log cabin, Jackson proved that almost any man could rise to the highest post in America. During his administration, he championed democratic ideals by attacking the Bank of the United States as a privileged monopoly and promoting rotation in office to broaden political participation. While creating new opportunities for some Americans, however, he curtailed the rights of others. His Indian policy satisfied land-hungry whites but victimized the Native Americans. The Cherokees, who had lived for hundreds of years in the southern Appalachians, suffered especially at Jackson's hands. In response to American policy, they had adopted many white customs early in the nineteenth century, only to be forced off their land in the 1830s to "protect" their native customs. Opportunity, it appeared, could damage one group while encouraging another.

Maj. Gen. Winfield Scott, a great admirer of the Cherokees, arrived at New Echota, Georgia, in 1838 commanding an army of seven thousand regular soldiers and state militiamen. Addressing his troops on May 17, Scott declared, "The Cherokees, by the advances they have made in Christianity and civilization, are by far the most interesting tribe of Indians in the territorial limits of the United States." He urged his soldiers to show the Indians "every possible kindness." These benevolent words might suggest that Scott was the leader of a mission of mercy designed to rescue the Cherokees from an impending calamity, but ironically, the kindly general was himself the agent of calamity. As Scott uttered considerate phrases, his men were busy constructing large wood pens with sixteen-foot walls. During the next month they would seek out fourteen thousand Cherokees, living in several thousand square miles of Appalachian valleys and mountainsides, and drive them like cattle into these log enclosures, holding them for shipment to a distant land in the West.

Scott's men divided into dozens of parties and spread out across Cherokee lands, finding the Indians, who had already been disarmed by other soldiers, engaged in domestic tasks. Men were in the fields, women at their spinning wheels, children at play, and families at dinner in their neat log or wood frame homes, when soldiers arrived with gruff voices and fixed bayonets to march them off with the clothes on their backs and the few possessions they could carry.

An old man listened stoically as the soldiers told him he must leave his home. Gathering his children and grandchildren around him, he knelt in prayer, then led his family away. A Cherokee woman used her last moments to feed her chickens. As the Indians left their homes, greedy men arrived to purchase their possessions for a pittance or to steal the remaining livestock and household goods.

Thousands of Cherokees were torn thus from their homes and driven from their lands, transformed in a sickening, brief moment from prosperous farmers and artisans into refugees. One night they slept in their own beds; the next they lay on the ground under crude shelters of boards and bark inside stockades. Among the efficient soldiers was a Georgia militiaman, who later served as a Confederate officer. "I fought through the Civil War," he later wrote, "and have seen men shot to pieces and slaughtered by thousands, but the Cherokee removal was the cruelest work I ever knew."

If the Cherokee removal had been the work of a totalitarian government in a country where individual or minority rights were lightly regarded and the state deified, we might regard it as an inevitable tragedy, sad but expected—consistent with the bloated authority of a dictatorial regime. But the American ideology, enshrined in the Declaration of Independence more than six decades before the Cherokee removal, rejects the totalitarian view of the state. Britain's threat to take a few pennies a year in tea taxes had provoked the colonists to revolt and establish a government more "likely to effect their safety and happiness." Andrew Jackson, then president of the United States, was a man who seemed particularly well suited to carry on the libertarian ideals of the founding fathers. "Old Hickory" regarded himself as a man of the people and claimed that any person was worthy of holding public office. On inauguration day in 1829 he had opened the White House and entertained a boisterous mob. Surely Jackson's appreciation of the needs, to say nothing of the rights, of the average citizen would lead him to sympathize with the Indians. Yet he and other Americans regarded the Cherokees as a people apart, not entitled to the same rights as other Americans.

To understand the Cherokee situation we need to review the tribe's early history, their adjustment to white settlers, and their condition on the eve of removal. In their story we can witness both the vitality of Native American cultures and the curiously insensitive Indian policies of the federal government.

Long ago, according to Cherokee legend, there was no earth, only a great body of water, and above it in the Upper World a multitude of animals, crowded together and longing for room. Finally "Beaver's Grandchild," the Water Beetle, offered to go down to the water and investigate. He skimmed over the surface but could find no land. So he swam to the bottom and came up with some soft mud, which began to grow and grow into a great flat plain. The delighted animals sent birds down to seek dry land, but everywhere the earth was still mud. Buzzard flew down and his wings struck the ground, breaking the earth into mountains and valleys. Finally the mud dried, and the animals came down from the Upper World and dwelt on the earth. The land where the buzzard's wings had struck became the Cherokee country.

Modern scholars have presented a more prosaic picture of Cherokee origins but agree that the Cherokees lived in the southern Appalachians for many generations. At some distant time, the Indians must have come from elsewhere, but the details of that prehistoric migration are uncertain. Scholars have traced a wide network of associations between the Cherokees and other peoples. Cherokee artifacts have turned up in burial mounds in Illinois and Indiana. Their language is Iroquoian, suggesting an earlier connection with Indians to the north. Their pottery is similar to that of Caribbean Indians. Their basketmaking bears a strong resemblance to the crafts of the Amazon and Orinoco Rivers in South America. During the thousands of years that Indians have lived in America such far-flung contacts were certainly possible.

By the time the first white men entered Cherokee lands in 1540, the natives had lived in the Appalachians for so many generations that they could imagine no other place as home. At the time, some thirty thousand Cherokees lived in loosely confederated villages, a strong, healthy people, nourished by rich soil and abundant wildlife. They planted corn and potatoes; gathered chestnuts and berries; and hunted deer, elk, buffalo, pheasants, and turkey. Cooking over open fires, they ate from earthenware vessels.

The Cherokees were well housed, many owning both summer and winter dwellings in close proximity. Summer houses were wood structures up to seventy feet long and two stories high, some housing several families. Winter dwellings were smaller, with floors three feet beneath the ground and thick circular walls composed of mud and timbers. Wood bedframes covered with finely woven mats and animal skins hugged the walls. A small fire in the middle warmed these tiny, efficient shelters.

Every Cherokee belonged to one of the seven tribal clans—the Bird, Wolf, Deer, Red Paint, Blue, Long Hair, and Wild Potato. The Indians protected themselves from genetic disease and created wide relational networks by requiring that every person marry outside his or her group. The clan was responsible for enforcing the law with the assistance of the town chief and the tribal council. There was no chief or assembly for all the Cherokees, but the cultural identity of the tribe made the Cherokees a single people.

The Cherokee religion taught the people that their land was a gift from the Great Spirit, Asga-Ya-Galun-lati. They did not "own" the land, strictly speaking, for it remained always the property of their god. But they did own the improvements on the land: houses, crops, and livestock.

Cherokee lives were animated by a perpetual sense of the proximity of sacred beings. "Little People" dwelt in nearby caves, and "Immortals" lived among the mountain peaks. The sun, moon, rivers, rocks, birds, animals, and trees—all were animate. The snowy owl was a star that had fallen to the earth to take a new form. The bears were Indians who had adopted animal form. They could talk to you if they wanted to, but perversely—or wisely—they remained silent.

The Cherokees loved to tell stories about the animals, many of which were later adopted by Joel Chandler Harris for his *Uncle Remus* tales and became part of the broader American folklore. The stories told how the deer got his antlers and why the mole lived underground. The most famous of all tells how a tortoise set out to race a hare. "I know I cannot beat a hare," said Tortoise, "but I can try."

The Cherokees celebrated their lives and honored their gods with periodic ceremonies, following the cycle of seasons in a land where nature announced the birth and death of the year with splendid impressions: the sweet scent of azaleas and other species of rhododendron in the spring and the bright colors of maple, oak, and cottonwood trees in the fall. The Indians observed the greatest of the celebrations, the Corn Ceremony, with prayers of thanks for good crops, a feast, music, dancing, and games. In such ways the people celebrated their lives under a Cherokee sky in a place that seemed ineffably their land.

The rhythms of Cherokee life were not affected by the arrival in the Caribbean in 1492 of three Spanish ships. Cortés conquered the Aztecs, and Pizarro overwhelmed the Incas before Europeans even entered Cherokee lands. The first visitor was Hernando de Soto, who made his way along the Winding Stair Trail through the Appalachians in 1640. His appearance must have impressed the Cherokees, who had never before seen men with horses, guns, and shining armor. But de Soto passed quickly onward, seeking treasures to rival those of the conquistadors. The comparative modesty of Cherokee holdings proved an asset in years ahead when the Spanish established their dominion in Florida. Having no incentive to loot the Cherokees, the Europeans left them alone. Only an occasional visitor moved among the natives, including a Jesuit priest who reported that the Cherokees were "sedate and thoughtful, dwelling in peace in their native mountains."

During the seventeenth century the Cherokees developed a taste for European goods and occasionally raided the Spanish for horses and guns. But they were slow to establish a stable trade with the whites. It was not until 1673 that the first Englishmen, James Needham and Gabriel Arthur, visited the Cherokees. They were such a curiosity that the Indians placed them on a platform for all the people to see. The visitors made a trade agreement with the Cherokees, and Gabriel Arthur returned to Virginia with a party of Indians to collect a store of goods. On their way back Arthur quarreled with one of the natives, a man remembered only as "Indian John," and in a moment Arthur lay dead on the ground, a bullet through his head. Indian John then did a curious and ominous thing: he drew his knife and cut out Arthur's heart. Holding it in his hand and turning east toward the English plantations, he said that "he valued not all the English." The words may be apocryphal, but they represent succinctly the Cherokee sense of independence.

Indian John nearly succeeded in having Needham killed as well, but a Cherokee chief came to the white man's defense, and during the next year Needham adopted Cherokee dress and accompanied the Indians on raids across the Southeast from the Ohio River to Florida. He returned safely to Virginia in 1674, but the English made no more attempts to establish trade with the Cherokees for the next two decades.

Early in the eighteenth century, however, an extensive trade did grow up between the two regions. In Charleston and other southern cities, large trains of packhorses were loaded with widely assorted trade goods: cloth, blankets, hoes, axes, beads, looking glasses, ribbons, guns, knives, hatchets, bullets, powder, flints, kettles, tobacco, pipes, and rum. They wound their way along the steep narrow trails through the Appalachians into Cherokee towns, where the traders exchanged their wares for pelts, beeswax, and bear oil. In 1708 alone, fifty thousand deerskins and other hides crossed the mountains.

Slowly the contacts with whites began to change Cherokee society. Not only did the Indians come to depend on English goods, but they also became familiar with English culture. White traders settled in many Indian towns, frequently building the largest houses in the neighborhood, marrying Indian women, raising families, and advising the natives on European ways. Among the resident traders were intelligent, sensitive men like Eleazar Wiggam and James Adair, who learned the Cherokee language and wrote descriptions of the people.

The Indian villages, which had always consisted of substantial dwellings, acquired the signs of white influence, and by the middle of the eighteenth century many Cherokees lived in log cabins like those of white frontiersmen. On cold winter nights, however, they sought the warmth of the tiny circular "hot houses" they had always known.

In 1735 there were sixty-four Cherokee villages with an approximate population of sixteen thousand. Each village consisted of between twenty and sixty houses, surrounded by gardens, orchards, and hogpens. The largest building in each town was a council house, capable of holding several hundred people for government councils or religious ceremonies. A sacred fire burned on an earthen mound in the middle of each council house.

The men frequently went away on war parties against the Creeks, the Iroquois, the Tuscaroras, and other neighboring tribes. In fact, warfare was so common among the Cherokees that they acquired a reputation with the English for being particularly fierce and regarding battle as a kind of pastime. Cherokee women were active participants in every aspect of life, including the military arts. They sat on war councils and even went on campaigns. They raised their children as warriors, forcing them to endure pain and hunger as preparation for warfare.

A softer side of Cherokee life was apparent, however, to most travelers. Eighteenth-century accounts of the Cherokees are filled with admiration. Hungry travelers who fed on Indian bread, corncakes, and hominy mush grew to admire Cherokee cooking. The Indians engaged in many crafts, including making baskets, mats, pottery, bows, clubs, and canoes. Observers commented on the natives' fine bearing and physiques. John Bartram, the naturalist, wrote: "They are tall, slender, erect and of a delicate frame; their features formed with perfect symmetry, their countenance cheerful and friendly, and they move with a becoming grace and dignity."

Having established trading relations with the Cherokees, the English wanted to secure them as allies in wars with other Indian tribes and with the French. In 1730 Sir Alexander Cummings persuaded the Cherokees to inaugurate one of their chiefs as an "emperor" of all the towns and to send representatives to England to negotiate a treaty. On May 4, 1730, he sailed to England with seven principal men of the tribe, including Attakullakulla, a short man known to his people as "The Little Carpenter," but distinguished as a statesman and orator.

In London these leading tribesmen were carefully coached in court etiquette and on June 18 were presented to the king at Windsor Castle. Everywhere they went in London—to the Tower, the Mermaid Tavern, the theater, St. James's Park, and the Houses of Parliament—they were observed with wonder as beings from an unimaginably remote region. They negotiated an agreement to become England's allies in war, to trade only with the English, and to return runaway slaves. The English promised, in turn, to punish anyone who injured the Cherokees.

Thomas Jefferson was on hand when another party of Indians set forth on a voyage to England. As a young man in Virginia, Jefferson was "very familiar" with the Cherokees. Years later in a letter to John Adams, Jefferson wrote:

> I knew much the great Ontasseté, the warrior and orator of the Cherokees; he was always the guest of my father, on his journeys to and from Williamsburg. I was in his camp when he made his great farewell oration to his people the evening before his departure for England. The moon was in full splendor, and to her he seemed to address himself in his prayers for his own safety on the voyage, and that of his people during his absence; his sounding voice, distinct articulation, animated action, and the solemn silence of his people at their several fires, filled me with awe and veneration, although I did not understand a word he uttered.

During the eighteenth century, the Cherokees and the English were closely allied, with the exception of a short period of warfare in 1760–1761, when English Capt. James Grant destroyed fifteen Cherokee towns, impressing upon the Indians the value of friendly relations with the English. In the years preceding the American Revolution, Cherokee–English relations were further improved by two able representatives of royal authority. One of the agents, John MacDonald, settled among the Cherokees at Chickamonga Creek and married Anne Shorey, the daughter of a white interpreter and an Indian woman. Their grandson, John Ross, would become one of the principal Cherokee leaders in the early nineteenth century.

Unfortunately, the friendship between Cherokees and English served the Indians poorly during the Revolutionary War. The Cherokees elected to remain faithful to their alliance but received little help from the English. In 1776–1777 American armies from Georgia, South Carolina, and North Carolina invaded Cherokee lands and destroyed more than fifty villages, forcing the Indians to accept the Carolina cession, whereby they lost large portions of territory.

Cherokee resistance to the new American government continued sporadically through the Revolutionary period and into the early years of the new nation, but by 1790 most of the Indians realized they would have to make peace with the Americans. The Treaty of Holston in 1791 ended hostilities and provided for the Indians' introduction to all the advantages of white society. Article 14 called for the Indians to advance their abilities in home industry and agriculture and guaranteed American tools and training to bring the Cherokees "to a greater degree of civilization."

During the next forty years, Native Americans, who had already been greatly influenced by European culture, adopted many customs and industries from their white neighbors. The change, known as the Cherokee Renaissance, was facilitated by white settlers. For several generations, traders of predominantly Scots, Irish, or Scots-Irish background had been living among the Cherokees, establishing their permanent homes in the Indian lands and marrying native women. As a matter of course, they brought with them some knowledge of literature and crafts.

The Cherokees were especially fortunate in the government's choice of Indian agents in the early nineteenth century. Benjamin Hawkins, who served in this capacity

CHEROKEE BOUNDARIES
—— Original Cherokee lands
—— Boundary in 1820

from 1796 until 1801, wanted to devote his life to the Indians and was particularly interested in seeing that the altruistic promise of Article 14 was implemented. Travelers in 1800 noticed signs of progress toward white standards of civilization: women at work at looms and men tending cattle in the fields.

Hawkins was followed by Return Jonathan Meigs, a Revolutionary War veteran and Ohio frontiersman, who began work as the Cherokee Indian agent in 1801 at age sixty and continued energetically in the post for twenty-two years. Under Meigs's direction, the provisions of the Treaty of Holston calling for American aid and training were carried out. The United States distributed plows, hoes, axes, and other tools. White blacksmiths, wheelwrights, carpenters, and other artisans settled in the Cherokee country and taught Indian apprentices their skills. Meigs also assisted the Indians by arguing their positions at treaty conferences and encouraging them to establish a unified tribal government, and he sought to expel whites who threatened the Indians' welfare—unscrupulous traders, fugitives, and squatters.

Meigs knew and liked the Cherokees well, lived among them, and won their respect. In times of famine or disease, he saw that the Indians received assistance quickly and attempted to persuade Washington that they should not be charged for such aid. His last act of kindness to a Cherokee symbolized his long consideration. In 1823 at age eighty-two he turned over his house to an elderly Cherokee chief on a cold night and slept in a tent. But the sacrifice proved too much for his aged body—he contracted pneumonia and died.

Meigs's dedication to the Cherokees was matched by that of many others, notably among a growing number of Christian missionaries. Early in the nineteenth century, Moravians, Presbyterians, Baptists, and Methodists established missions in the Cherokee lands, where they preached and conducted the first schools in the region. Many learned the Cherokee tongue, and Samuel Austin Worcester translated hymns into Cherokee.

Men like Hawkins, Meigs, and Worcester represented well the spirit of Article 14. They believed that the greatest benefit they could confer upon the Indians was to give them the knowledge and the tools to live as their white neighbors did. In the American government, however, there was a faction that espoused a different program for the Indians. From the earliest days of colonization many whites had regarded Native American lands as vacant lands, waiting to be properly settled by people of European descent. In the regions surrounding the Cherokees thousands of whites were beginning to feel the need for more land. The Cherokee territory was lightly settled: why not open it to whites?

The Indians were reluctant to part with any of their lands, but the federal government offered them many enticements. In exchange for vacant land the government would give the Indians money that could be used to improve the lands they occupied. If Cherokees were displaced when land was ceded to the federal government, they would be paid for their improvements and given land in the West. If they owned no land or improvements, the government would still give them rifles, blankets, and beaver traps so that they could make a start in the West. If they preferred to stay on their lands, they could each keep a 640-acre homestead, or "reservation," on ceded territory.

With such inducements the Cherokees made several land cessions in the early nineteenth century. By 1817 two thousand Cherokees, slightly more than 10 percent of the tribal population, had moved to a region beyond the Mississippi that became known as Cherokee West. But many Indians were worried about the loss of their native lands. They were confused by government policies that encouraged them to take up the plow and the loom and become "civilized" like whites but that also enticed them to go west with trap and rifle to live the traditional life of the Indian hunter. One missionary reported the Indian reaction to the two-sided American policies:

> The Indians say they don't know how to understand their Father the President. A few years ago he sent them a plough and a hoe—said it was not good for his red children to hunt—they must cultivate the earth. Now he tells them there is good hunting at the Arkansas; if they go there he will give them rifles.

In 1820 most Cherokees were committed to the first option. Their hunting lands were depleted anyway, and they recognized the need for raising cattle and growing more crops. Their loyalty to the United States was tested by the Creek War in 1814. The Creeks, a southern tribe, urged the Cherokees to join them in expelling whites from their native lands. But the Cherokees chose to side with the whites, sending eight hundred warriors against the southern tribe and helping Andrew Jackson win the decisive Battle of Horseshoe Bend.

The degree to which the Cherokees had assimilated white civilization was apparent to any person who journeyed through their lands. The Indian dwellings were log cabins or larger framed houses, usually surrounded by fields, orchards, and fenced pastures. Some of the more prosperous Cherokees owned black slaves and lived as gentlemen planters. Joseph Vann, one of the wealthiest men in the region, owned a fine two-story brick house featuring a veranda and imposing white columns.

In 1826 a Presbyterian church report surveyed the diverse holdings of the Cherokee people and arrived at these statistics: 7,600 houses, 22,000 cattle, 46,000 pigs, 2,500 sheep, 2,948 plows, 1,488 spinning wheels, 762 looms, 62 blacksmith shops, 31 gristmills, 10 sawmills, and 18 schools. These figures indicate the degree to which the Cherokees had assimilated white material culture. Another index is provided by the Indian claims filed after removal. Among the household items listed were dishes, cutlery, coffee pots, irons, churns, washtubs, chairs, tables, feather beds, and silk dresses. In addition, many Cherokees owned books written in English, and some even subscribed to English-language periodicals.

In government, too, the Cherokees were influenced by white practices. Although they retained their village chiefs, the Indians formed a central administration with a frame of government modeled on the U.S. Constitution. The Cherokee republic had a chief executive, a two-house legislature, and a supreme court. The Cherokees established New Echota in their Georgia lands as the capital; and it soon boasted a council house, a courthouse, a printing office, stores, and several frame houses.

The Cherokees preserved many tribal customs amid these signs of white influence. Although the leaders frequently dressed in suits, the standard dress for men was fringed buckskin shirts worn over cloth or buckskin trousers and possibly a calico turban and earrings. The traditional sports and ceremonies such as ball play, archery, and the Corn Ceremony endured.

No person better exemplified the Cherokee impulses to adopt white inventions and institutions and preserve native culture than Sequoya, who was born in 1775, the son of a Cherokee woman and a white trader. His relatives included great warriors, among them Old Tassel, the foremost Cherokee chief during the Revolutionary War. Sequoya grew up a solitary, energetic, and enigmatic young man, mastering the skills of silversmith, blacksmith, and trader. Interested in painting but unable to obtain store-bought supplies, he made brushes from horsehair and paints from earth and plant pigments.

Early in the nineteenth century, Sequoya became obsessed with the idea of creating an alphabet to represent the Cherokee language. Although other Indian languages had been put into print, the Cherokee sound patterns were so complicated that no one had been able to represent them with written characters. Sequoya was determined to try, but he disliked white influence and withdrew to a remote region of the Cherokee lands. He preferred hunting and trapping to farming and even moved away from his family into a small hut in order to pursue his study of the Cherokee tongue. His behavior was so strange that many Indians turned against him, considering him a witch. His detractors even burned his hut with all his linguistics notes.

In 1821, after twelve years of work, Sequoya completed a phonetic alphabet. Using the English alphabet, supplemented by other characters, he represented eighty-six distinctive Cherokee syllables, or sounds, thus arriving at a phonetic alphabet.

When other Cherokees heard about his accomplishment, they were incredulous but gave him the opportunity to demonstrate his system to the National Council. Because the characters were perfectly phonetic—unlike English—it was possible to learn to read quickly, and within a few hours he proved that he could teach children to sound out words. The rapidity with which the Cherokee people seized on the new method proved both their desire to learn and their attachment to their language. Some Indians learned to read Sequoya's writings in only a few days, and soon, thousands of Cherokees could read the printed words of their language. The National Council ordered the Cherokees' laws printed in the native language and established a printing press in New Echota. The missionary, Samuel Austin Worcester, carried the word of Sequoya's achievements to Philadelphia and Boston, raising large sums of money to buy a printing press and have Sequoya's alphabet cast in lead type. In 1828 the press in New Echota began to print a newspaper, the *Cherokee Phoenix*, in English and in Cherokee under the editorship of Elias Boudinot, a full-blooded Indian.

No achievement of the Cherokee Renaissance contributed more to tribal pride than Sequoya's alphabet. But Sequoya was still not comfortable with life on the fringes of white society, and in 1821, the year he introduced his invention to the National Council, he left his eastern homeland forever and moved to Cherokee West. Despite Sequoya's disaffection, however, the prospect of Cherokee life in the East was bright in the 1820s. While preserving tribal dress, law, and language, the Cherokees had successfully adopted many features of white civilization. They raised cattle and corn, built frame houses, sang hymns, and drafted legislation.

Despite their faithful adherence to the spirit of the Treaty of Holston, however, they would soon be torn from their tribal lands in a government program that made a mockery of the American policy of civilization and conciliation. With each year the white pressure on their borders increased, and the southern states, sensitive to their local "rights," began to demand control of tribal lands within their own boundaries. Andrew Jackson, who became president in 1829, was sensitive to their ambitions. As a westerner, he understood the frontiersman's desire for land; as a nationalist, he opposed the existence of autonomous enclaves within the United States. Having fought with and against Indians, he maintained a sentimental regard for the natives but believed that both they and the whites suffered from too close an association. He was glad enough to let the Indians live their own lives, as long as those lives were far removed from his own country.

Jackson set forth his Indian policy in his first annual message to Congress, on December 8, 1829, stating unequivocally that there could be no independent Indian nations within the United States. Sympathizing with Georgia's opposition to the Cherokee republic, he asked whether Maine would permit its Indians, the Penobscots, to form an independent country within the state's boundaries.

Although he opposed Indian autonomy within the states, Jackson recognized that previous Indian policy had been ambiguous. He believed that the natives could not preserve their integrity as tribes within the United States, even if the states granted their autonomy. Contact with whites inevitably doomed them to "weakness and decay." In the West, however, on a new land guaranteed to them for all time, they could

Sequoya and his alphabet. Sequoya created a Cherokee alphabet, enabling his people to publish a newspaper and write documents in their own tongue.

develop at their own pace, absorbing white culture as they chose, and eventually create "an interesting commonwealth, destined to perpetuate the race."

Jackson did not favor forced removal. "It would be as cruel as unjust," he said, "to compel the aborigines to abandon the graves of their fathers and seek a home in a distant land." Those who wished to remain could do so. But they must be subject to state law, and they could retain only the lands they had improved. They could not retain vacant tribal lands "merely because they have seen them from the mountain or passed them in the chase." Jackson anticipated that those who chose to remain on homesteads in the eastern states would receive, "like other citizens, protection in their persons and property. . . [and] ere long become merged in the mass of our population."

This was a complex statement. Our knowledge of subsequent history may incline us to simplify Jackson's address into a demand for forced removal. But Jackson distinguished between the tribe and the individual Indian. The natives who fully accepted American laws and American concepts of landownership should be allowed to remain on their present land. But the Indian nation within the nation, with its vast tribal lands and independent government, could not be allowed to continue. In short, the Indians must either accept white society in toto or go west and develop whatever blend of native and white society seemed appropriate.

Jackson's opposition to tribal autonomy seemed to invite the states to take over Indian lands. Georgia had already declared that whites living on Cherokee lands were subject to state law; soon after Jackson's message, that state declared Cherokee laws void and decreed Cherokee lands to be part of the state of Georgia. Because most Cherokee territory was in Georgia, this action threatened to destroy tribal autonomy. The state sent troops to take possession of gold fields recently discovered by the Indians, thereafter allowing whites, but not Indians, to mine the ore. In reprisal,

Cherokee warriors attacked and killed several whites, furnishing a pretext for further action by Georgia against the tribe.

In the meantime, an Indian removal bill was introduced in the U.S. House of Representatives on February 24, 1830, by Representative Wilson Lumpkin of Georgia. The bill called for an exchange of western land for Indian lands east of the Mississippi, compensation for improvements, and assistance in migration. It would apply equally to the five great southeastern tribes: the Choctaws, Chickasaws, Creeks, and Seminoles, as well as the Cherokees. The debate over the bill provoked a long and angry discussion about the proper character of Indian–white relations. Although many congressmen agreed with Lumpkin and Jackson that Indian removal was necessary, a substantial minority, including Daniel Webster, opposed the measure.

The opposition was dramatically summarized by Senator Theodore Frelinghuysen of New Jersey in a six-hour speech. Frelinghuysen began by examining the early history of the Native Americans, pointing out that they had been on their lands long before Great Britain, itself, had a political existence. The Indians, he said, "are men, endowed with kindred faculties and powers with ourselves... they have a place in human sympathy, and are justly entitled to a share in the common bounties of a benignant Providence." Whites had no right to take Indian land by force. "Where the Indian always has been," said Frelinghuysen, "he enjoys an absolute right still to be, in the free exercise of thought, government and conduct." The Indians' natural right to the land had been reinforced by a long series of treaties in which the Indian tribes were regarded as sovereign nations.

Historically, Native Americans had given up much land by treaty and purchase, but they had a right now to hold on to what remained. Frelinghuysen characterized whites as insatiably greedy: "Like the horse-leech," he said, "our insatiated cupidity cries, give! give!" Frelinghuysen pictured the white expansionist saying to the Indians: "Away! we cannot endure you so near us! These forests and rivers, these groves of your fathers, these firesides and hunting grounds are ours by the right of power, and the force of numbers." Such conduct was entirely inconsistent with the principles of liberty. We were "the wonder and praise of the world," he said, "freedom's hope, and her consolation." But now we were about "to become the oppressors of the feeble, and to cast away our birthright!" He urged his fellow congressmen to "place the White man where the Indian stands." Some years before "a few pence of duty on tea, that invaded no fireside, excited no fears, disturbed no substantial interest whatever" had excited in Americans a fear of unjust authority and precipitated the Revolution. During the years of war with Britain, the founding fathers had "contended for the very rights and privileges that our Indian neighbors now implore us to protect and preserve to them."

Frelinghuysen's eloquent speech won him national acclaim and summarized the key points in the arguments against removal: the priority of Indian claims to the land; the incompatibility of removal and American libertarian ideals; and the venality of the usurpers' motives. But he was not sufficiently persuasive to prevent the passage of the removal bill, and opportunism proved stronger than idealism; the bill was enacted into law in May 1830. In the meantime, Georgia had passed more legislation specifying that contracts between Indians and whites were null and void unless witnessed by two whites and that no Indian could testify against a white man in Georgia courts.

Apparently, Jackson's demand that eastern Indians live under white laws did not mean under the same laws that governed whites.

Despite these setbacks, the Cherokees, with the help of supporters throughout the United States, were determined to fight for their traditional rights. At a meeting of the Cherokee Legislative Council in July 1830, the Indians begged Jackson to uphold their treaties, telling him, "inclination to remove from this land has no abiding place in our hearts, and when we move, we shall move by the course of nature to sleep under this ground which the Great Spirit gave to our ancestors and which now covers them in undisturbed repose." The Cherokee opposition leader was John Ross, grandson of the British agent John MacDonald and son of the Scots trader Daniel Ross. Although he was only one-eighth Cherokee, Ross had been raised on Indian land and identified completely with the native cause. Since 1817 he had been the elected leader of the Cherokee Nation. A rather small man with dark hair, heavy eyebrows, and blue eyes, during the 1830s he worked unceasingly to prevent the removal.

For several years the Indians were in limbo, hardly able to believe that they might soon be forced to leave their homeland. Ross was a messenger of hope, periodically returning from battles in Washington and riding through Cherokee towns. The people came in from their farms and lined up for the chance to stand before John Ross and take him by the hand as he assured them that they would win.

Many Indians and whites helped Ross in the battle to retain the Cherokee lands. Elias Boudinot wrote stirring editorials against removal in the *Cherokee Phoenix*, exposing the hypocrisy of the removal policy: "Where have we an example in the whole history of man, of a nation or tribe removing in a body, from a land of civil and religious means, to a perfect wilderness, *in order to be civilized.*" Boudinot castigated the United States for failing to uphold its own promises. The Indians were driven off their lands even though "treaties are declared to be binding, and in them ample provisions are made for the protection of the Indians." He asked, "Who would trust his life and fortune to such a faithless nation?" No Cherokee *voluntarily* would. Stripped of its self-righteous rhetoric, the removal bill said to the Indian, "Go and perish."

Boudinot's essays not only helped unify Indian sentiment but also rallied white support and were reprinted across the United States. Influential men in Washington helped Ross find good legal counsel for the tribe. In 1832 the lawyers won a stunning victory before the U.S. Supreme Court in *Worcester v. Georgia*, a case that arose when Samuel Austin Worcester refused to register with the Georgia authorities as preacher in the Indian Territory. He argued that the new state law requiring such registration was unconstitutional because Georgia had no authority in Indian lands. The Court found in favor of Worcester, and Chief Justice John Marshall declared that the Cherokee Nation was "a distinct community, occupying its own territories, with boundaries accurately described, in which the laws of Georgia can have no force, and which the citizens of Georgia have no right to enter." The Court thus confirmed the Cherokee position. But President Jackson refused to uphold the decision, reputedly saying, "John Marshall has made his decision. Now let him enforce it." Whether or not Jackson ever made this statement, it accurately summarizes his attitude toward the Court's position. Without the president's support, the decision was a dead letter.

Georgia was so unimpressed by the Court's authority that the state held Worcester in prison for almost a year following the decision. Worse, the state began to distribute the Indian lands by lottery. In the next two years whites occupied John Ross's house, the Indian capital at New Echota, a Moravian mission station, and many other Cherokee dwellings. At the mission the Moravian chapel became a courthouse and the mission rectory was turned into a tavern.

In the face of these defeats, some Cherokees, including Elias Boudinot, began to waver. Boudinot admired many features of white civilization, but he was increasingly repelled by white prejudice. In 1826 he had married Harriet Gold, a white woman who lived in Cornwall, Connecticut, where he had attended a mission school. His cousin, John Ridge, also married a woman from Cornwall. The marriages, which must have seemed at first to confirm Boudinot's full acceptance into white society, soon produced the opposite effect. Anti-Indian racism erupted in Cornwall, and the mission school was forced to close. Boudinot, who had believed Native Americans could achieve equality through education, was bitterly disappointed. During the removal controversy he met with other expressions of racial animosity. Harassed by the Georgia Guard, he poured his anger and humiliation into a despairing question: "Would a white man have been treated as I have been?"

His experience with prejudice finally convinced Boudinot that the Indians' best chance lay in separating themselves from white civilization. Between two bad choices removal seemed the lesser evil. Assisted by Major Ridge and John Ridge, two of the Cherokees' foremost leaders, he formed a removal party and argued that because expulsion was inevitable the tribe should negotiate for the best possible terms. The other four nations had already signed removal treaties, so there appeared to be no alternative. In October 1835 a treaty council convened at Red Clay, Tennessee, the new Cherokee capital. Under Ross's leadership, the Indians overwhelmingly rejected a removal treaty. Even Boudinot and the other proponents of the treaty voted against it, fearing reprisals from the other Cherokees.

Exasperated by Ross's recalcitrance, Georgia authorities decided upon a desperate act. On the night of December 5, 1835, twenty-five members of the Georgia Guard rode across the Tennessee border and surrounded the small cabin that had served as Ross's home since his expulsion from his Georgia farm. They arrested Ross and a visitor, John Howard Payne, and made them ride through a cold rain back across the border to Camp Benton, Georgia, where they threw the two men into a small cabin that served as the jail. Inside the building, one Indian lay in chains and the body of another hung in the rafters.

Ross and his friend might never have escaped from the horror of their cell had the Guard not violated Tennessee territory, angering the authorities there. Their case was helped also by the fact that Ross's companion, John Howard Payne, was known throughout the country as the composer of a popular air, "Home, Sweet Home," and was occupied at the time in writing a history of the Cherokee Nation. His manuscript, written before this incident, referred to the Georgia Guard as "bandits." As he lay in the grotesque prison, Payne may have wondered whether the term was sufficiently strong.

The two men were released after thirteen days, but in the meantime, final preparations had been made for the last act in the legal maneuverings over the Cherokee removal. On December 29, Boudinot, the Ridges, and a hundred other proremoval Indians met and signed the Treaty of New Echota, purporting to represent the wishes of the Cherokee Nation. Ross went to Washington to fight the treaty and offered the government a document bearing the names of more than fourteen thousand Indians who opposed the treaty. Despite this evidence of its specious character, the document was ratified by the Senate by the narrow margin of one vote.

The Cherokees' defeat was complete. Ross continued to fight in Washington, and the Indians hoped for reversal of the government policy. The treaty gave them two years to move west. Before the end of that time, soldiers came onto Cherokee lands and disarmed all the natives. Having no choice in the matter, the Indians submitted peaceably. Some began to drift to Cherokee West, but most remained in their homes, unable to believe that the end was near.

Only the arrival of Gen. Winfield Scott's troops in spring 1838 convinced the remaining fourteen thousand Cherokees that the nightmare was a reality. Within a month most of the natives were imprisoned, suddenly reduced from citizens of a proud nation to a herd of refugees. Removing the Indians took almost a year; and although the federal government had promised to pay the cost, and General Scott attempted to provide well for the Cherokees, the migration decimated the tribe. In wagons and on foot the Indians made their way in large parties across Tennessee, Kentucky, Missouri, and Arkansas into the new lands in Oklahoma. They called their route the Trail of Tears.

Many whites saw them pass by on the road—their physical and spiritual suffering a ghastly sight. One traveler reported seeing Cherokees camped by the roadside, "under a severe fall of rain accompanied by heavy wind with their canvas for a shield from the inclemency of the weather, and the cold wet ground for a resting place." As the traveler moved through Kentucky, he came upon other parties of Indians, many of them laboring over "the sometimes frozen ground . . . with no covering for their feet except what nature had given them." At each camp Indians buried ten or a dozen comrades, the victims of cold, disease, and desolation. In all, four thousand Cherokees died on the Trail of Tears, including John Ross's wife, who, according to legend, gave her only blanket to a dying child. Not until spring 1839 did the last of the Indians reach Oklahoma.

Now only a few hundred Cherokees were left in the Appalachians, scattered bands of refugees hiding in caves in North Carolina. One of them was a man named Tsali, who had been wrongly accused of killing a soldier. Tsali struck a bargain with the government whereby he gave himself up in exchange for the promise that his people would be allowed to stay in the region. He was summarily executed, but the several hundred other Cherokees remained in the Appalachians where their descendants live today, keeping alive the memory of the martyred Tsali.

In the West, the Cherokee immigrants attempted to reconstruct their lives in a strange land. Animosity against the proremoval Indians who signed the treaty was so strong that their leaders—Major Ridge, John Ridge, and Elias Boudinot—were executed. But in Oklahoma, as in the Carolina mountains, the nation would survive hardships and divisions and preserve its tribal identity into the twentieth century, a goal both John Ross and Elias Boudinot had hoped to achieve.

To assess the Cherokee removal, one must confront the ugly ironies that lay at the heart of white policy. The government demanded that Indians adopt white standards of civilization; the Indians complied but then were told they must go west in order to preserve their Indian culture. The Indians lived in a nation that proudly considered itself, in Theodore Frelinghuysen's words, "freedom's hope, and her consolation," but were not even allowed the freedom to keep their own farms and remain in their own homeland.

They lived in an age that celebrated the rights and abilities of the common man, but they discovered that in Jacksonian America the common man was a white man, and greedy for Indian lands. The president said they could stay in the East if they accepted white laws, but white laws did not accept them as equals. They were told repeatedly that if they made concessions they would be guaranteed their lands forever; they made those concessions but found that "forever" meant at most a decade or a generation.

Often whites were as vehement as Indians in opposing such policies: Meigs at the Cherokee Agency, Frelinghuysen in the U.S. Senate, and Worcester on a mission station and in a Georgia prison. In addition to these and other whites who supported the Cherokee cause, many persons of Indian and white ancestry, men like John Ross and Sequoya, devoted their lives to the Cherokee Nation. All these men, as well as full-blooded leaders such as Elias Boudinot, wrestled with the complex problem of Indian and white identity. Two incidents in these years symbolize the elusiveness of the Indian's identity in Jacksonian America. In 1841 Sequoya, still seeking an ideal native society, became discontented with life in Oklahoma. Somewhere in the Far West, a legend told him, dwelled the Lost Cherokees, a precious remnant of the original tribe, living in the purity and splendor of the nation's past. At age sixty-six Sequoya set out to find that tribe somewhere in the mountains of Mexico. Sequoya's search ended a few years later with his death in the Mexican desert.

His fate finds a counterpart in the poignant effort of Christianized Indians to find consolation in the whites' deity. On June 17, 1838, ten Cherokee men and women stood in a river near Fort Butler, Georgia, with their white and their native ministers. There, in a ceremony described by witnesses as the most impressive they had ever seen, the ten were solemnly baptized. Then, under guard, they and their ministers were returned to the stockade where they were held prisoner with scores of other Cherokees, awaiting removal to Oklahoma.

Like the new immigrants of a half century later, the Cherokees wanted to preserve their ethnic identity while adjusting to white society. But for an Indian in the 1830s—and, indeed, in other periods of American history—that adjustment was made virtually impossible by the painful shifts of policy in a government that first fostered the Cherokee Renaissance and then forced the Cherokee removal.

Bibliography

Anderson, William L., Editor. *Cherokee Removal: Before and After* (1991). A collection of essays commemorating the 150th anniversary of the Trail of Tears.

Cumfer, Cynthia. *Separate Peoples, One Land: The Minds of Cherokees, Blacks, and Whites on the Tennessee Frontier* (2007). Thoughtful exploration of complex interaction between three ethnic groups.

Debo, Angie. *And Still the Waters Run* (1940). Classic account of the continuing plight of the Cherokees in Oklahoma focusing on ways they were defrauded after oil was discovered on their lands.

Gaul, Theresa Strough, Editor. *To Marry an Indian: The Marriage of Harriet Gold and Elias Boudinot in Letters, 1823–1839* (2005). The story of the marriage that led to race riots in Connecticut; Boudinot was a key opponent of the removal.

Halliburton, R., Jr. *Red Over Black: Black Slavery Among the Cherokee Indians* (1977). Describes Cherokee enslavement of African Americans.

Hudson, Charles. *The Southeastern Indians* (1977). Fine survey of the traditional cultures of the Cherokees and other southern tribes.

Mooney, James. *Myths of the Cherokees* (1900 and later editions). Based largely on oral interviews.

Moulton, Gary E. *John Ross* (1978). Biography of foremost nineteenth-century Cherokee leader.

Perdue, Theda, Editor. *Cherokee Editor: The Writings of Elias Boudinot* (1983). Fine collection of Boudinot's writings, including his antiremoval essays.

————. *Cherokee Women: Gender and Culture Change, 1700–1835* (1998). Cherokee history focusing on women as preservers of traditional culture.

Perdue, Theda, and Michael Green. *The Cherokee Nation and the Trail of Tears* (2007). Survey of Cherokee history leading up to and including the Trail of Tears

Remini, Robert V. *Andrew Jackson and His Indian Wars* (2001). Describes Jackson's relationship with Native Americans during his early years as a soldier and later as president.

Identification Topics

Winfield Scott, New Echota, Corn Ceremony, Return Jonathan Meigs, Andrew Jackson, Cherokee Renaissance, Treaty of Holston, Treaty of New Echota, Sequoya, *Cherokee Phoenix*, John Ross, *Worcester v. Georgia*, Ontasseté, "John Marshall has made his decision. Now let him enforce it"

Study Questions

1. Describe the early history and culture of the Cherokees. How did their past tie the tribe to the southern Appalachians?
2. Describe American Cherokee policies early in the nineteenth century. What were the major contradictions in American programs for the Cherokees?
3. Why did U.S. policy toward the Native Americans change from assimilation under the Treaty of Holston to forced removal under the Treaty of New Echota?
4. Why did so few Indians go to Cherokee West early in the nineteenth century? Do the Native Americans appear to have welcomed some aspects of white civilization?
5. Different white people and institutions influenced the Cherokees in different ways. Explain the role of these in Cherokee history: English traders, Return Jonathan Meigs, Christian missionaries, Andrew Jackson, Theodore Frelinghuysen, Georgia, the U.S. Supreme Court, and Winfield Scott.
6. The Cherokees could not agree among themselves on the proper course for their tribe. Describe how each of these influenced tribal history: Sequoya, John Ross, Elias Boudinot, and Tsali.
7. In his first inaugural address Andrew Jackson argued against forced removal, and yet under his administration most Cherokees were given no choice except to migrate west. Describe his initial policy and explain why it changed.
8. Describe the similarities and differences between John Ross and Elias Boudinot. Why did Boudinot first oppose, then favor removal?
9. Some Americans argued in favor of the Cherokee removal, some against. What were the major arguments on each side?

CHAPTER 10

Abolitionists and Antiabolitionists
William Lloyd Garrison and the Broadcloth Mob

During the nineteenth century, the greatest blemish on America's character as a free society was slavery, which grew ever more entrenched as cotton production expanded. Many Americans favored slavery, but abolition became a major reform impulse by 1835. In the Boston antiabolitionist riot of that year, we can see two facets of antislavery history: the ideals of a leading abolitionist and the persistent support for slavery, even in the North.

The ladies began to arrive at two o'clock on the bright autumn afternoon of October 21, 1835, for the meeting of the Boston Female Anti-Slavery Society. The building stood near the center of Boston and bore the sign "Anti-Slavery Rooms." In twos and threes the ladies ascended the stairs to the third floor, where a large barnlike hall was divided by wood partitions into a rude auditorium and a small newspaper office. As they took their seats, they could hear loud shouts in the street below, telling them that this would not be an ordinary gathering of their society.

That morning two merchants, Isaac Stevens and Isaac Means, had asked the *Boston Commercial Gazette* to print a handbill about the meeting—something to "wake up the populace," they said. The merchants had watched with approval as the editor, James L. Homer, worked "as fast as a horse can trot" to write a notice declaring that George Thompson, the British abolitionist, was in town and would deliver an address that afternoon. It was hardly a friendly announcement, for it called upon "the friends of the union" to "snake Thompson out" and offered a purse of $100 to "the individual who shall first lay violent hands on Thompson, so that he may be brought to the tar kettle before dark."

By noon Homer had printed five hundred copies of the handbill, and his apprentices ran through Boston's cobbled streets leaving the notice at hotels, reading rooms, offices, stores, and barrooms. Soon the town buzzed with the news. On Chatham Street an oil merchant read the notice and shouted for his men to get "a bucket of green tar" for use on the abolitionist. In the early afternoon hundreds of people from the shops and wharves and insurance offices strode excitedly through the streets, swelling into a crowd that choked Washington and State Streets near the antislavery headquarters.

As this hostile throng gathered in the street and jammed into the abolitionist building, a tall dark-haired man, purposeful in movement, pushed into the building and made his way upstairs to the meeting hall. Some of the intruders had gathered in a hostile knot at the rear. "That's Garrison," someone murmured.

William Lloyd Garrison walked quietly past them to the front of the room, took a seat near the ladies, then seemed to reconsider and walked back to the men who were milling noisily by the door. Affecting an air of friendly concern, he suggested that they must be confused. "This is a meeting of the Boston *Female* Anti-Slavery Society," he said. He assumed that they would not be so "indecorous" as to intrude but added disarmingly: "If, *gentlemen*, any of you are *ladies*—in disguise—why, only apprise me of the fact, give me your names, and I will introduce you to the rest of your sex, and you can take your seats among them accordingly."

Garrison was a man of such innocent and sincere expression that this outlandish proposition confused rather than enraged the intruders. For a minute they quieted down, but the tumult resumed with the arrival of more men who shouted and stamped in the hallway outside. Mounting one another's shoulders, they peered over the partition into the meeting room. They seemed uncertain what to do, and opened and slammed the door with aimless violence. The men were looking for Thompson, but he was nowhere to be seen.

The ladies were disturbed but not deterred by the noise. They would go on with their meeting even though many members, including Mrs. Garrison, would be unable to get through the crowd to the hall. Mary Parker, the society's president, called the meeting to order while the crowd was "howling with rage." She read from Scripture and offered a prayer asking for guidance, calling for the forgiveness of enemies and thanking God for preserving the members from fear. In the hall the men's rage seemed to abate as they listened to her "clear, untremulous" voice. Hearing her, Garrison was deeply moved. "It was," he said, "an awful, sublime, and soul-thrilling scene."

But on the street the mob, now increased to several thousand, shouted for the intended victim, their cry, "Thompson! Thompson!" filling the air. Boston's mayor, Theodore Lyman, came before the crowd. He told them that Thompson was not in the city and that they might as well disperse, but the crowd refused to depart. Lyman entered the abolitionist building with several constables and made his way to the upstairs meeting hall. He was no friend to abolitionism, but neither was he an advocate of violence, and he felt responsible for the safety of the women, whose best hope, he thought, lay in retreat.

He interrupted the meeting. "Ladies," he said, "do you wish to see a scene of bloodshed and confusion? If you do not, go home."

Maria Weston Chapman, the wife of an abolitionist merchant and guiding light of the ladies' society, answered: "Mr. Lyman, your personal friends are the instigators of this mob; have you ever used your personal influence with them?"

The mayor refused to acknowledge his association with the antiabolitionists. "I know no personal friends," he said, "I am merely an official. Indeed, ladies, you must retire. It is dangerous to remain."

Maria Chapman replied fervently, "If this is the last bulwark of freedom, we may as well die here as anywhere."

This prospect did not please the mayor, nor was martyrdom the immediate goal of the society, so Lyman was able to persuade Mrs. Chapman and her companions to adjourn the meeting. With his assurance that they would be escorted safely through the crowd, the women finally agreed to leave the building. Outside they were startled to see that the crowd extended far down the streets in every direction. But it was not so much the size of the throng as the familiarity of individual faces that alarmed the women. Maria Chapman records: "We saw the faces of those we had, till now, thought friends; men whom we never before met without giving the hand in friendly salutation; men whom till now we should have called upon for condemnation of ruffianism." The remarkable thing was that it was a "broadcloth" mob—named after the fashionable broadcloth coats worn by many of the "gentlemen of property and standing" who filled its turbulent ranks.

When the women realized that the hostile mob was not merely a gathering of malicious thugs but an assortment of presumably responsible citizens like themselves, they must have felt deeply apprehensive: If their proper defenders were members of the mob, who would help them? But they kept up a courageous bearing, carefully arranging themselves so that each black woman in the group was escorted by two white women, and walked through the hostile crowd to the sanctuary of Maria Chapman's house, where they continued their meeting.

In the meantime, thwarted in its attempt to capture Thompson, the mob turned to Garrison. "We must have Garrison!" they shouted as they pressed around the abolitionist headquarters. "Out with him! Lynch him!" A group of men rushed the door and were barely halted by the police. According to an observer, Samuel Sewall, their faces were "transformed with malice and passion."

The existence of such emotions in a town that characterized itself as the cradle of liberty demands an explanation. Massachusetts had been the first state to abolish slavery within its own boundaries and was the only state in which blacks enjoyed civil equality with whites. Why should it now be the scene of such hostility to abolitionism?

The answer lies in part in the state's economic history. In 1780 when slavery was ended by the Massachusetts Supreme Court, there had been relatively few blacks in the state; consequently, the cost of emancipation had been minimal. As the nineteenth century progressed, however, economic changes had made Massachusetts an active participant in the slave economy. The institution was not, of course, reestablished in the state, but with cotton production growing in the South, the prosperity of Massachusetts came to depend on the manufacture of textiles; and the mills that provided jobs and built fortunes in the North required southern cotton, a crop planted and harvested by slaves. New England manufacturers also sold goods in the South, and shippers carried cargoes between the two sections. The traders and manufacturers who dealt with the South controlled most of the large banks in the state.

Many northern businesses and their employees could thus be said to have had a stake in slavery, and their desire to protect that stake helps explain their support of human bondage. A second ingredient in their hostility to antislavery was a cultural phenomenon, a conservative mood that pervaded American society in the mid-1830s. On the one hand, the period brought change and reform, new churches and religious communities, and new ideas about disadvantaged Americans—prisoners, the insane, and women, as well as slaves. But it was also a time when many Americans cherished what they considered the traditional character of their society. In the North as in the South prejudice against blacks, slave or free, was common. Blacks were generally not allowed to vote, were required to ride in segregated railway cars, and were given the worst jobs. Few northerners were willing to risk disruption of the Union over the issue of slavery, and many took to the streets in violent defense of the traditional order. Such riots were especially frequent in 1835, and an antislavery convention was broken up in Utica, New York, on the same day as the Boston riot. The decade of the 1830s saw the mob lynching of Elijah Lovejoy, an abolitionist newspaper editor in Alton, Illinois, and the burning of an antislavery hall in Philadelphia. President Andrew Jackson characterized the abolitionists as fanatics; his postmaster, Amos Kendall, restricted their use of the mails; and after 1835 Congress adopted a "gag resolution" to table all antislavery petitions. Antiabolitionism was in fashion.

Boston had already taken a stand against the abolitionists in a meeting on August 21 attended by many of the city's leading citizens. For months southern newspapers and statesmen had been warning the North that unless the abolitionists were suppressed they would destroy the Union; the meeting, held in Faneuil Hall, was intended to demonstrate northern support for the Union and the South.

When he had learned of the planned gathering in a building that sixty years before had been the scene of Patriot gatherings, Garrison had denounced it in his newspaper, the *Liberator*. "The old cradle of liberty," he said, "it seems, is to be desecrated by a meeting of the friends of slavery and slaveholders! . . . No fiction, no sophistry, can hide the fact from the intelligence of an impartial posterity, that the contemplated meeting is a meeting to take sides with the *slaveholder*, and against his *victim*!"

Despite Garrison's protest, the meeting had been well attended. Mayor Theodore Lyman served as chairman and, with other speakers, used the occasion to chastise the abolitionists and praise the Union. The most vehement speaker, Peleg Sprague, a former U.S. senator, gestured toward a portrait of George Washington, a slaveholder who had helped Massachusetts win her freedom from Britain.

Southern newspapers reported the meeting with great satisfaction, the *Richmond Whig* declaring: "The people of the North *must* go to *hanging* these fanatical wretches, if they would not lose the benefit of Southern trade; and they *will* do it. They know too well which side their bread is buttered on." Events would soon bear out this prophecy.

On October 21, as the broadcloth mob gathered around the antislavery building, the citizens of Boston were about to accomplish by force what they had advocated by words two months before at Faneuil Hall. They would crush the reformers who threatened the Union, their traditions, and their trade. The first victim of their animosity was a symbol rather than a man, the sign reading "Anti-Slavery Rooms." Several men reached out through windows and detached the sign from its hooks, causing it to fall to the ground.

Mayor Lyman later declared that he had ordered the sign's removal. He feared that it would be pelted with rocks, which then might injure the observers, and he hoped the sign's removal would satisfy the crowd. Garrison, however, claimed that the mayor inadvertently encouraged the mob by condoning this "outrage upon private property." At any rate, the rioters quickly broke up the sign and snatched up pieces as souvenirs. One long fragment, measuring six feet by three inches, was carried to the *Commercial Gazette* office where James Homer, who had printed the announcement that instigated the riot, later cut it up and distributed it among friends as a memento of the antiabolitionist battle for stability and the Union.

While the world outside was in turmoil, Garrison was closeted with several friends in the abolitionist offices. Little in his appearance suggested that this man could have won the opprobrium of so many of his fellow citizens. Slightly under six feet tall, he had an erect bearing and a contemplative appearance: a receding hairline, a long, pensive forehead, heavy brows, and alert, quizzical eyes. He wore wire-frame glasses, stern black clothes and, on his face, an expression of calm rectitude.

Contemporaries and historians a century later castigated him as a narrow-minded fanatic, incapable of compromise, humorless, obsessed. His unrelenting hatred of slavery encouraged such characterizations, but he was also a warm human being, a devoted husband, and a propagandist who genuinely cared about the slaves. The English traveler, Harriet Martineau, described his face as "wholly expressive of purity, animation, and gentleness."

His brief lifetime—he was not yet thirty years old—had prepared him well for the martyr's role he seemed about to assume. William Lloyd Garrison was born in Newburyport, Massachusetts, in 1805. His father, an erratic and intemperate sea captain, deserted his family before the boy was three. He was raised by his hardworking mother, Frances Maria Lloyd Garrison, who, he declared, "loved me so intensely that no language can describe the yearning of her soul." Husbandless, diligent, and devoted, she served her son as a model of self-sacrifice.

William received little formal education, and in 1818 he was apprenticed for seven years to the editor of the *Newburyport Herald*. Like Benjamin Franklin, who had begun his career in a similar position a century before, Garrison practiced writing by composing anonymous pieces for the paper. When he was nineteen he became editor of the *Newburyport Free Press*; then worked as a printer in Boston; and in 1828 became coeditor of the *National Philanthropist*, a reform paper. In its pages he attacked a broad spectrum of social evils, including intemperance, war, gambling, and Sabbath breaking.

While in Boston he met Benjamin Lundy, who is credited with having turned his attention to antislavery. Lundy was a Quaker, whose humble existence showed Garrison that social reform was hardly a profitable enterprise: he walked from town to town and printed his small newspaper, *Genius of Universal Emancipation*, in any available printing office. Lundy's infectious dedication easily attracted Garrison.

Under Lundy's influence Garrison delivered his first antislavery lecture at Park Street Church on Boston Common in 1829, and that summer he visited Baltimore to help Lundy edit the *Genius*. His visit to Maryland convinced him that he should exercise his influence in New England, where he "found contempt more bitter, opposition more active, detraction more relentless, prejudice more stubborn, and apathy more frozen, than among slave-owners themselves." He founded a new paper, the *Liberator*, in Boston "within sight of Bunker Hill." The first issue, January 1, 1831, contained a ringing declaration of principles. Garrison had once approved of gradual emancipation but now demanded an immediate change. "I seize this opportunity," he said, "to make a full and unequivocal recantation, and thus publicly to ask pardon of my God, of my country, and of my brethren the poor slaves, for having uttered a sentiment so full of timidity, injustice, and absurdity."

Reporting that he had already been criticized for vehemence, he justified his radical abolitionism. "Is there not cause for severity?" he said. "On this subject, I do not wish to think, or speak, or write with moderation. No! No! Tell a man whose house is on fire to give a moderate alarm; tell him to moderately rescue his wife from the hands of the ravisher; tell the mother to gradually extricate her babe from the fire into which it has fallen;—but urge me not to use moderation in a cause like the present." He continued with a resounding phrase: "I am in earnest—I will not equivocate—I will not excuse—I will not retreat a single inch—AND I WILL BE HEARD."

In his blunt assertion that slavery must be ended without delay, Garrison took issue with northern gradualists as well as southern slaveholders. The movement against American slavery was already more than a century old in 1831, but its dominant tone early in the nineteenth century was moderate and conciliatory. During the Revolution slavery had been abolished in the northern states, and even in the South the Revolution's emphasis on freedom had borne fruit. Washington, Jefferson, and other Patriots regretted its existence, and the southern states passed laws legalizing manumission—the voluntary freeing of slaves by their master—thereby facilitating gradual emancipation.

In the nineteenth century the new cotton gin had increased the importance of slavery by making black production more profitable, but as late as 1827 more than half of the country's many abolitionist societies were in the South. Most antislavery organizations favored gradual emancipation, compensation for the slaveholders, and the return of free blacks to Africa. Within a few years, however, abolitionism in the North became more strident, and antislavery sentiment in the South all but vanished.

A single event, Nat Turner's Revolt, ended the southern antislavery movement. In that Virginia slave rebellion of 1831, fifty-seven whites lost their lives. The revolt was easily crushed, but the fear that had always been present was heightened and spread throughout the South. What had happened in Virginia could happen elsewhere; anyone who suggested that slavery was evil might well cause the next conflagration. In this spirit of dread, slavery proponents sought to drive the abolitionists from the South, prevented antislavery literature from entering the region, and posted rewards for the capture or execution of northern abolitionists such as Garrison. By 1837 there were no longer any abolitionist societies in the southern states.

This tough southern attitude led some northern abolitionists to become more strident in their hostility to the institution. Garrison was such a leader: he was not interested in preserving either the Union or the sensibilities of the slaveholder. The house was on fire, he said, and this was no time for moderation.

Garrison published his views in the *Liberator* and joined with others to form new societies dedicated to the immediate eradication of slavery. In 1831 he helped form the New England Anti-Slavery Society and in 1833 joined in creating a national organization, the American Anti-Slavery Association. These bodies cooperated with scores of local groups such as the Boston Female Anti-Slavery Society and the Massachusetts Anti-Slavery Society. The abolitionists believed that history was on their side when in 1833 they learned that in England, Parliament had abolished slavery in the British West Indies. The man primarily responsible for that act was George Thompson, who spent 1835 touring the United States and was the object of the crowd's attention in Boston.

Garrison's vociferous opposition to slavery and his stinging denunciation of moderation left him a natural target that October afternoon when the broadcloth mob could not locate Thompson. In a sense, his whole abolitionist career had led him to this moment, and he appears to have positively delighted in the attention of the mob. However, Garrison's abolitionist friends counseled him that discretion was wiser than vain heroics. With the mob howling in the hallway and the street outside, Garrison decided to depart through the back window, not an easy task for a man more adept at propaganda than gymnastics. When Garrison jumped from the third-story window onto a shed roof below, he landed hard and nearly pitched forward off the roof onto his head. But, catching himself, he found his way into a carpenter's shop behind the abolitionist headquarters. The owners obligingly hid him in an upstairs room while one of the local sheriffs pretended to search the building and then told the mob Garrison had escaped.

Unfortunately, some of the crowd had seen Garrison disappear into the shop. They searched and found the abolitionist hiding beneath a pile of boards. Accounts vary about how Garrison behaved when discovered. One newspaper claimed that he fell to his knees and begged for mercy. But Garrison claimed that he preserved his composure while the men shook him and tore at his clothes. "It is needless to make such extra efforts of violence," he recalled saying, "I shall go down to the mob unresistingly." His words may not have been so deliberate, but others later testified that he was calm. And this was, after all, his great moment.

His captors took Garrison to the window. Several wanted to hurl him to the ground, but another exclaimed, "Don't let's kill him outright!" This view prevailed. A ladder was raised to the window, and after bowing awkwardly to the crowd, Garrison descended with a rope coiled around his waist. He was now in the midst of a mob pressing in from every side, "as if eager to devour him," according to one abolitionist.

It was not yet clear what would occur next. Some rioters hoped to tar and feather the abolitionist and dye his face and hands black with indelible ink; others wanted to hang him or to club him to death. Suddenly a man tried to strike Garrison with a club, and two others defended him. The protectors were Aaron and Daniel Cooley, brothers who ran a transportation firm and were known for their antiabolitionist sentiments. For unknown reasons they grabbed Garrison by the shoulders and hustled him through the crowd, crying "He shan't be hurt! You shan't hurt him! He's an American!" It was a curious cry, but others in the street took it up. Apparently Garrison had one asset in the eyes of the mob that the Britisher George Thompson lacked. He might be a radical, but at least he was not a foreign radical. In 1835 that mattered. The Cooley brothers' muscles and rhetoric combined to soften the crowd around Garrison, and they were able to carry him toward the city hall, although the throng still pressed around.

Garrison had found temporary safety, but by now the center of Boston was in a state of total confusion. A few men, motivated by a sense of fair play rather than by any love of abolitionism, were attempting to save Garrison. A much larger group surged through the streets calling for his punishment. To onlookers, it was not clear who was in control.

Mayor Lyman had been at the front of the abolitionist building when Garrison was detected. As the men surged away from the building after Garrison, Lyman hurried toward city hall. Along the way a dozen people urged him to save Garrison. "They're going to hang him," said one, "for God's sake, save him!" As the mayor approached Garrison, he could hear people shouting, "To the frog pond with him!" Here was another possible punishment—a brutal dunking on Boston Common.

Garrison allowed himself to be carried along by the crowd. In the scuffle his hat and coat were lost, and his pants were ripped. Having removed his spectacles to protect them, he was nearly blind, yet maintained his composure. Charles Sprague, a banker and a poet, watched Garrison pass down Wilson's Lane. "I saw an exasperated mob dragging a man along without his hat and with a rope about him," he said. "The man walked with head erect, calm countenance, flashing eyes, like a martyr going to the stake, full of faith and manly hope."

As the crowd turned down State Street toward city hall, Henry Ingersoll Bowditch, a prominent physician, watched with a sense of outrage. He urged an acquaintance to help him oppose the rioters and was further incensed when the man refused, saying the authorities were on the side of the mob. "I was completely disgusted," Bowditch later wrote, "and I vowed in my heart as I left him with utter loathing, 'I am an abolitionist from this very moment.'"

Finally the crowd approached city hall and stood on the pavement where the Boston Massacre occurred sixty-five years before. Garrison saw the irony in his being made an object of "derision and scorn" on this "consecrated spot." As the Cooleys rushed him to the south door of city hall, the mayor arrived with supporters who covered Garrison's retreat into the building.

But Garrison was still not safe. The mob crushed around the building and poured into the north entrance. While Garrison was taken upstairs to the mayor's and aldermen's headquarters, Theodore Lyman addressed the crowd in the hall, saying that if necessary he would die to maintain law and order. Standing on a balcony over the south door, he repeated his speech to the swell of angry people outside. They listened but did not disperse. In the mayor's office a coterie of city officials considered what to do and decided that Garrison would be better off in the Leverett Street Jail. Garrison later claimed that the mayor was more interested in safeguarding the building than in protecting its inmate, but he agreed to go along with the plan on the understanding that he would not have to pay for his stay in jail.

Sheriff Parkman wrote out a writ for Garrison's arrest on the basis that he had disturbed the peace, perhaps to justify imprisoning him. When Garrison later learned that he, the victim of rioters, had been charged with instigating their actions, he was outraged. Nonetheless, the writ reflected public thinking about the abolitionists: their inflammatory rhetoric had created an atmosphere conducive to mob violence. Lyman may have approved of the writ of arrest on the theory that it would serve him well politically.

Now began a journey that Garrison himself described as "incredibly perilous." Because the crowd was still howling outside, the mayor created a diversion by sending a coach and guards to the south entrance while he took Garrison out the north. But he was seen, and Garrison had barely entered the carriage before it was surrounded by a crowd that reminded him of "the ocean, lashed into fury by the spirit of the storm."

Some pulled at the doors and wheels trying to get at him, and others placed a rope around the coach to tip it over. In the midst of this fray Garrison told an incredulous city official that he could win the crowd over if he could have just five minutes to speak to them. No one seemed eager to test his theory. Just as the coach was about to be pushed over, the driver lashed the horses and drew away. Rioters raced after the coach and clung to its sides while policemen pushed at them and the driver ran close to parked carriages to brush them away.

At Leverett Street Jail, police officers forced their way through a small group and escorted the prisoner to safety. Inside they locked him in a cell—"safe," as he said, "from my persecutors, accompanied by two delightful associates, a good conscience and a cheerful mind." During the evening, he had several visitors, including Isaac Knapp, publisher of the *Liberator*; Amos Bronson Alcott, essayist and educator; and John Greenleaf Whittier, poet. Whittier, one of the abolitionist's oldest friends, had published his first poems a decade before in Garrison's *Newburyport Free Press*. Whittier especially sympathized with his friend, having himself been the victim of an antiabolitionist attack a few weeks before when he had attempted to speak in Concord, New Hampshire, with George Thompson. Garrison seemed in good spirits and jokingly regretted that his cell was too small to accommodate his friends for the night. Although the abolitionists were greatly outnumbered in Boston in 1835, there were enough of them at least to enjoy a sense of shared participation in a great cause. After his friends left, Garrison fell quickly asleep in his small cell.

The next morning he ate "an excellent breakfast" and sought to immortalize his stay in the Leverett Street Jail with an inscription on the wall. It began: "William Lloyd Garrison was put into this cell on Wednesday afternoon, October 21, 1835, to save him from the violence of a 'respectable and influential mob,' who sought to destroy him for preaching the abominable and dangerous doctrine, that 'all men are created equal,' and that all oppression is odious in the sight of God."

That afternoon Garrison received a judicial hearing, conducted in the jail to ensure his protection. His indictment read: he "did disturb and break the peace of the Commonwealth, and a riot did cause and make, to the terror of the good people of the Commonwealth." The city did not press charges but required Garrison to leave Boston for a time to calm the public. Garrison agreed to do so, and that afternoon he was secretly conducted to the town of Canton, where with his wife, Helen, he boarded a train for Providence, Rhode Island. So ended Boston's great antiabolitionist riot.

Although the affair lasted only a few hours and caused little damage, it precipitated a debate in the New England press that has continued, in a fashion, to this day. The problem is that of fully understanding the character and motivation of each side in the conflict. As we have seen, the antiabolitionists were moved by economic self-interest—a knowledge of "which side their bread is buttered on" in the cynical phrase of the *Richmond Whig*—and by hostility to social change.

Like the previous meeting at Faneuil Hall, the Garrison riot testified to Boston's support of the Union and stability. The mob was composed mostly of merchants, bankers, shipowners, and their employees. Maria Chapman might be disturbed that many "gentlemen" were in the crowd, but so many members of Boston's ruling classes participated that no one had to apologize. Common wisdom in downtown Boston held that it was the right thing to do. Such was the view of the press, the business community, and many public officials.

Yet there was no unanimity of purpose among the antiabolitionists. They had varied in their opinions about how Garrison should be punished—some wanting him killed, others happy enough to tear down the abolitionist sign and give Garrison a scare. The Cooley brothers, who carried Garrison to city hall, had been antiabolitionists but risked their own skins to save Garrison. There were even some who were so shocked by the riot that they came to sympathize with abolitionism.

The position of Mayor Theodore Lyman during the riot is especially interesting. Lyman, we should recall, was an ardent antiabolitionist and had chaired the antiabolitionist meeting at Faneuil Hall. He refused to disperse the crowd or to press charges against individual rioters after the mob violence, even though he recognized many of the participants. But he neither encouraged the rioters nor watched idly as they did their work. He intervened personally to calm the multitude and protect Garrison, urging the abolitionist women to seek safety and encouraging Garrison to escape through a rear window in the antislavery building. He stood by Garrison on the steps of city hall and called upon the rioters to disperse. Having devised the plan to carry Garrison to Leverett Street Jail, he accompanied him to the coach in which he made the journey. In spite of Lyman's opposition to the abolitionist movement and his fear of offending the voters, he extended himself considerably for Garrison.

Clearly, opposition to abolition included many level-headed individuals. They believed that the antislavery movement was impractical, and they favored maintaining the social order. Some may have acted like thugs on the afternoon of October 21, 1835. But others with cooler heads—Mayor Lyman and the Cooley brothers among them— prevented William Lloyd Garrison from suffering great harm. What of Garrison's part in the day's events and his character as a political activist? When he reviewed the riot, Garrison was especially critical of the mayor for having allowed the destruction of the antislavery sign and for not using force against the rioters or pressing charges against those he recognized. Garrison was at his most ungenerous and dogmatic when he criticized Lyman, for his judgment focused on all the mayor's faults without recognizing his efforts on Garrison's behalf.

In such episodes Garrison appears fanatical and narrow. Further evidence for such a view might be taken from Garrison's behavior during the riot. If there ever was a man who appeared to welcome martyrdom, it was Garrison that day. Many observers mentioned his calm, saintly composure. Soon after the affair he wrote his brother-in-law and fellow abolitionist George W. Benson, "imminent as I felt the peril to be, my mind was placid and undisturbed throughout the trying scene; . . . I reposed as calmly in my prison-cell as if no uproar had happened." In his personal account of the riot he said, "I felt perfectly calm, nay, very happy."

Garrison took pleasure in the thought of persecution and remarked that other abolitionists felt the same. A month before the Boston uproar, his friend, Samuel May, had been mobbed in Haverhill, Massachusetts. May's letter describing the event was so buoyant that Garrison told a friend, "By the tone of it you would suppose he had done something better than making a fortune." Garrison said of Whittier's experience in New Hampshire: "His soul, being intangible, laughed at the salutation." Less than a month before the tumult in Boston, Garrison had learned that a price had been placed on his head in the South. Reporting the news to a friend, he said, "My mind is full of peace—I know what it is to rejoice in tribulation."

All this evidence suggests that two of the most serious charges against the abolitionists may be true: that they were psychologically disturbed fanatics, less interested in the well being of the slaves than in their own righteousness; and that they helped cause the Civil War by inflaming the public mind. According to these arguments the abolitionists were not involved in antislavery because they knew that slavery was wrong, but rather they cared about the slaves because, being misfits and malcontents, the abolitionists could not adjust to white society.

William Lloyd Garrison's character, however, belies the notion that the radical reformer was driven by a maladjusted personality. His own behavior during the days after the broadcloth riot demonstrates the stability of his personality and suggests the source of his abolitionism. After the events of October 21 he left Boston and traveled with his wife to Brooklyn, Connecticut, to stay with her father. Garrison's relationship with his wife furnishes clues to his character. Helen Benson Garrison was the daughter of George Benson, a retired merchant from Providence, Rhode Island, and an early opponent of slavery. Most of Benson's six sons and two daughters were ardent supporters of the antislavery movement. But Garrison claimed that he was attracted to Helen for familial rather than civic reasons. In 1835, on their first anniversary, he wrote her brother George: "I did not marry her expecting that she would assume a prominent station in the antislavery cause, but for domestic quietude and happiness." He continued: she "enables me to find exquisite delight in the family circle, as an offset to public adversity." Although he was a lion in public disputation, he claimed that in Helen's presence he was "as timid and gentle and submissive as a dove." Thus, recognizing his own tendency to become obsessed with the slavery issue, he counted on Helen to provide a humane ballast to the vessel of his ideals.

His experience in marriage intensified his loathing of slavery. On September 4, 1835, he wrote to his brother-in-law, George Benson, telling him how much he rejoiced

Helen Benson Garrison. Born into a family of abolitionists, she married a leader in the fight against slavery.

in his relationship with Helen. His pleasure in their attachment led him to contrast his own fortune with that of the slaves. "What faithful husband," he asked, "can think, for one moment, of having the object of his love torn from his arms by the might of oppression, and not feel indignation and horror swelling like a swift inundation in his bosom? What affectionate wife can imagine the sale of her beloved partner at auction, as a beast is sold, without shuddering as if smitten by the icy hand of death?... In this mirror, my dear George, how is the terrific image of the monster Slavery reflected! Should we not hate him with a perfect hatred?! Can we be too earnest for his destruction?"

Garrison's love for Helen may also have contributed to his self-awareness and given him a perspective on himself, a sense of humor, and a willingness to bend with the wind when necessary. When attacks on antislavery became common in the late summer of 1835, Garrison wrote a friend that the violence worried Helen. He suggested that while the atmosphere was heated, the abolitionists should be moderate and limit their discussions to ending slavery in the District of Columbia. But he was not personally bothered by threats. When he learned in September that a gallows had been placed in his front yard with an inscription from "Judge Lynch," he was unworried and simply asked his friends to try to secure it for the abolitionist museum.

William Lloyd Garrison was able to balance his antislavery with a sense of timing. He did not take the mobs too seriously; he could regard the mock gallows as a fine museum artifact and glory in the attention. But his opponents did force him to exercise discretion. He was a husband now and would soon be a father. It was decided that Helen should stay with her family in Brooklyn, Connecticut, while he returned to Boston to remove their furniture.

Garrison arrived back in Boston about three weeks after the riot that had forced him to leave. He rode north from Providence, Rhode Island, in an open railway car, exposed to wind and soot in order to save fifty cents—"no trifling sum" he wrote his wife, "in these days of penury and persecution." At the station he took a coach to a friend's house where he had supper. Then Joseph Tillson, a young helper in the antislavery office, guided him to the home of Joseph Southwick, president of the Massachusetts Anti-Slavery Society. There Garrison was delighted to find another refugee, his friend George Thompson, whose presence in Boston was a well-kept secret.

In a few minutes an abolitionist reunion was in progress. Garrison's brother-in-law, Henry Benson, arrived. Then came Mary Parker, the woman whose "clear, untremulous" voice had so moved Garrison on the day of the riot. She brought with her two antislavery friends, Anna Grew and Catherine Sullivan. Garrison found his reception "so kind and sympathetic and joyful, that one might almost covet to be mobbed, to obtain such a return." As his friends were talking, Garrison excused himself for a few minutes to go upstairs and write his wife a letter for the evening mail. Hearing his boisterous friends in the room below, he wrote, "What a collection of raving fanatics and dangerous incendiaries! A happy meeting this!"

Later that evening Garrison went to his own house with several friends. In another letter to Helen he described the return to "the house that we fondly expected to call our home, in which we have spent so many happy hours, but which can be our home no longer." He had married Helen to create with her a domestic shelter from the turmoil of his work. The house embodied that ideal of repose. Everything, he said, "seems dearer to me than ever." The carpets, tables, chairs, looking glasses—all seemed "almost to have found a tongue, to welcome my return, and to congratulate me upon my escape out of the jaws of the lion." He continued, "The clock ticks an emphatical and sonorous welcome. As for puss, she finds it a difficult matter, even with all her purring and playing, to express her joy."

The return to the house at 23 Brighton Street in Boston was one of the most poignant and serene evenings in Garrison's life. Here was fulfillment in the midst of privation—the warmth of friendship to balance the fury of the mob and the comfort of domestic bliss transcending the knowledge of imminent removal. That night Garrison slept with deep satisfaction. "As you were absent," he wrote Helen, "I permitted puss to occupy the *outside* of the bed, as a substitute. We reposed very lovingly until morning, without any alarm from mobs without, or disturbance from rats within."

Garrison was cautious during the next few days, not wishing by his presence to become the object of another riot. At his first visit to the antislavery office he saw evidence of the city's continuing animosity to abolitionism. He heard a noise outside, and from a window he watched a procession moving through the street behind a band. The marchers carried a large board with drawings of George Thompson and a black woman. Above Thompson's head were the words, "The Foreign Emissary." The black woman was saying, "When are we going to have another meeting, brother Thompson?" Unaware that Garrison was in the building, the marchers continued on through the city streets, giddy with pleasure at their infantile joke.

The opponents of abolition were still active, it was clear, but the riot had created a backlash of sympathy for abolitionism. Garrison received an anonymous contribution of $45, new subscribers ordered the *Liberator*, and his name was placed in nomination for the state legislature. He belittled the danger of life in Boston, writing facetiously in one letter that his cat was outside and might have "fallen into the hands of Judge Lynch."

But Boston was no place for his pregnant wife, and wanting to be near her, he made arrangements with friends to run the *Liberator* in his absence, packed his and Helen's belongings, and boarded a train for Brooklyn. On the train he sat near two ladies, "one a fat dowager-looking female—the other younger and less corpulent—probably mother and daughter." In Canton a gentleman jokingly expressed his surprise that these ladies should be on the train rather than attending a local ladies antislavery meeting, then in progress.

"Oh," they said quite emphatically, "we are not antislavery."

They spoke as if they were testifying to something more than their view on the great social question of the day. They were testifying to their own character, indicating that they were stable, sensible, and respectable—as if no one of any consequence could possibly be an abolitionist.

The loud rattling of the cars and Garrison's sense of propriety kept him from joining the conversation, but he wanted to draw out the implication of their remarks and say to them: "What! Not antislavery? Do you mean to say that you are in favor of slavery? Or what do you mean? If you are not antislavery, then you are for concubinage, pollution, robbery, cruelty; then you are for making merchandise of God's image, for setting aside the forms and obligations of marriage, for darkening the human intellect, and debasing the soul." He was pleased that a few miles away in Canton, Massachusetts, there were other women, "high-souled, intellectual, courageous, devout females," who were at that moment meeting to express their hostility to slavery.

Garrison arrived back in Brooklyn at the end of November. His first son, named George Thompson Garrison, was born in February. The family spent most of 1836 in Brooklyn where Garrison wrote frequently for the *Liberator* while leaving its publication to friends in Boston. In September 1836 it appeared safe to return to the city, and the family reestablished themselves in New England's largest metropolis.

In the ensuing years Garrison continued to be the most outspoken figure in the abolitionist movement, advocating not only an end to slavery but also civil rights for blacks and full participation by women in the abolitionist movement. Whereas more conservative abolitionists objected to allowing women like Angelina and Sarah Grimké to address their meetings, Garrison encouraged their participation. In 1840 he refused to take part in the World Anti-Slavery Convention in London because women were not allowed to attend.

His views on politics were even more controversial than his support for women. He believed that political action led to corruption and, consequently, voted only once in his life. The Union itself was sinful, he reasoned, because it allowed slavery to exist. In a dramatic gesture of hostility to the federal government he once burned a copy of the Constitution.

Many abolitionists refused to accept Garrison's views on women and the Union, and when his supporters gained control of the American Anti-Slavery Society in 1840, many withdrew under the leadership of Arthur Tappan and formed the more conservative American and Foreign Anti-Slavery Society. Such divisions were disturbing, but Garrison could take consolation in the fact that the abolitionist movement continued to gain support. In the 1850s, after enactment of the Fugitive Slave Law (1850), which provided for the return of escaped slaves to the South, Boston—the town that had rioted against Garrison two decades before—was the scene of riots in support of runaway slaves.

It was Garrison's good fortune to live to see the fruition of his agitation in the Emancipation Proclamation in 1863. At the end of the Civil War he was one of a group of honored guests at Fort Sumter, South Carolina, at the raising of the American flag. Time had not diminished the vehemence of his rhetoric, nor did the charm of the scene soothe his temper. "I hate slavery as I hate nothing else in the world," he said. "It is not only a crime, but the sum of all criminality."

Bibliography

Dixon, Chris. *Perfecting the Family: Antislavery Marriages in Nineteenth-Century America* (1997). Focuses on eight abolitionist couples, including the Garrisons and the Stantons, and explores the relationship between their abolitionism and their marriages.

Harrold, Stanley. *The Abolitionists and the South, 1831–1861* (1995). An account of the least known, and arguably the most courageous, of the abolitionists.

———. *The Rise of Aggressive Abolitionism: Addresses to the Slaves* (2004). Argues that by the early 1840s, abolitionists, including William Lloyd Garrison, were advocating slave rebellion.

Jeferey, Julie Roy. *The Great Silent Army of Abolitionism: Ordinary Women in the Antislavery Movement* (1998). Explores ways that ordinary women, many living in small towns and on farms, took part in the abolitionist movement.

Kraditor, Aileen S. *Means and Ends in American Abolitionism* (1968). Sympathetic assessment of supposed fanaticism of Garrison and other radical abolitionists.

Mayer, Henry. *All on Fire: William Lloyd Garrison and the Abolition of Slavery* (1998). Evocative account of Garrison's passion for reform by a writer who was a devoted activist during the 1960s.

Mccarthy, Timothy Patrick, and John Stauffer, Editors. *The Prophets of Protest: Reconsidering the History of American Abolitionism* (2006). A collection of essays demonstrating the wide-ranging backgrounds of the abolitionists.

Merrill, Walter M., and Louis Ruchames, Editors. *The Letters of William Lloyd Garrison* (1971–1981). Well-edited multi-volume collection with many rich and informative letters.

Richards, Leonard L. *"Gentlemen of Property and Standing": Anti-Abolitionist Mobs in Jacksonian America* (1970). Description and analysis of northern hostility to abolitionists.

Thomas, John L. *The Liberator* (1963). Prize-winning biography of Garrison.

Walters, Ronald G. *The Antislavery Appeal* (1976). Discusses the character of the abolitionist supporters.

Identification Topics

Boston Female Anti-Slavery Society, William Lloyd Garrison, Mary Parker, Theodore Lyman, Faneuil Hall, gradual emancipation, abolitionists, Benjamin Lundy, the *Liberator*, Nat Turner's Revolt, American Anti-Slavery Society, Helen Benson Garrison, Fugitive Slave Law, "I will be heard"

Study Questions

1. Who were the antiabolitionist rioters? Describe their social background and reasons for supporting slavery.
2. William Lloyd Garrison has sometimes been regarded as a fanatic. What evidence in this chapter supports and what evidence contradicts that accusation?
3. Describe the role of Boston mayor Theodore Lyman in the broadcloth riot. Should he have done more to protect William Lloyd Garrison? Or did he do all that he could in view of the fact that many of the city's leaders were in the mob?
4. What part did women play in the abolitionist movement, and what special difficulties did they encounter?
5. Garrison favored active women's participation in the abolitionist movement but married a woman who would stay at home and tend the family. Is this a contradiction? Did he fail to apply his principles to his own life?
6. Were abolitionist spokesmen too strident and inflammatory, or did they make an appropriate response to an unjust institution?
7. Discuss William Lloyd Garrison's motivation in devoting his life to abolitionism.

CHAPTER 11

The Texas Revolution
Lorenzo de Zavala and Sam Houston

The American frontier, with its promise of inexpensive land and the opportunity to get ahead, attracted thousands of settlers during the early nineteenth century. Although initially a Mexican state, Texas became a favorite destination of many of these settlers, including Sam Houston. In 1835 Texans would revolt against Mexican rule and establish a separate country, modeled on the United States. The revolt was in some respects a movement of Americans intent on wresting Texas from Mexico and turning it over to the United States. But the Texas Revolution also had roots deep in Mexican history, and one of its leaders, Lorenzo de Zavala had been one of the foremost reformers in Mexico itself during that country's early years of independence. The careers of Lorenzo de Zavala and Sam Houston epitomize the blending of American and Mexican sources in the history of revolutionary Texas.

On March 1, 1836, a force of 187 rebels was barricaded behind the walls of the Alamo, a former mission in San Antonio, Texas. They flew a flag bearing the numbers 1824, commemorating the date of constitution of recently independent Mexico. In the surrounding countryside, an army of four thousand federal soldiers led by General Santa Anna, the dictator of Mexico, prepared to attack the garrison. As the two sides squared off, other men were assembled a few miles away in a small Texas town called Washington-on-the-Brazos, drafting a declaration of independence and a constitution for Texas—a republic whose existence would depend on defeating Santa Anna.

On one level, the Texas Revolution pitted newly arrived Americans against native Mexicans. But among the men who sought an independent Texas were many Mexicans, and their reasons for seeking independence from Mexico included roots in Mexican values and traditions. One of the leaders in the convention at Washington-on-the-Brazos was a man named Lorenzo de Zavala, who had been raised in the

Merida on the Yucatán Peninsula. Another important leader of the Revolution came from entirely different roots: Sam Houston was born in Virginia and raised in frontier Tennessee. These two men grew up in different worlds, and yet in the movement for Texas independence from Mexico, and in this initial American expansion into the Southwest, their similarities were more apparent than their differences.

Mérida, the capital city of Yucatán, is in the heart of the Mexican region where Mayan culture flowered long before the arrival of the first Europeans. In 1542 Spanish conquerors tore down the buildings of an ancient Mayan town and used the rubble to lay the foundations for the town of Mérida. Soon afterward they began work on a huge cathedral, completed in 1598. Almost two centuries later a Mexican couple of Spanish and Indian descent brought their infant son, Lorenzo de Zavala, to be baptized in the cathedral. The boy had been born a month before on October 3, 1788, the year in which a new constitution was ratified in the United States. At that time Mexico was still a colony of Spain. As an adult Zavala would take part in two revolutions and help draft two constitutions, one for Mexico and one for Texas.

During his youth Zavala's parents hoped that Lorenzo, the fifth of their nine children, would become a priest, and accordingly he attended seminary until he was nineteen. But he disliked the rigid curriculum and favored books and ideas not approved by the church. When he was twenty, Zavala married Teresa Josefa Correa, the thirteen-year-old daughter of his godparents. A year later she bore him a daughter, María Manuela, and four years later a son, Manuel Lorenzo Jr.

In 1810 when Lorenzo de Zavala was learning to be a husband and father in Mérida, Father Miguel Hidalgo, a Mexican priest in the village of Dolores near Mexico City, was beginning the movement that would lead eventually to Mexican independence. Inspired by his leadership, thousands of peasants, mainly Indians, rose in revolt. Hidalgo's revolutionary career was short: he was captured and executed less than a year after his revolt began. But other Mexicans kept alive the possibility of revolution.

In Mérida Zavala joined with other reform-minded citizens to discuss the works of Rousseau, Voltaire, and Locke—philosophers whose writings had also inspired Thomas Jefferson and other leaders of the American Revolution. Known as the *Sanjuanistas*, these men brought a printing press to Mérida in 1813, and Zavala became editor of a succession of reform publications, advocating help for the Indians and political and religious reform. The Sanjuanistas founded their own college, taught constitutional law, and fought against church taxes. Their activities were made possible in part by events in Spain, where a liberal government briefly replaced traditional conservative rule. But in 1814 absolute monarchy was restored to Spain, and the effects reached from Madrid to Mérida.

On the night of July 26, 1814, Lorenzo de Zavala was arrested at his home and threatened with a firing squad. But he was sent instead to the prison of San Juan Ulúa in the harbor at Vera Cruz. This prison was one of the most notorious in all of Mexico. The prison contributed, however, to Zavala's growth and education. There he learned English, read medical texts, and was introduced to Freemasonry, a society dedicated to fellowship, religious toleration, and political reform. In the United States many founding fathers had been Freemasons. Released from prison in 1817, Zavala returned to Mérida with a new dedication to reform.

In 1820 he was elected as a representative from Yucatán to serve in the *Cortes*, the Spanish parliament. But while he was abroad, Mexico declared its independence.

Zavala returned to Mérida and was elected in 1822 to serve in a provisional congress in Mexico City, whose work would be to draft a constitution. Mexico City fell into turmoil soon after Zavala arrived: a mob ran through the streets demanding that the leader of the army, Agustín de Iturbide, be made emperor of Mexico. Iturbide assumed power and immediately arrested fifteen members of the congress for opposing his rule. Despite the danger of arrest, Zavala refused to trade Mexican tyranny for Spanish tyranny. He denounced Iturbide and called for a government of checks and balances modeled on the U.S. Constitution.

Fortunately for Zavala others joined in opposition to the empire. In 1823 Iturbide abdicated and left the country. A new congress was elected, with Lorenzo de Zavala again as a member. Soon a new constitution was drafted with Zavala as one of its chief architects. One faction, centralists, favored a strong central power and the other, federalists, preferred to leave significant power in the states. Zavala was a leader of the federalists; they prevailed and created a three-branch government with a chief executive elected to a four-year term of office. The new constitution was adopted in 1824.

Eager for an administrative role in the new republic, Lorenzo de Zavala moved to the state of Mexico, the region surrounding the capital city, and in 1827 he was elected governor. In this role he worked on improving roads, schools, and libraries. He also set out to provide land for the Indians, taxing absentee landlords to raise the necessary funds. Because of his liberal programs, Lorenzo de Zavala has been referred to as a reformer "with a revolutionary fervor and an insight into political realities which have rarely been surpassed in the history of his country."

But events cut short Zavala's reform career. The second presidential election under the new Mexican constitution involved fraudulent ballot-counting. Zavala was one of the chief critics of the results. Another opponent was a general based in Vera Cruz named Antonió Lopez de Santa Anna. Once again Zavala's principles brought him danger, and in order to avoid arrest, he fled from his governor's mansion into the hills, where he remained in hiding until he could slip unnoticed into Mexico City.

There he led a brief uprising that brought a reformer, Vicente Guerrero, to the presidency. As a reward for Zavala's support Guerrero appointed him secretary of the treasury. Unfortunately for Zavala, his proposals for raising revenue, such as an income tax and a series of license fees, created enemies. Additionally, his one-time ally Santa Anna turned on him when an article allegedly by Zavala appeared in a Mexico City newspaper warning against Santa Anna's dictatorial ambitions. Zavala was forced to resign from the cabinet. Friends warned him that his life was in danger, and he fled across the mountains to Vera Cruz, his career and his fortune in ruins. In Vera Cruz he learned that a friend in Mexico City had been condemned to death for political activities. Zavala might be next. He embarked on an American merchant ship, the *United States*, bound for New Orleans, and the start of a long tour through the young American republic.

Lorenzo de Zavala was a good writer, and with time on his hands he began work on an account of his travels through the United States. The resulting book, *Journey to the United States of North America*, has been compared to Alexis de Tocqueville's *Democracy in America*. Like his French counterpart, Zavala combined vivid portraits of American people and places with his own musings on American political culture. Having experienced firsthand all the idealism and all the confusion of Mexican independence, Zavala was eager to study the American experiment in democracy, now in its fifth decade. He declared that he was writing out of "an unquenchable desire for the public good and an insatiable love of liberty."

Zavala's American journey began in New Orleans, a city that he described as boasting seventy thousand residents. He described the central market as a "Tower of Babel." "There one hears blacks, mulattos, Frenchmen, Spaniards, Germans, and Americans," he wrote, "hawking their merchandise in different languages." Zavala discovered quickly that amid this diversity, African Americans were treated differently than other peoples. In the Protestant churches, for example, blacks were "separated in one corner by bars or railings." In contrast, the Catholic church seemed more embracing: "The paving stones of the cathedral are filled with people of all colors." According to Zavala this mingling brought "a temporary unawareness of all human distinctions."

Other locales in New Orleans, however, brought a grim reminder of American slavery. The institution had already been abolished in Mexico. During his short stay in New Orleans, one thousand slaves were offered for sale in that city alone. When a master wished to punish a slave he could send him to jail with a note indicating the number of lashes the victim should receive: "Often as one passes by the jail in the morning," Zavala wrote, "the cries and laments of those unfortunate people can be heard." On June 15, 1829, Lorenzo de Zavala boarded the steamship *Louisiana*, bound up the Mississippi for Pittsburgh and the continuation of his American journey.

Only a few weeks before Zavala visited New Orleans another notable politician, Sam Houston, had been on the Mississippi River steaming in the opposite direction. Like Lorenzo de Zavala, Sam Houston had reached a turning point in his life. Like Zavala, Houston had only recently been a state governor. And like Zavala, Houston was now an exile.

Sam Houston was born in Virginia in 1793, about five years after Lorenzo de Zavala. His father died when he was thirteen, and soon afterward his mother moved with her nine children and five slaves to frontier Tennessee. Sam proved himself a poor farm hand, and so his mother sent him to clerk in a nearby store. He did not like that job either, and one day he simply disappeared. His mother heard a rumor that her son was living with Cherokees a few miles away on the Tennessee River, so she sent two of his brothers to fetch him.

They found young Sam sitting beneath a tree reading a copy of the *Iliad*. Houston had received little formal schooling, but he was so taken with Homer's epic tale of Greek heroes that he read and reread the book until he had learned most of it by heart. At the moment when his brothers caught up with him, he was living in two worlds, both far from the drudgery of life at home: one a world of imagination in ancient Greece and another the actual world of the Cherokee village life.

In response to their urging that they return home, Houston told his brothers that he preferred "measuring dear tracks" to measuring tape—no more clerking for him. "I liked the wild liberty of the Red men better than the tyranny of my own brothers," he later recalled. "I told them to go home and leave me in peace." Houston stayed with the Cherokees for three years, learning their language and their customs. The band he joined consisted of about three hundred members who lived on an island in the Tennessee River. Their chief, Oo-loo-te-ka, grew fond of Sam Houston and adopted him as an honorary son, giving him the Indian name "Colonneh," meaning "The Raven." Houston later admitted that "this running wild among the Indians, sleeping on the ground, chasing wild game, living in the forests, and reading Homer's *Iliad* withal, seemed a pretty strange business." People predicted that he would "either be a great Indian chief, or die in a madhouse, or be governor of the State." Eventually he would become the governor of *two* states—the only American ever to accomplish that feat. But in his youth, the prospect of Houston ever being elected governor of a state seemed remote.

He was, however, learning lessons that stayed with him throughout his life. Sam Houston reckoned that his teenage sojourn with the Indians "implanted" in him "a principle enduring as life itself. That principle was to protect the Indian against wrong and oppression, and to vindicate him in the enjoyment of rights which have been solemnly guaranteed to him by this Government." He took seriously his connection to the Cherokees, and in the future he would live among them again. But first he returned to his birth family and faced the problem of earning a living.

There were no state-supported schools in Tennessee at that time; individuals simply set themselves up as teachers and recruited fee-paying students. Lacking much formal schooling, Houston decided to transform a liability as an asset. He announced that "one who had graduated at an Indian university ought to hold his lore at a dearer rate" than other teachers, and so he charged about 30 percent more than the going rate for instruction, the fees to be paid in cash, corn, and cotton cloth. Houston even dressed the part of the "Indian Professor," wearing colorful calico hunting shirts and arranging his hair in a long queue down his back. The hairstyle, he noted, "added somewhat to the adornment of my person." Houston soon filled his classroom with students who apparently responded well to his theatrics. As a teacher, he later wrote, "I experienced a higher feeling of dignity and self-satisfaction than from any office or honor which I later held."

Before long, national events drew Houston from the classroom to the battlefield. In 1812 the United States went to war with Britain. Tennesseans supported the war heartily because they blamed Britain for inciting the Indian attacks on the frontiers. They signed up in such numbers that Tennessee acquired its permanent nickname as "The Volunteer State." One of those volunteers was Sam Houston, who signed up at Knoxville in 1813, a few days after his twentieth birthday. His familiarity with forest life may have set him apart from other soldiers; additionally he was an imposing figure, standing six feet two inches tall at a time when American men were typically about eight inches shorter. Then too there was his experience as a schoolmaster. He quickly rose in the ranks to sergeant and then to lieutenant. He marched off to war in 1813 after a listening to a parting speech from his mother: "I had rather all my sons should fill one honorable grave, than that one of them should turn his back to save his life," she said. "Go and remember too that while the door of my cottage is open to brave men, it is eternally shut against cowards." Within a few months Houston came very close to filling an honorable grave rather than returning home at all.

The Tennesseans were drawn into combat when Creek Indians massacred some 500 settlers at Fort Mims in Alabama. The Creek War is usually considered part of the larger War of 1812 because the Creek were allied with the British. The culminating battle against the Creeks came at Horseshoe Bend in Alabama on March 27, 1814. A young military officer named Andrew Jackson led a force of 1,500 whites and 500 Cherokees against the Creeks, who had built a fortification on a peninsula in the river. Houston charged over breastwork and was immediately hit with barbed arrow in his thigh. Blood gushing from his wound, he stumbled back to the camp to have it dressed. There he met Andrew Jackson who told him his fighting was over for that day. But as the battle raged on, Houston could not bear to watch from safety. He returned to the fray, charged a well-fortified Creek post and was wounded again, this time by bullets in the arm and shoulder.

Sam Houston's heroism at Horseshoe Bend won him the lifelong admiration and friendship of Andrew Jackson, but it also came close to ending his life. That evening the army surgeon extracted one of the bullets, but left the other, explaining that the pain of the operation would be excruciating, and Houston would likely be dead by morning anyway. So Houston was left to die, while the surgeon turned his attention to other less severely wounded men. "It was," he later wrote, "the darkest night of my life." But Sam Houston was still alive the next morning. During the following weeks he was carried on a litter through the wilderness toward his home, barely clinging to life. He was so gaunt when he reached Tennessee that his mother hardly recognized him. For months Houston lingered near death. But after more than a year of convalescence he finally recovered his health.

Houston remained in the army, where one of his most notable assignments was to represent the Cherokees in negotiations with the government about relinquishing their land and moving west. He appeared in Washington to meet with Secretary of War John C. Calhoun. In an effort to show his sympathy for the Indians, Houston dressed in Cherokee clothing. This made a striking appearance, but resulted in a reprimand from Secretary Calhoun. Soon afterward Houston resigned from the Army.

Back in Tennessee Houston studied law and gained admission to the bar after only six months of study. Following a brief career as an attorney, he turned to politics, and in 1823 he ran for congress. Houston's popularity as a war hero and his friendship with Andrew Jackson helped him win election that year and two years later. He was advancing quickly in politics, and in 1827 he decided to run for governor. By now Houston was a seasoned orator with a flair for colorful speech and colorful dress recalling his time among the Cherokees. In other ways his attire was conventional, but he wore an "Indian hunting-shirt" fastened at the waist by a large red sash "covered with fancy beadwork." Houston won the governorship in a landslide.

In Houston's first address to the legislature he advocated canal-building, cheap land, and public support for education. Schooling, he said, should be "equally open to all the youth of our country whose ambition may urge them on." Houston's own popularity and his friendship with Andrew Jackson, who was elected president in 1828, made him one of the most powerful men in Tennessee. Reelection in 1829 seemed certain, but then disaster struck.

In January of that year he married a young woman named Eliza Allen. She was 20, and he was 35. Her parents favored the match, but she was less enthusiastic, and was perhaps in love with another man. Being the first lady of Tennessee was not enough to make Eliza a loving wife, and after less than three months with Houston, she left the governor and returned to her family. The governor was humiliated and heart-broken. In a gesture echoing his decision of two decades before to leave home, he decided once more to live among the Cherokees, now residing in Arkansas. Houston resigned the governorship of Tennessee. Wearing common clothes with an Indian blanket thrown over his shoulders, and carrying only a few belongings, he boarded a steamer bound for Arkansas.

Sam Houston was unaware that a Mexican leader named Lorenzo de Zavala was at that moment in New Orleans. Within a few years they would meet in Texas and lead a revolution, but in the mean time Houston would rejoin his Cherokee family, and Zavala would continue his study of the United States.

Traveling north on the Mississippi, Lorenzo de Zavala began assembling notes on how Americans lived and worked. Along the banks of the river were little communities of squatters who gathered firewood to fuel the hundreds of steamboats that plied the river. Making its way up the river, the *Louisiana* steamed past numerous rafts, up to six hundred feet long, floating downstream with lumber and other goods bound for New Orleans. Having helped draft his own country's constitution, Zavala was keen to learn about the governments of the various states through which he passed. In Cincinnati he saw a remarkable example of the democratic style of American public life. Just as the *Louisiana* came to town, President Andrew Jackson was arriving for a visit. In Mexico Zavala might have expected battalions and artillery to accompany the president, but in Cincinnati "there was none of that."

> Instead one saw many people running along the banks of the river in order to welcome their first citizen, this venerable man who had liberated Louisiana and gave Florida to the United States, and who now guided the destinies of the country with prudence and benevolence. They greeted him with music, banners, flags, applause, and shouts of happiness. Everything was natural, everything spontaneous. It seemed more like the fiestas in our towns and cities when the people, of their own accord, celebrate a saint than the ceremonies concocted [in Mexico] to pay homage to the rulers, events in which the people show no signs of genuine respect.

The next day Zavala had the chance to meet the president. He found Jackson in a "modestly furnished" house, seated in an armchair. Gathered nearby were some thirty persons "who by their dress seemed to be workmen and craftsmen, thus making for him the simplest court in the world." In contrast, when Agustín de Iturbide had come to power a few years before in Mexico, he had surrounded himself with titled followers including "a corps of gentlemen and ladies of the imperial bedchamber." Upon meeting the Mexican visitor, Jackson asked about "his friend" General Vincente Guerrero, whose removal as president of Mexico had lead to Lorenzo de Zavala's exile. Jackson regretted Guerrero's fate and told Zavala he hoped that "the people's cause which he was defending would have a complete triumph." Zavala, of course, shared that wish, but in the meantime he was still a refugee, studying America.

From Cincinnati, Zavala continued up the Ohio River to Pittsburgh. From there he traveled on to New York City. While he was in New York, Lorenzo de Zavala saw another example of American devotion to liberty. Word arrived of the brief but successful revolution of 1830 in Paris, which brought Louis Philippe, the "Citizen King," to the throne. Former president James Monroe presided over a meeting of citizens at New York's Tammany Hall to plan a huge parade. "The procession," Zavala wrote, "was one of the most brilliant gatherings that I have ever seen." Zavala interpreted the parade, which took three hours to pass any given point, as a visual manifestation of the American republic.

There were printers carrying their type, tailors, shoemakers, silversmiths, ironworkers, blacksmiths, businessmen, sailors, lawyers, doctors, students, each group beneath its banner. Finally there were legislators, magistrates, and diplomats, all the most brilliant and respectable people. . . .The order and decorum that ruled from beginning to end were signs of the prosperity of the community, the grand event they were celebrating, and the majesty of the American nation.

While admiring the "majesty" of America, Lorenzo de Zavala was an honest reporter, and he observed one great exception to the democratic atmosphere of the republic—the treatment of African Americans. Blacks, he noted, were denied political and economic opportunities even when free and were "living to a certain degree as though excommunicated." He told the story of a wealthy Haitian who had come to New York expecting to be treated with the same respect he received at home. The man got off his ship and ordered his luggage carried to the finest hotel in the city. But New York's best hotel refused his business because he was black. The visitor went to hotel after hotel and received the same reception: "The young Haitian was humiliated, all the more so because he was dressed elegantly and adorned with gold chains and glittering rings and buttons." He finally found refuge in a house run by an African American. Everywhere the Haitian visitor went, he received the "same insults." He could not even sit beside white New Yorkers in church or at the theater. Zavala admired many things about the United States, but he did not admire slavery and he did not admire segregation. "This situation," he wrote, "is not very natural in a country where they profess the principles of the widest liberty."

Apart from the glaring exceptions of slavery and prejudice, Zavala was impressed with democracy in America. He reprinted in his book many public documents on subjects such as religious freedom as examples to the people of Mexico. He was also impressed by the progress of the two hundred thousand European immigrants arriving annually in the United States: "With active and robust arms they soon find work, and within a few months they become proprietors of land that rewards their sweat. They soon populate places that recently had been the habitat only for wolves, bears, and other wild beasts."

Zavala contended that the example of the United States furnished many useful lessons for Mexico. His homeland, he argued, was hampered by tyranny and chaos. Instead of the freedom and stability of its neighbor to the north, Mexico was a land tormented by "bloody despotic systems" and "disastrous cataclysms." Mexico could grow prosperous by following the example of the United States, "that practical school of free and independent politics, which is today the model of all civilized peoples." In the concluding chapter to his *Journey to the United States*, Zavala summarized the features of American life that made it in his view such a good model for other nations to imitate:

There is not, nor has there ever been, a community in which the rights of citizenship were more respected, where the people participated more fully in their government, and where they were more perfectly equal in all social enjoyments.

This people, full of life and movement, is steadfast in its course, and from the frontiers of Nova Scotia to those of New Mexico, the American upholds these principals: *the dignity of work and the rights of citizenship.* His code is succinct, but clear, pure, and tangible.

In 1832 events in Mexico created an opportunity for Lorenzo de Zavala to return to his homeland. General Santa Anna—sometime friend, sometime foe of Zavala—had begun a revolution in Vera Cruz. Zavala took a ship to Vera Cruz, arriving on August 12, 1832. On shore he immediately penned a letter to Santa Anna seeking to make amends for past differences, and soon afterward Zavala, Santa Anna, and a third man, Gómez Pedraza, came to an agreement. Pedraza would become acting president of Mexico, Zavala would become governor of the state of Mexico, and Santa Anna would lead the army to put them in power. Soon after making this agreement, on November 1, 1832, Zavala was installed as governor; but he held the post for only thirty-five days before opponents forced him to flee to the hills, as he had in 1828. Zavala had an advantage, however, in local politics. He was popular in the state of Mexico due to his reform efforts during his earlier term as governor. He soon gathered a thousand followers and recaptured the state capital—a victory that won him the title "General."

Back in power as governor, Zavala spent much of 1833 promoting reform in his state and country. As governor he confiscated the property of absentee landlords to provide holdings for poorer Mexicans and to raise revenues for roads and schools. He took fertile land from the church and sold it at a nominal price to small farmers. All of these measures created enemies, and in 1833 he faced another revolt. In a dramatic speech he told the citizens of his state that they faced a choice between slavery and liberty, ignorance and enlightenment. The revolt faltered.

Zavala's reform ideas continued to earn him enemies, especially among the powerful clergy and aristocrats. Soon the enemies worked out a scheme to reduce his influence while appearing to honor his talents. During the fall of 1833, Zavala was appointed minister to the French court, an honor certainly, but one that would take him far from Mexico City. Nonetheless, he accepted the appointment and after a journey of several months he and his family arrived in Paris in March 1834. But soon after his arrival in Paris, Zavala learned that Mexican politics had taken yet another turn toward illegal and despotic rule. Santa Anna, who had been vacillating for years between liberalism and conservatism, depending on which seemed more powerful, allied himself with the conservative elements in Mexico. With the army behind him, he took control of the government, abolished recent reforms, and disbanded congress. When several state legislatures protested his action, he disbanded those bodies as well. In Paris, Zavala was completing his account of his journey through the United States, and the developments in Mexico may have contributed to his admiration for American political success. He wrote, for example:

In America it is another thing. Although monarchic principles are not formally outlawed, it is evident that the spirit of a new republic is almost exclusively democratic. In America there are no government takeovers, nor conspiracies, nor diplomatic intrigues, nor financial corruption, nor any group of dissidents strong enough to create a monarchy.

On August 30, 1834, Zavala sent a letter to Santa Anna, resigning as minister to France, and urging the dictator to mend his ways and abandon "the monarchial form." The letter was not well received in the capital. Mexico's foreign secretary wrote Zavala that Santa Anna was outraged with him. Zavala was ordered to return to Mexico City, but he realized that returning might well be prison or death.

What should he do?

Given his admiration for the United States as well his allegiance to Mexico, it was natural that Lorenzo de Zavala should turn his eyes upon Texas. It was a Mexican state, or more accurately a part of the larger political entity known as Coahuila-Texas. In his *Journey to the United States* Zavala had noted that northern Mexico was destined to profit by immigration from its neighbor. At the time, he explained, more than ten thousand Americans per year were settling in Mexican territory. These "enterprising guests" would inevitably influence his native land with their ideas about work and politics. He predicted that within a few years Mexico would be "molded to a combined regimen of the American system and Spanish customs and traditions."

Perhaps in northern Mexico, far from the corrupting influence of the capital and safe from Santa Anna's clutches, Zavala could help create a community that would combine the best of Mexico and the best of the United States. He had already been involved in Texas land deals and so now he decided to settle in Mexico's northern territory. His son, Lorenzo Jr., was in Texas and had identified an attractive homestead for the family. It was located on high ground overlooking Buffalo Bayou, near the mouth of the San Jacinto River. Lorenzo de Zavala moved to Texas soon afterward. As he stood on the porch of his new house, surveying the countryside, he could enjoy a broad view over miles of grassland and river. Shortly before he had been living in one of the great cities of the world; now he was on a frontier full of possibility. At that moment he could hardly have imagined that within a few months this landscape would be filled with the cries of dying men, and that his own house would become a hospital for the survivors of a great battle.

While Lorenzo de Zavala was exploring the United States, governing in Mexico, and serving as Mexican ambassador to Paris, Sam Houston was slowly rebuilding his life in Arkansas. Upon resigning as governor of Tennessee and leaving that state, he was heartily welcomed by his Cherokee friends when he arrived in their new country in spring of 1829. His adoptive father, Oo-loo-te-ka and other tribal leaders were prospering on great tracts of land cultivated by slaves and large herds of cattle. Houston lived with the Cherokees and again adopted their dress. All was not well, however, with the Cherokees. Houston learned that they were regularly cheated by the agents who stole from the allotments of food and supplies owed them by the government. Still a close friend of Andrew Jackson, Houston could pass on Cherokee complaints to the highest levels of the government. In 1829 he officially became a Cherokee citizen; dressed in native garb including a colorful turban, he went to Washington, D.C. Through Houston's influence several corrupt Indian agents were dismissed.

Back at home among the Cherokees, Sam Houston poured out his feelings of support for the Indians in a series of articles in the *Arkansas Gazette*. He went beyond the specific grievances of the Cherokees and asked his readers to consider the entire history of white oppression of the Indians:

Where stood the Indian of other days? He stood on the shore of the Atlantic, and beheld, each morning, the sun rolling from the bosom of its green waves. In that sun he beheld his God, and bowed in homage to the shrine. He felt that no intermediate creature could usurp the favor of his Divinity. He was monarch of the wilds, and his buoyant step proclaimed him, "every inch a king." That age has long gone by—the aboriginal character is almost lost in the views of the white man, or by a series of impositions. A succession of injuries has broken his proud spirit, & taught him to kiss the hand which inflicts upon him stripes.

These were strong words and Houston's defense of the Indians. Many whites in the Old Southwest were glad enough to see the "proud spirit" of the Indians broken. Houston made many enemies, which may be one reason that in 1830 his personal life fell into shambles. Always a drinker, Houston became, quite simply, a drunk. He ordered ten *barrels* of liquor from a nearby fort and began working his way through them. Even his Cherokee brethren adopted for him the nickname "Big Drunk."

Nonetheless, in 1832 Sam Houston accompanied a delegation of Cherokees back to Washington. In the capital Congressman William Stanbery of Ohio delivered a speech claiming that Houston was trying to use government contracts to defraud the Indians. Stanbery was an opponent of President Andrew Jackson and hoped to strike at Jackson by discrediting Houston. In response Houston began carrying a hickory cane through the streets of Washington, announcing that he would beat Stanbery if he met him. The congressman, in turn, armed himself with two pistols and a knife. On the night of April 13, 1832, they met on Pennsylvania Avenue. Houston struck the first blow with his cane; Stanbery drew a pistol and tried to shoot his assailant. But the gun misfired and Houston struck Stanberry again and again with his cane. This was not Sam Houston's finest hour.

Bruised and outraged, William Stanbery persuaded the House of Representatives to regard his humiliation as an attack on Congress as a whole. By a vote of 145 to 25 the House called for Houston's arrest and trial. Within a few days the trial began with Houston acting for the most part as his own defense. On the night before he was due to deliver his final statement Houston drank heavily, but the next day he had recovered sufficiently to make his speech. At noon when the trial resumed the House was packed, with chairs in the aisles of the chamber and men standing packed by the walls. Houston was a seasoned orator, and he rose to the occasion.

What was at stake here, he claimed, was liberty itself. The audience that day knew Houston had once been a congressman and the governor of a state. He acknowledged freely his fallen condition, quoting these dramatic lines from a poem: "The thorns which I have reaped are of the tree I planted; they have torn me and I bleed." Houston's humility appealed to the audience. The citizens in the galleries applauded, someone threw a rose bouquet at Houston's feet, and a woman called out: "I had rather be Sam Houston in a dungeon than Stanbery on a throne!" Encouraged, Houston delivered a long, passionate discourse on the history of liberty and tyranny. Looking at a flag hanging on the wall, he concluded:

So long as that proud emblem . . . shall wave in the Hall of American legislators, so long shall it cast its sacred protection over the personal rights of every American citizen. . . . When you have destroyed the pride of American character, you will have destroyed the brightest jewel that heaven ever made.

Many in the audience cheered wildly that day. The House nonetheless voted to reprimand Houston for beating one of its members, but the condemnation was half-hearted. Unsatisfied, Congressman Stanbery filed a civil complaint against Houston and won a $500 judgment, but Houston prevailed in another trial alleging he was guilty of misconduct in Indian affairs. The experience of those weeks was important for Houston in that it sobered him up—literally and figuratively. He later wrote that at this time he was "dying out," but trials gave him a "national tribunal for a theater, and that set me up again."

Sam Houston soon found a new sphere for his enterprise. While in the East, he visited New York and met with businessmen who had formed the Galveston Bay and Texas Land Company, hoping to make money by selling land in Texas. They wanted Houston to go there and gather information. That arrangement came to nothing, but then with Sam Houston interested in Texas anyway, he received an assignment from President Jackson to visit the region and learn more about the Indian tribes of it, especially the Comanches, the most powerful tribe in the region. In December, 1832, Houston crossed the Red River into Texas.

For centuries Texas had been claimed as part of Mexico, which was in turn controlled by Spain, and in 1682 Yselta, near present-day El Paso, became the first Spanish settlement. But for more than a century afterward Texas remained a lightly populated frontier. In the early 1700s San Antonio de Béxar, with a mission and a military post, became the administrative center. Other posts were soon established at Nacogdoches, Goliad, and El Paso.

During the eighteenth century five missions were built in the San Antonio region by Franciscan friars. The mission San Antonio de Valero, later known as the Alamo, was typical of these. On the mission grounds were a chapel, monastery, guest rooms, school, jail, and factory. Most of the Indian tribes in Texas, notably the powerful Comanches and Apaches, resisted conversion. But another tribe, the Coahuiltecans, supplied many converts, men and women who moved to the missions, became Christians, and learned European trades and agriculture. On the mission grounds Coahuiltecan women spun yarn for cloth, while the men worked in fields nearby or tended cattle and horses or built the mission itself. Toward the close of the century the missions, such as San Antonio de Valero, were secularized, and turned over to private ownership. The Alamo itself became a military garrison. The civilian population grew slowly as farmers and ranchers moved into the region. By 1800 the population in the San Antonio region was about 1,700; another 1,000 settlers in the rest of Texas could be counted citizens of Spain.

With independence, the Mexican population of Texas was less than five thousand, and during the 1820s the government of Mexico decided to encourage immigration from the United States. In 1820 American Moses Austin went to San Antonio, where, in exchange for land, he offered to bring three hundred immigrants to Texas, all of whom would agree to become Mexican citizens. Moses Austin won approval for his plan but died en route to Missouri, where he had hoped to recruit settlers. His son Stephen Austin took over the colonizing plan. Austin was twenty-seven at the time, slight of build, an intellectual, and a musician. He was tolerant and honest, calm and diplomatic, an ideal leader among the frontiersmen he would attract to Texas.

Needing to confirm title to his father's grant, Stephen Austin traveled to Mexico City, where he met with various public officials, including the head of the colonization committee of the federal congress, a young legislator from the Yucatán named Lorenzo de Zavala. The grant as confirmed in 1823 allowed Austin to bring to Texas families who would pay him 12.5 cents per acre for their land. At this time the American Land Act of 1820 dictated a price of $1.25 per acre, so Austin had no trouble finding recruits. By 1832 Austin had established several colonies, inhabited by eight thousand immigrants. Land developers such as Austin were known in Spanish as *empresarios*. Many of the empresarios were American, but Mexicans, including Zavala himself, also received contracts. By 1832 "Texas fever"—the lure of inexpensive land—had brought roughly twenty thousand immigrants to Texas from the United States, and thousands more came during the next few years. In 1835 Anglo Texans greatly outnumbered native Mexicans: of thirty thousand residents less than 15 percent were Mexican by birth.

Most of the early settlers took seriously their obligation to become Mexican citizens. Stephen Austin served, for example, in the Coahuila-Texas legislature, and when a group of Americans in Fredonia, Texas, revolted against Mexican rule in 1826, an

Stephen Austin. He was the foremost empresario in Texas and supervised the immigration of many Americans into what was then Mexican territory during the 1820s and 1830s.

Anglo force from Austin's land grant joined a Mexican force from San Antonio in putting down the uprising. In 1832 Austin supported the movement that brought Santa Anna to power and Lorenzo de Zavala back from his first exile. He became a close friend of Mexicans in San Antonio, and he urged his fellow colonists to learn Spanish.

But there were points of friction between the new Mexican citizens and their government. Technically only Catholics were allowed to worship freely in Mexico; the law was not strictly enforced, but for the mainly Protestant immigrants the laws against freedom of worship were an affront. Ironically, the same Mexican government that restricted personal freedom in matters of worship annoyed Americans by being, from the immigrant standpoint, too liberal in another area. In 1829 the Mexican government abolished slavery. Many immigrants came from the American South to Texas, looking for land to grow cotton with slave labor. The newcomers found ways, often with the connivance of local Mexican officials, to avoid the rules against Protestantism and slavery, but such rules accentuated the difference between American and Mexican values.

During the 1830s Mexican policy toward American immigrants was in constant flux. Immigration from the United States would be encouraged, then outlawed; new tariffs on trade to the Texas colonies would be imposed, then lifted. When the settlers resisted paying the tariffs, soldiers were sent to support the customs collectors. At the same time the army was too close, the government was too remote: the state legislature and supreme court were seated hundreds of miles from Texas to the south in Coahuila. Like the American colonists of 1776 and the Mexicans in 1820, the Texans felt themselves governed by a remote and unfriendly regime.

In 1832 a convention of Texans at San Felipe drafted a document calling for reforms. One of the members was Lorenzo de Zavala. The Texans wanted the Mexican government to reduce tariffs, fund primary schools, and create a separate state of Texas. Delegates met at San Felipe again in 1833 to draft another petition. Zavala was there again along with Sam Houston, newly arrived to Texas, but a leader already thanks to his military career and his background as former American congressman and Tennessee governor. Shortly after completing his Indian mission for Andrew Jackson, Houston had received a grant of land from Stephen Austin. He wrote Jackson that he intended to make Texas his "abiding place," thus casting his future with Mexico, although he promised Jackson he would "never forget" the country of his birth, meaning the United States. At San Felipe in 1833 Houston, Zavala, and other members of the convention chose Stephen Austin to take their petition of grievances to Mexico City. In particular, he was to request that the government set up a separate Texas administration within the Mexican federation. But Austin failed to win support in the capital, and in response to this disappointment he wrote an ill-fated letter to friends in Texas suggesting they go ahead and create their own legislature. The letter was intercepted by government agents and Stephen Austin found himself in jail in Mexico City. In the meantime, Santa Anna had outlawed the state legislatures throughout Mexico.

Discontent with Antonio López de Santa Anna was not merely a Texas phenomenon. Santa Anna was a tough political survivor, who would eventually head eleven of the fifty governments that ruled Mexico during its first thirty years of independence. A proponent of strong central government (under his leadership), in 1834 he curtailed state legislatures and dissolved the Mexican national congress. When Joel Poinsett, an

American minister to Mexico City, chided him for abandoning his earlier commitment to freedom, Santa Anna replied that he had indeed once favored liberty, but "very soon found the folly of it." He argued the Mexican people were "unenlightened" and incapable of self-government.

Many Mexicans disagreed with Santa Anna's assessment of their capability for self-government. In Zacatecas, north of Mexico City, the local militia refused to follow the dictator's order to disband. On May 11, 1835, Santa Anna personally led 3,500 troops to the city, quickly defeated the militia, then turned his troops loose for an orgy of rape, robbery, arson, and murder. Two thousand civilians lost their lives in the carnage. Soon afterward the governor of Coahuila-Texas was arrested and jailed for resisting Santa Anna's policies.

Thus, the unrest in Texas was part of a wider Mexican opposition to tyranny. In 1835 tensions in Texas led to outright insurrection at Gonzales, where residents had been given a cannon to use in defense against Indian attacks. Fearing rebellion, the Mexican authorities demanded its return, and so a force of about one hundred soldiers was sent to reclaim the cannon. In the meantime the residents of Gonzales loaded their weapon with scrap iron and designed a flag with a picture of the cannon and the in-your-face slogan, "come and take it." On October 2, 1835, the soldiers came, the defenders fired their cannon, and the soldiers fled. This was the shot heard around Texas, if not around the world, and with it the revolution began. Texans feared rightly that Santa Anna would attempt to handle them the same way he had handled the rebels at Zacatecas. One Texan had reason to be especially worried: when Santa Anna came, his object would be not only to conquer the Texas rebels, but to arrest his enemy, Lorenzo de Zavala.

Stephen Austin, newly released from prison, returned to Texas on September 1, 1835. In a report to the people of Texas, he argued that in Texas and throughout the nation, Mexicans were rightly resisting the effort to "destroy the Federal Constitution of 1824." In Austin's view, resistance to tyranny was the citizen's duty:

> How can I, or any one, remain indifferent when our rights, our all, appear to be in jeopardy, and when it is our duty, as well as our obligation as good Mexican citizens, to express our opinions on the present state of things and to represent our situation to the government?

Austin called for a "general consultation" of the people of Texas to meet in the fall of 1835 and discuss resistance. Soon afterward he circulated a letter with a long list of grievances against Santa Anna's government; he mentioned specifically as a sign of his despotism the orders the government had issued to arrest Lorenzo de Zavala, a "patriotic and virtuous citizen" who had come to Texas seeking asylum. "His offense we know not," Austin wrote, "except that he is the known friend of free institutions."

In November 1835, delegates including Lorenzo de Zavala and Sam Houston met in San Felipe at a gathering they called the Consultation. Partly at the urging of Zavala the members rejected an outright declaration of independence, preferring to adopt a statement "setting forth to the world the causes that impelled us to take up arms." This declaration stressed the Mexican roots of the rebellion: the Texans rose up to defend their "rights and liberties" against "the encroachments of military despots."

His work at the Consultation completed, Zavala enjoyed a brief interlude of domestic life at the end of 1835. His wife Emily arrived in December with their three children and an Irish maid. Emily unpacked furniture and household goods from New York; Lorenzo worked on a history of Mexico. Three French-speaking men were hired to begin farming the Zavala estate. While relaxing, the family could sit on the wide covered porch, looking down the San Jacinto estuary toward the Gulf of Mexico.

In the mean time, Sam Houston was settling into his new life in Nacogdoches, Texas, earning a living as an attorney. In discussions about how to handle the crisis with Mexico City, Houston like many other Anglo Mexicans, favored resistance in the name of the Mexican Constitution of 1824, rather than independence—reform rather than revolution. But events took a new turn as Santa Anna marched with an army toward Texas. He bragged that if necessary he would take the war all the way to Washington, D.C., where he would raise the Mexican flag above the Capitol. The Texan hope that Mexicans in other states would join their resistance was frustrated by Santa Anna's brutal suppression of the movement in Zacatecas. Feeling the need to act alone, Texans elected delegates to a new convention, which set up a provisional government and elected Sam Houston the commander of a Texas army, to be formed later.

During the next few months Houston visited soldiers in the San Antonio region, urging them to withdraw to an area more remote from Santa Anna's line of march. Made bold by cocky notions of their ability not only to defend the Alamo, many stayed on. Because they were not part of an official Texas army, Houston could not order them to withdraw. Soon afterward he was elected to yet another convention, this one at a place called Washington-on-the-Brazos, where one of his fellow delegates was Lorenzo de Zavala. The place, soon to be the scene of a Texas declaration of Independence, was merely a collection of rude homes and shops clustered on a single street. Thirty of the fifty-one delegates slept on the floor of a twenty-by-forty-foot room in a tavern, which served also as their independence hall. Here, beginning on March 1, 1836, they deliberated on the new government. Most of the delegates were Anglo Texans, but San Antonio sent two native Mexicans, José Antonio Navarro and Francisco Ruíz. Neither spoke English and so Zavala befriended and translated for them.

One of the members arrived at the convention with a declaration of independence already drafted, and on March 2, 1836, it was adopted without alteration by a unanimous vote of the convention. The Texas Declaration of Independence followed closely the ideology of the American declaration, but focused on circumstances in Mexico and Texas. Just as Thomas Jefferson had followed John Locke by insisting on the right of rebellion against tyranny, the delegates at Washington-on-the-Brazos used Lockean arguments to prove that they were the victims of despotism. The Mexican government had ceased to protect "lives liberty and property." In the place of republican government the usurpers had set up "a consolidated central military despotism in which every interest is disregarded but that of the army and the priesthood." The declaration decried the arrest of Stephen Austin, the threatened arrest of Lorenzo de Zavala, the lack of trial by jury and public education, the disbanding of the militia, prohibitions on freedom of worship, and the dissolution of the government of Coahuila-Texas.

The delegates argued that Texans had begun their revolution as loyal Mexicans seeking reform and calling to their "Mexican brethren" for assistance. In 1776

Americans had made the same statement about calling to their "British brethren" for help against King George. In each case the appeal had gone unheeded. Just as the revolutionaries of 1776 had addressed their declaration to "a candid world," those of 1836 concluded by declaring their independence from Mexico and calling upon "a candid world" for approval. On March 3, 1836, Lorenzo de Zavala and Sam Houston along with all the other delegates signed the declaration.

The delegates then turned to drafting a constitution. Zavala's assignments included chairing the section on the executive branch and serving on committees on defense, naval affairs, and flag design. While discussions of these and other matters were taking place in the tavern in Washington, Texas, messengers arrived every few days with news from the Alamo.

On Sunday, March 6, a note from William Travis at the Alamo reached the delegates as they were eating breakfast. Written three days earlier, the letter reported that although Travis and his men had repelled Santa Anna again and again, their future looked bleak. Outnumbered by more than fifteen to one, low on ammunition, they expected the worst. At one point Travis had drawn a line in the sand inside the fortified walls of the Alamo, telling his men that only those who agreed to fight to the finish should cross over the line. All of the defenders stepped over the line except James Bowie, inventor of the Bowie knife, who was desperately ill: unable to walk he arranged to be carried across the line in his bed.

News traveled slowly in frontier Texas, and so the delegates at Washington had no way of knowing that while they were eating breakfast and listening to the report from Travis, Santa Anna's troops were shooting, bayoneting, and clubbing to death the last defenders of the Alamo, including Travis, Bowie, and Davy Crockett.

As military leader of the new republic, Sam Houston rode out toward the Alamo with three others, hoping for a clearer idea of what was happening there. On the broad plains in the direction of San Antonio, it had been possible to hear the cannon from the Alamo dozens of miles away from the fighting. But waking up one morning near the fortress, Houston could hear no cannon fire. Rightly, he suspected the worst.

In the mean time, Lorenzo de Zavala and his colleagues worked for another eleven days, drafting the Texas constitution and electing officers. On their last full day of deliberations the delegates received news of the fall of the Alamo—and of the approach of two thousand Mexican cavalrymen, who were now within one hundred miles. The latter information was incorrect, but the danger to the delegates was real. Lorenzo de Zavala was already a marked man. And now any of the delegates at Washington-on-the-Brazos, all signers of the Declaration of Independence, could imagine a violent death at the hands of Santa Anna. They rushed to complete their work on the constitution, staying awake most of the night following the grim news from the Alamo. The delegates elected David Burnet as president of the new republic and chose Lorenzo de Zavala as vice president. Zavala accepted the post at the urging of his colleagues, who argued that his presence in the administration would help demonstrate that the Texas revolution had Mexican as well as American supporters. At 4:00 A.M. Burnet and Zavala finally took their oaths of office. The exhausted delegates then went to sleep for a few hours.

On the morning of March 17, 1836, President Burnet delivered a rambling inaugural address that must have made some of the delegates regret his election. Among other ill-phrased sentiments, he urged the citizens of Texas to "gird up the loins of our minds" in the fight against Santa Anna. By now most of the delegates were more concerned with putting their legs than their minds to work and getting out of the reach of Santa Anna. As they scattered for their homes, they joined the flight of thousands of fellow citizens toward east Texas.

The general panic following the fall of the Alamo was made worse by news of another slaughter. On a plain outside of Goliad, Texas, four hundred soldiers under James Fannin were surprised by a large Mexican army. Unable to defend themselves, they relied on promises that their lives would be spared if they surrendered. On March 27, 1836, they were imprisoned in a nearby mission; that night, expecting to be released within a few days, the men sang "Home Sweet Home." Early the next morning, Easter Sunday, following orders from Santa Anna, they were roused from their blankets and marched off, supposedly to gather firewood or to board ships for home. But instead they were divided into groups and shot in cold blood by their captors. Men who survived the first volley were cut down by cavalrymen with lances or killed by soldiers with bayonets or butcher knives. In all 342 men died in what came to be known as the Goliad Massacre.

Following the Alamo and Goliad, rumors spread throughout the region that Santa Anna had given orders to "kill everything" to the eastern border of Texas. The resulting flight of civilians came to be known as the Runaway Scrape. "It seemed as if the whole country was panic struck" wrote an observer. One of the refugees, a man named Noah Smithwick, wrote a vivid account of the countryside:

> The desolation of the country through which we passed beggars description. Houses were standing open, the beds unmade, the breakfast things still on the tables, pans of milk moulding in the dairies. There were cribs full of corn, smoke houses full of bacon, yards full of chickens that ran after us for food, . . . all abandoned. Forlorn dogs roamed around the deserted homes, their doleful howls adding to the general sense of desolation.

As Smithwick pushed on, he came to a notice stuck on a tree "reporting the surrender and subsequent massacre of Fannin's men. We then understood the precipitate flight of the inhabitants, and realized the fate in store for us should we fall into the hands of the enemy."

While soldiers died at the Alamo and Goliad and civilians fled Santa Anna, Sam Houston was not inactive—although many Texans questioned his leadership. Why had he failed to field an army to halt Santa Anna? In retrospect, the answer is simple. He saw no benefit in fighting too soon, without enough resources, and suffering the fate of the Alamo and Goliad. Shortly before the "Runaway Scrape" he had urged James Fannin, now dead at Goliad, to withdraw to a better position for the fight against Santa Anna. "It is better," Houston wrote, "to do well, *late*, than *never*." These would prove to be wise words, but for families forced to abandon their homes, Houston's tactics seemed more cowardly than wise.

Lorenzo de Zavala had reached home a few days before the Goliad Massacre. A Virginia land agent, visiting at this time, found the family relaxed. The visitor came to know Lorenzo de Zavala's story of intermittent triumph and exile and admired his

Map showing the location of the Battle of San Jacinto. Note proximity of the Zavala home to the battlefield; the house was used as a hospital for the wounded after the battle.

courage. In the house there were no extra beds, and so the visitor slept on blankets on the floor, but he rested comfortably "under the roof of this remarkable man."

On March 25, 1836, on the eve of the Goliad Massacre, Zavala traveled west to meet with President Burnet and members of the Texas cabinet at Harrisburg. Soon after Zavala's arrival news came that Santa Anna was approaching; so Burnet and Zavala boarded a boat and steamed back down Buffalo Bayou toward their homes. The steamer was loaded with refugees and towed five other boats also filled with fleeing Texans. A few days later Santa Anna himself arrived in Harrisburg and burned the town. The dictator sent a colonel on with orders to arrest Burnet and Zavala.

In the meantime the president and vice president gathered their families and went by steamer to Galveston Island, where Santa Anna would have trouble reaching them. Zavala, Burnet, and members of the Texas cabinet stayed aboard their vessels, while other, less fortunate refugees hunkered down in tents and driftwood huts on the desolate island. A few miles away, Santa Anna had marched to within a few miles of the Zavala homestead and burned a neighbor's farm.

While Santa Anna was marching unopposed across Texas, Sam Houston had been retreating ahead of the dictator, gathering an army as he went. The general sought to keep up the spirits of his men with promises that they would soon be fighting. On April 7, 1836, he told them: "The victims of the Alamo, and the names of those who were murdered at Goliad, call for cool, *deliberate*, vengence." Among his troops was Lorenzo de Zavala Jr., who served Houston as translator. Both armies came to rest near the confluence of Buffalo Bayou and the San Jacinto River, opposite the Zavala house. Having been told that his family's home would be commandeered as a hospital for the wounded, young Zavala returned and made an inventory of household goods, expecting that many of the possessions would be lost.

The two armies were camped near each other on the night of April 20. Santa Anna slept comfortably in a tent, while Sam Houston slept on the ground with a coil of rope as a pillow. The next morning Santa Anna's force was swelled by the arrival of 550 additional troops. That gave him 1,350 soldiers compared to Houston's 900. Confident of victory the dictator invited the newcomers to eat and rest in the early afternoon, not even posting guards by his camp. In the American camp, the soldiers prepared themselves for battle. A troop of *Tejanos*, native-born Mexicans from San Antonio de Béxar, placed slips of paper in their hats with the slogan, *recuerdo el Alamo*, remember the Alamo, to distinguish them from Santa Anna's troops.

In the mid-afternoon Houston's men faded into the tall grass separating them from Santa Anna's camp. Suddenly, they appeared among the Mexicans, firing their rifles and shouting, "Remember the Alamo!" Houston was hit in the ankle with a bullet, but fought on. In just eighteen minutes the battle was over. Six hundred of the enemy were killed, another six hundred captured. The Texans lost only nine men in the Battle of San Jacinto. Santa Anna hid near the camp, but was captured the next day. He surrendered to Houston, who was lying propped up against a tree, unable to walk because of his shattered ankle.

A few days later Lorenzo de Zavala visited the battlefield and met with Santa Anna. Unfortunately, we have no record of what the old adversaries said to each other. But we do know that Zavala favored humane treatment for the fallen dictator. Many Texans wanted him killed in revenge for the Alamo and Goliad, but Houston, Zavala, and others prevailed in allowing Santa Anna to live. Santa Anna negotiated two agreements with the Texans, recognizing their independence. The Mexican government did not recognize these as valid treaties, but Texas would maintain its independence for almost a decade before joining the United States.

Zavala learned that among the fallen at San Jacinto was an old friend, Gen. Manuel Fernández Castrillón. He arranged to have the body carried to a cedar grove near his house for burial, little realizing that he would soon be resting in the same graveyard.

During the summer of 1836, Zavala was again suffering from malaria, unable to attend meetings of the government. He was relieved when new elections were held and Mirabeau Lamar replaced him as vice president. At his inauguration Lamar praised his predecessor as a gentleman, scholar, and patriot. "Zavala," he said, "has been the unwavering and consistent friend of liberal principles and free government."

Zavala was in better health by the fall of 1836 and took his five-year-old son Agustín rowing on Buffalo Bayou. The boat overturned. Zavala pushed the boy onto the hull and got back to shore, but in his condition, weakened by malaria, the accident was fatal. Zavala died of pneumonia on November 15, 1836, at the age of forty-eight. The only newspaper in the republic, *The Telegraph and Texas Register*, hailed Lorenzo de Zavala as an "enlightened and patriotic statesman." "Texas," the paper said, "has lost one of her most valuable citizens." Soon after his death, the Texas navy named one of their ships after Zavala, and a Texas county as well as the Texas archives bear his name. In Mexico City he is recognized as one of the leaders of the early republic but is regarded as a traitor—"the Mexican Benedict Arnold"—for signing the Texas Declaration of Independence. In his native Yucatán, however, a province that entertained its own independence movement during the nineteenth century, a memorial was erected in Mérida to honor Zavala.

Sam Houston too would die of pneumonia, but long after Zavala. He received lifelong fame in Texas and throughout the United States as hero of San Jacinto. Texas was an independent nation for nine years, and during that time Houston was twice president of the republic. In 1845 the United States annexed the region, making Texas the twenty-eighth state. Houston was senator from 1846 to 1859, and in 1859 he became governor of the state. He retained the ability, despite his popularity, to stand up for causes he considered just, even if unpopular. As president, senator, and governor he continued to support the Indians; and as the sectional crisis worsened, he supported the Union, even when Texas seceded in 1861. The legislature insisted that he take an oath of allegiance to the Confederacy, which he refused to do, ending his term as governor. During the final months of his life, Houston settled into retirement and watched from afar as the Civil War unfolded. He was somewhat infirm, troubled by pain from the shoulder wound he had received almost a half century before at Horseshoe Bend. He contracted pneumonia and died on July 26, 1863, shortly after the Battle of Gettysburg. Like Lorenzo de Zavala's name, Houston's is memorialized in Texas, not the least in the names of a university and a city.

In retrospect, looking at the varied paths that brought the two men to the Texas Revolution is remarkable, given the differences in their lives that they found a common ground in the Texas Revolution. A Mexican from the Yucatán and an American from Tennessee shared a belief in good government, human rights, and simple justice.

Bibliography

Campbell, Randolph B. *Sam Houston and the American Southwest* (2007). Well-written brief biography of Houston.

Gregory, Jack, and Rennard Strickland. *Sam Houston with the Cherokees, 1829–1833* (1967). Detailed account of Sam Houston's life among, and services to, the Cherokees after his departure from Tennessee.

Hardin, Stephen L. *Texian Iliad: A Military History of the Texas Revolution, 1835–1836* (1994). Well-researched narrative history of the Texas war of independence.

Henson, Margaret Swett. *Lorenzo de Zavala: The Pragmatic Idealist* (1991). Solid biography of a "man who was willing to take risks to achieve his republican goals."

Matovina, Timothy M., Editor. *The Alamo Remembered: Tejano Accounts and Perspectives* (1995). Accounts written by native-born Mexicans present during the siege of the Alamo.

Ramos, Paul A. *Beyond the Alamo: Forging Mexican Ethnicity in San Antonia, 1821–1861* (2008). Valuable account of relationships between Mexican-born and American-born Texans before, during, and after the Texas Revolution.

Zavala, Lorenzo de. *Journey to the United States of North America* (1980). Translation by Wallace Woolsey of Zavala's important observations made during his travels through Jacksonian America.

Identification Topics

Mérida, Lorenzo de Zavala, *sanjuanistas*, San Juan Ulúa, the Mexican Constitution of 1824, Antonió Lopez de Santa Anna, Sam Houston, Oo-loo-te-ka, the Raven, William Stanbery, Andrew Jackson in Cincinnati, Stephen Austin, *empresarios*, Gonzales, the Texas Declaration of Independence, the Texas Constitution, the Alamo, Goliad Massacre, the Runaway Scrape, San Jacinto

Study Questions

1. What roles did Lorenzo de Zavala play in Mexico City and the state of Mexico during the early years of the Mexican republic? How did these activities gain him a reputation as a liberal reformer?
2. Why did Zavala become an exile in 1829? In 1835?
3. What features of Sam Houston's early life made him a successful politician in Tennessee?
4. Why did Houston become an "exile" in 1829? Why was his relationship to the Cherokees important to him?
5. What information did Lorenzo de Zavala accumulate about slavery and discrimination in the United States? What evidence did he find of democracy at work?
6. Why did Zavala decide to immigrate to Texas? Why did Houston make the same decision?
7. In what ways did Anglo Texans act as loyal Mexicans on the eve of their revolution? Later for what reasons did they (a) complain about Mexican policies and (b) decide to declare independence?
8. What roles did Zavala and Houston play in the Texas Revolution?

CHAPTER 12

Reform in the Early Republic
The Seneca Falls Convention of 1848

In antebellum America, reformers adopted many causes. Besides trying to eradicate slavery, they advocated temperance and favored improving schools, hospitals, and prisons. Women were involved in each of these movements and sometimes discussed their own disadvantaged status while meeting to help other groups. But it was not until 1848 that the first American women's rights convention convened in Seneca Falls, New York. The meeting highlighted how law and custom placed women in an inferior position and exposed the inconsistency between the egalitarian ideals of the young republic and the injustice of sexual discrimination. The resolutions adopted at the meeting would influence the women's rights movement for more than a century.

Charlotte Woodward, a nineteen-year-old farm girl in upstate New York, read the July 14, 1848, issue of the *Seneca County Courier* with growing excitement. After a tedious day of sewing gloves for a local manufacturer, she was intrigued by a small notice that caught her eye:

> WOMAN'S RIGHTS CONVENTION—A Convention to discuss the social, civil, and religious rights of women, will be held in the Wesleyan Chapel, Seneca Falls, New York, on Wednesday and Thursday, the 19th and 20th of July, current; commencing at ten o'clock A.M. During the first day the meeting will be held exclusively for women, who are earnestly invited to attend. The public generally are invited to be present the second day, when Lucretia Mott, of Philadelphia, and other ladies and gentlemen will address the meeting.

The young girl hardly knew what the announcement meant, and she had probably never considered seriously the question of the "social, civil, and religious rights of women." She was not accustomed to thinking of her status in terms of large social and political issues, but she clearly felt the sorrow of her condition, and the notion of a women's convention struck a sympathetic chord.

The young men of her age were already embarking on challenging careers—as lawyers, merchants, or bankers; as boatmen on the Erie Canal; or as farmers with land of their own. The nation was growing rapidly, and they were helping it grow. But Charlotte Woodward and other women in early America could hope to play only a subordinate part in the vital world that both encompassed and excluded them.

While the men she knew set out to make their fortunes, Charlotte stayed at home and earned a little money by sewing gloves, each day stitching together the precut panels of leather that were sent to her in packages from nearby Gloversville. The tedious job left her mind free to wander—untested, undeveloped, and unnourished. She would rather have worked in a printing office, setting type, but her prospect for such a job was as remote as that of becoming a banker or a lawyer. All such work was considered outside "the woman's sphere." Even the money she earned was not legally her own but her father's; and later, after she was married, anything she earned would belong to her husband.

And so the small notice in the *Seneca County Courier* was tantalizing, allowing women like Charlotte Woodward to give their own meaning to the notion of the "rights of women," hinting that she and others might deserve a more promising life. Charlotte was so enthusiastic about the convention that she ran over to a neighbor's to share the news with other girls. They, too, had read the notice, and soon a group of Charlotte's friends decided to go together to the meeting.

On July 19 she and six other women set out for Seneca Falls in a wagon pulled by sturdy farm horses. As they neared the town, they were joined on the main road by other wagons, carriages, and surreys bound, like them, for the meeting at the Wesleyan Chapel. Charlotte was surprised and pleased to see that men as well as women had joined the procession. In town they came upon a large crowd gathered in the churchyard.

None of the people who stood outside the Wesleyan Chapel on that summer morning in Seneca Falls had ever before attended a convention on women. The subject of women's rights had occasionally been discussed in the past half century, and new legislation sometimes affected the position of women, but this was the first time a convention had ever met in the United States to consider the general problem of women's rights. Even those who had called the meeting were not certain what would happen; but among them was a woman named Elizabeth Cady Stanton, who had considered more fully than most the position of women in a democratic nation. She and a few friends had suggested the meeting and drafted a preliminary resolution. Her background illustrates the history of women in early America and helps explain both the large social forces and the personal aspirations that came into play at Seneca Falls.

Elizabeth Cady Stanton, who was the guiding light of the Seneca Falls Convention and a leading figure in the early movement for women's rights, was born into a conservative, upper-class household in Johnstown, New York, on November 12, 1815. Her father, Daniel Cady, was a lawyer, legislator, and judge; her mother, Margaret Cady, was a stern Presbyterian woman who bore six children.

Like Charlotte Woodward and other women whose lives she would influence, Elizabeth Cady was aware from her earliest years that she had been born into a man's world. It was all very well for women like her mother to bear daughters—the biological survival of the race demanded the existence of both sexes, after all. But a woman's greatest achievement was to bear a son. Elizabeth's first memory was a conversation she heard in her fifth year when her mother's friends had gathered after the birth of her sister, Katherine. Although everyone was undoubtedly pleased at the good health of mother and child, there was sorrow in the house. The friends commiserated with her parents for not having produced a boy.

From her early childhood Elizabeth grappled with the problem of being a female in a society that favored boys and men. The dichotomy between the two worlds was reflected in the development of her personality. She was a lively, intelligent child with sparkling eyes, a pretty face, and a vibrant sense of humor, but beneath this animated exterior she was depressed, given to dark thoughts and frightening nightmares. Although well behaved, she believed that she was tainted with evil. This anxiety may have also developed from her Presbyterian upbringing, with its emphasis on humankind's innate sinfulness, and from the rigorous standards of conduct imposed by her parents.

But her uneasiness must have fed also on her sense of discontent with her gender role. She was attracted to male activities. As a child, she was a tomboy—a phrase used then and today to describe a young girl who enjoyed sports. As she grew older, she longed for educational and vocational opportunities that were provided only for boys. What was the source of these outlandish longings? Surely they were not a woman's ideas.

It did not initially occur to her that her ambitions might be natural human aspirations, and she feared that their source must be an evil force. As a child, Elizabeth had a recurrent dream in which she had been fathered by Satan, and he wanted to reclaim her. After such dreams she would awaken with horror and with a troubled mind would creep to the top of the staircase where she could listen to the adult voices from the room below. These human sounds calmed her, returning her to her daily world.

If, however, the real world was not as disturbing as her dream world, it did contain disquieting problems for a young girl like Elizabeth. Her yearning after manly opportunities was not merely a whim; it was a part of her makeup. She was as bright and resourceful as the boys she knew. She played chess and at school was an able student of Latin, Greek, and mathematics.

When she was not at school, she often visited her father's law offices. Comfortable in that adult, male world, she could read legal cases and listen to his conversations with clients. In 1826 when Elizabeth's only brother, Eleazer, died shortly after graduating from college, her grief-stricken father told her, "Oh, my daughter, I wish you were a boy." The statement is more complex than it sounds. Daniel Cady was a sensitive man and was well aware of his daughter's abilities. He did not simply wish that she had been a completely different person, for she already had the energy and ability he would have wanted in a son. If she had been a boy, however, she could fill the worldly role for which her character and intellect so well prepared her. He wanted that for her sake as well as for his.

But Elizabeth was a girl, and early in the nineteenth century this meant that however strong or smart or energetic she might be, much of life was closed to her. On her visits to the law office, where she saw women shackled to dissolute husbands, unable to free themselves by divorce or even to control their own money or children, she learned a great deal about these limitations. In marriage a woman quite literally lost her legal personality and became in a real sense the property of her husband, who gained complete control of her possessions and ownership of anything she might earn during wedlock. He could even beat her if he so chose, and she had no legal redress. She could not testify in court, because she was considered to have no legal character separate from that of her husband. Realizing that Elizabeth objected to laws discriminating against her sex, the young men who studied law under Daniel Cady teased her by pointing out many such rules in statute books. One Christmas Day they made a point of telling her that a fine coral necklace and bracelets she had just received would someday belong to her husband. More than sixty years later she remembered one of the students saying: "Now if in due time you should be my wife, these ornaments would be mine; I could take them and lock them up, and you could never wear them except with my permission. I could even exchange them for a box of cigars, and you could watch them evaporate in smoke."

The fact of inequality grew even more evident when Elizabeth graduated from the local academy. At school the girls and boys had been able "to study and play together with the greatest freedom and harmony," and she and other girls had competed successfully with boys in all things. But at the end of the academy years, the boys went off to Union College in Schenectady, proud and handsome in their new clothes, while the girls remained behind. When, said Elizabeth, "I learned of the barrier that prevented me from following in their footsteps—'no girls admitted here'—my vexation and mortification knew no bounds."

Though she could not go to Union College, Elizabeth was able to find other opportunities for growth. An academy for young girls had recently opened in Troy, New York, under the direction of Emma Willard. Most women's academies in the nineteenth century were "finishing schools" that taught women to be ladies and wives; but Emma Willard believed that girls should have the same educational challenges as boys and modeled her curriculum after that in men's colleges. Elizabeth attended Emma Willard's school and graduated in 1832.

She received further education in the company of her cousin, Gerrit Smith, whom she frequently visited in Peterboro, New York. A wealthy landowner who devoted much of his time to reform causes, Smith taught Elizabeth about abolitionism and temperance reform. She saw fugitive slaves, whom Smith sheltered and sent to Canada; she attended antislavery meetings; and she associated with people who believed that the world could be changed. Her parents had espoused a static view of reality. There were facts of life that one must simply learn, and the mature person adjusted to the world as it was. But Smith and his friends believed society was changeable, that if the individual and the community were in conflict, the community might be to blame rather than the individual.

Among the reformers who visited Gerrit Smith's house was an abolitionist lecturer and organizer named Henry Brewster Stanton. Ten years Elizabeth's senior, he was widely regarded as the most eloquent antislavery orator of his time. During autumn 1839 he and Elizabeth conversed by her cousin's fireside and traveled together to local reform meetings. One day while they were horseback riding through the bright autumnal woods, Stanton surprised Elizabeth with "one of those charming revelations of human feeling which brave knights have always found eloquent words to utter, and to which fair ladies have always listened with mingled emotions of pleasure and astonishment." The description of Stanton's proposal, written by Elizabeth fifty years after the event, invokes the image of a strong, assertive man and a weak, submissive woman. But if such feelings accompanied the proposal, they hardly characterize the marriage.

In their years together Elizabeth frequently displayed her resourcefulness and initiative, having to contend first with her parents, who opposed the match because of Stanton's abolitionism. Antislavery had not yet become fashionable in the North, and people like Stanton were frequently regarded as deluded fanatics whose utopian schemes endangered the Union. But Elizabeth persisted in her attachment despite their opposition.

On May 10, 1840, the young couple stood before a Scottish clergyman, Hugh Maire, and were joined in marriage. Even the ceremony reflected Elizabeth's independent temperament. With some difficulty, but with her husband's approval, she persuaded the minister to omit the promise to "obey" her husband from the wedding ceremony, because, as she later wrote, "I obstinately refused to obey one with whom I supposed I was entering into an equal relation." Both husband and wife were strong-willed individuals whose personal ambitions would test one another's patience in the years ahead. But after nearly a half century of marriage, Elizabeth could write that she and Henry had lived together "without more than the usual matrimonial friction."

After the ceremony the Stantons sailed for England, where Henry was to be a delegate to the World's Anti-Slavery Convention, held in London. While there, Elizabeth Stanton furthered her education through discussions with women delegates to the convention. Many opponents of slavery opposed the inclusion of women as participants or speakers in organizations exclusively for men, and the first issue debated at the London convention was the seating of female delegates. Henry Stanton and William Lloyd Garrison, among others, favored including women, but they were outvoted. Garrison was so disgusted that he refused to participate in the meeting, joining the ladies in an observation gallery instead. "After battling so many long years," he said, "for the liberties of African slaves, I can take no part in a convention that strikes down the most sacred rights of all women." Henry Stanton was annoyed but was not sufficiently outraged to boycott the convention.

In London, Elizabeth Stanton met Lucretia C. Mott, a Quaker minister from Philadelphia. Mott and other Quaker women, nourished by the liberal atmosphere of a faith that encouraged women to speak in church, were active in various reform movements. She and Elizabeth Stanton immediately became good friends. Walking arm in arm through the streets of London, they discussed the idea of an American women's rights convention. In Mott's company Elizabeth realized for the first time in her life that her discontent about her place in the world could be transformed from a personal grievance into a program for change.

The proposed convention was delayed for eight years, but when the Stantons returned to the United States, Elizabeth's education in reform movements continued. For two years she and Henry lived in Johnstown, where Daniel Cady received Henry Stanton

Henry Stanton. A reformer himself, he usually supported his wife, Elizabeth Cady Stanton, when she fought for women's rights.

as a student in his law offices, hoping perhaps that the legal profession would mute the radicalism of his new son-in-law. In 1843 the Stantons moved to Boston, where Henry opened a law office and Elizabeth devoted her attention to rearing her first three children. Her work at home gave her confidence in her own abilities. When she properly diagnosed why her first child cried constantly, she claimed that she had learned "another lesson in self-reliance." While raising a family she maintained her interest in reform by associating with local abolitionists, including Frederick Douglass, William Lloyd Garrison, Lydia Maria Child, and Maria Weston Chapman. In Boston, as in her cousin's house at Peterboro, she met people who believed that the world could be improved by reform activity.

In 1847 the Stantons left Boston and returned to rural upstate New York where Henry opened a law office in Seneca Falls. The change was discouraging, for here Elizabeth was occupied with a seemingly endless round of trivial household tasks. "My duties were too numerous and varied," she later wrote, "and none sufficiently exhilarating or intellectual to bring into play my higher faculties. I suffered with mental hunger, which, like an empty stomach, is very depressing." As she observed the "wearied, anxious look" of other women, she recognized that they, too, felt weighted down by immediate cares and excluded from the real excitement and challenge of life. She wanted to do something to improve their condition and hers.

During this troubled time she visited Lucretia Mott, who was staying with a friend in nearby Waterloo, New York. Recognizing that she would find a sympathetic audience in Lucretia Mott and three other Quakers, Jane Hunt, Mary Ann McClintock, and Martha C. Wright, Elizabeth poured out her feelings of "long accumulating discontent." They were so moved by her complaints that they decided to hold a meeting on women's rights the following week. That evening they wrote the announcement for the *Seneca County Courier*.

While women like Charlotte Woodward, the glove seamstress, were reading the notice, Elizabeth Stanton and her friends began to plan the meeting, assembling on Sunday at Mary Ann McClintock's house to draft an agenda and proposals. At first they expected this to be an easy task, for their grievances were many. As Stanton later wrote, "They had felt the insults incident to their sex, in many ways, as every proud, thinking woman must, in the laws, religion, and literature of the world." But how could they express their ideas in a plain, forceful resolution? The task seemed overwhelming, and "They felt as helpless and hopeless," wrote Stanton, "as if they had been suddenly asked to construct a steam engine."

They resigned themselves finally to reviewing various "masculine productions," including statements from temperance and antislavery conventions. But these "seemed too tame and pacific for the inauguration of a rebellion such as the world had never before seen." Finally, one of the women read the Declaration of Independence. Here, at last, was a suitable model. Sitting around a mahogany table in the McClintock parlor, the women rewrote the Declaration. The villain of the piece became "all men" instead of George III, and the specific complaints of the founding fathers gave way to a list of women's grievances culled from statute books, church practices, and social customs. With the completion of this document they were ready to conduct America's first women's rights convention.

On the morning of July 19 Elizabeth Cady Stanton, Lucretia Mott, and three hundred other men and women gathered at the Wesleyan Chapel at Seneca Falls. They found the church door locked—perhaps the local minister had suddenly grown faint of heart at the thought of this extraordinary meeting in his church—but soon a small boy was lifted through a church window, and he unbolted the door. As the large crowd entered the building, the women leaders quickly and somewhat apprehensively reviewed the situation. The number of Quaker reformers, working women, and towns-people greatly exceeded their expectations. The women had initially planned on an all-female meeting for the first day, but they were glad now to discover forty men in the audience. Their declaration called for a revolt against male rule, but several "well disposed men," including Henry Stanton, had helped draft the document; other men, among them James Mott, Frederick Douglass, Ansel Bascom, and Samuel Tillman, had come to the convention. In deference to male familiarity with public meetings, the women appointed Lucretia Mott's husband, James, to moderate. Later generations of reformers might regard this decision as a failure of nerve, a retreat to male domination in the very moment of revolt. But Elizabeth Stanton and other women recognized that one need not be a slave to oppose slavery, or a woman to oppose injustice to women. And so they felt comfortable with support from a "well disposed" male.

The meeting began with speeches. Lucretia Mott summarized the condition of her sex and called for the education and elevation of women. Ansel Bascom, a New York politician, described a bill that had just passed the state legislature giving property rights to married women. And Samuel Tillman, a law student, read objectionable statutes affecting women. Elizabeth Cady Stanton spoke briefly but was so overawed that she felt like "running away" and spoke in a timid voice that could hardly be heard. The next day, however, she redeemed herself.

On the second day the convention began with a reading of the Declaration of Sentiments, which provides a concise summary of the laws and attitudes that defined a woman's position in nineteenth-century America. The preamble followed almost exactly the wording of the American Declaration of Independence and thus identified the issue of women's rights with the principles of the founding fathers. It began: "We hold these truths to be self-evident: that all men and women are created equal; that they are endowed by their Creator with certain inalienable rights; that among these are life, liberty, and the pursuit of happiness; that to secure these rights governments are instituted, deriving their just powers from the consent of the governed."

These inalienable rights had been continually abused by men: "The history of mankind," the declaration read, "is a history of repeated injuries and usurpations on the part of man toward woman, having in direct object the establishment of an absolute tyranny over her."

The Declaration of Sentiments continued, like the Jeffersonian original, by listing specific grievances. Some of these were political. The government denies woman "her inalienable right to the elective franchise," taxes her without her own consent, and forces her to submit to laws "in the formation of which she had no voice." Even the most "ignorant and degraded men" received these same rights without question.

Woman's disabilities were even more pronounced in her status in marriage. Wedlock was a repressive institution in which men had the right to rule as absolute monarchs. By law, a married woman was "civilly dead"—without rights to property, or even to her own wages. She was not even considered morally responsible, because if she committed a crime in the presence of her husband, he was considered culpable on the presumption that he was her master. Moreover, men were free to beat their wives, and in a divorce the law favored male claims to guardianship of the children.

Woman's position was further weakened by laws and customs that denied her an equal place in society. She could not receive "a thorough education, all colleges being closed against her," and she was barred from the professions; even the path to the ministry was closed on the claim of "apostolic authority." She received "but a scanty remuneration" for the humble jobs she was allowed to perform. Even the moral code was easier on men, among whom such activities as drunkenness and fornication were regarded as peccadilloes.

In all these ways men attempted to destroy woman's "confidence in her own powers, to lessen her self-respect, and to make her willing to lead a dependent and abject life." Elizabeth Cady Stanton had not suffered from many of the worst outgrowths of woman's subordination. Her husband did not beat her or misuse his legal control of her property, nor was she one of those women whose husbands sold their jewels for money to spend in the local saloon. But since her early childhood she had felt humiliated by the knowledge that she occupied an inferior position in society. She had seen men with less intelligence than hers leaving for a college she could not attend, voting when she could not vote, and working where she could not work. She knew the many ways in which her society undermined women's confidence and self-respect. Her solution, expressed in the declaration, was simple and direct: women must have "immediate admission to all the rights and privileges which belong to them as citizens of the United States."

Lucretia Mott. Taught self-reliance by the Quakers, she in turn encouraged Elizabeth Cady Stanton to take up the fight for women's rights.

To reach this goal the Declaration of Sentiments called for supporters to educate the American people about the wrongs women suffered. Toward that end the delegates passed resolutions for specific reforms. They condemned all laws that conflicted with "the true and substantial happiness of women" and prevented a woman from "occupying such a station in society as her conscience shall dictate." Such laws were contrary to nature and hence were invalid. The delegates condemned the "double standard" in moral precepts and claimed "the same amount of virtue, delicacy, and refinement of behavior that is required of women in the social state, should also be required of men." The convention resolved that God intended woman to be man's equal. Accordingly, she should speak out on social issues; participate in "trades, professions, and commerce"; and move beyond the "circumscribed limits" imposed upon her by "corrupt customs," thus entering into "the enlarged sphere which her great Creator has assigned her."

All these proposals passed the convention by unanimous vote. But one other resolution encountered stiff opposition. This was the declaration that "It is the duty of the women of this country to secure to themselves their sacred right to the elective franchise." A substantial portion of the delegates were unwilling to accept the idea of woman suffrage. Some were Quakers who opposed it because they did not favor political activity by men or women; others believed that the measure was too radical. Henry Stanton, who had favored other reform proposals, refused to attend when woman suffrage was discussed. Apparently, many of those who favored equality for women in education, professions, and marriage wanted to preserve some vestige of male supremacy.

But Elizabeth Cady Stanton and her supporters felt that the right to vote furnished the key to all other rights, because men passed the laws that circumscribed women's rights. In defense of the famous ninth resolution—the first woman suffrage proposal to be voted on in an American convention—she delivered an eloquent address, urging the importance of the measure. She received impressive support from Frederick Douglass, who had come to the convention from his home in nearby Rochester. Douglass, the great black abolitionist, was fully occupied with writing and speaking for the antislavery cause. Having suffered beatings, hunger, and other trials in his youth as a slave, he might easily have thought little of the oppression of women. But he was a highly principled man and believed that one could not denounce one form of oppression while accepting another. He spoke forcefully in defense of Stanton's suffrage proposal, linking his cause with hers. In the end the measure passed by a close vote.

The convention adjourned late in the evening of the second day. It had been a gathering of men and women who believed that many current laws and customs were unfair to women and that their declaration and resolutions were statements of common sense. But to the nation at large, the events at Seneca Falls seemed either ridiculous or threatening. In 1848 most Americans believed that a woman's "natural" sphere was the home. Her sole obligation to society was to create a comfortable domestic environment for her children and husband. Men should be engaged in worldly activities: they developed new industries, built railroads, designed canals; they settled the West, removing obstacles with ax and rifle; they fought in the Mexican War, acquiring new territory for America. A woman's role in all these manly activities should be dependent and supportive. She must provide an oasis of tranquility for the businessman back from his work, the farmer home from the fields, and the soldier returned from the battlefield.

The public reaction to the Seneca Falls Convention reflected the predominantly conservative attitude of the nation as a whole toward the question of women's rights, many newspapers declaring that the gathering had been inappropriate and outlandish. The meeting was dubbed "The Hen Convention," and its participants were described as cranks, amazons, and frustrated spinsters. The women had attended their convention "at the expense of their appropriate duties."

The demand for women's rights was so startling that many editors had trouble explaining specifically in what ways it was wrong. They tended to fall back on their own version of natural law. No well-balanced woman would demand more rights, they said. "Every true hearted female will instantly feel that this is unwomanly." The demand for women's rights would destroy "things established at the creation of mankind." An editor in Philadelphia declared that in his city women already influenced human affairs through their control over men's souls. "They soar to rule the hearts of their worshippers," he said, "and secure obedience by the sceptre of affection." Continuing his romantic description of female influence, he said, "A woman is nobody. A wife is everything. A pretty girl is equal to ten thousand men, and a mother is, next to God, all powerful." In such ways the idealized power of woman was used as an excuse for making her powerless.

In general, the press also sought to ridicule the Seneca Falls Convention by pointing out seemingly absurd implications of women's rights. If the proposed revolution were to occur, society would have to be "radically remodeled" and its "organic laws" overturned. If women wanted to participate in some traditionally male occupations, they must participate in all and not just "those employments only which require the least exertion and are exempt from danger." Thus, in what one editor regarded as the ultimate absurdity, she would be required ultimately to put on "the panoply of war."

To balance out the intrusion of women into man's sphere, men would have to engage in women's work. One journalist wrote that the Seneca Falls Declaration implied that men must "wash dishes, scour up, be put to the tub, handle the broom, darn stockings, patch breeches, scold the servants, dress in the latest fashion, wear trinkets, look beautiful, and be as fascinating as those blessed morsels of humanity whom God gave to preserve that rough animal man, in something like a reasonable civilization."

Although such criticisms dominated the press, a few newspapers welcomed the women's rights proposals as part of the general "democratic progression" of the age. The editor of the *Rochester Daily Advertiser* wrote that "nature" did not require women to be confined exclusively to "the drudgery of raising children, and superintending the kitchens, and to the performance of the various other household duties which the cruelty of men and the customs of society have so long assigned to them." He welcomed the idea of an exchange or blending of roles. "Can not women fill an office," he said, "or cast a vote, or conduct a campaign, as judiciously and vigorously as men? And, on the other hand, can not men 'nurse' the babies, or preside at the washtub, or boil a pot as safely and as well as women?"

Despite such scattered support, however, the signers of the Seneca Falls Declaration and resolutions were generally condemned. Many former participants were surprised and dismayed by the widespread press criticism and sheepishly withdrew their names from the convention documents, concluding, apparently, that personal ridicule was too high a price to pay for their goals. But others were encouraged by the start they had made. Many of the Seneca Falls supporters would remain staunch backers of the women's reform movement in the years ahead. Others heard about the convention in the papers and were encouraged to communicate with Stanton and Mott. One of these new recruits was Susan B. Anthony, who read about the convention and eventually became one of the nation's outstanding women's rights organizers.

A new movement had been launched, and in small ways women could begin to live according to its ideas. Elizabeth Cady Stanton began to see herself in a new way, as something more than the appendage of a man. She could not yet vote or hold office, but she could at least declare her independence by insisting on being called by her own name rather than by her husband's. Her defense of this practice in a letter to a friend, Rebecca R. Eyster, a year before the Seneca Falls Convention, is one of her clearest statements of her quest for personal identity. She wrote: "I have very serious objections, dear Rebecca, to being called Henry. There is a great deal in a name. It often signifies much, and may involve a great principle. Ask our colored brethren if there is nothing in a name. Why are the slaves nameless unless they take that of their master? Simply because they have no independent existence. They are mere chattels, with no civil or social rights. . . . The custom of calling women Mrs. John This and Mrs. Tom That, and colored men Sambo and Zip Coon, is founded on the principle that white men are lords of all. I cannot acknowledge this principle as just; therefore, I cannot bear the name of another."

Elizabeth Cady Stanton lived until 1902. She remained married to Henry Stanton and reared seven children, but the Seneca Falls Convention changed her life.

For the next half century she devoted much of her time to speaking and organizing on behalf of women's rights. She and Susan B. Anthony formed one of the most creative partnerships in the history of American reform movements and laid the foundation for the woman suffrage amendment and many other reforms.

Just as Stanton had startled some of her friends by proposing a suffrage resolution at Seneca Falls, she continued to keep her friends off balance with new proposals. She advocated, for example, easier divorce laws and condemned the church for its subordination of women. "To be eternally politic and polite," she said, "was to do violence to yourself." She was reluctant to allow women to become too complacent about the character of their movement. Women's demands had to be continually reevaluated and restated. With her keen intellect, bright charm, and sparkling humor, she was a leading figure in the women's movement in America for five decades.

The issue articulated at Seneca Falls in 1848 was one of the most complex in the history of American reform. It was a revolt against male domination in which many "well disposed men" participated. It began a women's rights movement that many women were afraid to embrace. It occurred at a time when Americans supported many reforms, and yet it was ahead of its time. In the year of the Seneca Falls meeting the New York legislature did pass a bill granting women more control over personal property in marriage, but few Americans in 1848 were willing to consider the idea of equal employment or suffrage for women.

The Seneca Falls Convention reflected the disposition of Americans in the early republic to question every institution and reevaluate every social convention. But the response revealed the bedrock of conservatism that left many reforms such as emancipation, racial integration, and women's rights to the future. For leaders like Elizabeth Cady Stanton and followers like Charlotte Woodward, however, it was exciting to have taken the first step on the road to equality.

Bibliography

Banner, Lois W. *Elizabeth Cady Stanton: A Radical for Woman's Rights* (1995). Fine brief biography.

Dixon, Chris. *Perfecting the Family: Antislavery Marriages in Nineteenth-Century America* (1997). Focuses on eight reform-minded couples, including Elizabeth Cady Stanton and Henry Stanton.

Du Bois, Ellen. *Feminism and Suffrage: The Emergence of an Independent Women's Movement in America, 1848–1869* (1978). Development of the women's rights movement after Seneca Falls.

Griffith, Elizabeth. *In Her Own Right: The Life of Elizabeth Cady Stanton* (1984). Well-researched and admiring biography.

Matthews, Jean V. *Women's Struggle for Equality: The First Phase, 1828–1876* (1997). Explores the many ways that women enhanced their lives during the half century surrounding the Seneca Falls Convention.

McMillen, Sally. *Seneca Falls and the Origins of the Women's Rights Movement* (2009). Fine narrative history and survey focusing on the lives of four leaders of the movement, including Elizabeth Cady Stanton.

Stanton, Elizabeth Cady. *Eighty Years and More* (1898). Stanton's vivid autobiography.

Stanton, Elizabeth Cady, et al. *History of Woman Suffrage* (6 vols., 1899–1922). Useful survey with Seneca Falls documents.

Stanton, Theodore, and Harriot Stanton Blatch, Editors. *Elizabeth Cady Stanton as Revealed in Her Letters, Diary, and Reminiscences* (1922). Includes many valuable Stanton letters.

Wellman, Judith. *The Road to Seneca Falls: Elizabeth Cady Stanton and the First Women's Rights Convention* (2004). Explores the background of the convention, including abolitionist influences and preexisting women's support networks.

Identification Topics

Charlotte Woodward, Elizabeth Cady Stanton, Daniel Cady, Susan B. Anthony, Henry Brewster Stanton, World's Anti-Slavery Convention (1840), Emma Willard, Lucretia C. Mott, Seneca Falls Convention, Declaration of Sentiments, Frederick Douglass, "A dependent and abject life"

Study Questions

1. What disadvantages as women did persons like Charlotte Woodward and Elizabeth Cady Stanton experience in the early 1800s?
2. Why do you think Stanton was dissatisfied with her lot as a woman in 1848? Why could she not be content to be a wife and a mother?
3. In what ways did Stanton assert her independence prior to the Seneca Falls Convention?
4. Why were Quaker women better prepared to assert themselves in public gatherings than non-Quaker women?
5. What did men in the 1840s think about women's rights? In what ways did men support and oppose the movement—especially at Seneca Falls?
6. What specific grievances were aired at Seneca Falls, and what solutions were offered?
7. Why were many participants at the convention opposed to the woman suffrage proposal?
8. Describe the press reaction to the convention and explain why it was generally so hostile. How did opponents of women's rights justify their position?
9. What was accomplished at Seneca Falls?

CHAPTER 13

Manifest Destiny
Down the Santa Fe Trail with Susan Shelby Magoffin, 1846–1847

During the 1840s, American expansionists dreamed of occupying the continent from sea to sea. The Southwest belonged to Mexico and the Northwest was jointly controlled by England and the United States, but supporters of "manifest destiny" argued that God had ordained these lands for exclusive use by the American people as a showcase for liberty and democracy. Through diplomatic negotiations in 1846 the United States was able to gain the Oregon Territory, then a wilderness. The Southwest, however, had been settled for more than two centuries by immigrants from Mexico and could not be won by peaceful negotiation. In 1845 the United States annexed Texas, which had fought for its independence from Mexico in 1836, and in the next year the United States went to war with Mexico. By 1848 the United States had gained a million square miles of territory, all carved out of Mexico. The moral problem inherent in spreading democracy by the sword was evident in the experience of a trader's wife, Susan Shelby Magoffin, and other American civilians and soldiers who entered New Mexico in 1846 with Gen. Stephen Watts Kearny and the Army of the West.

As the sun sank low over the Kansas plains on the evening of June 12, 1846, Susan Shelby Magoffin, a young bride, busied herself gathering wildflowers. The prairie blossoms were so abundant that she repeatedly filled her arms with flowers, discarded them, and filled her arms again. At last she grew tired of her grasslands ramble and returned home to feed the chickens. As twilight fell over the prairie, she heard the barnyard sounds of dogs, cows, and mules, mingling with men's voices. She finished her work and stepped inside for supper.

These events suggest moments in the ordinary routine of nineteenth-century rural life, linking Susan Magoffin with thousands of other farm wives in the United States. But nothing else in Susan's life on that night in 1846 was the least bit conventional. Her "house" was a tent; her neighbors slept in freight wagons; and the men outside were Mexicans as well as Americans. Susan Magoffin was beginning a trip that no other American woman had made. Her husband, Samuel, was a merchant who made his living by carrying goods overland from Missouri to northern Mexico along the Santa Fe Trail. The trade was twenty-five years old, but Samuel was the first trader ever to bring an American wife along on the rugged journey. That night in the tent Susan revealed the spirit of adventure underlying her journey when she wrote in a notebook: "My journal tells a story tonight different from what it has ever done before. . . . From the city of New York to the plains of Mexico is a stride that I myself can scarcely realize."

Susan Magoffin's journey would have been extraordinary at any time, but in 1846 political events would add to her adventures. In 1844 James Polk had been elected to the presidency on a platform promising to expand America's boundaries westward. He capitalized on a national mood of "manifest destiny"—belief that American institutions were so inherently righteous that the United States would, with God's blessing, occupy the continent from sea to sea. In 1845 Polk annexed Texas, which had recently won its independence from Mexico. He then opened negotiations with the Mexicans, hoping to persuade them to sell the remainder of the Southwest to the United States. But Mexico was unwilling to give up half its territory, so Polk used a border skirmish as a pretext for war, which was declared on May 13, 1846. During the next two years American armies would knife into Mexico through Santa Fe, Matamoros, and Vera Cruz. The nationalist dream of 1844 would be a reality in 1848: American flags would flutter over scores of Mexican villages from Texas to California.

What was it like to be in Mexico in the presence of a conquering army? How did the Mexicans feel about the American conquest? Susan Magoffin's experience suggests that during the era when the United States absorbed a large portion of Mexico, Americans were also absorbed by Mexico, acquiring Mexican habits of speech, thought, dress, and diet. Her journal reveals the American capacity for both openness and ethnocentrism.

By the 1840s several hundred men set out each year by wagon and horseback from Missouri carrying merchandise to Santa Fe. Two of the foremost traders were Samuel Magoffin and his brother James. James entered the trade in 1825, the year the United States sent a party to mark the Santa Fe Trail, and three years later Samuel joined him. James traveled as far south as Mexico City, and the brothers established stores in Chihuahua and Saltillo, hundreds of miles south of Santa Fe. They liked the Mexican people. In 1830 James married a wellborn woman from Chihuahua, Doña Maria Gertrudes Valdez. Her brother Gabriel Valdez was also a trader, and her cousin Manuel Armijo was a merchant from Albuquerque who would become governor of New Mexico.

The Magoffin brothers exemplify the close relations that American merchants were able to establish with the Mexicans. James was at various times consul to Saltillo and American commercial agent in Chihuahua and Durango. Samuel was trusted to carry the payroll for the Santa Fe garrison. The people of northern Mexico welcomed the goods from the United States, which included books, clothing, drugs, and printing presses. They in turn exported silver and furs to America. The famous "Missouri mule" was really an import from Mexico, and in parts of Missouri the Mexican peso circulated as freely as the American dollar.

In 1846 Susan and Samuel Magoffin were in Independence, Missouri, making their final preparations for the overland journey. Independence, a town of trim wood-frame houses, stood at the threshold of the American wilderness. Steamboats arrived from St. Louis loaded with traders, gamblers, speculators, Oregon-bound immigrants, Native Americans, fur trappers, and slaves. At Independence the travelers saw Mexicans in sombreros and French-Canadian mountain men in buckskin. The clang, clang of hammer on iron filled the air as a dozen blacksmiths shoed horses and repaired wagons.

Samuel and Susan left Independence in a carriage, protected from the elements. Their party included Susan's servant Jane, who went in another carriage, and a number of Mexican servants and teamsters, who drove the freight wagons with Samuel's merchandise. Little in Susan Magoffin's background suggests that she would undertake such an arduous trip. Her parents were wealthy Kentuckians, and her grandfather, Isaac Shelby, was the first governor of the state. A photo taken in 1845, when Susan was eighteen, shows her wearing an elegant brocade dress. Long black hair and dark eyebrows accentuate a pretty oval face, and a look of quiet contentment brightens her eyes. The photo may have been taken for her fiancé, Samuel Magoffin, whose portrait was painted on an ivory medallion at roughly the same time. He is forty-five years old, twenty-seven years older than his wife, and looks like a respectable judge. A roll of fat above his bow tie gives him a second chin, sideburns curl from his ears almost to his lips, and a receding hairline accentuates his thoughtful forehead. He looks pleased and self-assured: a hardworking man whose life is about to be crowned with marriage to an attractive and wellborn young lady.

The Magoffins were married in Kentucky on November 25, 1845, and went to New York for their honeymoon. In the ordinary course of life, Susan would then have settled down in Kentucky or Missouri while Samuel set off alone to attend to his business interests in Mexico. Susan does not explain why she decided to accompany her husband, but several reasons are evident. She had been interested in that remote region since her schooldays, when she learned about the "table plains" of the Southwest—we call them mesas. She hoped the prairie air would be good for her health. And she and Samuel cherished each other's company. Susan's journal begins with almost fifty pages of love poems. Her first words of Spanish in the account are *mi alma* (my soul), her nickname for her husband.

On the first night out the Magoffins stayed in a house ten miles from Independence. The next day they left the settlements behind. "Now the prairie life begins!" wrote Susan. Morning brought the noise of teamsters cracking whips and "whooping and hallowing" over the mules and oxen. Their fourteen wagons of trade goods were pulled by twelve oxen each; a baggage wagon was pulled by four oxen; and the Magoffins' and the maid's carriages were pulled by two mules each. Two men on mules drove the "loose stock"— another nineteen oxen. The men were Mexican and American teamsters.

In 1846 the Santa Fe Trail was busier than usual, for the merchants shared the road with fifteen hundred soldiers belonging to the U.S. Army and to various volunteer companies, all on their way to the Mexican War. One of the soldiers, John Taylor Hughes of the First Regiment of Missouri Cavalry, poetically described the army's line of march: "As far as the vision could penetrate the long files of cavalry, the gay fluttering banners, and the canvas-covered wagons of the merchant teams, glistening like banks of snow in the distance, might be seen winding their tortuous way over the undulating surface of the prairie."

No paved highway led to Santa Fe, but only a vague route across 750 miles of dirt, sand, rocks, and mud. Wagons bogged down in the mud, and oxen had to be hitched in double or triple teams to move them at all. One of the Magoffin wagons got stuck so badly that twenty-two oxen were hitched to it, and even they were unable to move it. Finally the teamsters "whipped out" the wagon by beating the oxen with their whip handles, "yelling all the time," wrote Susan, "till one is almost induced to believe their throats will split."

At the creeks and rivers the party found no bridges, only fords. The wagons made their way down slippery banks and plunged into the streams, hurrying sometimes to get across before a rainstorm could swell the river. On a good day they covered twenty or twenty-five miles. Often they made only ten, traveling one mile an hour or slower.

During the night the Magoffins stopped at customary resting places. No hotels or shops or taverns graced these spots; only the convenient supply of wood and water distinguished them from the rest of the prairie. They were usually named for a geographic feature or local event. "The Lone Elm" was, naturally, a place with one elm tree. "Council Grove" was the scene of a meeting between Indian and white leaders in 1825. "Big John's Spring" was named for an early pioneer who liked to carve his name on trees with a tomahawk.

Susan traveled comfortably in her carriage, protected from the elements. On cold, rainy days she wrapped herself in a buffalo robe and looked out at the countryside. When the sky cleared, she got out to walk, easily keeping up with the slow-moving wagons. She picked prairie flowers, which she pressed in her diary, and she gathered gooseberries to eat. At night Susan and Samuel slept in their army tent. A table was fastened to the center pole, and above it was a stand holding their mirror and combs. The rug was made of sailcloth, and their chairs were portable stools with seats of carpet. Outside lay their dog, a greyhound named Ring, whom Susan called "a nice watch for our tent door."

When days of heavy rain stalled the wagons, Susan stayed in the tent and knitted, read books, and wrote letters. One rainy afternoon she and her husband sat comfortably in bed as a stream flowed through the tent. Samuel rested his head in Susan's lap and "dozed a little and talked a little." Her contentment shines through the early pages of the journal. "Oh, this is a life I would not exchange for a good deal!" she wrote, "There is such independence, so much free uncontaminated air, which impregnates the mind, the feelings, nay every thought, with purity. I breathe free without that oppression and uneasiness felt in the gossiping circles of a settled home." Camped one evening in a bed of wild roses—with rosebushes at the door and inside the tent—she wrote, "It is the life of a wandering princess mine."

Day after day the Magoffins worked their way westward, sometimes alone, sometimes in company with other merchants or soldiers. Parties would split up as one segment fell behind to repair wagons; a few days later the lagging traders might pass their former comrades, now repairing their own wagons. Susan faithfully recorded the changes along the trail. On the Kansas plains the wagons moved through grass so tall "as to conceal a man's waist." One evening Susan walked out on the prairie at sunset. To the west all that she could see was "a waving sea of tall grass." She had never seen "a more imposing sight."

Along the way they came to "tourist attractions." No billboards advertised these sites, and no merchants ran souvenir stands nearby, but word of mouth and descriptions in Josiah Gregg's *Commerce of the Prairies*, the classic account of the Santa Fe trade, told travelers what to expect. Susan particularly enjoyed "Dog City," a community of prairie dog burrows near the Arkansas River. As the wagons passed, "the little folks like people ran to their doors to see the passing crowd. They could be seen all around with their heads poked out, and expressing their opinions I supposed from the loud barking I heard." It was, she thought, "a curiosity well worth seeing." At Pawnee Rock, another "curiosity," Susan celebrated Independence Day and literally made her mark on the trail by carving her name in stone. The rock already bore the names of hundreds of other travelers.

The Santa Fe Trail passed through stunning vistas and amusing curiosities, but it also brought peculiar hardships. The heat was the first and most persistent obstacle. Between the watering places even muddy water collected from gullies in the tall grass could seem to Susan "a luxurious draught." The oxen staggered under their burdens, and when released from the yoke some "absolutely crept under the wagons for shade." Sunsets brought some relief, but in the hot tent Susan slept uncomfortably in her slip. "Even that would have been sent off without regret," she wrote, "had not modesty forbid me."

Fear was a constant companion on the prairie. A week out of Independence the Magoffins first encountered wolves. Just as Susan was falling asleep in the tent "The delightful music began. . . . It was a mixture of cat, dog, sheep, wolf, and the dear [Lord] knows what else." Ring, the greyhound, rushed out barking fiercely at the wolves, scaring them off. They came back later, however, and Susan wished Samuel, who was accustomed to wolves and slept peacefully at her side, was not "so well engaged."

Indians, too, inspired fear. During the past two decades a dozen men had been killed on the trail by the natives—not a large number out of the hundreds who had made the trip, but enough to breed caution. When Susan carved her name in Pawnee Rock, Samuel had watched carefully for signs of hostile Indians—and Susan worked quickly.

Neither wolves nor Indians attacked the Magoffins, but they did suffer other mishaps. One day as their carriage was descending a riverbank, it flipped over, crushing the sides and top. Bruised, Samuel carried his stunned wife to the shade of a tree, rubbed her face and hands, and poured whiskey into her mouth. Slowly she regained consciousness. The wagon was a mess: books, bottles, baskets, and pistols were spilled onto the ground, but neither of the Magoffins was seriously injured.

Even the mosquitoes posed a threat. They were a common annoyance, something to be endured. But one evening they were a positive menace. Susan knew something was wrong when the mules pulling her carriage became restless and ran past the wagons, shaking their tails, desperate to rid themselves of the pests. The Mexican driver struggled to hold them in. "*Holà, los animales!*" he shouted, "*Como estande bravos!*" (Ho, animals! How wild you are!) When they stopped for the night at ten o'clock the mules were "perfectly frantic" to escape their tormenters. Unable to hold them, the driver let them free to "shift for themselves" for the night. Samuel covered his face and neck with pocket handkerchiefs and directed the men setting up the tent. Meanwhile Susan hid in the carriage with her face smothered in a shawl and "listened to the din without." "Millions" of mosquitoes swarmed against the sides of the wagon. It "reminded me of a hard rain. It was equal to any of the plagues of Egypt. I lay almost in a perfect stupor, the heat and stings made me perfectly sick."

The mosquito attack and the carriage wreck were the most dramatic episodes in Susan's "rite of passage" into the wilderness. In such ways she experienced the great distance between the settled parts of the United States and the new lands in the West. Now she was realizing facts that before had been only images, lessons in school, and reports from her husband.

For hundreds of miles the Magoffins saw no hotels, no habitations of any sort. Then in southeastern Colorado a building appeared in the distance that looked like an ancient castle. It was Bent's Fort, a private trading post that carried supplies for mountain men and Santa Fe traders and served as a depot for American soldiers. Constructed in 1833, it was a massive structure, 135 by 180 feet, with walls 4 feet thick and 15 feet high. At diagonal corners stood two round watchtowers, and over the gateway was a room with windows on all sides and a telescope mounted on a pivot, with which sentries could scan the countryside for hostile Indians. The fort was built in the Mexican style of adobe bricks, made of sun-dried mud and straw. An interior well provided crystal-clear water. Around the courtyard were two dozen rooms—kitchen, dining room, blacksmith shop, barbershop, and billiard room. There was also an icehouse that received, according to Susan, "perhaps more customers than any other." Soldiers, trappers, Indians, and traders mingled in the courtyard. After the quiet of the prairie the noise seemed incessant; chickens cackling, mules braying, blacksmiths hammering, children crying, and men shouting.

Samuel arranged for lodging, and soon the Magoffins were installed in a large room on the second floor, furnished simply with bed, chairs, washbasin, and table. They could look out at the courtyard on one side, the prairie on the other. The ceiling was of timber, but the floor was dirt, and Susan had to throw water on it several times a day to keep down the dust.

The Magoffins stayed in Bent's Fort for two weeks. Samuel was eager to press on, but the traders could not move until the army was ready. Finally Gen. Stephen Watts Kearny arrived with his soldiers. "It seems the whole world was coming with him," wrote Susan. James Magoffin, Samuel's brother, also arrived at Bent's Fort on his way to a conference with the governor of Santa Fe.

Within a few days the Magoffins set out again on the Santa Fe Trail. Soon they crossed the Arkansas River, which they regarded as the southern border of the United States. No signs or border guards, however, separated the United States and Mexico. Nor were there towns on either side of the border to distinguish the people and cultures of the two regions. Ahead lay more wilderness. The wagons moved through a dry land of sandhills and mirages—the first Susan had seen. At first they traveled quickly, covering eighteen miles in a day. From the plains they worked their way into stony hills, then up into mountains. They passed piñon trees and wild cherry blossoms. One night they found themselves among "stupendous mountains, forming an entire breastwork to our little camp." Susan spotted a snowcapped peak in the distance; she was hardly able to believe she had seen snow in August.

In the mountains they feasted on wild turkeys, prairie chickens, and rabbits. The nights were so cold that they needed to cover themselves with two blankets and a thick quilt. The Raton Pass, which they were now crossing, was the roughest part of the Santa Fe Trail. The men worked the wagons down the pass by locking the brakes and standing six on a side to steady each wagon over the worst places. Inevitably, wheels were broken, and sometimes so many were being repaired at once that the trail seemed "like a regular shipyard."

A rider approached the train from the south and told them that James Magoffin had arrived in Santa Fe and was negotiating with the governor of New Mexico. If James was successful, the Mexicans would allow the American army to enter Santa Fe. If not, an army of four thousand Mexicans might, at this moment, be preparing to fight Kearny's force of fifteen hundred.

But for the moment the Magoffins continued south toward Santa Fe. Just beyond Raton Pass they were approached by three *rancheros*, selling cheese, bread, and *aguardiente*, a native brandy. These were the first Mexicans they had met since crossing the border, and Susan did not like them. To her they seemed like "huckster-women after a steamboat." Nor did she like their food. The bread was hard, and the cheese was "very tough, mean looking, and to me unpalatable."

In fact, Susan seemed to like nothing at all about the first Mexicans they met. She described the *casa grande*, the biggest house in the village of Mora, as "a little hovel, a fit match for some of the genteel pig sties in the states." The people seemed even stranger than their dwellings. They swarmed around Susan "like bees," and she felt like the prize exhibit in a "monkey show."

Susan felt disdain as she looked from behind her veil at this new world. The children were in "a perfect state of nudity," and their mothers were poorly clad, wearing only petticoats, chemises, and buckskin moccasins. "The women slap about with their arms and necks bare," wrote Susan. Their dresses were too short, barely covering their calves, and worse still, when the women crossed a creek, they would pull the hems "up above their knees and paddle through the water like ducks, sloshing and splattering everything about them."

The Magoffins stopped for a midday meal at Las Vegas, New Mexico. The usual crowd gathered, and much to Susan's disgust they followed her into a dining room, seating themselves on chairs and the floor, enchanted at the presence of this light-skinned American lady. Susan, however, was less than enchanted with her first meal in New Mexico. The men and women chattered and smoked "little cigarritas"—tobacco wrapped in corn husks. Mothers held their babies under their shawls—"I shan't say at what business," reported an embarrassed Susan. Someone brought out a tablecloth, "black with dirt and grease," followed by a half dozen tortillas wrapped in a dirty napkin along with a bowl of meat, green peppers, and onions. No cutlery arrived, and Susan was appalled to learn that she was supposed to dip the tortillas into the meat and eat with her hands. "My heart sickened, to say nothing of my stomach."

Back in the carriage she watched with relief as the village with its motley collection of "men, women, children, and dogs" disappeared around a curve. "Joy beat in my heart," she recalled, "to think that once more I was at liberty to breathe the pure air of the prairie, and to sit alone in my little tent, unmolested by the constant stare of those wild looking strangers!"

When Susan Magoffin entered New Mexico in 1846 the United States was on the verge of a new kind of cultural contact. In the past the United States had occupied lands that were previously home to non-Europeans. In many of these lands the tribes were nomadic or lived in simple bark shelters. They could easily be moved from one section of the country to another ahead of the white settlers. But the Mexicans were different. Many lived in substantial houses of brick and timber and worshiped in large, well-built Catholic churches. The invading Americans could not easily move them, out of sight or out of mind. But would the invaders recognize the Mexicans for who they were: men and women with distinctive customs and beliefs, as aware of their own heritage as the Americans were of theirs? Was manifest destiny a doctrine of conquest merely, or could American expansion accommodate the distinctive qualities of native peoples?

Santa Fe, the capital of New Mexico, was established by Spain in 1610, ten years before the Pilgrims landed at Plymouth Rock and just three years after the English established Jamestown. The Spaniards laid out the new town on a plateau on the north bank of a fast-running stream that flowed from the nearby Sangre de Cristo Mountains. As their seat of government, they built the Governor's Palace, an adobe structure on a public square; today it is the oldest public building in the United States. The governor, legislature, and court met at the palace to develop and administer policies for a territory that eventually included Colorado, Arizona, Utah, and New Mexico.

The Spanish conquerors collected annual tribute of corn and blankets from the local Indian *pueblos*, or villages. During the seventeenth century, however, their hold on the region was tenuous; in 1680 the Pueblo Indians rebelled and drove the colonizers out of New Mexico. For a dozen years Indians inhabited the Governor's Palace, leaving traces of their occupation—such as holes in the floor where they stored their corn—that can still be seen today. The Spaniards reconquered New Mexico in 1692, but Indian wars continued on the frontier for almost two centuries.

By 1800 the population of Santa Fe had grown to about 2,500, and it doubled to 5,000 by 1846. Half of the male inhabitants were farmers; the remainder were adobemakers, carpenters, blacksmiths, barrelmakers, lumbermen, muleskinners, shoemakers, weavers, tailors, and hunters. In the central plaza—a surface of sun-baked mud—Indians camped and traders left their wagons. As in many American towns at the time, the streets of Santa Fe were made filthy by stagnant pools of water and piles of garbage thrown from houses. The dwellings were built of adobe bricks, with pine beams supporting the flat roofs. Sheets of mica served as windowpanes, and door hinges were made of leather. Men wore buckskin pants and homespun shirts, and women wore full skirts and low-necked blouses and covered their heads and shoulders with shawls called *rebosos*.

In 1810 the Mexicans began a decade-long struggle for independence from Spain. News that an independent government had been established in Mexico City reached Santa Fe in the fall of 1821. The Santa Feans, who were remote from events in the capital, waited several months to confirm the news of the nation's independence; then in January 1822 they celebrated with speeches, processions, music, masses, patriotic dramas, musket fire, and *fandangos*, or balls.

In the year of Mexican independence, the borders were opened to trade with the United States. Long before General Kearny and his troops arrived at the border, Santa Fe had come under the influence of the United States. During the trading season, American merchants rented adobe houses on the south side of the plaza and sold cloth, mirrors, furniture, tools, medicines, and other American products. Manuel Armijo, governor of New Mexico in 1846, lined the wall of his office in the palace with dinner plates manufactured in the United States.

More than a thousand miles away in Mexico City, a long period of civil disorder followed independence. Between 1833 and 1855 the presidency changed hands thirty-five times. Ambitious Mexican generals kept their armies close to the capital, hoping for advancement during periods of turmoil. As a result they left the frontiers unguarded, and Indian raids on the scattered settlements of New Mexico became increasingly common. "We are surrounded on all sides by heartless barbarians," a settler complained, "and our brothers, instead of helping us, are at each other's throats in their festering civil wars."

In the meantime, New Mexico was being drawn into an American orbit; along with economic ties came social ties. American traders and trappers made friends with the settlers and married into Mexican families. Some became citizens, served in municipal offices, and fought in the Indian wars. In California, where a similar process was under way, a worried official of the Mexican government noted that the local inhabitants were beginning to regard Americans as "brothers." The same could be said of New Mexico, where Mexicans had prospered in the American trade. Additionally, the Hispanic residents were impressed by the wealth and the political stability of the people they called *Norte Americanos*. In the 1830s a Santa Fe newspaper predicted that the American influence would grow because of American "industry [and] their ideas of liberty and independence." A decade earlier a paper in Mexico City had warned that citizens who lived near the northern border "cannot remain unaware of the fortune enjoyed by citizens of the United States."

Given these facts, a modern historian has noted that the American annexation of northern Mexico was the "culmination of a process" that was under way long before 1846. As General Kearny and the Magoffins approached Santa Fe, however, no one could predict whether their invasion would culminate in a bloody conquest or in the peaceful commingling of two peoples.

At the very moment when Susan was entering northern New Mexico, her brother-in-law James was in Santa Fe, negotiating with Governor Manuel Armijo. Although the Mexicans greatly outnumbered the Americans, Magoffin persuaded Armijo to disband his army and retire from New Mexico. We cannot be certain why Armijo gave up without a fight. He may have been awed by stories of American military valor; he may have been bribed. But James was able to persuade Armijo to leave. On the trail into Santa Fe he had joked with another trader, a Mexican named Gonzales, about "the thousand advantages to being conquered" by the United States—not the least, he said, were "liberty and equality." James had a gift for mixing humor and persuasion. It was fortunate also for the Americans that James was, through his Mexican wife, a cousin of the New Mexican governor. At any rate, his negotiations with Armijo cleared the way for the American army to enter Santa Fe without bloodshed.

A few days later General Kearny reached the first Mexican settlements. At the village of Las Vegas he organized a ceremony that he would repeat again and again in other villages: he called together the religious and civil leaders of the town, explained that New Mexico was now American territory, and administered an oath of allegiance. In Las Vegas he stood on one of the flat-roofed adobe buildings with two Mexican army captains and the *alcalde*, or mayor, and addressed a crowd of 150 villagers. He had come by order of the United States to take possession of New Mexico, he told them. He had a strong force with him, and another American army would soon join the first. The people were absolved of allegiance to Governor Armijo and Mexico and now must give their allegiance to the United States. Kearny emphasized the advantages they would gain with American citizenship. The United States would protect them from Indian raids, which were common throughout New Mexico, and would guarantee their personal and religious liberties. The American government, he declared, would "protect the poor man as well as the rich man." The alcalde and the two captains then swore an oath of allegiance to the United States. Kearny shook their hands and turned to the crowd. "I shake hands with all of you through your alcalde," he said, "and hail you as good citizens of the United States."

Several soldiers in the Army of the West wrote accounts of the public reaction to the ceremony. One said that the people appeared "perfectly friendly," another said that they raised "a general shout," and a third said they raised a "faint shout." But several observers observed some hesitation on the part of the Mexicans. One soldier noted in his journal that the oath was clearly taken under compulsion. "These poor creatures," he wrote, "were evidently compelled to take it for fear of giving offense to our army." Another soldier recorded with irony that "the great boon of American citizenship," was thrust "by the mailed hand" upon the Mexicans.

But Kearny and many of his men regarded themselves as emancipators rather than conquerors. The general was confident that as American citizens the people of New Mexico would enjoy more freedom than under Mexican rule, and he demanded that his men treat the Mexicans as fellow citizens. He issued an order declaring that "humanity as well as policy requires that we should conciliate the inhabitants by kind and courteous treatment." He assured the Mexicans that not even "an onion or a pepper would be taken from them without a full equivalent in cash." When the army camped at Las Vegas he told the men that if any soldier so much as let his horse wander unattended into a Mexican cornfield, that soldier would walk the next day.

Word of Kearny's behavior preceded the army, and as he approached Santa Fe, each village seemed friendlier than the last. The people embraced one another "in token of their joy at the change of government," one soldier reported. An alcalde told Kearny that "God ruled the destinies of men," and because he "had come with a strong army among them to change their form of government, it must be right."

On the afternoon of August 18, 1846, the Army of the West reached the adobe city of Santa Fe. They marched four abreast down the hill to a plaza at the center of town. The streets were cluttered with dogs, but many of the people had fled. One soldier recalled that on side streets, "men, with surly countenances and downcast looks, regarded us with watchfulness, if not terror; and black eyes looked through latticed windows at our column of cavaliers, some gleaming with pleasure, and others filled with tears." Despite Kearny's earlier professions of friendship, the residents of Santa Fe, many of whom had close ties to the government, feared that the soldiers had come to pillage their city. The Mexican men had been told they would be branded on the cheek by the Americans with the letters "U.S."

At the plaza the soldiers stood around a hastily erected flagpole, a bugle sounded and, as the sun dropped behind the mountains, the Americans raised their flag above Santa Fe. Cannons on the hilltop boomed a thirteen-gun salute. Over the din of men and horses the soldiers could hear a "wail of grief" from the houses as "the pent-up emotions of many of the women could be suppressed no longer."

Susan and Samuel Magoffin heard the news from Santa Fe as their wagon train worked its way through little villages beyond Las Vegas. That night they camped alone in a pine forest at the foot of a mountain. The next day Susan's attitude toward the Mexicans suddenly seemed to change from disdain to respect. Perhaps the knowledge that they could pass safely into the capital made this strange land seem less hostile. Perhaps the villages were less squalid as they drew closer to Santa Fe. Perhaps the shift was internal: after a few days in the unfamiliar culture its strangeness had worn off, and Susan was ready to accommodate herself to the new land.

She seems to laugh at herself as she describes her change in attitude. The carriage tongue broke by a little creek outside the village of San Miguel, forcing the Magoffins to halt while two army carpenters worked on it. The usual assembly of Mexicans soon crowded around. "I did think the Mexicans were as void of refinement, judgment, etc., as the dumb animals till I heard one of them say '*bonita muchachita*' [pretty girl]." This compliment caught Susan's attention, and one can almost see the twinkle in her eye as she writes: "Now I have reason and certainly a good one for changing my opinion; they are certainly a very *quick and intelligent people!*"

Suddenly the whole business of meeting the Mexicans took a new tone. Many of the *mujeres* (women) came to the carriage to shake hands and talk with Susan. One brought her some tortillas, goat's milk, and stewed goat meat with onions. And Susan actually liked it. "They are decidedly polite, easy in their manners, perfectly free." Suddenly she was viewing the people in a different way—dropping her guard, letting herself experience the Mexican culture.

A few days later the Magoffins came to the top of a hill, and there below them were streets, churches, and houses—the first real city they had seen in almost two months of travel. Night had fallen, and so Susan could not see Santa Fe clearly, but she felt the significance of the moment. "I have entered the city in a year that will always be remembered by my countrymen, and under the 'Star-Spangled Banner' too."

Santa Fe was a city of six thousand people, the largest in New Mexico. The road-ways were crooked and narrow. Along the main street were flat-roofed adobe houses, one story high. Some blocks were devoted to cornfields—"fine ornament to a *city*, that," wrote Susan. A mountain stream ran through Santa Fe; irrigation canals carried water from its banks past the houses and into the fields, gardens, and orchards. People washed their clothes in the irrigation ditches in front of their own houses. The markets sold fresh fruits and vegetables, including fine ripe grapes brought in from local vineyards in wicker baskets carried by burros. The main plaza was a large open square fronted by the government palace, a cathedral, houses, and shops. Roofs hung over the sidewalks. "It makes a fine walk," Susan noted. "And in rainy weather there is no use for an umbrella."

The Magoffins moved into a Mexican house opposite a church. Susan described it as *nuestra casa* (our house), "quite a nice little place." The main room was long with a dirt floor, plank ceiling, and whitewashed adobe walls. Cushioned benches of adobe along the wall provided seating, and a screen behind protected backs from whitewash. One side of the room was carpeted and served as a parlor, where the Magoffins received their many guests. The other side was bare earth with a table—the dining room. Nearby was *la cocina* (the kitchen). The bedroom was "a nice cool little room" with two win-dows. It could be darkened at midday, enabling Susan and Samuel to indulge in one of the most agreeable local customs: "I must say it is truly pleasant to follow after the Mexican style, which is after dinner to close the shutters and take a short siesta."

Susan soon settled into the role of housewife. She began her days by "superin-tending the general business of housekeepers, such as sweeping, dusting, arranging and re-arranging of furniture, making of beds, ordering dinner." She went shopping, worked on a dress, and taught the servants their jobs. "Mine is a quiet little household," she wrote. "The servants are all doing their duty, the great bugbear to most house-keepers;

and if I can do my duty so well as to gain one bright smile and sweet kiss from my good, kind husband on his return, my joy will be complete."

In such moments Susan might almost have been in her native Kentucky, but many reminders told that she was in a foreign land and that in 1846 Santa Fe was an occupied city. The church bells, which seemed to be chiming day and night, mingled with the "everlasting noise" of the army. Soldiers were camped near the Magoffin casa. "From early dawn till late at night they are blowing their trumpets, whooping like Indians, or making some unheard of sounds, quite shocking to my delicate nerves."

The army, however, furnished one of Susan's pleasantest diversions, the society of other Americans. The officers regularly called on the Magoffins, the only American couple in Santa Fe. Their agreeable society was a reminder to Susan of the difference between the Mexican community and the Americans. Their company, she said, was "quite desirable to be sought after in this foreign land where there are so few of our countrymen and so few manners and customs similar to ours, or in short anything to correspond with our national feelings and fireside friendships."

General Kearny's chief activity during the early months of the American occupation of New Mexico was to secure his position by tact and force. Upon entering Santa Fe he promised the people that he would not change their customs or threaten their religion. He then toured the region, bearing the news of American conquest. One evening after returning from his diplomatic mission, he stopped by to visit the Magoffins and gave them a "graphic account" of his reception in the Mexican towns. On his diplomatic mission he had attended feasts, balls, and Indian "sham battles." In one village he and his officers followed a train of priests, carrying candles "lighting the train of the Virgin Mary." He told Susan he felt as if he was "making a fool of himself." But by this gesture and others he indicated that Americans would respect Mexican customs and beliefs.

The United States hoped to pacify New Mexico through gestures of good will, but General Kearny did not take it for granted that parades and banquets alone would enable him to control the prize that had fallen so easily into American hands. This was apparent one morning when Kearny, riding "a splendid bay charger," came by to take Susan on a tour of the city's defenses. She mounted her horse, and they rode off through the "clogged streets" of Santa Fe. He showed her his artillery, arranged in two rows on the outskirts of town, and guided her past Armijo's army barracks, now occupied by Americans. Then they climbed a steep hill. At the summit men were building a fort out of massive adobe blocks. Susan stood at the edge and looked at the city and the plains and mountains beyond. The fort stood one hundred feet above Santa Fe and only six hundred yards from its center. Its presence guaranteed that Santa Fe would remain in American hands. Susan reported that from the hilltop "every house in the city can be torn by the artillery to atoms."

The Americans did not want to appear as conquerors in New Mexico. They preferred to regard themselves as offering an attractive alternative to government by the distant and sometimes corrupt regimes in Mexico City. But tensions were created by the behavior of American soldiers. Kearny instructed them to treat the Mexicans well, but liquor, prejudice, and the fact of occupation made some of the men misbehave. Susan saw some of this in her own house. One day an officer wandered into the parlor uninvited and tried to treat Susan like an old friend. He "staggered to a seat where he sat and ran on with foolishness and impudence." Fortunately, Samuel was home and took him off her hands. Another drunken officer "went off into ecstasies about the war." He was "all eagerness for a fight," wrote Susan, "and says he has done all things in his power to provoke one."

Most of the soldiers could communicate with the Mexicans only with simple gestures and a few Spanish words. The awkwardness of the language barrier was apparent when soldiers were billeted with a Mexican family. "My Spanish friends are very courteous," writes William Richardson, a Missouri volunteer, "but there is little to relieve the monotony of our intercourse, as from my ignorance of the language I am unable to converse with them." The frustrated soldiers often changed Spanish words to English for the sake of convenience, finding similar-sounding American words as substitutes. *Frijoles* (beans) became "free-holders," the *Rio Purgatoire* (Purgatory River) became the "Picket Wire," and *aguardiente*, the Mexican brandy, became "the ingrediente."

The Mexican reaction to the Americans took many forms, but naturally they were as unsettled as the soldiers by the foreign army suddenly intruding into their midst. New Mexico had traditionally maintained a degree of independence from Mexico City. Only a few years before, in 1837, the people had risen against an appointed governor, Albino Perez, who tried to change the laws, collect taxes, and appoint new government officials. Governor Perez and sixteen of his assistants died in the rebellion. The American presence inevitably disrupted life in Santa Fe. Rumors flew that Armijo would soon return with an army of five thousand and retake the capital. These tales frightened his former followers, some of whom fled the city fearing a triumphant Armijo would persecute them as traitors. Other Mexicans, remaining in Santa Fe, lamented that they might never again see their departed friends. Hostility to Mexico City did not guarantee enthusiasm for American government, especially when it was not yet clear what sort of government that would be. Kearny's aide-de-camp, Abraham Johnston, recalled a Mexican soldier's remark on seeing the American army marching toward Santa Fe. "My God!" he said, "What is to become of our republic!" Another soldier thought that some Mexicans welcomed the American presence but said that they were "far from receiving us generally as deliverers."

Within a few weeks of Kearny's occupation of Santa Fe another two thousand American soldiers arrived, Missouri volunteers and members of a Mormon battalion recruited from immigrants on their way to Utah. Gibson reported that with all the soldiers in Santa Fe, "the grogshops do a thriving business." The Americans made noise, got drunk, and chased after Mexican women. In theory, they were the agents of liberation and progress. In practice, the soldiers were often obtrusive and insensitive. A huge cannon was fired off in the center of Santa Fe to welcome newly arrived soldiers. The blast shattered the few precious panes of real glass in the city.

The Americans probably did more damage and made more enemies through carelessness than hostility. One morning Pvt. William Richardson was camped near a Mexican village. Suddenly a group of villagers came into camp "in a great rage about something." It turned out that the captain had broken the bank of the local millpond the night before to ensure that it would not overflow and dampen his tent floor. Richardson reports, "The water of course rushed out with great force, tearing the embankment down, and washing the earth away for a considerable distance, stopping their mill, and leaving many families destitute of water." Richardson was disgusted with the captain's behavior, which he says, "met with little favor from his men, to their honor be it spoken." But when a lieutenant sought volunteers the next day to repair the damage, the men were unwilling to stand in the cold water and work without compensation.

A few months later an English adventurer, George Frederick Ruxton, traveled through New Mexico and found "that the most bitter feeling and most determined hostility existed against the Americans, who certainly in Santa Fe and elsewhere have not been very anxious to conciliate the people, but by their bullying and overbearing demeanor towards them, have in a great measure been the cause of this hatred." He spent one evening on the way to Taos with a Native American family. His hostess fixed him a meal, but seemed reserved until she discovered he was an Englishman.

"*Gracias a Dios* [Thanks to God]," she exclaimed, "a Christian will sleep with us tonight and not an American!"

Such instances of provocation and hostility were not, however, universal in New Mexico. Among both Americans and Mexicans were many types of people. In the United States there were outspoken war opponents as well as enthusiastic expansionists. Henry David Thoreau and Abraham Lincoln, among others, questioned whether the United States belonged in Mexico. Even among the soldiers there were dissenters. One of the armies sent into Mexico included many Irish Catholics who were so disgusted with camp life that they were persuaded by their fellow Catholics in Mexico to desert and serve in the Mexican army in the "San Patricio Brigade."

Among the Mexicans, too, were many varieties of opinion. Some Mexicans had enjoyed their contacts with the American merchants during the twenty-five years of the Santa Fe trade and believed that the United States would govern justly. One soldier visited a priest's house, where he saw curtains decorated with pictures of American presidents. The Mexicans were impressed too by Kearny's respect for the Catholic Church and his reappointment of Mexican civil officials in the new government. When Kearny toured northern New Mexico to administer the oath of allegiance, eighty Mexican horsemen rode with him as a sign of support. Along the way hundreds of villagers fell in with the line of march.

In meeting the Mexicans Susan Magoffin had an advantage over most of the soldiers. Ever since leaving Independence, Missouri, she had been in daily contact with Mexicans, and she was soon learning Spanish. In Santa Fe, Spanish words and expressions grew frequent in her diary: *la niña* (the little girl), *muchacha* (girl), *una señora* (a lady), *bastante* (enough), *duraznos* (peaches), and *El Señor Vicaro* (the priest). Along with the American traders and soldiers who found their way to the Magoffin parlor, Susan and Samuel welcomed many Mexicans to the house. Some were old friends of Samuel's; others were new acquaintances. Shortly after they arrived Doña Juliana called. "She is a woman poor in the goods of this world," wrote Susan, but "a great friend to the Americans and especially to the Magoffins whom she calls a *muy buena familia* [very good family]." Susan was proud that she had carried on a conversation in Spanish for half an hour with Doña Juliana. "Whether correct or not, she insists that I am a good scholar."

Many of Susan's encounters with the people of Santa Fe reflect eagerness on both sides to befriend the other. The Mexicans wanted to know about her "*madre, padre, hermanos, hermanas* [mother, father, brothers, and sisters]." They examined her knitting and sewing, and Susan reported, "in an instant they can tell me how it is done, though perhaps 'tis the first of the kind they have ever seen. What an inquisitive, quick people they are!"

Susan and Samuel mingled with the people on public occasions. They went to a dress ball given by General Kearny as a gesture of friendship toward the Mexicans. The room was decorated with American flags, and the people were brightly dressed in "the seven rainbow colors." The women wore dresses of silk and satin, fine *rebozos* (shawls), and "showy ornaments, such as huge necklaces, countless rings, combs, [and] bows." A guitar and violin furnished lively music. Men and women circled the floor in a "mazy dance." Others sat along the wall, puffing cigarettes and filling the room with a cloud of smoke. A plump, short priest was there, dressed in bright robes. He was "a man rather short of stature, but that is made up in width." And "Doña Tula" was there, a wealthy and independent woman who ran the most prosperous card rooms in Santa Fe. One of the soldiers jokingly held out a handful of corn husks and a horn of tobacco for Susan to roll a cigarette. The Mexican women were smoking, but Susan's acculturation did not include the seemingly unladylike practice of puffing a cigarette, and she politely refused. Susan's friends from the army danced with the Mexican women and drank aguardiente. On the wall was a portrait of General Kearny, draped with an American flag that flew during the day from a hundred-foot flagpole in the city plaza. The picture showed Kearny handing a constitution to the Mexican people. Below it was a single word: *Liberdad*—Liberty.

On such occasions the Mexicans and Americans seemed more like cousins at a large family reunion than the peoples of two warring nations. This easy mingling was apparent to Susan a few days later at their first Mexican dinner. She and Samuel were invited to dinner by the Leitendorfers, an American trader and his Mexican wife, along with General Kearny and other guests. During the meal General Kearny offered an interesting toast. Raising his glass he declared, "The U.S. and Mexico—They are now united; may no one ever think of separating." These words suggest an attraction between two peoples rather than the triumph of a conquering nation. Forgotten for the moment were the guns of Fort Marcy or the American soldiers camped nearby. Kearny expected that with a little encouragement, such as he had shown in carrying candles in a Mexican procession, the people would be delighted to become Americans. To Kearny and other expansionists of 1846 America was not an aggressive nation imposing its culture on other peoples; it was rather a liberal system of government that made room for men and women of many nations and religions.

On December 15, 1846, President Polk expressed a similar idea when he declared that America was in Mexico due to "a patriotic desire to give the inhabitants the privileges and immunities cherished by the people of our own country." Like Kearny he could think of Mexico as "now united" to a larger America that was still growing, still making its way westward. Kearny and Polk, living in the age of manifest destiny, assumed that other peoples would appreciate being absorbed by the United States. And about some people, like the guests at the Leitendorfer dinner party, they were correct. The Mexicans at the table were not resentful or lukewarm at Kearny's toast. Instead they greeted his words with enthusiastic shouts of *viva! viva!* ("long live" or "hurrah").

But not every Mexican was as eager for union as were these friendly guests. To the south American and Mexican armies were maneuvering, preparing for battles in a war that was far from over. And in the villages around Santa Fe Mexican patriots were at this moment trying to arouse the populace to rebel against the Yankee invaders. Susan Magoffin's until-now peaceful sojourn in New Mexico would soon be filled with anxiety and with the threat of imprisonment or death.

At the end of September in 1846 the markets in Santa Fe were selling fresh vegetables and "the most delightful" peaches, grapes, and melons. But Susan knew the growing season would soon end, for she could see snow on the mountains nearby. General Kearny saw the snow, and it may have encouraged him to quicken his departure for California. On September 25, just a month after he had entered Santa Fe, he divided his army, leaving some men in New Mexico and taking the rest on a difficult march toward Los Angeles. Another force, under Col. Alexander William Doniphan, would soon march south to El Paso and Chihuahua.

Assured of protection by Doniphan's army, the American merchants resumed their journey into the interior of Mexico, where they would continue their trading. Susan reported in her diary, "Lo, we are camping again!" She had enjoyed her "casa" in Santa Fe, but she relished being back in the one "house" that was her own. "It is quite cool and our little tent is comfortable enough. It is a fine thing." The oxen struggled along the sandy road, which followed the Rio Grande. In the distance Susan could see the flat mountains that she called "the table-plains of Mexico."

The people along the road south of Santa Fe were as eager as their northern cousins to study the Magoffins. The Pueblo Indians, whose villages lined the road, crowded around "as thick as some flocks of sheep and goats" and peered under the tent, calling it *la casa bonita* (the pretty house). "They are certainly the most inquiring, prying, searching people I ever saw." At times Susan was annoyed by the persistent curiosity of the natives, but more often she was wonderfully open to new people. An old woman came by one day just after the Magoffins had set up their tent. She and Susan sat together for a half hour and talked about "all family concerns from the children down to the dogs." The woman asked about Susan's parents. "I ran off from them just for a husband," she replied. "*Pues, es mejor no?*" (Well, is it not better?) The old woman laughed heartily.

"*El marido es todo del mundo a las mujeres,*" Susan added. (The husband is the whole world to a woman.)

The old woman laughed again in agreement. "She thinks though I am young, I am old enough," wrote the nineteen-year-old Susan.

Ordinarily Samuel would have led his wagon train straight through El Paso into Chihuahua, about five hundred miles south of Santa Fe. But these were not ordinary times. Word came from the army that the traders should wait until Doniphan could clear the way into El Paso. The Magoffins decided to rent a house in San Gabriel, a tiny village along the trail. Expecting to spend the winter there, Susan planned to familiarize herself with local customs. "I must learn a good many of the New Mexican ways of living, manufacturing serapes, rebozos, [and] making tortillas, chili peppers, and chocolate."

While they were in San Gabriel, Samuel served as the local doctor. The medicines he carried cured some illnesses, and soon he was regarded as a "skillful *médico*." Samuel charged little or nothing for his work, though some patients gave him gifts of food in return. "It shows a feeling of pure gratitude," Susan remarked, "which I constantly see manifested among these people for any little kindnesses done them." On Saint Gabriel's feast day, the Magoffins' landlord came by the door, telling them to prepare no dinner. Later he brought chili with *carne de carnero* (mutton), stewed chicken with onions, and a dessert made of bread and grapes. The people of the village, Susan observed, had been preparing their dishes for a week. They apparently enjoyed sharing their creations. "The home folks would think me a great favorite if they could see how the good people of the village are sending me tortillas, *quesos* [cheeses], *dulces* [sweets], and the like."

In such encounters the American entry into New Mexico was a meeting of cultures rather than one people subjugating another. But even as the Magoffins lived peacefully in San Gabriel, tensions underlying the American occupation were working their way to the surface. First came news that James was robbed by Apaches who occupied the wild countryside flanking the thin ribbon of Mexican settlement along the Rio Grande. He lost his carriage, mules, clothes, and trade goods.

Then came rumors from the south that a large Mexican army was on the march toward Santa Fe. The main body of traders, stopped thirty miles beyond San Gabriel, were said to have circled their wagons and sunk the wheels to the hubs as a breastwork against the enemy. One trader decided to give up, selling his goods for what he could get and returning to Santa Fe. Others were "crazy to get on" and make a profit on their merchandise, whatever the risk.

A few weeks later news arrived that James, now in Chihuahua, had been arrested by the Mexicans as a spy. Then came rumors that an army under General Santa Anna had been formed to reconquer New Mexico. Santa Anna was a seasoned commander who had led the Mexican army during the fighting in Texas in the 1830s. In a battle with French invaders at Vera Cruz in 1838 he lost his left leg below the knee; he sent the leg to Mexico City with a patriotic greeting as a sign of his devotion to the cause. Santa Anna would not be easily defeated.

Susan worried that if Santa Anna beat the American forces in the south, she and Samuel would have to flee to Santa Fe for safety at Fort Marcy. His victory would "inspire this fickle people with such confidence as to his superior and almost immortal skill that en masse they will rise on our heads and murder us." Suddenly the Mexicans were "fickle people." This is not the Susan Magoffin who had come to know and like individual Mexicans. For a moment, she is a member of a conquering nation, who is shocked that a defeated people might still be loyal to their native land.

The Magoffins were elated to hear a few days later that Doniphan had defeated the Mexicans at Brazito, outside of El Paso. The victory opened the way to El Paso, and Americans seemed in complete control of New Mexico. Soon, however, conditions changed once more. The Magoffins learned that a general uprising had been planned in the north by the Mexicans, with the intent of retaking Santa Fe and killing or expelling all Americans. Charles Bent, who had been appointed governor of New Mexico by General Kearny, learned of the planned uprising from friendly Mexicans. Governor Bent was able to thwart the rebellion by arresting seven of its leaders, but tensions remained.

On January 17, 1847, Governor Bent was in Taos, fifty miles from Santa Fe, visiting his family. Bent was one of the brothers who had built Bent's Fort; he had moved to New Mexico in 1829 and settled in Taos, marrying a Mexican, Marie Ignacia Jaramillo. Long a resident of New Mexico, he knew the country and its people well, but he was unprepared for the events now surrounding him. Early in the morning a crowd of Indians marched through Taos demanding the release of two men who had been arrested for robbery. The American sheriff refused, and the Mexican prefect called the Indians all thieves. Soon the sheriff and prefect were dead.

Meanwhile, Charles Bent was at home with his wife, their three children, his wife's sister (who was married to frontier scout Kit Carson), and two other women. Warned that the crowd was after him, Bent dressed quickly and armed himself. He then tried to quell the rioters by reminding them of his friendship with them over the years. But they would not listen. They attacked the house and tried to dig in through the roof. Bent's wife and children begged him to defend himself, but he hesitated to fire, perhaps fearing he would only make matters worse.

A French-Canadian neighbor and his Mexican wife had dug a hole through a wall dividing his house from Bent's. The governor's family escaped through the hole, but Bent hesitated and was shot by a Pueblo Indian. Badly wounded, he crawled through the hole, and in his last moments he tried to write a note for his weeping family. Bent's attackers swarmed after him, filling him with arrows and shooting him with his own pistols. They then scalped the dead governor and paraded their trophy around the village.

Susan and Samuel Magoffin were horrified by the news from Taos. "My knowledge of these people has been extended very much in one day," wrote Susan. She conceded that there were "some good people" among the Mexicans but feared that most would "murder without distinction every American in the country if the least thing should turn in their favor." The Magoffins prepared hastily to leave San Gabriel. During their last hours in the village Susan looked at everyone with suspicion.

The Magoffins, their wagoners, and another trader played a dangerous game of bluff, trying to demonstrate to the townspeople their confidence without provoking a confrontation. Samuel stood on the rooftop surveying the countryside; other men scouted the town; they all examined and fired their guns. At last they were ready to leave San Gabriel. "In truth we are flying before them," wrote Susan. That night the men remained on guard. In the Magoffin tent Samuel laid out a double-barreled shotgun and several pistols, including "one of Colt's six barreled revolvers." If they were attacked by Mexicans or Indians, Susan would stand beside her husband, gun in hand.

For the next few days, however, their greatest enemy was the land rather than its people. Deep sand clutched the wagon wheels. The winter nights were cold enough to freeze a cup of water in the Magoffin tent. Then came the Jornada, an eighty-mile stretch of arid land where mountains forced the wagon trail away from the Rio Grande. Most of all they worried about the Apaches, who made no distinction between Mexicans and Americans. They had attacked James's party and even raided Doniphan's livestock. Samuel warned Susan that she should not even venture two hundred yards from the wagons.

The Magoffins spent one night at Doña Ana, the one Mexican village between the Jornada and the town of El Paso. The danger from Indians had been so acute that the village, though Mexican, seemed a haven. It had been attacked recently by the Apaches, and as a sign of common cause against a shared enemy, Doniphan had given the people a cannon. Unfortunately, this gesture of friendship was wrecked by some wagoners, who got drunk and stole the cannon and brought it into camp, claiming it was "unfit for Mexicans." The alcalde sent off a protest to El Paso, and Samuel took his side, insisting that the cannon be returned. Resentful, the thieves drove a spike into the cannon's touchhole so that it would not fire. Samuel apologized to the mayor, and took the names of the bigoted men who had ruined Doniphan's friendly gesture.

Farther along the trail the Magoffins passed through the battleground of Brasito, where Mexicans and Americans had fought only a few weeks before. Riding over the flat plain Susan discovered two cartridges, one Mexican, one American. Despite this sign of conflict, however, the Magoffins did not anticipate hostility as they entered El Paso. Samuel's friends in the city sent word that he should "come on without fear" and "that they have always been friendly to him and they still are." They moved in with the family of a local priest.

The trader's wife was again at home among the Mexican people. But the war and the danger of American defeat could not be forgotten. Rumors reached El Paso that Santa Anna had assembled a great army to attack Doniphan and to recapture Texas. Susan and Samuel worried that they might be robbed, imprisoned, or murdered. But living with a Mexican family, they did not see threats everywhere as they had in San Gabriel. In fact, they shared a unique bond with the curate's family. Samuel's brother James was a prisoner of the Mexicans—and the curate himself was a hostage of Doniphan, carried off with several other leading citizens to ensure the good behavior of the Mexicans in El Paso. "Our situations are truly similar," wrote Susan, "I shall regret deeply when we have to leave them; 'twould be injustice to say that I like one more than another, for I love them all."

On the morning of March 5, 1847, Don Ygnacio Roquia, a wealthy friend of Samuel's, came to the curate's house with news of the war. Don Ygnacio was one of the men Susan most admired in El Paso. She had visited his fine casa and saw his garden, where he raised oranges, figs, apricots, and almonds. His wife was "a lady easy in her own house," whose well-behaved children were studying English and French. Don Ygnacio was a dignified-looking man, who reminded Susan in appearance of George Washington. But on the morning of his visit to the curate's house he stepped through the door "with his hair somewhat on ends and his features ghastly." He took Samuel by the hand and led him from the room. Then with tears in his eyes he told his American friend that "he was a Mexican, and it pained him to the heart to know that the American army had gained the battle and taken possession of Chihuahua."

Visions of imprisonment and death faded from Susan's imagination, and she confided to her diary, "I am delighted with the news." But although she was relieved, she was not triumphant. A few days before, her Mexican friends had offered her consolation when it appeared that Doniphan would lose. Now she wrote in her diary, "I would not for the world exult or say one word to hurt the feelings of this family."

Both families were soon reunited with their imprisoned kinfolk. With Chihuahua in his possession Doniphan released his hostages, and soon *El Señor Cura*, the curate, was home. In the meantime James had gained his release from the Mexicans by cleverly using his affable tongue—and by judiciously distributing some two thousand bottles of champagne. Following Doniphan's victory Susan and Samuel made their way to Chihuahua and then the Mexican coast, and from there by ship back to the United States. Doniphan joined forces with Gen. Zachary Taylor and defeated Santa Anna at the Battle of Buena Vista. General Kearny marched his army across Arizona to California and fought two small battles, consolidating American control of California. In New Mexico the Taos rebels were defeated in battle, and the leading conspirators were hanged.

The war came to an end in September 1847, when Gen. Winfield Scott, after winning several battles in the environs of Mexico City, led the triumphant American army into the capital. In 1848 the United States and Mexico signed the Treaty of Guadalupe Hidalgo, by which Mexico ceded the Southwest to the United States and received in exchange a payment for $15 million.

Few Americans questioned the justice of the Mexican War. Although some opposed annexation of northern Mexico, most, including the Magoffins, assumed that everyone would benefit from the new arrangement. But one day while she was still in El Paso Susan had been confronted frankly with the moral problem of America's invasion of Mexico. Don Ygnacio, the man who had brought the news of Chihuahua, told Susan he was an admirer of George Washington, "whose name is ever dear to the hearts of the American." This statement was pleasant enough, but then her Mexican friend said something disturbing that Susan carefully recorded: "He says the course Mr. Polk is pursuing in regard to this war is entirely against the principles of Washington, which were to remain at home, encourage all home improvements, to defend our rights *there* against the encroachments of others, and never to invade the territory of another nation."

She could find no satisfactory rebuttal to this argument, now that the invasion of Mexico was an accomplished fact. But the effects of the invasion were yet to be determined. Whether, as the United States claimed, its institutions could embrace and encourage men and women in all walks of life would depend on American willingness to be tolerant of people with different cultures. Susan Magoffin's experience showed the possibilities for both prejudice and accommodation. In El Paso Susan seemed to grow more tolerant, more understanding of all elements in Mexican culture. During her days of travel she had been unhappy that she could not attend church and carry out other traditional Sabbath observances as in her Protestant home in Kentucky. She read the Bible quietly in tent or room, and tried to think about her soul and God. But religious observances were difficult without institutional support. On the trail the wagoners seemed to swear less on Sunday, but no religious services were held. In Mexico on the Sabbath church services were held, but otherwise it was business as usual. When Samuel himself sold goods on Sunday, Susan remarked, "It hurts me more than I can tell."

Finally on January 21, 1847, after more than half a year without attending a religious service, Susan began going to the Catholic church in El Paso. In her diary she struggled to explain why she had done something so unusual for a Protestant in an unecumenical age. She should not judge the Mexicans, she wrote, for "I am told to 'judge no man but to bear the burden of my brother.'" She must first purify herself before trying to reform someone else. At the least, she said, "they are sincere in what they do." And so she went to church and stood among a foreign people and listened to a foreign service. But it was all right. "This morning I have been to mass not led by idle curiosity, not by a blind faith, a belief in the creed there practiced, but because 'tis the house of God."

Susan could never have written those words a year before, could never have found this common bond between American Protestant and Mexican Catholic, but exposure to a new culture changed and broadened her. It was a small thing in the whole history of the Mexican War, but it was an example of the personal growth and flexibility that could provide the only possible justification for manifest destiny.

Catholic church in El Paso where Susan Shelby Maggofin, a Protestant, went to worship.

President Polk and General Kearny might speak glowingly about the amalgamation of the Mexican and American peoples, but without growth in understanding and toleration between the two peoples, their words were hollow promises.

One of Samuel's best friends in El Paso, a dignified old man named Don Agapita, described Susan's experience well when he told her that on her journey she was "learning a lesson that no one could have taught... but experience, the ways of the world." She thought about the words of this "philosophical" old man. "'Tis true all he says," she wrote, "I have seen and read of Kentucky till I know it all by heart, but who could by telling me, make me sensible of what I have seen and felt since I left home to travel."

Bibliography

Boyle, Susan Calafate. *Hispano Merchants and the Santa Fe Trade* (1997). Shows that these Santa Fe traders established contacts from Chihuahua to Philadelphia and beyond.

Brack, Gene M. *Mexico Views Manifest Destiny, 1821–1846* (1975). Mexican thoughts about American expansionism.

Cather, Willa. *Death Comes for the Archbishop* (1927 and later editions). Hauntingly beautiful novel based on the life of the first American archbishop of New Mexico.

Chalfant, William Y. *Dangerous Passage: The Santa Fe Trail and the Mexican War* (1994). Narrative history of the trail with an emphasis on Indian conflicts.

Drumm, Stella M., Editor. *Down the Santa Fe Trail and into Mexico* (1926, 1962). Susan Shelby Magoffin's colorful description of life on the Santa Fe Trail and in northern Mexico in 1846 and 1847.

Duggard, Martin. *The Training Ground: Grant, Lee, Sherman, and Davis in the Mexican War, 1846–1848* (2008). History of the war emphasizing lessons learned by future Civil War officers.

Hyslop, Stephen G. *Bound for Santa Fe: The Road to New Mexico and the American Conquest, 1806–1848* (2002). An economic and cultural history of the Santa Fe trade, exceptionally thorough and compelling.

Smith, George Winston, and Charles Judah, Editors. *Chronicles of the Gringos* (1968). Documentary history of the Mexican War based on eyewitness reports.

Weinerg, Albert K. *Manifest Destiny* (1935). Classic account of the philosophy and practice of manifest destiny.

Winders, Richard Bruce. *Mr. Polk's Army: The American Military Experience in the Mexican War* (1997). Explores the American army in the framework of contemporary American society— an example of the new military history.

Identification Topics

Susan Shelby Magoffin, Samuel Magoffin, Stephen Watts Kearny, Army of the West, Santa Fe Trail, manifest destiny, Independence (Missouri), Bent's Fort, Pueblo Revolt, "Dog City," Santa Fe, Alexander William Doniphan, Apaches, Taos Revolt, the Jornada, Don Ygnacio Roquia, Governor's Palace, Manuel Armijo

Study Questions

1. In 1846 New Mexico was distant from the United States, both geographically and culturally. Summarize the difficulties a traveler experienced in journeying from Missouri to New Mexico, and describe the most obvious cultural differences between the two regions. Consider particularly Susan Magoffin's experience.

2. In what ways did Gen. Stephen Kearny attempt to persuade the people of New Mexico that he came as a liberator, not as a conqueror?

3. Why were some New Mexicans receptive to annexation by the United States, and how did they express their approval?

4. Why were some New Mexicans opposed to annexation by the United States, and how did they express their disapproval?

5. In what ways and for what reasons did American soldiers contribute to Mexican feelings for and against the occupation? Did their behavior justify President Polk's claim that the United States intended to give the people of New Mexico "the privileges and immunities cherished by the people" of the United States?

6. Susan Magoffin sometimes treated the New Mexicans with friendship and respect, sometimes with hostility and contempt. Cite examples of each attitude and try to explain why her attitudes changed several times.

7. "Manifest destiny" is a complex idea. From your reading, how would you define it? What did it mean to Susan Magoffin? To General Kearny? To other American soldiers?

8. Was the United States justified in annexing more than half of Mexico? Did the Americans who came to New Mexico in 1846 show any respect for the residents of the region?

CHAPTER 14

A Slave's Story
Abd Rahman Ibrahima's Journey
from Slavery to Freedom

The individual lives of most American slaves are lost to history. Diaries, letters, autobiographies, and oral histories allow us to explore the lives of a few, but we can seldom follow the lives of even the most articulate slaves back to Africa. The dark hold of the slave ship is an apt symbol for the obscurity from which the African seemingly emerges into American history. But in reality each African came from a vital world in which he or she lived before enslavement. The story of Abd Rahman Ibrahima is an exception to the pattern of uncertainty. We come to know him as an African and a Muslim before we know him as an enslaved person. As we follow his story, we gain a deeper appreciation for the African background of enslaved Americans, and we also gain a valuable perspective on the system of slavery itself and on those Americans who saw beyond it.

D uring autumn of 1790 an African named Abd Rahman Ibrahima was living alone in the forest a few miles from Natchez, Mississippi. A few weeks earlier he had been a slave on a small tobacco farm. And a few months before that he was a colonel leading a troop of cavalry in Africa. Defeated in battle and enslaved by other Africans, Ibrahima endured an Atlantic crossing and was sold to an American planter named Thomas Foster in Natchez. This new master knew nothing of the African's background or his military career. All that mattered to Foster was that Ibrahima refused to recognize him as his master.

First there had been a struggle over the slave's hair. To Ibrahima long hair was a sign of manhood and dignity, a status he possessed as a member of the Muslim elite in his homeland. But Thomas Foster experienced the hair as an annoyance. Other slaves wore their hair short, and so should this new slave. Ibrahima struggled against the shears but was knocked down, tied to a tree, and shorn. After this humiliation, the African faced another affront. He was told to work in the tobacco fields, following behind a more experienced slave who cut the leaves, which Ibrahima was to gather and carry. To Thomas Foster, this was a simple job that any slave could be expected to do. But to Abd Rahman Ibrahima it was a degradation worse than losing his hair. His people in Africa, the Fulbe, took pride in pastoral labor and regarded field labor with contempt. A lower caste of Africans, the Jalunke, tilled the fields in his homeland.

In America Ibrahima might be forcibly shorn, but no one could force him to carry those tobacco leaves. He refused even to go to the fields. In response, Thomas Foster used the age-old method to bully an enslaved person into a recognition of his or her status. He brought out the whip. But even under the lash Ibrahima would not be broken. The historian Terry Alford has carefully reconstructed these and other events in Ibrahima's life. In his book *Prince among Slaves*, Alford describes what happened next: "A single avenue led out of the maddening cycle into which master and slave had fallen, and Ibrahima took it resolutely. He slipped away from his bed one night and crossed to the woods beyond the field. Another minute, and he was racing away through the darkened forest."

In that instant Abd Rahman Ibrahima escaped from slavery. Searchers checked the forests and streams in the neighborhood but could not find the runaway. After a few weeks they gave up the search, assuming that Ibrahima had been killed by a wild animal, captured by Indians, or died of starvation. And yet somehow Ibrahima survived. Thousands of miles from home, he had no way of getting back to Africa and no way of knowing whether some other part of America might be more hospitable. His world had been reduced to a few homesteads and small towns near the Mississippi River and the forest in which he hid. He must have sensed that he would do no better on another farm than with Thomas Foster. If he sought help from any of the white men, he would probably be tied up and returned to Foster and beaten again. So for a time Ibrahima simply endured the hardship of living outdoors and without regular meals. He stayed near the Foster plantation, watching and pondering his choices.

Ibrahima might stay in the forest, but how long could he endure hunger and exposure, especially with the days growing shorter and colder? He might kill himself rather than accept the cruel humiliation of slavery. But the Quran, which he had studied and memorized from childhood, told him that Allah did not approve of suicide.

The Quran did offer, however, another possibility:

> And reckon not those who are killed in Allah's way as dead; nay, they are
> alive and are provided sustenance from their Lord. (Quran 3.169)

If Ibrahima were to revenge himself on Thomas Foster and his wife Sarah, and if he were killed in resisting enslavement, Allah would surely take note of his bravery. During Ibrahima's long weeks in the forest, he came to the most important decision of his life. He decided to act as he had been trained to act with his heart fixed on Allah. He came out of the forest and walked toward the little house where the Fosters lived. Thomas was away but his wife Sarah was in the house. Ibrahima opened the door and walked toward her.

He knew what he must do. . . .

While alone in the forest, Abd Rahman Ibrahima must have thought often of his former life in Africa, now so far away. His people, known collectively as the Fulbe, and Pullo as individuals, were Muslim and raised cattle. They lived among an agricultural people, the Jalunke, who were animists, worshiping many gods. That region of Africa in the interior of present-day Senegal became known as Futa Jalon, from the names Fulbe and Jalunke. For a time the two peoples subsisted in peace, but their differences produced tensions. The Fulbe tended to look down on the Jalunke, considering agricultural labor inferior to tending cattle. When later Ibrahima refused to gather tobacco leaves on the Foster plantation in Mississippi, he was expressing a Pullo's distaste for fieldwork.

The Jalunke were more numerous, and at first they had the upper hand. They forbade the Fulbe to pray in public or possess the Quran. Just as English Protestants had been forced to hide their Bibles during the early years of the Reformation, the Fulbe were forced to hide their sacred writings, sometimes in caves. Eventually a Muslim cleric named Karamoko Alfa proclaimed a holy war, a *jihad*, against the Jalunke. The leader of the Fulbe forces was a man named Ibrahima Sori Mawdo, the father of Abd Rahman Ibrahima.

In the 1970s historian Terry Alford visited the region of Africa near the scene of Sori's rebellion. "In a traditional story still cherished in the mountains of Guinea," Alford writes, "Sori, in one swift, dramatic act, slashed open the great ceremonial drum of the farmers, thus beginning the war." Sori won victory after victory, and by 1730 the Muslim Fulbe took control of Futa Jalon. Slave traders on the coast came to know the Fulbe as a wealthy and orderly people: as Muslims the Fulbe did not drink. They brought ivory, gold, rice, cattle, and slaves to the Europeans to trade. The Fulbe acquired the slaves in a succession of wars with non-Muslim neighbors. They would never enslave fellow Muslims. They kept some of the slaves to work the fields in Futa Jalon and sold others. The slave trade routes ran into the interior to Timbuktu and north to Morocco and also to the Atlantic coast and America.

For a time Karamoko Alfa, the cleric, ruled the Futa Jalon. Then in 1748 Sori himself came to power and assumed the title *almaami*, chief ruler. Sori took four wives, one of whom gave birth to Abd Rahman Ibrahima in 1762.

During Ibrahima's childhood his father fought a succession of campaigns against non-Muslim Africans who succeeded in burning Timbo, his capital, to the ground. The conquerors were forced to withdraw from Timbo, but controlled other parts of Futa Jalon and forced many of the Fulbe to do fieldwork. Despite the incessant warfare and its disruption of Fulbe society, Ibrahima received a traditional Muslim education.

His schooling began when he was seven and followed a pattern observed throughout the Islamic world. He and other children practiced writing verses in Arabic from the Quran onto tablets of wood. Paper was available in Timbo at this time, brought from Europe as a trade item, but was rare and expensive. The students gathered around a *marabout*, or cleric, sometimes beside a fire, for their studies.

Ibrahima's education led not only to proficiency in reading and writing, but also to a thorough knowledge of the Quran: students were expected to memorize the sacred texts. In the words of Terry Alford: Ibrahima's training "put the stamp of his culture upon him, opening him to the Islamic vision and teaching him the omnipotence of God and the importance of the community of believers." Ibrahima was deeply impressed with the lessons of Islam and as he later reported, he studied the Quran "forty-eight hours per day."

In 1795 the Scots explorer Mungo Park would explore the Niger River region of Africa and report on Islamic schooling in a region near Timbo. Park was impressed with the rigor of the local education. "By establishing small schools in the different towns," Park wrote, "where many of the pagan as well as Mohammedan children are taught to read the Quran, and instructed in the tenets of the Prophet, the Mohammedan priests fix a bias on the minds, and form the character, of their young disciples, which no accidents of life can ever afterwards remove or alter. Many of these little schools I visited in my progress through the country, and I observed with pleasure the great docility and submissive deportment of the children." Among the passages that Ibrahima and other Muslim Africans learned was this from the second chapter of the Quran:

> Yes! whoever submits himself entirely to Allah and he is the doer of good
> (to others) he has his reward from his Lord, and there is no fear for him
> nor shall he grieve. (Quran 2.112)

Impressed with his son's devotion to learning at home in Timbo, Sori decided to send Ibrahima away for more schooling in Islamic religion and science. In 1774 when colonial Americans were arguing about the Intolerable Acts and arming for a possible conflict with Great Britain, Ibrahima left home for the kingdom of Macina, several hundred miles east of Timbo, in present-day Mali. Macina was the ancestral home of the Fulbe, and merchants carried goods regularly between Macina and Futa, including tobacco, silver, ivory, and slaves. For the twelve-year-old Ibrahima the journey was an introduction to a wider world. He went by boat down a tributary of the Niger River, then hundreds of miles down the Niger to another tributary leading to the city of Djenne, in Macina.

Djenne in 1774 was a city of about thirty thousand inhabitants—about twice the size of Boston at that time. Explorer Mungo Park approached Djenne about twenty years later. His account of the Niger gives an idea of the country through which Ibrahima traveled in 1774. The land was fertile, reminding Park of places in England. He encountered lions in the countryside and went through towns with large mosques. Near Djenne, Ibrahima's destination, Park observed "twenty large canoes, most of them fully loaded, and covered with mats to prevent the rain from injuring the goods."

The people of Djenne grazed cattle on islands, protected from the lions. The city was at the center of a wide-reaching commercial network. Merchants traded gold dust, carried overland from the South, and locally manufactured cloth and dried fish along a trade route north to Timbuktu and beyond to the distant shores of the Mediterranean. Djenne was also a center for Islamic learning. Ibrahima studied at Djenne and then went on to Timbuktu, further along the Niger, for more advanced training.

Timbuktu was for centuries a center for Islamic learning. According to the Islamic faith, in the year 610 the archangel Gabriel appeared to Muhammad, and through Gabriel over the course of twenty-two years Allah revealed the words of the Quran. Muslims regard the Old and New Testaments also as holy writ, but they especially revere the Quran as consisting of words directly from God. By 750 Islam had spread across North Africa from Egypt to Morocco. Berber merchants carried Islam south to sub-Saharan Africa, where they made many converts. Timbuktu was the principal city of several empires that grew up in the region of the Niger River, including the fourteenth-century Kingdom of Mali. In 1424–1425 the best-known ruler of Mali, Mansa Musa, made a famous hajj, a pilgrimage, to Mecca. According to legend sixty thousand people accompanied him, and he took along so much gold that the economy of Egypt was affected for years to come. By 1500 the Mali Empire was in decline and the Songhay Empire replaced it as the regional power in control of Timbuktu. When the young Abd Rahman Ibrahima came to Timbuktu in the late 1700s the city was in control of a group of Berber tribesmen known as the Tuaregs. By then Timbuktu had been a center of Islamic learning for many centuries.

Ibrahima would remember the city as a trading center where "caravans were continually arriving." The wealthy lived in two-story houses made of mud bricks and painted white. He attended a school associated with one of the three ancient centers of learning in Timbuktu. Along with two hundred other pupils he studied geography, astronomy, law, and mathematics.

At the age of seventeen Ibrahima returned to Timbo. His father, Sori, was engaged in a bitter struggle with neighboring tribesmen and had sent out a plea for help from other Muslims. In 1778, when George Washington fought the British to a standstill at Monmouth in New Jersey, Sori led troops into battle in Futa Jalon. His force was forty thousand soldiers, more than the number of men who fought on *both* sides at Monmouth. During the next several years Sori took the offensive, sending armies hundreds of miles on a jihad for the expansion of Islamic Africa. One of his ablest soldiers was his son Ibrahima, who became a commander of cavalry.

In the Quran, Ibrahima read:

> If you are in danger, then say your prayers on foot or on horseback; and when you are secure, then remember Allah, as He has taught you what you did not know. (Quran 2.239)

In 1781 Ibrahima was in grave danger. He was second in command of an army led by his uncle, a man named Sulimina. They were up against an enemy force of at least five thousand and were badly outnumbered. Sulimina was killed in the opening engagement, leaving Ibrahima—not yet twenty years old—in charge. The Muslim soldiers wanted to retreat to Timbo rather than fight under an inexperienced leader, but Ibrahima persuaded them to wait for three days. He devoted the time to preparing a trap for the enemy. At the end of the three days Ibrahima appeared to be fleeing with his men into a cane field. The enemy charged in after them and came to a large opening within the field. This was Ibrahima's trap. His men attacked from several sides and set the cane aflame, destroying most of the enemy. Ibrahima found the leader, an elderly soldier, sitting on the ground. Ibrahima asked him what punishment he deserved. "I must die," the old man said, "and I rejoice! I have been defeated by a boy!"

Unknown to Ibrahima, in another world another soldier won a great victory against his enemy in this same year. George Washington defeated the British in 1781 at Yorktown, the last major battle of the Revolutionary War. The great anthem of the American Revolution, "Chester," celebrates the role of "beardless boys" in defeating the British.

Toward the end of the year Ibrahima met an unusual person at Timbo, a man with white skin. He was John Coates Cox, a one-eyed Irish surgeon from a ship that had touched the coast a few score miles away. While on shore he had become separated from his shipmates, and the vessel left without him. Cox had wandered lost through the countryside until he ran into a group of Fulbe, who brought him to Timbo. Sori welcomed John Cox and assigned a woman to attend to his leg, which Cox had injured on his travels. Ibrahima befriended Cox, rode horseback with him in the countryside, and learned a few English phrases from him. Cox apparently married Ibrahima's sister and fathered a child. But after six months in Timbo, he was eager to return home. Sori gave Cox some gold and assigned fifteen men to accompany him to the coast—warning them, however, not to board a ship, for fear that they might be enslaved. Luckily Cox found the very ship from which he had been separated months before and sailed back to his own world.

In Timbo a period of peace followed Ibrahima's victory in the cane field. Sori built ten houses on the summit of a fortification overlooking the town. Ibrahima occupied one of these, married, and fathered a son, al-Husayn. An important trade route for the Fulbe followed the Rio Pongas down from the high plateau of Futa Jalon to the lower country to trade for European guns and other manufactured goods, including paper. The Fulbe paid for these with gold, ivory, hides, and slaves. In 1788, as Americans were debating the merits of a new constitution—designed in part to improve their ability to trade successfully in a trans-Atlantic world—the Fulbe found their own access to the Atlantic hampered by a people known as Hebohs who were raiding commerce in the region.

Ibrahima was by now a colonel in his father's army, and led a force of 2000 men, including 350 cavalry, intending to punish the Hebohs. The enemy fled and the Fulbe burned several of their villages. Satisfied with the campaign, Ibrahima sent the infantry home and followed more slowly with his cavalry. In the meantime the Hebohs had arranged themselves along the sides of a narrow pass through which the Fulbe would pass. Ibrahima's men were leading their horses up a slope when gunshots rang out on all sides, killing and wounding many Fulbe. Ibrahima and his comrades were badly outnumbered. Hebohs armed with muskets surrounded him. They could easily have killed him, but they reversed their weapons, a sign that they wanted to take him prisoner. He struck one with his sword, but then a rifle barrel cracked across the back of his head and Ibrahima fell unconscious.

When he recovered, Ibrahima told his captors that he was the son of a king, who would gladly pay a ransom for his freedom. But the Hebohs refused to listen, even though Ibrahima's clothing and ornaments did indicate his high station. They may have feared that a freed Fulbe colonel would make war against them in the future. Besides they had another way of making money off of Ibrahima and their other captives. In that region there were many Mandinka *slatees*, or slave traders, who bought prisoners to sell on the coast to the European slavers. The Hebohs sold Ibrahima to these men for two flasks of powder, several muskets, some tobacco, and two bottles of rum. Hearing of his son's capture, Sori came and burned the Heboh lands in revenge, but by then the Mandinka had herded Ibrahima and fifty fellow Fulbe to the Gambia River. There they sold them to Capt. John Nevin, an Englishman, who loaded them aboard the slave ship *Africa*.

Only recently a prince, a colonel, a husband, and a father in Timbo, Ibrahima was now a chattel, part of the cargo on a trading vessel. With him were about 170 other Africans, mainly adult males, along with several hundred pounds of beeswax and some ivory tusks. He was chained below decks and probably heard but did not see the anchor being raised and felt but did not see the motion of the ship as it set sail. The *Africa* began its voyage to America with a journey of a hundred miles down the Gambia River past Bara Point to the open Atlantic. We have no diary, letters, or oral account from Ibrahima describing his feelings as he left behind the entire world he had known. In the dark space where he was chained he had one resource that he carried with him from his homeland: his mind with its store of memories and lessons. In the night he may have repeated this verse:

Those who trust in Allah have no fear. (Quran 10.62)

In heavy seas when the ship pitched wildly, and terror filled the hold, he may have clung to this verse:

Allah is nearer to you than your jugular vein. (Quran 50.16)

The voyage of the *Africa* in 1788 was, by the standards of the slave trade, unusually healthy. Few slaves died during the passage and most were rated in good health when they arrived at their first port of call, the Caribbean island of Dominica. Here the slaves were "refreshed" with shore provisions. Ibrahima might well have been shipped to another of the Caribbean islands and put to work on a sugar plantation. But another long voyage lay ahead. He and fifty-six other slaves from the *Africa* were purchased by Thomas Irwin, a slave dealer from New Orleans. They left Dominica on May 2, 1788, and sailed on the *Navaroo* for more than a month across the Gulf of Mexico to New Orleans, then about two hundred miles up the Mississippi to Natchez.

Once the homeland of the Natchez Indians, the region had already seen more than two hundred years of European contacts. In 1540–1541 Spanish explorer Hernando De Soto fought the Natchez on his way across the lower Mississippi. In their wake Spaniards left diseases that decimated the Indians. The region was "discovered" again by the French in the late 1600s. The French stayed and finally won decisive battles against the Natchez. When the *Navaroo* approached Natchez with its slave cargo the town was part of Spanish Louisiana. A dilapidated old fort on a bluff over the river housed the Spanish administrative offices and the jail.

In a policy somewhat like the Mexicans would practice several decades later in Texas, the Spaniards offered inexpensive land and religious toleration to lure American settlers to the region. One of these immigrants was Thomas Foster, who immigrated to Natchez from South Carolina in 1783 along with his three brothers and their mother. Thomas had married another immigrant, Sarah Smith, the daughter of a local farmer. She immediately bore two children and was pregnant with a third in 1788.

In mid-August 1788 Thomas Foster went into town to inspect the African cargo recently unloaded from the *Navaroo*. He needed slave labor to clear the land and expand his tobacco plantation. Foster liked the look of Ibrahima, a man of his own age, and also noticed another Pullo, who was captured with Ibrahima, a man named Samba. Ibrahima's body may have been oiled, as was the custom in slave auctions, so that his muscles stood out.

In Foster's eyes Ibrahima's strength and his long hair would have been his most notable features. The African would have been able to present no résumé indicating that he was a Muslim, a scholar, a husband, a father, a cavalry colonel, and a prince. For the price of $930 Thomas Foster purchased the human being known in Futa Jalon as Abd Rahman Ibrahima and also Ibrahima's compatriot, Samba. In the Spanish record of the sale, the Africans were referred to as "dos negros brutos."

On August 17, 1788, as Americans on the Atlantic seaboard were preparing to elect George Washington as the first president of the republic, Ibrahima followed Foster along an old Indian trail up a bluff over the Mississippi then eastward through rolling countryside toward the Foster homestead at a place called Pine Ridge. Not many months before, the African had sat astride a horse leading hundreds of other men in battle. But on this day Thomas Foster rode a horse and Ibrahima walked behind. After a few miles they reached their destination. Terry Alford writes: "There were probably no more than five acres in fence and a few simple buildings, surrounded by piles of brush, stumps, and muddy sod of newly cleared land. . . . Unclaimed, unsettled lands stretched out from it in trackless distances of forest."

Soon afterward, as we have seen, the beatings began. Ibrahima had lost his family, his home, his authority. Next he lost his hair, and then, with the demand that he work in the fields, he was to be denied the last shred of his dignity.

This was too much.

So Ibrahima had chosen to resist, first by enduring the beatings rather than work, next by escaping into the forest, and finally by determining upon an even more courageous gesture: he had decided to return to the farm, and to act the part of a Fulbe prince, a Muslim, and a man.

Those who trust in Allah have no fear. . . .

And so Ibrahima walked to the house, opened the door, and stood face to face with Sarah Foster. Then, as he had concluded to do, he threw himself on the floor before her, clasped one of her feet in his hands, and placed it on his neck.

With this simple gesture Ibrahima put his fate in the hands of Sarah and Thomas Foster, his mistress and master. In the days, months, and years to come, Abd Rahman Ibrahima would labor diligently on the Foster plantation. In all of the literature on slavery, there is no more poignant episode than this, than Ibrahima's taking upon himself the character of a slave by prostrating himself before Sarah Foster. The man born to rule had agreed to be ruled.

Scholars have argued for generations about the psychological nature of slavery. Did enslaved persons simply become what their masters required them to become? Did they bring from Africa customs and values that they nurtured even in slavery? Did they enjoy any measure of freedom, any opportunities for initiative, even while enslaved? On one level Ibrahima seems to provide an example of a human being who simply became what his master required him to become. Back from his forest hideaway, Ibrahima went to work in the fields beside his fellow Africans. Seemingly he abandoned his dignity and accepted the only life open to him.

Or did he?

Another possibility is that when Ibrahima began working for the Fosters, he retained precisely the values he had learned in Timbo and Djenne and Timbuktu. As we will see, evidence is strong that he was the same person among the crops of Mississippi that he had been in that cane field where he won his first battle in Futa Jalon. Islam provides the thread. The precepts that ennobled his life as a prince and an officer told him that Allah was still there so many thousand miles from home. Of course, Ibrahima did not want to be a slave, but his enslavement did not mean that Allah had forgotten him. Islam itself calls on a Muslim to put his or her life in the control of God. In fact, the word Islam means "submission to God," and Muslim means "one who submits." Ibrahima had learned from the Quran:

Nothing will happen except that which Allah has decreed. (Quran 9.51),
and Allah is with you wheresoever you may be. (Quran 57.5)

Ibrahima was an enslaved person, and yet he was not simply a slave. The word "slave" does not fully describe who he was or what he could do. The evidence of this inner strength would be apparent during his life in servitude. Once he had accepted his enslavement, Ibrahima acted in a way that was far from merely *servile*. He understood at least as well as Thomas Foster what needed to be done to transform the little homestead into a prosperous farm. He carried himself in a way, worked with a purpose, and showed an aptitude for leadership that won him a nickname on the farm and in Natchez that echoed his former position in Africa: in Natchez Ibrahima came to be known as "Prince."

When Thomas Foster came home on the day of Ibrahima's return from the forest, he was so pleased with the return of his "property" that he did not beat the African. Soon four men, Foster and three slaves, were working in the field planting and harvesting tobacco. In 1789 Spain offered a good price for the crop and Foster doubled his yield. But the next year the crown's support declined and so did Foster's profits. In 1791 he began planting cotton. Ibrahima was familiar with this crop. In Timbo it was cultivated in small plots near the houses. There women—slave and free—picked the cotton, removed the seeds by hand, and spun it into thread. Local weavers then made it into cloth. The process of picking and processing cotton was essentially the same in Natchez in 1791, except that men as well as women did the work. But that would soon change.

In 1792 a New Englander, Eli Whitney, was visiting Mulberry Grove, near Savannah, Georgia, a plantation owned by Catherine Greene, widow of Revolutionary general Nathaniel Greene. Whitney impressed her with his inventiveness when he built a frame for holding her needlework. One day neighboring planters were lamenting the lack of a machine to remove the seeds from upland cotton. Catherine Greene volunteered Eli Whitney for the job. Whitney had never even seen a cotton boll, but during 1793 he spent six months producing a working model of a machine to remove seeds. He used the materials at hand, including wire from a birdcage in the Greene parlor, and built a "gin"—the word most likely comes from "engine"—with which one laborer could clean as much cotton as ten laborers without the gin. Whitney returned to the North and applied for a patent from Secretary of State, Thomas Jefferson.

The new cotton gins were easy to build and revolutionized southern agriculture. In 1790 the South had produced three thousand bales of cotton. In 1810 it raised 178,000 bales, and by 1860 cotton production had surged another twentyfold to four million bales. Between 1810 and 1860 the population of Alabama, Mississippi, Louisiana, and Arkansas—the heart of the cotton country—vaulted by almost 2,500 percent from 117,970 to 2,898,958.

Ibrahima and Foster supplied some of the actual life behind those statistics. Foster was ginning his cotton by 1795. Already he was prospering. In 1791 he bought a new slave, and in 1794 he purchased four more, including a woman named Isabella. She was American-born and came from South Carolina. It is hard to know exactly what she made of Ibrahima or he of her. Contemporaries described Isabella as "an interesting, fine-looking woman." She had known slavery all of her life; he had known freedom most of his life. The attraction between them was strong and would prove to be enduring.

Slave marriages were susceptible to many pressures, some inherent in the relationship between a particular man and woman and others resulting from the system of slavery. Servitude sometimes posed insurmountable difficulties to couples. In fact, slaves could not even be legally married. They could engage in informal ceremonies such as joining hands and jumping backward over a broomstick—a time-honored way of signifying a bond between man and woman. And some of these informal marriages were sanctified in religious ceremonies. Some owners were callous about the marital relationships of their slaves; others were highly solicitous. The latter sometimes bought the spouse of one of their slaves if that person belonged to another owner. Others specified in their wills that a slave couple or family was not to be broken up after the owner's death. Slaves were sometimes treated to a marriage ceremony in the big house, the bride wearing the hand-me-down wedding dress of her mistress.

By 1794 Thomas and Sarah Foster held Ibrahima in such high regard that they arranged a proper ceremony for his marriage to Isabella. On Christmas day Thomas read passages from the Bible to sanctify the marriage, and provided a feast including brandy and a roast in celebration. Soon Isabella gave birth to the first of Ibrahima's American-born children, a son whom they named Simon.

The choice of a Biblical name suggests Isabella's influence. She was a devout Christian. This might suggest that Ibrahima abandoned his own Islamic faith, but reports from those who knew him indicate that he did remain a Muslim. The fate of African Muslims in America varied greatly from one owner to another. Many whites considered Islam simply another form of "heathenism," forcing their slaves to worship in secret. At the other extreme some owners of larger plantations encouraged Muslim slaves to build traditional African villages on their estates and to worship freely.

In 1730 a young Muslim named Ayuba Suleiman Diallo was captured by Mandinkas and sold into slavery on the Gambia River a few score miles from where Ibrahima began his journey to America. Ayuba was from Bondu, in the interior, and like Ibrahima he was raised a Muslim. He became a slave in Maryland and resisted doing fieldwork for the same status reasons as Ibrahima had. His master then assigned him to tend cattle, a task that was more appropriate to his African background. While at work he would kneel and pray toward Mecca, according to the rules of Islam. But a white boy would see him at prayer and throw dirt in his face. Finally, like Ibrahima, Ayuba ran away. He was captured some fifty miles from his plantation, and his captor called in an African who could translate for Ayuba. They learned that the runaway was a Muslim, and they returned him to his master with this information.

On another plantation Ayuba might have been beaten and then told to abandon his Islamic faith. But in the words of a man named Thomas Bluett, who befriended Ayuba and described these events, his master "fetched him home, and was much kinder to him than before; allowing him a place to pray in, and some other conveniencies, in order to make his slavery as easy as possible." Through Bluett's influence, English philanthropists purchased Ayuba's freedom and brought him to England, then arranged for his return to Africa.

The story of Ayuba Suleiman Diallo is unusual, but it does suggest the actual range of possibilities open to a Muslim slave. Although few Muslim slaves would win their freedom, many were allowed to worship freely. This could be inconvenient to an owner because a Muslim needed to pray five times daily and should not eat pork, a plantation staple. But the Muslim training nurtured a gift for self-discipline and leadership. Muslim Africans often became overseers on southern plantations. The inconveniences of Islamic worship were a small price to pay for a good overseer.

Thomas Foster apparently encouraged Ibrahima to practice his Muslim faith, and insofar as possible Ibrahima did so. He had no copy of the Quran, but had many passages committed to memory. Ibrahima had no writing paper, but scratched Arabic characters in the dirt for practice. Of the Five Pillars of Islam, the essentials of the faith, Ibrahima would have been able to practice all but one in Natchez. First, he could confess his faith in Allah and his prophet Muhammad. This he could do silently in the field or while at prayer, or in conversation with his wife Isabella. Second, he was obligated to perform ritual worship, consisting of five periods of prayer, the first before sunrise and the last two after sunset. The prayers in the dark would not interrupt his fieldwork, but prayer at midday and mid-afternoon would. Thomas Foster apparently accepted these breaks in Ibrahima's work as a small price to pay for his usefulness.

A third pillar of the faith held that Muslims should give alms for the poor and needy. Since Ibrahima was himself now poor, we might not expect him to engage in charity. But then again, with Foster's approval he did earn some money of his own, and he may have given some of that to others. At any rate, when later in life he needed to go to the townsfolk of Natchez with an appeal for charity, they responded to Ibrahima with remarkable good grace. The fourth pillar was fasting during the holy month of Ramadan. During each day of the ninth lunar month, Muslims are required to go without food from sunrise to sunset. Here again, it is likely that Ibrahima continued this practice in America. Records of other plantations include notations of Muslim slaves observing Ramadan. And two Mississippians who knew Ibrahima both used the phrase "adhered strictly" in describing the African's Muslim practices.

The final pillar of the faith was impossible to observe while Ibrahima was in America. A Muslim is encouraged to make the pilgrimage, or hajj, to Mecca once in his or her lifetime. Muhammed was born in Mecca, and Muslims pray in the direction of Mecca. But for reasons of distance and poverty many Muslims could not make the hajj. It is doubtful that many Africans managed to travel all the way from Timbo or even Timbuktu to Mecca. Mansa Musa's famous journey in 1424–1425 is a notable exception. And certainly a slave in Natchez was not likely to reach Mecca. But on the subject of the hajj, Islam is forgiving, accepting that not all Muslims will be able to make the journey. Allah could be worshipped in Mecca, certainly. But he could also be worshipped in Timbo and Natchez. In his studies in Africa Ibrahima may have read this Islamic saying:

There are as many ways to Allah as there are human beings.

Life on the Foster plantation unfolded year by year. There must have been a sameness to many of the days. Always there was cotton to plant or harvest. But there were changes as well. Ibrahima's family grew and so did Foster's. By 1798, when Americans were arguing about the Alien and Sedition Acts, Thomas Foster owned about ten slaves. He was also building a herd of cattle. That year Natchez became an actual part of the United States. In Pinckney's Treaty of 1795 Spain had turned over the region to the United States, and three years afterward the first American governor arrived to administer the Mississippi Territory.

A few years later the United States purchased Louisiana from France, and Lewis and Clark led their expedition to the Pacific. The Fosters and their slaves continued to plant and harvest cotton.

In addition to working their master's land, Ibrahima and Isabella planted garden crops that they carried to Natchez to sell. A slave was legally the property of his or her master. And a piece of property could not be said to own property any more than a cow could own the bells around her neck or a dog his collar. One code described the slave's position bluntly: "The master may sell him, dispose of his person, his industry, and his labor: he [the slave] can do nothing, possess nothing, nor acquire anything but what must belong to his master."

So much for the legal description of a slave's position. The reality was often more complex than the codes suggested. A slave named Polly Turner Cancer told an interviewer during an oral history project in the 1930s: "'Marster used to let us raise our own chickens and sell dem at de tavern. . . . He let us make some money too by pickin' cotton at nite by de moonlight; we didn't hav' to do hit, but he'd let us ef we wanted to."

On a famous journey through the South, Frederick Law Olmsted described how free enterprise functioned on one plantation. The slaves could raise poultry and pigs of their own. The plantation owner bought all his eggs and poultry from his own slaves. In addition, the slaves hunted and sold the master the game they shot. To encourage his slaves to purchase goods on the plantation instead of in town, the master sold them products at wholesale prices. He held the profits from their produce until they wanted to spend the money. When Olmsted visited this plantation the owner was $500 in debt to his own slaves.

Private economic activity by slaves was common throughout the South. The goods bought and sold by slaves included shirts, jackets, coats, chickens, scarves, hats, linen, ribbons, tableware, fish, ducks, melons, vegetables, berries, hay, nuts, candies, and cakes. A slave owner in northern Virginia provided three acres for each of his slave families; those who produced their own food received a $10 bonus at Christmas. Southern whites disagreed about the propriety of "allowing" slaves to buy and sell goods. Some thought that it encouraged thievery—a slave might sell his or her owner's property as his or her own—but others argued the opposite. A slave who was allowed to raise his or her own food beyond what the master supplied was less likely to raid the plantation stores.

When Ibrahima went into Natchez to the market he carried his own vegetables to trade. He also collected Spanish moss from the trees and dried it for sale to make mattresses. In Natchez he met newly arrived slaves from Africa, some of whom brought news from Futa Jalon. Once a man recognized Ibrahima as a prince from Timbo and fell on the ground in respect. From such men Ibrahima learned that his father had died, his brother had been crowned ruler, and a rebellion had led to the brother's death. All this had occurred during the first seven years of Ibrahima's captivity. He might himself have been killed in the insurrection if he had stayed in Timbo. But then again, had he been able to stay, he might have ruled in such a way that the rebellion would have been crushed or not taken place. He would never know.

One summer day in 1807, during the presidency of Thomas Jefferson, Ibrahima went to market, carrying a large basket of sweet potatoes on his head. He was struck by the appearance of a middle-aged white man on a horse. Here was someone he had known long ago—in Africa. To catch the man's attention and have a closer look he called out to him to come and look at his potatoes.

"Were you raised in this country," the man asked.

"No," said Ibrahima, "I came from Africa."

"You came from Timbo?"

"Yes, sir."

The man was Dr. John Cox, the Irish surgeon who had wandered into Timbo a quarter-century before. Various stories in Natchez provide different versions of Ibrahima's reaction to this meeting. He was said to have bowed or jumped or danced. Cox was equally excited, leaping from his horse and embracing Ibrahima. The doctor was living nearby and immediately invited the African to his house. In his excitement he also invited the territorial governor to meet Ibrahima and hear the story of their earlier acquaintance. Then he went to Thomas Foster, told him the story, and tried to purchase Ibrahima's freedom.

While these events were unfolding, Ibrahima must have allowed himself to hope for something that until then would have seemed impossible, the opportunity to return to his native land. For reasons he could not comprehend, Allah had placed him in the hands of the Hebohs and he had been delivered into slavery. Perhaps now Allah would now reward him for his long years in servitude by bringing him to freedom.

But it was not to be. Thomas Foster refused to sell Ibrahima, even when John Cox offered more than his market value. Foster explained that even if he were free Ibrahima was probably better off at Pine Ridge. He would be no better off anywhere else in America, and he had little chance of getting back to Africa. More importantly, in terms of Foster's personal interests, his plantation would suffer without Ibrahima as overseer.

For Ibrahima there was at least some consolation in John Cox's arrival in the neighborhood. The doctor welcomed him to visit his house and made certain that the people of the region knew about Ibrahima's African background and about his father's kindness to a lost European.

More years passed and Thomas Foster built a new house for his family and continued to add to his lands, his slaves, and his cattle. James Madison was elected president in 1808, and a few years later he presided over the War of 1812. In 1815 Andrew Jackson met the British forces down river at New Orleans and won one of the most lopsided victories in American history. By 1810 on the eve of the war, Foster owned forty slaves, and in 1819 he owned more than one hundred. Isabella and Ibrahima had more children—five boys and four girls in all—and their children began to have children.

Foster's slaves lived in a community beside a stream a few hundred feet from the main house. Slave housing in the South varied considerably from one plantation to another, and many former slaves left accounts of their unique dwellings. Booker T. Washington recalled that the holes in the walls of his slave home in Virginia were so wide that the cat could walk through them. Henry Daniels said of his slave home in Georgia: "You could take a dog by de heels an' throw him through de cracks in our house." An ex-slave from Texas went one step further in describing the frailty of his cabin: "The cold winds of winter went through the cracks between the logs like the walls was somewhere else."

Other slaves were better housed. Some lived in comfortable quarters in their owner's homes. A New Orleans household slave named Phoebe lived in the back bedroom of the house, slept on a bed made of cherry wood, and kept her clothes in a cherry wood armoire. In the antebellum era most estates with fifty or more slaves (about eleven thousand by 1860) had separate slave quarters, typically laid out in a rectangular pattern some distance from the main house. The houses were usually frame or brick and often had fireplaces. A common type consisted of a single large room with a loft above. Whether from prudence in protecting an expensive asset or humanity in caring for fellow human beings, some masters built substantial quarters for their slaves.

The quarters on Thomas Foster's plantation varied from simple shacks to more substantial frame houses built of one-foot wide boards. As the foremost member of the slave community at Pine Ridge, Ibrahima would have occupied one of the more substantial houses.

In 1818 Ibrahima began to attend regularly the local church of the Mississippi Baptist Association. He did not become a Christian, nor did he abandon his Islamic practices, but something about the church attracted him. In part, it was a matter of his relationship to other enslaved men, women, and children. Isabella was a Christian, and their children followed her faith. It is hard to imagine how Ibrahima could have brought them up as Muslims, given the lack of Islamic schools or even a copy of the Quran. Additionally there was much in the Christian services that was familiar, in particular the stories of Old Testament patriarchs, such as Abraham and Isaac, who were as revered by Muslims as by Christians. Finally, many Christian precepts would have sounded familiar. Just as Protestant Susan Magoffin began attending Catholic services in El Paso during the Mexican War for lack of a nearby Protestant church, Ibrahima, while not converting to Christianity, took some satisfaction in hearing Christian preaching.

During the 1820s Ibrahima no longer worked in the fields. He often went to Natchez to sell his own and Foster's vegetables at the market. By now John Cox had passed away, but his son William Cox remained a friend and continued the Cox effort to buy Ibrahima's freedom. Fortunately they secured a new ally, Andrew Marschalk, the editor of a local newspaper, the *Mississippi State Gazette*. Marschalk was impressed with the story of Ibrahima's royal lineage and saw in the man himself evidence for the truth of the story. "I did not look upon Prince, or Ibrahim," he wrote, "as a mere biped slave, but as a dignified captive, a man born to command, unjustly deprived of his liberty."

In 1826, at Marschalk's urging, Ibrahima wrote a note in Arabic, which they hoped would help win his freedom. Marschalk scribbled a cover letter explaining Ibrahima's circumstances, and they sent it to a Mississippi senator, who carried it to the state department. From there the letter was posted to the United States consul in Tangier, Morocco. Ironically, a mistake in identifying Ibrahima's African roots helped with this petition. Understanding of African geography was poor at the time in the United States. Ibrahima had never been within fifteen hundred miles of Morocco, but America was interested in improving relations with that nation. American seamen were sometimes shipwrecked on the Moroccan shores, and often endured long periods of enslavement before being released, if indeed they ever were released. The consul saw the advantage of freeing an apparent Moroccan captive enslaved in America. He wrote to Secretary of State Henry Clay, who brought the name of Abd Rahman Ibrahima to the attention of President John Quincy Adams in 1827. Impressed, Adams gave his approval for the freeing of Ibrahima.

Negotiations then took place to work out the details. Thomas Foster had grown to admire Ibrahima over the years. They were now both in their sixties, and together they had seen Foster's holdings grow remarkably during the past four decades. Foster declared that he would not sell Ibrahima. Instead he would give the man his freedom if the government would provide funds to return him to his home. Knowing that these negotiations were taking place, Ibrahima was delighted, and those who knew him remembered the enslaved African as seemingly becoming thirty years younger as this new possibility of freedom was discussed. He spoke about the subject with "a countenance beaming with joy."

Finally in February of 1828 a letter arrived in Natchez from the secretary of state. Henry Clay announced that the United States wished to return Ibrahima to Africa and that arrangements should be made for his travel to Washington, D.C. Thomas Foster signed a document freeing his slave on February 22, 1828. This was the moment that Ibrahima had longed for during all of four decades since he awakened in Africa from the blow to the head from a Heboh musket. He was overjoyed. And yet at the same time he was deeply distressed. Perhaps he had never allowed himself to think of this hoped-for freedom as a reality because now that he was free, he came to the hard realization that his wife Isabella and their children would be left behind.

Andrew Marschalk approached Foster about freeing Isabella, and Foster's reply was not entirely discouraging. He noted that she was an essential presence on his plantation: she was the "obstetrick practitioner and doctress." Nor could he afford simply to give her freedom. But he would sell her for $200, about $100 below her fair price. Unfortunately, the federal government had not provided any extra money. And so Foster devised a scheme to raise the money—the equivalent of about $8000 today. A document was drawn up, which citizens could sign to make a donation toward the freeing of Isabella. Ibrahima himself would have to take the paper to the market stalls and offices of Natchez to seek the funds.

Given the common view of slavery and prejudice as inexorable in the Old South, what happened next is quite remarkable. Within twenty-four hours 140 citizens had subscribed to free Isabella, raising a total of $293 for the fund—almost 50 percent more than was required. Their donations ranged from $1 to $20, equivalent to about $40 to $800 today. This gesture cannot cloak the fact that thousands of Africans remained in bondage in Mississippi. But at the same time, it does provide a striking example of the capacity of human beings to transcend the prejudices of their age and to engage, from time to time, in acts of transcendent decency.

On April 11, 1828, Ibrahima and Isabella boarded the steamboat *Neptune* for a voyage up the Mississippi River. Their children came to the dock, "genteely dressed," and bid their parents farewell. The children tried to appear cheerful, but an observer noted "a look of silent agony in their eyes." Ibrahima hoped to raise money in the East to buy their freedom as well, but neither parents nor children could be certain they would see each other again.

Ibrahima and Isabella went by boat to Wheeling, West Virginia, and then by stagecoach along the National Road to Baltimore. By now the eastern press had gotten word of the journey and were billing Ibrahima as the "King of Timbuctoo." In Baltimore they stayed in the home of Benjamin Lundy, publisher of the abolitionist newspaper *Genius of Universal Emancipation*. Ibrahima went on to Washington and

Thomas Hopkins Gallaudet. He was one of several philanthropists who helped Ibrahima raise funds to purchase the freedom of his children.

met with President Adams. He had hoped that the government would raise funds to free his five children and eight grandchildren, but Adams declined in part because Ibrahima, was not, as he had anticipated, a MoorMorocco.

The attraction of Liberia, recently established as a refuge for free blacks from the United States, was that it was much nearer to Timbo than Morocco. Despite the disappointment at the White House, Ibrahima had supporters in Washington who wanted to help him reunite with his children. The American Colonization Society, founded in 1816, was dedicated to resettling free blacks in Liberia. Its members saw the attraction of helping the now-famous Ibrahima in his quest.

Ibrahima's supporters tried a variety of strategies to raise funds. He was a key attraction at a "panorama" of Niagara Falls at the capitol. The panorama was a huge painting of Niagara Falls on a five-thousand-square-foot canvass, so realistic, it was said, that you could get wet if you stood near it. According to the advertisements, Ibrahima was to appear "in Moorish costume." He came, signed autographs, wrote passages in Arabic, and received 50 percent of the entrance fees. In an effort to raise money, Ibrahima went from Washington to Philadelphia, Boston, New Haven, and

New York. Everywhere his name was by now well known among abolitionists, including Arthur and Lewis Tappan, his foremost supporters in New York City.

The story of Ibrahima added to a growing body of anecdotal information about slavery, Africa, and blacks circulating in antebellum America. Here was Ibrahima, a prince and an educated man, who had been a slave. And despite forty years of servitude he had not lost the stately bearing and the quiet dignity apparent to all who saw him. Through the stories of men like Ibrahima, and the escaped slaves of the *Amistad* a few years later, and later still the riveting drama of *Uncle Tom's Cabin*, Americans came increasingly to think of the enslaved Africans of the South as much more than an abstraction. The lesson in each of these stories was that a slave was not merely a slave, but rather an *enslaved person*, a human being in chains.

After months of work, Ibrahima raised more than $3000, enough at least to buy the freedom of some of his Natchez progeny. Leaving those transactions in other hands, he boarded the *Harriet*, a ship chartered by the American Colonization Society. He anticipated that Isabella and the children would follow later. On February 9, 1829, the ship sailed into the Atlantic. More than forty years before Ibrahima had made this journey in chains, below decks. This time, as a guest of the United States, he occupied a fine cabin.

After thirty-seven days at sea the ship arrived in Monrovia, Liberia. It was a small town of wood frame houses, the center of a planned community of Africans returned from America. Ibrahima was still several hundred miles from Futa Jalon. Eager to see his old home, he was also eager for the arrival of the remainder of his American family. In 1830 the Tappan brothers were able to buy the freedom of eight of Ibrahima's children and grandchildren. Later that year they and Isabella sailed for Liberia.

We can only imagine what it might have been like for Ibrahima to take them to Timbo, where they would meet cousins and perhaps uncles and aunts who would speak a strange language. We can imagine Ibrahima sitting beside a fire, telling these relatives and friends about his inconceivably long journey of body and spirit into another continent and society. It was a story of terrible tragedy and profound triumph. He who had been born to rule had spent most of his sixty-six years as a common laborer and a slave. He who had married and fathered a son at Timbo had been separated from the wife of his youth, never to enjoy raising a family with her. But then he had seen wonders and known successes. He had become the overseer of a great estate near a great river in the United States. He had married an African woman in America, fathered children, and became a grandfather. He had known the greed and cruelty of white men; and he had known their generosity and kindness. He had met the president of the United States in his house. These and other tales would have fascinated his African audience. But Ibrahima would never tell these stories in Timbo because, on July 26, 1829, he died of disease in Monrovia. Thus he would never see his American or his African families again.

There is an inner compactness to Ibrahima that is impressive, that stands out above his premature death. His tough spiritual core was never lost in the turmoil of his enslavement or in the celebration of his freedom. While on his tour of New England he was persuaded to accept Christianity, perhaps in gratitude to his many benefactors, perhaps as a way of insuring more support, or perhaps out of a genuine respect for Christian beliefs. But the faith of his upbringing was finally more congenial to him.

On one level in America Ibrahima was dead and "Prince" (as the enslaved man was called) was born in his place. And yet Ibrahima continued to live in the regal bearing of this African, in his dignity, in his leadership, and ultimately in his desire to return home.

After crossing the Atlantic for the second time, Ibrahima first spotted the rich green shore of Africa at Cape Mesurado in Liberia. At that moment he resumed his Islamic worship. In his youth, in Timbo, he had learned and in America he had not forgotten his fundamental faith:

> Nothing will happen except that which Allah has decreed.

Bibliography

Alford, Terry. *Prince among Slaves* (1977). Excellent research and wonderful writing—the definitive account of the life of Abd Rahman Ibrahima.

Austin, Allan D. *African Muslims in Antebellum America* (1997). A comprehensive history of Muslim slaves in America.

Barry, Boubacar. *Senegambia and the Atlantic Slave Trade* (1998). The slave trade and the rise of Islam in the region that includes Ibrahima's homeland.

Blassingame, John W. *The Slave Community* (1972). Description of slave society based largely on slave narratives.

Curtin, Philip D. *Africa Remembered: Narratives by West Africans from the Era of the Slave Trade* (1967). Accounts by and about slaves, including Ayuba Suleiman Diallo, describing their experience in Africa and America.

Genovese, Eugene D. *Roll, Jordon, Roll* (1975). Describes a "black nation" in the Old South based on familial and religious ties.

Gutman, Herbert G. *Black Family in Slavery and Freedom* (1976). Extensive analysis of the black family.

Hogan, William Ranson, and Edwin Adams Davis. *William Johnson's Natchez* (2 vols. 1951). The remarkable diary of a wealthy free black in antebellum Natchez.

Kolchin, Peter. *American Slavery, 1619–1877* (1993). Comprehensive history of the development of slavery in the United States.

Levine, Lawrence W. *Black Culture and Black Consciousness* (1977). Survival of African culture in black America.

Martin, Jonathan D. *Divided Mastery: Slave Hiring in the American South* (2004). Argues that most slaves were hired out at some point during their lives and describes the hiring-out practice.

West, Emily. *Chains of Love: Slave Couples in Antebellum South* (2004). Like Ibrahima and Isabella, many other slave couples forged strong marital bonds despite the obstacles imposed by their enslavement.

Identification Topics

Ibrahima Sori Mawdo, Abd Rahman Ibrahima, Timbo, Futa Jalon, Niger River, Djenne, Timbuktu, Islam, Muslim, hajj, Mungo Park, John Coates Cox, the Hebohs, John Nevin, the *Africa*, Thomas Foster, Sarah Foster, Samba, Eli Whitney, Ayuba Suleiman Diallo, Five Pillars of Islam, Andrew Marschalk, John Quincy Adams, the American Colonization Society, Arthur and Lewis Tappan, Liberia, Monrovia, the *Harriet*

Study Questions

1. What were the essential elements of Ibrahima's education in Africa?
2. How did Ibrahima become a slave?
3. What were some of the key tenets of Ibrahima's faith as a Muslim? In what ways were he and other Muslim slaves able to continue practicing their faith in America?
4. Why did Ibrahima "accept" his enslavement after running away to the forest?
5. In what ways did Ibrahima preserve his culture and individuality even while filling the role of a slave?
6. What was the nature of free enterprise for slaves on some southern plantations, and why would a planter allow it to exist?
7. Why were John Quincy Adams and Henry Clay interested in freeing Ibrahima?
8. Why would 140 Mississippians in 1828 contribute to a fund to buy the freedom of Ibrahima's wife, Isabella?
9. The author makes a distinction between a slave and an enslaved person, sometimes choosing the latter term to describe Ibrahima. What is the meaning of this distinction? How does the story of Ibrahima give meaning to the distinction?
10. Why were abolitionists interested in Ibrahima? How did he help their cause?

CHAPTER 15

The Civil War
Two Soldiers and Their Worlds

During the American Revolution, Loyalist opponents of independence had claimed that the colonists could never create a unified nation because the economic and cultural differences between North and South would lead to civil strife. But the two sections were able to lay aside their differences while they fought the Revolutionary War, drafted the Constitution, and began the new government. Even as they cooperated in some enterprises, however, they disagreed over tariffs, slavery, and western lands, widening the breach that Tories had discerned almost a century before. Antagonism between the two sections exploded into war in 1861, each side believing in the righteousness of its cause. The Civil War not only revealed the depths of sectional differences, but also demonstrated the underlying similarities between the sections. The careers of William Wheeler and Charles Colcock Jones Jr. personify both the brutality of warfare and the common humanity of North and South.

The Civil War occupies a unique position in American history. No event, not even the Revolution, holds a higher place in the national regard. Its battles were the bloodiest ever fought on American soil, and its people were at once the most human and resourceful of American heroes. The names of its events and leaders read like a patriotic litany: Abraham Lincoln, Ulysses S. Grant, William Tecumseh Sherman, Thomas ("Stonewall") Jackson, and Robert E. Lee; the Gettysburg Address and the Emancipation Proclamation; the *Monitor* and the *Merrimack*; and the Battles of Bull Run, Antietam, Chancellorsville, Gettysburg, Vicksburg, and the Wilderness. The history of the war includes stories of recruitment, war industries, supplies, military leadership, politics, diplomacy, and civilian morale. It is really not one tale but many separate histories, each complex and elusive.

The Civil War can, however, be reduced to human scale by the very soldiers who fought in it. Each had his own history, personal experiences that reflected in some fashion

247

the larger forces of the war. Although most soldiers left no record of their thoughts and activities beyond the brief notices they received in troop lists, casualty reports, and other public records, some wrote diaries and letters that allow us to observe closely their personal histories. Two such men were William Wheeler, captain of New York's Thirteenth Artillery, and Charles Colcock Jones Jr., lieutenant colonel of the Georgia Artillery. Their Civil War letters help explain why northerners and southerners took up arms against one another and describe how they spent their days during the hard years of the war.

In spring 1864 William Wheeler was an artillery captain in a northern army marching toward Atlanta, Georgia, under the command of William Tecumseh Sherman. Wheeler had been in the army for three years and fought at the Second Battle of Bull Run, Chancellorsville, Gettysburg, and Chattanooga. The army had become so much his way of life that after his infrequent leaves he actually enjoyed returning to camp. Recently back from a trip home, he wrote his mother that he rejoined his men with "a quiet feeling of satisfaction and contentment, a happiness in being back at my work again."

By this time Wheeler was a seasoned professional, a soldier's soldier. We can understand him and his work best if we look at his early years as a civilian and as a raw recruit. William Wheeler was born in New York City on August 14, 1836. He developed an early interest in literature, reading when he was four and improvising stories to entertain neighborhood children when he was eight. Wheeler absorbed literature easily and could recall lines from Shakespeare, the Latin and Greek classics, and contemporary poetry. He developed a love of outdoors and became a skilled fisherman, catching seventy-two trout as a boy on a two-day trip to the Catskill Mountains.

In 1852, at age sixteen, Wheeler entered Yale College. His undergraduate letters combine prudery and playfulness. As a freshman he wrote home that four older boys had been "caught in the interesting occupation of cementing up the bell." His mother "need not fear" that he would be found in any such "scrapes." On a "stupendously cold" morning in January, he wrote her, "The fire itself froze the other morning. I would send you a piece, but . . . fear it would burn a hole in the paper." In fall 1854, when he was a senior, he attempted to grow whiskers; finding, however, that his beard's "powers of increasing were exactly the opposite of Jack's bean-stalk," he gave it up.

At college William Wheeler enjoyed his studies and nature equally. He excelled in classics and mathematics and formed a secret society for scholars. He observed closely the patterns of nature around the college—the spring when green and purple mosses came out upon the hills; the fall when the thick woods seemed painted by "unearthly artists, in earth-surpassing colors"; and the winter when he took sleigh rides over the snow through the valley between East and West Rocks, two hills that overlooked New Haven "like ermine-clad giants."

After completing his undergraduate program he studied law at Yale until 1857, then made a grand tour of Europe, a common postgraduate activity for well-to-do young men of his day. Wheeler's zest for life, his most appealing quality, was especially evident in his letters on the trip. His sailing ship, *Australia*, ran into a storm of rain, wind, and mountainous waves; while other passengers cringed in fear, Wheeler found that the threat of destruction gave the sea "a more sublime and lofty" character and reminded him of his "own littleness in comparison with this greatest of God's works." When the sea was calm on the long journey, he loved to watch the "snowy canvass" of the great sails, the moonlight's "flood of glory" on the water, and the glow of phosphorescence shining in the sea "like stars rolled out" of an angel's cloak.

Wheeler delighted in such scenes. He was drawn also to literary and historical grandeur. As the *Australia* sailed past Gibraltar into the Mediterranean, he thought of the great seamen whose keels had "furrowed" these waters. Here the fleets of Rome and Greece had fought, the Crusaders had sailed for the Holy Land, and Nelson had won the Battle of Trafalgar. And now along their path came William Wheeler, "not to strike a blow for Grecian or Italian Independence, but bound for Marseilles, in the merchant ship *Australia* consigned to Ribaud Brothers & Co., and oh! horror, laden with alcohol (I smell it now), stores, wheat, and bacon." Despite his amusement at the common circumstances of his arrival in Europe, Wheeler made the most of his year abroad, hiking through the Swiss Alps, studying in Berlin, and visiting Paris, Florence, and London.

He returned to America in 1858 and resumed his legal studies at Harvard. After graduating in 1860, he moved to New York, where he took an apartment and studied for the bar, alternately reading Shakespeare's plays and legal tomes to fight the sleep-inducing effects of "cramming up the Revised Statutes" for his examination.

Wheeler was absorbed by the year's political events. He was intensely interested in the outcome of the 1860 presidential election. Describing himself frankly as belonging to "the extreme Abolition edge of the Republican party," he worked hard for the election of Abraham Lincoln. As the outcome of the election became clear and the southern states began to move toward secession, Wheeler actually hoped for war so that slavery could be ended once and for all. If a civil war occurred, he wrote, "then the

Civil War encampment. Yankee and Confederate soldiers slept in crude huts of canvas and wood, often with pork-barrel chimneys.

country will emerge from that chaos of fire and blood, fresh and free, its dross purged away, and its great sin expiated." As the conflict drew near he decided that he would join the army rather than hire a substitute, as many wealthy young men did. "I do not suppose that I am very well fitted for a soldier," he wrote, "but still I have a good deal of fight in me, and think that I shall never see a holier cause to fight for."

That spring New York City was ablaze with patriotism, recruits marching up and down to the sound of fife and drum and the streets "a long arbor of flags." Full of excitement and hoping not to miss the first engagements of the war, Wheeler joined the Seventh Regiment in New York; purchased a uniform, blankets, and mess kit; and had his hair cut to regulation length. On May 9, 1861, he boarded the steamer *Mantanzas*, having written his mother, "For myself, I cannot see how a life could be more worthily given up, unless it were for God's sake, though is not this God's cause?" He was twenty-four years old; a practicing lawyer; a scholar proficient in Latin, Greek, Hebrew, German, and French; and now a soldier going forth on his greatest adventure.

The soldiers aboard the *Mantanzas* were crazed with exuberance, and Wheeler feared that "the younger ones seem to look upon the whole affair as a gigantic spree, and to form no true conception of the serious character of the undertaking." Yet it was Wheeler who led the men in giving three cheers when the steamer passed a ship bearing the Italian flag "under which Garibaldi achieved the freedom of Italy." Soon afterward he and the others cheered an English ship called the *Union* and joined in singing verse after verse of "The Star-Spangled Banner." The next day the spirit of patriotism was still ablaze as the ship streamed up the Potomac past Mount Vernon, her flag at half-mast, her bell tolling, and her men standing respectfully with heads uncovered, a traditional sign of respect for George Washington.

On May 14, 1861, Wheeler was stationed at Camp Cameron, the first of dozens of posts where he would spend the next three years sleeping in tents, in makeshift cabins, and beneath the stars. When his regiment made camp on its long marches and countermarches in Virginia, Tennessee, and Georgia, the soldiers normally slept under canvas, a perfectly adequate arrangement when the elements were at rest. But there were nights when gales ripped through the camp and Wheeler's tent "rocked like a boat on the waves." In the winter the shelters became so cold that "the only way was to lie [in bed] and take it." After a particularly cold night Wheeler wrote home, "ten degrees below zero is not exactly comfortable in a tent." To make matters worse, the fragile dwellings caught fire with alarming regularity.

The more resourceful soldiers made an occupation of improving their tents. Sometimes Wheeler had stone fireplaces built in his, using pork barrels as chimneys and lining the floors with boards. But such efforts were often frustrated by the need to move on, and moving frequently meant sleeping outdoors. Wheeler rather liked camping out, even in the cold, when he could lie beside a roaring fire with the stars overhead. But when he had to sleep in the rain and the mud, then, he said, "the fun ceases to be perceptible."

The food was no better than the shelter. Men often had nothing more than crackers and coffee for breakfast and supper, with meat and soup for lunch. Worse, there were days of "salt horse and hard bisquit." On good days the diet might be improved with mutton or chicken purchased or stolen from southern farmers, but on bad days Wheeler had to make do with a handful of horse's grain, a meal he called "maize au naturel." Worn down by poor shelter and food, he wrote his mother that he had become "a shabby, muddy soldier."

Wheeler and others attempted to improve the tone of camp life with ceremonies, song, and even learning. On Christmas Eve in 1862, when the regiment was camped near the Stafford courthouse in Virginia, he went out into the woods and found "a most beautiful little holly-tree, with splendid leaves and full of berries," which he planted at the foot of a flagpole. In the war's early months, before he became disillusioned with the army chaplains, he organized well-attended prayer meetings at which the men sang "ever so many hymns." He enjoyed, too, the songs men sung by campfires. Wheeler's men, mainly German immigrants, sang fine old songs from their fatherland, while black servants sang camp-meeting tunes, "in a minor and melancholy key."

Such moments softened the hard outlines of camp life. Wheeler sought also to uplift his surroundings by establishing a school for the soldiers. The schoolhouse was a collection of desks and chairs made from split logs and arranged around a tree; the teacher, an old corporal chosen by Wheeler; the pupils, "rough, wild" enlisted men, many of whom did not know how to read. Some forty men came to classes of their own accord, and Wheeler hoped they would soon sign their own payroll slips. But before he could strike a blow for literacy, the regiment had to move on again, leaving behind its latest encampment and Wheeler's improvised school.

Despite the disruption of each move, Wheeler generally welcomed the chance to break camp. "I am twice as buoyant, and hopeful, and happy," he wrote his mother, "on a hard march, as when vegetating in camp." Wheeler especially liked traveling through the mountainous parts of Virginia, where the soldiers "went fishing, blackberrying, and cherry-picking, and where at times it seemed more like a charming summer picnic 'long drawn out' than anything else." Pleasant, too, was the train journey from Virginia to Tennessee on the Baltimore and Ohio Railroad, through the "mysterious lights and shadows of a perfect moonlight autumn night," and across Indiana where the citizens cheered the soldiers at each stop and ladies gave them cakes, cold meats, doughnuts, handkerchiefs, towels, and soap. In such moments the whole war seemed a glorious adventure, made all the more exciting by "the inspiring prospect of a conflict with an enemy a few miles ahead."

Wheeler's regiment was never required to wait long for that next engagement. For two years they fought indecisive skirmishes and battles in Virginia. Then one day in 1863 the army began to move north, following Robert E. Lee into Pennsylvania. The men, who had lived for months in the South, were pleased by their reception as they marched through Frederick County, Maryland. Children waved handkerchiefs and tiny flags; hotels were wrapped in red, white, and blue bunting; an old lady stood at her door handing out cups of cold water to thirsty soldiers; her gray-haired husband stood at her side, his eyes half filled with tears. "Good luck to you boys," he murmured, "God bless you."

On the morning of July 1, 1863, Wheeler's artillery battery was eleven miles from Gettysburg, Pennsylvania, moving along at a deliberate pace, when a messenger arrived urging speed. The men flew toward the town, gun carriages rattling and bouncing over the stony road, food and kettles breaking loose from the caissons, and cannoneers running to keep up. When they reached Gettysburg, tens of thousands of men in gray and blue were gathering their forces in a vast pattern of artillery, infantry, and cavalry. Wheeler's battery rushed from one point to another in this scene of noise, movement, and confusion. Hurrying through town, the soldiers passed ladies waving handkerchiefs and cheering them on and stopped at a place called Cemetery Hill, where the Union forces concentrated their artillery.

During the next three days the two armies mauled one another with cannon, rifle, and bayonet. Lee unleashed the greatest artillery barrage ever known in America. "The air," said Wheeler, "was literally alive with flying projectiles." Cemetery Hill was hit with a hailstorm of shot, ranging from six-pound missiles the size of cricket balls to Whitworth rifle shot so huge they gave "rise to the story of the rebs firing railroad iron." Most dangerous of all were the Confederate charges that drove right in among the Union ranks. When the enemy came close, and the Federal infantry drew back leaving the artillery dangerously exposed, Wheeler abandoned the large shells used against the Confederate artillery and aimed small canister shot at the infantry.

"Wheeler," said another officer, "which *are* the rebels and which are our men?"

"You pays your money," said Wheeler, "and you takes your choice."

The Confederates were driven back, then and in other efforts to break the Union lines. Both armies rested on July 4, and the next day Lee began the dismal march back to Virginia. He had failed to win the northern victory that would have meant so much to his cause.

William Wheeler's role at the Battle of Gettysburg was like that of hundreds of other junior officers. He stuck to his post, opposed the enemy advance, and kept up a strong fire. He was a minor actor in an epic drama. Yet he loved his role. "Somehow or other," he told his friends at home, "I felt a joyous exaltation, a perfect indifference to circumstances, through the whole of that three days' fight, and have seldom enjoyed three days more in my life."

Strange words, perhaps, for a man who admired the classics, led prayer meetings, and established a camp school. But battle had become a way of life to Wheeler. Not that he was unaffected by suffering; in his mind he carried images of the devastation of war: trees speckled with bullets and bored through by shells; a fellow artillery officer killed when a shell plowed through his horse; an infantryman's leg, blown off at Gettysburg, whirling "through the air like a stone, until it came against a caisson with a loud whack." Worse still was the sight of his own men hospitalized with mortal wounds. One of the hardest to bear was a "fine-looking young Irishman, with a . . . deep suscep-tibility to both pain and pleasure," whom Wheeler visited in the hospital. "One of his wounds had affected the nerves," he wrote, "and the pain came in great wrenches and spasms that made him gnash his teeth and beat his feet on the bed in agony. I became so sick that I could hardly get to the door."

Despite his familiarity with the reality of injury and death, Wheeler appears to have had few worries about his own fate. He admitted that he felt anxiety at the approach to battle, before his guns were in place. He said that he "would prefer to be either in the midst of the affair or else entirely absent." When he had to set up his guns while the enemy was firing at him, he felt "unpleasantly"; but once the battery was ready and he was busy loading, aiming, and firing, his chief sensation was excitement. He enjoyed the challenge of his work as well as "the sense of bodily danger and of continual escape from it." In these engagements, death and injury were so common as to be unin-timidating. At Gettysburg, he wrote, "the danger was so great and so constant that, at last, it took away the sense of danger." Wheeler even found that he slept especially well on the night before a battle. When conflict was inevitable, one might as well rest.

Different men accommodated to battle in various ways. Some were armed with the giddy assurance that they could never be shot. Others refused to speculate about their prospective fortunes. Wheeler's resolution came from another source—the certitude that he *would* be killed. In the first years of the war he had looked at the magnitude of the conflict and concluded that almost everyone who stayed in the army for the duration would die. He wrote home in 1861, "This is emphatically a war deadly to officers, and I have fully made up my mind never to see any of you again." In the next year he predicted that "few of the army now in the field will ever see their homes again; the new conscripts will win the glory of finishing the war." He disliked thinking about the possibility of survival, because such imaginings weakened his resolve. "I prefer to accept the belief that I must fall," he wrote. "The question with us is not whether we shall die or not, but how we shall die and among what surroundings."

The expectation that he would die a soldier in the field intensified his relationship to the army. It was, quite literally, his life's work. "My battery," he told his cousin, "is my plighted bride." His weapons, a half dozen three-inch rifled guns, were to him "as a sweetheart, yea, as many sweethearts." When he lost one of his guns in an engagement at Gettysburg, he went out on the field after the battle, found the gun, and repaired it, glad in the recovery of an old friend. He was equally fond of his horse, who ate sugar from his hand, followed him like a dog, and bore the name Barry, after Wheeler's artillery chief. Then, too, there was the pleasure of leadership. When he was elevated from the rank of lieutenant to captain in 1863, he wrote home, "I like to have the command of men, and to say, like the centurion, 'Go! and he goeth.'"

As much as Wheeler enjoyed the craft of artilleryman, the war's purpose excited him more than its process. He called himself an "extreme Emancipationist" determined to see the end of slavery. Men fought in the Civil War for many reasons: some because they were drafted, others for adventure, and others to save the Union. Wheeler and soldiers like him fought with the moral fervor of medieval knights on a crusade, their goal the eradication of slavery. The war, he told his mother, "has become the religion of very many of our lives, and those of us who think, and who did not enter the service for gain of military distinction, have come more and more to identify this cause for which we are fighting, with all of good and religion in our previous lives." His hero was Gen. Ulysses S. Grant, whom he called "a steam engine in pantaloons." He had no patience with men who gave sparingly for the cause and rejoiced when the timorous McClellan, a "softy warrior," was dismissed from command. Disgusted at the news of draft riots in New York City, he proposed a simple solution: he would set up his battery at a place on Broadway he knew where "the balls would ricochet splendidly on the hard pavement."

The Union cause simply must prevail. It was to him "the same that the quest of the Holy Grail was to Sir Galahad." He would endeavor, like Tennyson's Ulysses, "to strive, to seek, to find, and not to yield." After Gettysburg he acknowledged that the war might last many years, but he and his fellows would endure. "I am, in this matter," he said, "like St. Paul's Charity, ready to bear, believe, hope, and endure all things for the cause, knowing that if we do, we also, like Charity, shall never fail."

Wheeler was able to inspire others with his enthusiasm. He said little about his influence, but his men seem to have rallied around him in many circumstances: on the battlefield, in hymn singing, or in the creation of a school. When time came for reenlistment early in 1864, the men of his company wanted first to be reassured that Wheeler would stay in. When he agreed to do so, almost all of them followed him.

Wheeler's influence and his personal success as a soldier owed much to his devotion to his work and his cause. That commitment so hardened him to the attractions of home that he did not like to think a great deal about his civilian life. He even hesitated to visit his family, saying, "If I should go home, the parting would be most painful, the crust of insensibility and of absorption in my duty would be cast off,—I should be like a soft-shell crab, who had cast his shell prematurely."

He acknowledged, however, that when he was not occupied by present duties, a longing for home swept through him. On a "beautiful Sabbath afternoon" in the South he thought of his mother walking through the autumn leaves on her way to church. He missed good conversation and domestic surroundings: "a quiet supper with a chosen crowd . . . and then a sensible chat over the apples and Madeira until the small hours." He begged his family and friends to fill their letters to him with the details of daily life. "It is the neat little touches thrown skillfully in," he wrote, "that make the home picture glow with life, and make the heart of the absent member beat warmly as he looks at it."

Affected as he was by memories of his home, he found himself sympathizing with the people whose lands the northern armies occupied. He could speak facetiously of "fried secessionists for breakfast," and he fired cannon shot at the enemy with unbridled enthusiasm. But when he came face to face with southerners his feelings changed. As the soldiers marched along, they often saw women "dressed in black and weeping as if their hearts would break." In Virginia Wheeler sought to prevent excessive demands on the local farmsteads, interfering in one case, "in favor of a sheep, some bee-hives, and the potato patch" and winning in return an invitation to dinner. He was solicitous of enemy soldiers wounded in battle. At Gettysburg he walked among the southerners where they "lay scattered over the field in groups of twenty, fifty, or even a hundred." Wheeler brought water to one, propped another on his side, and rigged up a bed of straw for a third. On one occasion, having driven off some Union soldiers who were about to pillage a southern house, he was rewarded by being invited in. In a letter to his mother he tells how he nearly lost his heart to a rebel:

I met the prettiest girl I have seen in Virginia,—a real stunner, with light brown hair and perfect features, . . . I grieve to say that I was quite enthralled by this she-rebel, and the next night, being out foraging for hay, I stayed to supper, and came home so late that I found a party just saddling to go out and rescue me from the bush-wackers. The captain gave me three days on guard, but I think that it was worth it on the whole. Then, to cap the climax, being sent down to Culpepper after stores, I stopped there yesterday morning on my way back and took breakfast. If we have occasion to retreat, I shall manage to get wounded near that house and have "sweet Maud Muller" (I don't know her real name), take care of me. . . .

I picked up a letter on the battle field the other day, from a young married lady in Georgia to her two brothers in the army, and it might have been from you, so pleasant and naïve was the style. She chatted about her little baby, and how it resembled its young uncles, etc., and my heart smote me when I thought that perhaps their life-blood had soaked the very ground where I stood.

In such moments Wheeler was struck by the "common humanity" of Confederate and Yankee. He mixed easily with the people of Virginia and Tennessee, arguing at one moment with an old Presbyterian clergyman in Virginia about secession and at the next singing hymns at the piano with him and his family. He and his men often visited, played games, discussed books, sang, and ate melons with civilians, then ended their visits with a chorus of "The Star-Spangled Banner," which, he said, "ought to do a secessionist's ears a great deal of good." In Tennessee he spent a pleasant evening visiting a fine old house where an aristocratic young lady sang "Union songs, and secesh airs, darkey melodies and opera morceaux with equal facility."

It was a curious war, and Wheeler's life reflected all its ambiguities—the shabby encampments, the heroic aims, the brutal battles, the moments of reconciliation, and the furtive thoughts of home. Now in spring 1864 William Wheeler was engaged in a new phase of the conflict, marching south in one of the columns of troops that Sherman sent into Georgia. Soldiering was a way of life to which he had grown accustomed, and he operated with routine efficiency: bringing his battery into play in a series of engagements; writing home while bullets flew overhead; and enjoying, in moments of respite, the honeysuckles, jasmines, and roses of this fertile southern land.

A few miles away from Sherman's army another soldier, Charles Colcock Jones Jr., was preparing to resist the invaders of his homeland. His background prepared him to see southern virtues that Wheeler could never perceive and to excoriate northern vices that Wheeler would never acknowledge. Jones was as dedicated to the Confederacy as Wheeler was to the Union. The two men were on opposite sides of a bitter struggle. Yet in retrospect, we can see that they shared many thoughts, aspirations, and experiences.

Jones was born on October 28, 1831, in Savannah, Georgia. His father was a Presbyterian minister who owned three plantations in nearby Liberty County. Jones grew up with many advantages and pleasures of plantation wealth: private tutors who nourished his interest in literature and history; lessons in riding and weekly "cavalry parades" with other children; and opportunities to hunt duck, deer, raccoon, rabbit, and alligator in the countryside near his home.

During the 1850s Jones observed the North firsthand and so became aware of his distinctive southern heritage. He was an undergraduate at Princeton and studied law at Harvard, graduating in 1855, three years before Wheeler's arrival. Jones enjoyed his Harvard years—admired his teachers, indulged his "passion" for books, and won the respect of his professors and fellow students. At times he was positively attracted to New England, especially to "all the glories" of her Indian summers. But he was reminded, too, of his attachment to the South, finding tiresome the northern climate, with its sharp temperature changes, and disliking the noise of the local Fourth of July celebrations, all firecrackers and rockets, instead of the fine orations he associated with southern celebrations.

Jones was particularly repelled by the abolitionists, who abounded in Massachusetts, even in the staid halls of the law school. He was engrossed by the Burns case in May 1854. Anthony Burns was an escaped slave owned by a Virginian, Col. Charles F. Suttle. A hearing to determine whether Burns was in fact Suttle's property provided a focal point for antislavery sentiment. After attending the hearing, Jones wrote his parents that "Mob law, perjury, free-soilism, and abolitionism are running riot." The courtroom was filled with armed men, and even the attorneys carried guns and bowie knives. The mob in the street had to be cleared every hour. Even then, the confused noise of the soldiers and abolitionists nearly drowned out the voices of the litigants.

Jones befriended Suttle, the object of this vituperation, and found him "a perfect Virginia gentleman, of high standing, well educated, of fine, commanding, prepossessing appearance." The abolitionists considered him a vicious slavemaster bent on exploiting his fellow man, but Jones came to admire him with "such an attachment as only a Southerner can know for his brother Southerner." From such incidents and attachments Charles Colcock Jones Jr. and thousands of other southerners like him developed a sense of the beleaguered righteousness of their own region. Twenty years earlier he could have witnessed the mobbing of William Lloyd Garrison by an antiabolitionist citizenry, but the past two decades had seen popular sentiment swing against slavery. Jones noticed with dismay that some of the bitterest antisouthern diatribes came from New England's pulpits. He was treated well enough by his classmates at Harvard, but he sensed that he and his "brother" southerners were different from these harsh, misguided northerners.

Jones returned to Savannah in 1855 and practiced law, soon becoming a partner in the firm of Ward, Owens, and Jones. Like other aspiring young attorneys, he engaged in civic affairs, joining the volunteer Chatham Artillery Company and serving as a city alderman. In 1858 he married Ruth Berrien Whitehead, whom he called "a noble specimen of a young woman of the most generous impulses, and of remarkably good judgment." Two years later he was elected mayor of Savannah.

Jones's letters in this period do not mention the continuing northern campaign against slavery, but his ideas about the institution and about blacks continually appear in his correspondence. He and his family were exemplars of a benevolent, paternalistic relationship between the master and the slave. His mother spoke of slaveownership as bringing "responsibilities not only for time but for eternity." The family owned 129 blacks in 1860. Jones's father was so effective as a Presbyterian evangelist among the slaves that his region was famed throughout the South for its Christianized blacks. He wrote two books, *Catechism of Scripture Doctrine and Practice* (1837) and *The Religious Instruction of the Negroes in the United States* (1842), both widely used for evangelical work. The younger Jones inherited his father's sense of responsibility for the slaves. He opposed as cruel the reopening of the slave trade and was appalled when a southern commercial convention entertained such a notion. He believed that if slaves had to be sold at all they should be sold with their families and regarded slave trading as "the lowest occupation" in which men could engage.

His letters described scenes in which the lives of blacks and whites mingled in common sentiment. On June 30, 1858, he attended the funeral of the late mayor of Savannah, Richard Wayne, a solemn occasion at which volunteer organizations—the artillery company, the fire brigades, the Odd Fellows, the Irish societies, and other groups—marched through the streets past silent crowds and flags at half-mast. They formed a great procession a half-mile long, but what most impressed Jones was not the column in which he marched but the singing of hundreds of blacks, who stood near the grave. As he and the other mourners entered the cemetery, the blacks began singing "that beautiful and solemn funeral hymn, 'We Are Passing Away.'" They sang with "a depth of feeling" that awakened "a sad echo in every breast."

In Jones's mind, master and slave in Georgia constituted a genuine community. Yet there was no question but that white authority must prevail. He disliked the arrangement that allowed slaves in Savannah and other southern cities to "live out," hiring their labor and seeing their masters only on payday. The practice, said Jones, "exerts a most injurious influence upon the relation of master and slave." If necessary he was willing to uphold slavery with the sword, as he tacitly admitted when he told his parents that the Chatham Artillery, which he had recently joined, was organized to "quell sudden insurrection or domestic lawlessness."

In 1850, when the memory of Nat Turner's Revolt was still fresh in southern minds, the blacks themselves seemed to threaten violence to the "peculiar institution" of slavery. But at the close of the decade the rise of the Republican Party and the increasing stridency of the abolitionists suggested an even greater danger from the North. Private military companies such as the Chatham Artillery offered a means of preparing southerners for the eventuality of sectional warfare. Jones and his company made an unusual out-of-state trip in 1859 to Nashville, Tennessee, to encourage formation of a similar company there. His group had been "privately" assured that they would receive a warm welcome and made the railroad journey in force—fifty men in uniform with six cannon. They were cheered along the route, and in Nashville they were greeted by an enthusiastic crowd, including fifteen hundred children dressed in white who threw roses in their path. A series of banquets and artillery demonstrations highlighted their visit. Before they left, the gentlemen of Nashville had begun to form an artillery company of their own.

Within a few months the value to the South of such companies would become apparent. At the news of Abraham Lincoln's election, South Carolina seceded from the Union and declared itself an independent state. Charles Jones wrote his parents, "We are on the verge of heaven only knows what." At first, the thought of secession may have frightened him, but he was soon a leader of the movement in Georgia.

On October 12, 1861, he presided over a secession meeting in Savannah. The crowd that gathered was too large for any hall, so Jones and others addressed it from a balcony. The throng before Jones seemed to "sway to and fro on every hand like the sea lifted by the breath of the tornado." Mad with excitement, the people cheered and fired cannon and rockets when they heard the secession proposals. After the tumult quieted, Jones asked whether there were any nay votes. The throng was silent; then someone shouted, "There's *narra no*, Mayor Jones!"

Jones wholeheartedly supported the secession movement, believing that there could be no reconciliation between the sections. He wrote his father: "I have long since believed that in this country there have arisen two races which, although claiming a common parentage, have been so entirely separated by climate, by morals, by religion, and by estimates so totally opposed of all that constitutes honor, truth, and manliness, that they cannot longer coexist under the same government. Oil and water will not commingle. We are the land of rulers; fanaticism has no home here. The sooner we separate the better."

As mayor of Savannah, Jones observed the disposition of troops in the area and the strengthening of the city's defenses. He wrote with pleasure that "the ladies of Savannah" were busy making cartridges, bandages, and shirts. A spirit of sectional patriotism had swept the South, and his father declared the Union's opposition to secession to be "an outrage upon Christianity and the civilization of the age, and upon the great and just principles of popular sovereignty." He had no doubt that "The law-abiding mass of the American people lies south of Mason's and Dixon's line." Father and son agreed that the Civil War had been brought on by a mass of lawless, godless fanatics. But they would prevail. "Heaven forbid," said the younger Jones, that the Yankees should "ever attempt to set foot upon this land of sunshine, of high-souled honor, and of liberty."

At this moment of buoyant optimism, tragedy struck Charles Jones in the death of his wife and his first daughter. He was despondent for weeks, haunted by the memories that filled his empty house. "Oh, my dear parents," he wrote, "What voices dwell in these vacant chairs, this silent piano, this desolate bed, these folded garments, these unused jewels, these neglected toys, these noiseless rooms." In his despair he had a prophetic sense that God might have taken them away to spare them from the "evil to come."

But in the summer months of 1861 his grief gave way to optimistic thoughts about the Confederacy. He welcomed news of the Battle of Manassas as a great southern victory. "Surely the God of Battles is with us," he wrote. His bereavement removed the sole impediment to his joining active service. He announced that he would not seek a second term as Savannah mayor at the expiration of his term on October 15, 1861, and accepted the rank of first lieutenant in his old company, the Chatham Artillery, now a branch of the Confederate army. He embraced the southern standard with his "whole heart," and he told his parents he would gladly give his life in the "sacred cause."

At the end of October 1861 Lt. Col. Charles Colcock Jones Jr. moved to Camp Claghorn, on a bluff on the Isle of Hope nine miles from Savannah. The encampment was picturesque: pure white tents set amid a cluster of dark overhanging oaks, "burnished" guns gleaming brightly in the sun, a garrison flag waving overhead, a "bold river" flowing past, and the soft waves of the ocean sounding in the distance. This was one of several camps near Savannah. In the morning Jones could hear the sound of reveille from other camps along the river.

On November 7, a few days after Jones's arrival at Claghorn, the Union launched an attack from the sea on nearby Port Royal and the rich Georgia Sea Islands. Jones and his company expected to be moved at any moment to support the Confederate batteries on the islands, but within a few hours the Union fleet had swept around the island defenses and occupied Port Royal. The Yankees now threatened Savannah herself, and anticipating a deadly battle, Jones wrote his parents that he would gladly give his life in support of southern "honor, nationality, and principles" and in opposition to the "infamous pollution of a lawless and inhuman enemy." He anticipated that despite this initial defeat, in Georgia the Yankees would find that "a people armed in the holy cause of liberty, and in such a country as this which we possess, are invincible by any force which they may send against us." Although Jones did not say so, his phrase was derived from Patrick Henry's famous Revolutionary oration in which he said, "give me liberty or give me death." Jones, like many other southerners, believed that the principles of 1776 and 1861 were identical. And as the earlier patriots had, his people, too, would prevail.

Despite the proximity of the Union forces to Savannah, the battle Jones expected did not occur. The Yankees, controlling the seas, were impervious to threat on the Sea Islands and used their hold on this Atlantic outpost of southern plantation society as an opportunity to experiment with the reconstruction of black life through education and economic opportunity.

Nonetheless, the Union encampment necessitated stationing batteries such as Jones's on the Georgia coast. Jones was offered the command of a volunteer company fighting in Virginia, but the threat to his native region kept him in Georgia. Small skirmishes occasionally erupted, and at times Savannah residents could see northern ships with the naked eye; but the wait for conflict stretched on month after month, and the situation acquired an aura of unreality. One day in early spring 1862 Jones rode out to an abandoned battery on nearby Skidaway Island. In the still evening the sea gulls and pelicans played above the gentle sea. The scene seemed "emblematic of perfect peace." But only a short distance away five Union ships stood in full view. When would the enemy attack?

For the present the artillery companies were left to the day-to-day work of camp life. Sometimes the men left the orderly rows of tents at Camp Claghorn and bivouacked in the country to practice the fatigues of march. One December evening they slept with only blankets in the cold clear air and awakened with frost on their caps and lumps of ice in their canteens. Sometimes they went farther afield and had to contend with bedbugs and crowded quarters. But, anchored as they were to their base near Savannah, they never had to endure the hardships of a long march.

Jones hoped for the opportunity to confront the enemy, but the Yankees at Port Royal seemed contented to stay on the Sea Islands, and the great engagements of the war took place in distant places. Jones was forced to follow the war from afar, drilling his artillery company and hoping for a chance to strike a blow for the cause.

He viewed the war with the strong religious sensibilities taught him by his Presbyterian father, believing that the South must recognize its dependence upon God in order to defeat the Union armies. When his state or the Confederacy called for days of fasting, Jones observed them strictly, halting all drills and encouraging his men to "feel their sins and their dependence upon God." Jones regarded southern defeats as scourges from God, designed to purify the southern people and draw their hearts to Him. Despite their sins and temporary setbacks, they were on the side of virtue and order, and in time God would punish the North with a "day of retribution."

But after the defeat of General Lee at Gettysburg and the Union victories on the Mississippi, the prospect of a southern victory began to dim. Still, the northern victories did not undermine Jones's sense of Yankee villainy and southern rectitude. When the Federal navy bombarded Charleston, South Carolina, in August 1863, he was appalled at this attack on a civilian population. "Can history furnish a parallel to such an act of inhumanity?" he asked. He regarded the Emancipation Proclamation as the "crowning act" in a "series of black and diabolical transactions." He wrote his father that Lincoln intended to "subvert our entire social system, desolate our homes, and convert the quiet, ignorant, dependent black son of toil into a savage incendiary and brutal murderer."

Believing, as most southerners did, that slavery was the natural and proper condition for blacks, he thought the northern promise of freedom misguided. Not understanding their own best interests, many blacks would be attracted to the Union side. "Ignorance, credulity, pliability, desire for change, the absence of the political ties of allegiance, the peculiar status of the race"—all these factors would make slaves unduly susceptible to northern enticements, contrary to their best interests. He advised his father to offset the appeal of freedom with harsh penalties for unruly slaves. Any black who incited others to run away or acted as a spy should be summarily executed. Those who sought the Union lines should be met with "terrible corporal punishment" and imprisoned in the county jail. "If insensible to every other consideration," he wrote, "terror must be made to operate upon their minds, and fear prevent what curiosity and desire for utopian pleasures induce them to attempt." In his anger at northern efforts to undermine slavery he even suggested that Yankee captives should not be treated as prisoners of a legitimate war but as robbers and murderers.

Before the end of 1864 Jones's characterization of the Yankees as vandals was borne out by the behavior of many of the soldiers who marched through his native Georgia with General Sherman. The necessity of obtaining food on the expedition and the animosity of some soldiers toward the planters led to countless acts of violence and looting. Among the victims was Charles Jones's mother, Mary. In January 1865 her house was repeatedly plundered. Union soldiers looking for food and valuables broke open every room, closet, trunk, bureau, and box in the house. They took grain, livestock, clothing, jewelry, cutlery, and everything else worth carrying. She dared eat by candlelight only before dawn, lest the invaders take her remaining food. The children could play outside only under close supervision; at the appearance of Yankee soldiers they would "rush in and remain almost breathless, huddled together in one of the upper rooms like a bevy of frightened partridges."

No person could have prevented the suffering experienced by the civilians on Sherman's route. But one of the officers who opposed the gratuitous destruction of southern property was William Wheeler, whose path almost crossed that of the other artilleryman, Charles Jones. One wonders what the two men would have thought of one another had they met. Both were lawyers, Harvard graduates, devotees of literature, sensitive officers, and artillerymen. Each believed he was fighting for God's cause against a sinful foe.

They never had the chance to meet. On June 23, 1864, Wheeler had moved his artillery company into position for another of the skirmishes that had become a routine part of his life. This engagement, however, was different. As he stood on the battlefield, giving orders, a bullet caught him squarely in the chest. In that instant he may have thought of his boyhood in New York, the ocean voyage to Europe, his years in college, his soldier's life, and his family at home. Then the sound of battle faded, and he was gone.

Charles Jones survived the defeat of the South. His opportunity for battle came finally in December 1864 when he commanded the batteries that tried unsuccessfully to defend Savannah from Sherman. He must have known already that the Confederacy's end was near. His land had endured defeat after defeat, and food had been scarce for months. The North had been too powerful for a Confederacy that fought with fewer men, little industry, and no navy.

In 1865 Jones began the long work of accommodation to the new order of affairs. He counseled his mother to accept the fact that the slaves were now free. He found himself engaged in manual labor, loading cotton for shipment to market, his hands peculiarly hardened and tanned by the unaccustomed labor. He soon decided that he could not earn a good living in his homeland, because the plantation economy was devastated by Sherman's destruction and the effects of emancipation were uncertain. Legal and business opportunities in Savannah had become problematical, and in 1866 Jones joined a friend in establishing a law office in New York City, remaining in the heart of Yankeeland for eleven years. Eventually he returned to Georgia and became a lawyer and one of the state's leading historians.

If Wheeler had lived, he, too, might have combined writing and the law. The parallels between his and Jones's life are intriguing but not surprising. North and South might be "oil and water," as Jones had said. But ties of common character and experience bound the two sections together. It was curious but not entirely improbable that the story would end as it did—with Jones at work as a lawyer in New York and Wheeler killed in a battle outside of Atlanta.

Bibliography

Aamodt, Terrie Dopp. *Righteous Armies, Holy Cause: Apocalyptic Imagery and the Civil War* (2002). Shows that both the North and South claimed that God was on their side in the war.

Berlin, IRA, Joseph P. Reidy, and Leslie S. Rowland, Editors. *Freedom's Soldiers: The Black Military Experience in the Civil War* (1998). Letters and memorials from the National Archives providing firsthand accounts of the meaning of the war to black soldiers and sailors.

Breshears, Guy, Editor. *Loyal till Death: A Diary of the 13th New York Artillery* (2003). Includes William Wheeler's letters from the war years and other documents relating to the history of his battery.

Crane, Stephen. *The Red Badge of Courage* (1895 and later editions). The classic Civil War novel about a young man's maturation in battle.

Foote, Shelby. *The Civil War* (3 vols., 1958–1971). Beautifully written narrative history.

Leonard, Elizabeth D. *All the Daring of the Soldier: Women of the Civil War Armies* (1999). Argues persuasively that women played an important role in the war as soldiers and spies.

Myers, Robert Manson, Editor. *The Children of Pride* (1972). Contains letters of Charles Colcock Jones Jr. and his family.

Perry, Mark. *Conceived in Liberty: Joshua Chamberlain, William Oates, and the American Civil War* (1997). Study of a southern and a northern officer who fought over Little Round Top at Gettysburg.

Sharra, Michael. *Killer Angels* (1974). Novel about the Battle of Gettysburg.

Wheeler, William. *In Memoriam: The Letters of William Wheeler* (1875). Wheeler's letters as student, traveler, and soldier.

Identification Topics

William Wheeler, Republican Party, Robert E. Lee, Gettysburg, Ulysses S. Grant, Charles Colcock Jones Jr., Anthony Burns, Chatham Artillery, Sea Islands, William Tecumseh Sherman

Study Questions

1. How did William Wheeler justify suppression of the South in the Civil War? What did he believe he was fighting for?
2. What were Wheeler's attitudes toward the following: the Union, army life, battle, the enemy, southern civilians, and home?

3. Describe Charles Colcock Jones Jr.'s attitude toward slaves. In what ways did he display warmth toward the blacks, and in what ways did he exhibit sternness? How did he explain the slave reaction to the Emancipation Proclamation?

4. How do you imagine that the Joneses treated their slaves? Would they have considered Thomas Foster a good master?

5. What were Jones's attitudes toward these: the North, the South, secession, and the Emancipation Proclamation?

6. Compare the views of Charles Colcock Jones Jr. and William Lloyd Garrison on slavery. How is it possible for two people to have such different views on the same institution?

7. What connections did Jones and Wheeler make between their cause and God?

8. What were the main similarities and differences between Jones and Wheeler?

9. What really divided Wheeler and Jones? Had their cultures made them completely different kinds of people? Or did the war create an artificial and impermanent hostility between them?

10. Would you describe either Wheeler or Jones as an "extremist"? What role did extremism play in the Civil War?

CREDITS

INDEX